Esse

of **PSYCHOLOGICAL ASSESSMENT** Series

Everything you need to know to administer, score, and interpret the major psychological tests.

I'd like to order the following
ESSENTIALS OF PSYCHOLOGICAL ASSESSMENT:

All titles are $34.95* each

- ❏ WAIS®-III Assessment / 0471-28295-2
- ❏ WISC-III® and WPPSI-R® Assessment / 0471-34501-6
- ❏ WJ III® Cognitive Abilities Assessment / 0471-34466-4
- ❏ Cross-Battery Assessment / 0471-38264-7
- ❏ Cognitive Assessment with KAIT & Other Kaufman Measures / 0471-38317-1
- ❏ Nonverbal Assessment / 0471-38318-X
- ❏ PAI® Assessment / 0471-08463-8
- ❏ CAS Assessment / 0471-29015-7
- ❏ MMPI-2™ Assessment / 0471-34533-4
- ❏ Myers-Briggs Type Indicator® Assessment / 0471-33239-9
- ❏ Rorschach® Assessment / 0471-33146-5
- ❏ Millon™ Inventories Assessment, Second Edition / 0471-21891-X
- ❏ TAT and Other Storytelling Techniques / 0471-39469-6
- ❏ MMPI-A™ Assessment / 0471-39815-2
- ❏ NEPSY® Assessment / 0471-32690-9
- ❏ Neuropsychological Assessment / 0471-40522-1
- ❏ WJ III® Tests of Achievement Assessment / 0471-33059-0
- ❏ Individual Achievement Assessment / 0471-32432-9
- ❏ WMS®-III Assessment / 0471-38080-6
- ❏ Behavioral Assessment / 0471-35367-1
- ❏ Forensic Assessment / 0471-33186-4
- ❏ Bayley Scales of Infant Development—II Assessment / 0471-32651-8
- ❏ Career Interest Assessment / 0471-35365-5
- ❏ WPPSI™-III Assessment / 0471-28895-0
- ❏ 16PF® Assessment / 0471-23424-9
- ❏ Assessment Report Writing / 0471-39487-4
- ❏ Stanford-Binet Intelligence Scales (SB5) Assessment / 0471-22404-9
- ❏ WISC®-IV Assessment / 0471-47691-9

Please complete the order form on the back

TO ORDER BY PHONE, CALL TOLL FREE 1-877-762-2974
To order online: www.wiley.com/essentials **WILEY**
To order by mail refer to order form on next page

Essentials

of **PSYCHOLOGICAL ASSESSMENT** Series

Order Form

Please send this order form with your payment (credit card or check) to:

John Wiley & Sons, Inc.
Attn: J. Knott
111 River Street
Hoboken, NJ 07030-5774

Name _____

Affiliation _____

Address _____

City/State/Zip _____

Phone _____

E-mail _____

❏ Please add me to your e-mailing list

Quantity of Book(s) ordered _____ x $34.95* each

Shipping charges:	Surface	2-Day	1-Day	
First Item	$5.00	$10.50	$17.50	
Each additional item	$3.00	$3.00	$4.00	**Total $**_____

For orders greater than 15 items, please contact Customer Care at 1-877-762-2974.

Payment Method: ❏ Check ❏ Credit Card (*All orders subject to credit approval*)
❏ MasterCard ❏ Visa ❏ American Express

Card Number _____ Exp. Date_____

Signature _____

* Prices subject to change.

TO ORDER BY PHONE, CALL TOLL FREE 1-877-762-2974
To order online: www.wiley.com/essentials ⊗**WILEY**

Essentials of KABC-II Assessment

Essentials of Psychological Assessment Series

Series Editors, Alan S. Kaufman and Nadeen L. Kaufman

Essentials

of KABC-II Assessment

Alan S. Kaufman

Elizabeth O. Lichtenberger

Elaine Fletcher-Janzen

Nadeen L. Kaufman

John Wiley & Sons, Inc.

Published by John Wiley & Sons, Inc., Hoboken, New Jersey.
Published simultaneously in Canada.

This publication is designed to provide accurate and authoritative information in regard to the subject matter covered. It is sold with the understanding that the publisher is not engaged in rendering professional services. If legal, accounting, medical, psychological or any other expert assistance is required, the services of a competent professional person should be sought.

Designations used by companies to distinguish their products are often claimed as trademarks. In all instances where John Wiley & Sons, Inc. is aware of a claim, the product names appear in initial capital or all capital letters. Readers, however, should contact the appropriate companies for more complete information regarding trademarks and registration.

For general information on our other products and services please contact our Customer Care Department within the United States at (800) 762-2974, outside the United States at (317) 572-3993 or fax (317) 572-4002.

Wiley also publishes its books in a variety of electronic formats. Some content that appears in print may not be available in electronic books. For more information about Wiley products, visit our website at www.wiley.com.

Library of Congress Cataloging-in-Publication Data:

Essentials of KABC-II assessment / Alan S. Kaufman . . . [et al.].
   p. cm. — (Essentials of psychological assessment series)
  Includes bibliographical references (p.) and index.
  ISBN 0-471-66733-1 (paper)
   1. Kaufman Assessment Battery for Children. I. Kaufman, Alan S., 1944– II. Series.
  BF432.5.K38E87 2005
  155.4'1393—dc22

                                                       2004054210

Printed in the United States of America

10 9 8 7 6 5 4 3 2 1

CONTENTS

SERIES PREFACE

In the *Essentials of Psychological Assessment* series, we have attempted to provide the reader with books that will deliver key practical information in the most efficient and accessible style. The series features instruments in a variety of domains, such as cognition, personality, education, and neuropsychology. For the experienced clinician, books in the series will offer a concise yet thorough way to master utilization of the continuously evolving supply of new and revised instruments, as well as a convenient method for keeping up to date on the tried-and-true measures. The novice will find here a prioritized assembly of all the information and techniques that must be at one's fingertips to begin the complicated process of individual psychological diagnosis.

Wherever feasible, visual shortcuts to highlight key points are utilized alongside systematic, step-by-step guidelines. Chapters are focused and succinct. Topics are targeted for an easy understanding of the essentials of administration, scoring, interpretation, and clinical application. Theory and research are continually woven into the fabric of each book but always to enhance clinical inference, never to sidetrack or overwhelm. We have long been advocates of what has been called intelligent testing—the notion that a profile of test scores is meaningless unless it is brought to life by the clinical observations and astute detective work of knowledgeable examiners. Test profiles must be used to make a difference in the child's or adult's life, or why bother to test? We want this series to help our readers become the best intelligent testers they can be.

In *Essentials of KABC-II Assessment,* the authors have attempted to provide readers with succinct, straightforward, theory-based methods for competent clinical interpretation and application of the second edition of the test that we developed in 1983. Unlike the original K-ABC (for ages 2.5–12.5), the KABC-II is normed for children and adolescents between 3 and 18 years. This book helps ease the transition of examiners who have been longtime K-ABC users and provides a solid foundation for new examiners who are first discovering the Kaufman approach to cognitive assessment. The KABC-II reflects the blend of its 20-year history with the latest neuropsychological and psychoeducational theories. The second edition of the K-ABC offers innovative new subtests and allows examiners to choose the theoretical model that best meets the child's individual needs. This book thoroughly integrates theory, research, clinical history, and clinical inference with sets of guidelines that enable the examiner to give, and then systematically interpret and apply, this thoroughly revised and restandardized instrument.

Alan S. Kaufman, PhD, and Nadeen L. Kaufman, EdD, Series Editors
Yale University School of Medicine

Essentials of KABC-II Assessment

One

At the time of its development, the original Kaufman Assessment Battery for Children (K-ABC; Kaufman & Kaufman, 1983a, 1983b) was innovative as a theory-based, empirically grounded clinical instrument. However, since the K-ABC's inception, many other tests have entered the field to provide clinicians with a plethora of tests that are theory based and empirically sound (e.g., Woodcock-Johnson III [WJ III; Woodcock, McGrew, and Mather 2001]; Cognitive Assessment System [CAS; Naglieri & Das, 1997]). The Kaufman Assessment Battery for Children—Second Edition (KABC-II; Kaufman & Kaufman, 2004a) takes assessment to a new level by basing the test on a dual theoretical model and allowing clinicians to select the model for each child that is best suited to that particular child's background and reasons for referral. The KABC-II also focuses more on specific, rather than global, constructs that provide useful insights into children's learning abilities and problem-solving strategies. The KABC-II represents a substantial revision of the K-ABC, with only 8 of the original 16 K-ABC subtests retained for the KABC-II, and with 10 new subtests joining the revised battery.

This book was developed for those who test children within the 3- to 18-year-old age range and wish to learn the essentials of the KABC-II in a direct, nononsense, systematic manner. The main topics covered here are administration, scoring, interpretation, and clinical use of the instrument. Important points are highlighted throughout the book in "Rapid Reference" boxes, "Caution" boxes, and "Don't Forget" boxes. Each chapter contains questions that are intended to help you consolidate what you have read. After reading this book, you will have at your fingertips in-depth information to help you become a competent KABC-II examiner and clinician.

This chapter reviews the history of the K-ABC, the development of the KABC-II and the theoretical foundations of the test, and provides a thorough description of the test, its reliability, and its validity. In addition, we highlight changes from the K-ABC to the KABC-II as well as noting general uses for the test. However, before delving into these details of the KABC-II, we feel it is important to emphasize some important facts about the test. The KABC-II is founded in two theoretical models: Luria's (1966, 1970, 1973) neuropsychological model, featuring three blocks, and the Cattell-Horn-Carroll (CHC) approach to categorizing specific cognitive abilities (Carroll, 1997; Flanagan, McGrew, & Ortiz, 2000). The KABC-II yields a separate global score for each of these two theoretical models: The global score measuring general mental processing ability from the Luria perspective is the Mental Processing Index (MPI), and global score measuring general cognitive ability from the CHC perspective is the Fluid-Crystallized Index (FCI). The key difference between these two global scores is that the MPI (Luria's theory) *excludes* measures of acquired knowledge, whereas the FCI (CHC theory) *includes* measures of acquired knowledge. Only one of these two global scores is computed for any examinee. Prior to testing a client, examiners choose the interpretive system (i.e., Luria or CHC) that best fits with both their personal orientation and the reason for referral. Deciding which interpretive system to use will dictate which global score is reported and also whether measures of acquired knowledge are included from the core battery (see Rapid Reference 1.1).

The authors of the KABC-II clearly state in the manual (Kaufman & Kaufman, 2004a, p. 4–5) that "the CHC model should generally be the model of choice, except in cases where the examiner believes that including measures of acquired knowledge/crystallized ability would compromise the validity of the Fluid-Crystallized Index." In those cases, the Luria global score (MPI) is preferred. The first Don't Forget box reviews when it is advisable to administer the FCI and MPI.

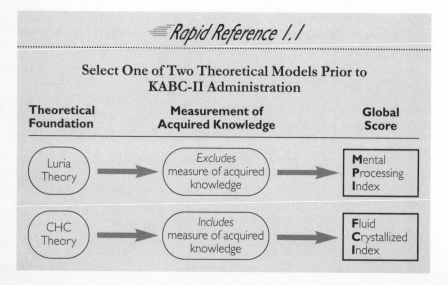

Rapid Reference 1.1

Select One of Two Theoretical Models Prior to KABC-II Administration

Theoretical Foundation	Measurement of Acquired Knowledge	Global Score
Luria Theory	*Excludes* measure of acquired knowledge	**M**ental **P**rocessing **I**ndex
CHC Theory	*Includes* measure of acquired knowledge	**F**luid **C**rystallized **I**ndex

DON'T FORGET

When to Administer the FCI or MPI

CHC Model is Preferred (FCI)	Luria Model is Preferred (MPI)
• In the majority of cases. • If a child has (or is suspected of having) a disability in reading, written expression, or mathematics. • If a child has mental retardation. • If a child has Attention-Deficit/Hyperactivity Disorder. • If a child has an emotional or behavioral disturbance. • If a child may be gifted.	• If a child is from a bilingual background. • If a child's nonmainstream cultural background may have affected his or her knowledge acquisition and verbal development. • If a child has known or suspected language disorders (expressive, receptive, or mixed). • If a child has known or suspected autism. • If a child is deaf or hard of hearing. • If the examiner has a firm commitment to the Luria processing approach and believes that acquired knowledge should be excluded from any cognitive score.

Note. Examiners must select either the Luria or CHC model before testing the child or adolescent. The global score that the examiner decides to interpret should be based on referral and background factors. Both Luria and CHC theories are equally important as foundations of the KABC-II. Neither is deemed theoretically superior to the other.

HISTORY AND DEVELOPMENT

The K-ABC was developed in the late 1970s and early 1980s and was published in 1983, during a time when IQ was largely a Wechsler-Binet monopoly; anti-IQ sentiments were rampant, with racial inequities at the forefront of most discussions; and the gap between theories of intelligence and measures of intelligence was a chasm. The Binet tradition was empirical and practical in contrast to the clinical tradition spawned by Wechsler the man and Wechsler the test developer. Neither orientation paid more than lip service to the burst of theories in cognitive psychology, neuropsychology, intelligence, and learning. Even the original Woodcock-Johnson Psycho-Educational Battery (WJ; Woodcock & Johnson, 1977), whose subsequent revisions became the quintessential application of intelligence theory to practice, was developed from a decidedly practical, nontheoretical foundation. And when old tests were revised (Wechsler, 1974, 1981) or new tests were developed (McCarthy, 1972), there were precious few novel tasks to supplement the traditional tasks developed during the early 1900s. The 1978 WJ was indeed replete with novel subtests, but for years the cognitive portion of this instrument was primarily a test used by special educators, not psychologists.

Although more than a half-century's worth of brain-related and thinking-related theories were obviously related to the measurement of intelligence, they did not invade the domain of IQ assessment until the 1980s with the advent of the K-ABC in 1983. The K-ABC broke from tradition, as it was rooted in neuropsychological theory—Sperry's (1968) cerebral specialization approach and the Luria-Das successive-simultaneous processing dichotomy. Both the Sperry and the Luria-Das models are characterized by a dual-processing approach that has been well supported by a large body of cognitive and neuropsychological research (Das et al., 1979; Neisser, 1967).

Shortly after the publication of the K-ABC, other tests were developed with theoretical underpinnings, such as the Stanford-Binet IV (Thorndike, Hagen, & Sattler, 1986) and the Woodcock-Johnson—Revised (WJ-R; Woodcock & Johnson, 1989). In the 1990s and early 2000s, further clinical tests with strong empirically grounded theoretical foundations were developed: the Kaufman Adolescent and Adult Intelligence Test (KAIT; Kaufman & Kaufman, 1993), the WJ III, and the CAS.

In addition to the K-ABC's theoretical underpinnings, its fairness in assessing children from diverse minority groups made it stand out above other tests, such as those developed from the Binet-Wechsler tradition. The size of group differences on tests of cognitive ability between white children and minority children is thought to reflect, in part, the cultural fairness of a test. Tests such as the Wechsler scales have typically yielded differences of about 15–16 points in favor of white children versus African-American children, but the K-ABC cut those differences in half (Kaufman & Kaufman, 1983b). Numerous research studies have shown that Latino or Latina children and Native American children also tended to score higher on the K-ABC than on conventional measures, resulting in reduced differences between white and minority children (e.g., Campbell, Bell, & Keith, 2001; Davidson, 1992; Fourqurean, 1987; Valencia, Rankin, & Livingston, 1995; Vincent, 1991; Whitworth & Chrisman, 1987).

The innovative features of the K-ABC did not shelter it from controversy, with many psychologists and educators expressing strong positive and negative comments about the test. Voicing the diverse and varied responses among professionals was a special issue of the *Journal of Special Education* that was devoted to the

K-ABC (Miller & Reynolds, 1984). Kamphaus (1993, 2003) has reviewed and summarized the various perspectives on the K-ABC. The K-ABC's psychometric qualities were recognized as a clear strength, as well as its use of teaching items and the implementation of several novel subtests (Kamphaus, 2003). In contrast, the limited floor and insufficient ceiling on some subtests were noted as negative aspects of the K-ABC. Additionally, some professionals questioned whether the K-ABC's scales measured their intended mental processes (sequential and simultaneous) as opposed to measuring other abilities, such as semantic memory and nonverbal reasoning (Keith & Dunbar, 1984).

In revising the K-ABC and developing the KABC-II, the Kaufmans consid-

DON'T FORGET

Inspiration for KABC-II Subtests

Subtest	Inspiration
Atlantis	Memory for Names of WJ-R (Woodcock & Johnson, 1989)
Atlantis—Delayed	Talland (1965)
Block Counting	Cube Analysis (Yoakum & Yerkes, 1920)
Conceptual Thinking	Columbia Mental Maturity Scale (Gurgemeister, Blum, & Lorge, 1954, 1972)
Expressive Vocabulary	Stanford-Binet Picture Vocabulary task (Terman, 1916)
Face Recognition	Kagan and Klein (1973)
Gestalt Closure	Gestalt Completion Test (Street, 1931)
Hand Movements	Luria (1966)
Number Recall	Binet and Simon (1905)
Pattern Reasoning	X-O Test (Yoakum & Yerkes, 1920)
Rebus Learning	Visual-Auditory Learning of *Woodcock Reading Mastery Tests* (Woodcock, 1973)
Rebus Learning—Delayed	Talland (1965)
Riddles	Conceptual Inference (Kagan & Klein, 1973)
Rover	Tower of Hanoi (Cook, 1937)
Story Completion	DeCroly (1914)
Triangles	Kohs (1927)
Verbal Knowledge	Stanford-Binet Pictorial Identification task (Terman, 1916)
Word Order	McCarthy (1972) and Das, Kirby, & Jarman (1979)

ered several factors: the perspectives of psychologists and educators on the original K-ABC, the enormous amount of research on the test, and the current needs of clinicians as dictated by political, social, economic, and educational concerns. The second chapter of the KABC-II Manual (Kaufman & Kaufman, 2004a) details the goals for the test's revision. As we review in Rapid Reference 1.2, the goals for the KABC's revision included strengthening the theoretical foundations, increasing the number of constructs measured, enhancing the test's clinical utility, developing a test that fairly assesses children from minority groups, and enhancing fair assessment of preschoolers. In Rapid Reference 1.2 we also describe how each of these goals was achieved. Each of the subtests that was retained from the K-ABC, or newly developed for the KABC-II, was included to help meet the goals of the second edition (the Don't Forget box lists the inspiration for each KABC-II subtest).

THEORETICAL FOUNDATIONS OF THE KABC-II

The following sections describe the theoretical traditions that contributed to the development of the KABC-II.

Luria's Neuropsychological Theory

Luria (1970) believed that three main blocks or functional systems represented the brain's basic functions. These three blocks are responsible for arousal and attention (block 1); the use of one's senses to analyze, code, and store information (block 2); and the application of executive functions for formulating plans and programming behavior (block 3). Rapid Reference 1.3 explains how these blocks map to particular areas of the brain. Empirical research strongly supports Luria's clinical documentation of the three functional units (see, for example, Das, Naglieri, & Kirby, 1994; Naglieri, 1999; Naglieri & Das, 1997).

In his theory, Luria emphasized that the integration and interdependence of these blocks into functional systems is necessary in order to be capable of complex behavior; this integration is a key feature of Luria's approach to brain functioning (Naglieri, 1999; Reitan, 1988). The joint operation of several brain systems is crucial for children to learn new material efficiently. The Kaufmans focused on the integrative aspects of Luria's theory, rather than on each block's specific functions, in the construction of the KABC-II.

Indeed, the KABC-II was designed primarily to measure high-level, complex, intelligent behavior. Conceptually, the integration of Luria's blocks captures that complexity. Luria's theory emphasizes the integration of the incoming stimuli

≡ *Rapid Reference 1.2*

Revision Goals of the KABC-II

1. Strengthen theoretical foundations	• Recognized that multiple theories were needed to explain the concepts measured by KABC-II scales • Retained original Luria-based interpretations of scales • Added CHC-based interpretation of scales • Linked neuropsychological and psychometric theories with the dual theoretical foundation • Developed subtests that measure more than one aspect of children's ability, allowing alternative theoretical interpretations of scales
2. Increase number of constructs measured	• Considered the forthcoming changes in IDEA guidelines • Recognized that several specific abilities, rather than global abilities, are needed to help identify process disorders and to target interventions • Enhanced measures of learning and planning in addition to sequential and simultaneous processing
3. Enhance clinical utility	• Extended age range to 3 years through 18 years • Strengthened floors for young children and ceilings for older children • Kept achievement (Gc) as a distinct construct, apart from general cognitive ability, and allowed clinicians to decide when to administer the Knowledge/Gc subtests to clients. • Added qualitative indicators (QIs) for each subtest that allow examiners to record pertinent clinical observations during the evaluation • Is suitable for inclusion in a neuropsychological assessment battery
4. Fairly assess children from minority groups	• Allowed examiners to exclude measures of verbal ability and factual knowledge when appropriate • Retained teaching items to ensure that a child's performance is not due to lack of understanding the test's directions • Simplified instructions • Offered a nonverbal scale
5. Enhance fair assessment of preschoolers	• Retained teaching items • Simplified administration and scoring procedures • Limited verbalizations required for preschool children • Constructed child-oriented, gamelike test stimuli • Developed adequate floors for low-functioning preschoolers

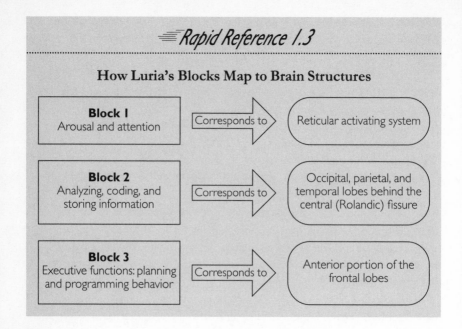

≡ *Rapid Reference 1.3*

How Luria's Blocks Map to Brain Structures

Block I Arousal and attention	Corresponds to	Reticular activating system
Block 2 Analyzing, coding, and storing information	Corresponds to	Occipital, parietal, and temporal lobes behind the central (Rolandic) fissure
Block 3 Executive functions: planning and programming behavior	Corresponds to	Anterior portion of the frontal lobes

and the responsibility of block 2 to make connections with block 3. Thus, the KABC-II includes subtests that require synthesis of auditory and visual stimuli (e.g., Word Order, Atlantis, Rebus Learning, and Rover). To capture the linkage between blocks 2 and 3, the KABC-II includes measures of simultaneous processing that not only require the analysis, coding, and storage of incoming stimuli but also demand executive functioning and problem solving for success (e.g., Rover, Conceptual Thinking).

Cattell-Horn-Carroll (CHC) Theory

Whereas Luria's theory was driven by his own clinical and neuropsychological research and his respect for the work of others, the CHC model is a psychometric theory that rests on a large body of research. Thus, CHC theory represents a data-driven theory, in contrast to the distinctly clinical origins of Luria's model (although Luria's theory has also been empirically validated).

As explained by Kaufman and Kaufman (2004a), two theories were merged into a single model in the late 1990s to create CHC theory: (1) Raymond Cattell's (1941) original two-pronged *Gf-Gc* theory, which was expanded and refined by John Horn (1965, 1989) to include an array of abilities (not just *Gf* and *Gc*); and (2) John Carroll's (1943, 1993) half-century of rigorous pursuit to satisfy "the field's need for a thoroughgoing survey and critique of the voluminous results in the factor-analytic literature on cognitive abilities" (Carroll, 1993, p. vii).

Both the Cattell-Horn and Carroll models essentially started from Spearman's (1904) g-factor theory, and ended up with consistent conclusions about the spectrum of broad cognitive abilities. Horn and Carroll ultimately merged their separate but overlapping models into a unified theory called Cattell-Horn-Carroll (CHC) theory. The details of CHC theory have been articulated by Dawn Flanagan, Kevin McGrew, and Samuel Ortiz (2000; Flanagan & Ortiz, 2001; McGrew, Woodcock, & Ford, 2002).

Cattell's (1963) system revolved around the concept of general intelligence (g), as he posited two types of g abilities, not just one: Fluid intelligence (Gf), the ability to solve novel problems by using reasoning, which Cattell considered to be largely a function of biological and neurological factors and to be vulnerable to the effects of aging; and crystallized intelligence (Gc), a knowledge-based ability believed to be highly dependent on education and acculturation and resistant to the impact of aging.

Horn collaborated with Cattell on a series of studies to enrich and validate the two aspects of g (Cattell & Horn, 1978; Horn & Cattell, 1966, 1967). However, Horn believed that the psychometric data, as well as neurocognitive and developmental data, were suggesting more than just these two general abilities. Early in his collaboration with Cattell, Horn (1965, 1968) identified four additional abilities—Short-Term Acquisition and Retrieval (Gsm), Long-Term Storage and Retrieval (Glr), Visual Processing (Gv), and Speed of Processing (Gs). Horn subsequently refined the definition and measurement of these factors and added additional factors, so that by the late 1980s to mid-1990s his model included 9 to 10 Broad Abilities (Horn, 1989; Horn & Hofer, 1992; Horn & Noll, 1997). Although the theory continued to be called Gf-Gc theory, the multiple Broad Abilities were treated as equals, not as part of any hierarchy.

Based on his in-depth survey of factor-analytic studies, Carroll (1993, 1997) developed a hierarchical theory composed of three levels or strata of abilities, which are detailed in Rapid Reference 1.4. Horn's Gf-Gc theory always focused on the Broad Abilities, and he discussed the more specific or narrow abilities as well, but the g construct had no place in his Gf-Gc theory. Otherwise, the Carroll and Cattell-Horn theories were similar enough to warrant their merger into the new CHC theory. Differences between the theories have been spelled out elsewhere (Flanagan et al., 2000; Flanagan & Ortiz, 2001; McGrew et al., 2002).

When CHC theory is applied to the KABC-II, the g level is not intended as a theoretical construct but as a practical one to provide a summary score. There are five CHC Stratum II abilities (corresponding to five KABC-II scales) that are

≡ Rapid Reference 1.4

Carroll's Three-Stratum Hierarchy

Level of Hierarchy	Number of Abilities	Description
Stratum III (general)	1	A Spearman-like g, which Carroll (1993, 1997) considered to be a valid construct based on overwhelming evidence from factor analysis
Stratum II (broad)	8	Correspond reasonably closely to Horn's (1989) Broad Abilities and "show rough correspondences to Gardner's [1993] seven 'intelligences'" (Carroll, 1997, p. 127)
Stratum I (narrow)	70	Organized by the Broad Ability with which each is most closely associated, many of which indicate the person's "level of mastery, along a difficulty scale," "speed with which the individual performs tasks," or "rate of learning in learning and memory tasks" (Carroll, 1997, p. 124)

measured by the KABC-II (*Glr, Gsm, Gv, Gf,* and *Gc*). An additional sixth Broad Ability, Quantitative Knowledge (*Gq*), is also tapped by the KABC-II because the Narrow Ability of Mathematical Achievement is measured by two subtests as a secondary ability (Rover and Block Counting both require the child to count). Four Broad Abilities and their respective Narrow Abilities are excluded from the KABC-II: Reading and Writing (*Grw*), Auditory Processing (*Ga*), Processing Speed (*Gs*), and Decision/Reaction Time/Speed (*Gt*).

Separate measures of *Gq* or *Grw* were not included on the KABC-II because the authors view reading, writing, and mathematics as more appropriate for tests of academic achievement than for tests of cognitive ability (these abilities are measured by both the Brief and Comprehensive Forms of the Kaufman Test of Educational Achievement—Second Edition (KTEA-II; Kaufman & Kaufman, 2004b). Auditory Processing (*Ga*), Processing Speed (*Gs*), and Decision/Reaction Time/Speed (*Gt*) were also not included on the KABC-II because they lacked the requisite complexity for inclusion in the Kaufmans' test battery. When the KABC-II is administered alongside the KTEA-II Comprehensive Form, then the number of Broad Abilities measured by the combined set of subtests increases from five to eight, and the number of CHC Narrow Abilities measured more than doubles (see the section in Chapter 6 on integrating the KABC-II and KTEA-II).

PURPOSES AND USES OF THE KABC-II

The KABC-II can be used to assess preschool-age and school-age children, as well as adolescents. The types of assessments that it may be used for include psychological, clinical, psychoeducational, and neuropsychological evaluations. The results from such evaluations may be used in making clinical and educational diagnoses, in educational and treatment planning, and in making placement decisions. Like the original K-ABC, the KABC-II is quite useful for the assessment of African American, Hispanic, Native American, and Asian-American children and adolescents within a wide variety of settings.

The number of children in prekindergarten through 12th grade who were served under the Individuals with Disabilities Education Act and Chapter 1 of the Education and Consolidation and Improvement Act in 2000–2001 numbered nearly 6.3 million (U.S. Department of Education, 2002). That number indicates that approximately 13% of students enrolled in public education problems are considered disabled and receive some type of special programming. Thus, a very large number of children need assessments to create effective educational and psychological interventions.

When the KABC-II is administered as part of a larger battery of tests, it is optimally useful. To identify mental retardation, for example, the KABC-II can be used in conjunction with measures of adaptive behavior. When it is combined with informal measures of creativity and talent, it can identify intellectual giftedness. To better understand brain-behavior relationships in individuals with brain dysfunction or damage, the KABC-II can be administered along with measures of specific neuropsychological functioning. To evaluate students with known or suspected learning disabilities, administer the test with measures of achievement.

For children across the spectrum of cognitive ability, the KABC-II helps identify an individual's strengths and weaknesses in cognitive ability and mental processing. It helps identify disorders of basic psychological processing, a key aspect of the definition of learning disabilities. Educational interventions and treatment plans can be developed based on the results of KABC-II profile analyses.

DESCRIPTION OF THE KABC-II

The KABC-II is a measure of the processing and cognitive abilities of children and adolescents between the ages of 3 years 0 months and 18 years 11 months. It is organized into three levels (age 3, ages 4–6, ages 7–18). The KABC-II yields from one to five scales depending on the age level of the child and the interpretive approach that the clinician chooses to take. At age 3, there is only one scale, a global measure of ability, composed of either five subtests (MPI) or seven subtests (FCI). For ages 4–6, subtests are organized into either three scales (Luria model) or four scales (CHC model): Sequential/*Gsm,* Simultaneous/*Gv,* and Learning/*Glr* are in both models, and Knowledge/*Gc* is only in the CHC model. For ages 7–18, four scales (Luria) or five scales (CHC) are available, with the Planning/*Gf* scale joining the aforementioned KABC-II scales. The KABC-II scales for each age level are shown in Rapid Reference 1.5. The Don't Forget box provides additional information about the KABC-II.

From the Luria perspective, the KABC-II scales correspond to learning ability, sequential processing, simultaneous processing, and planning ability. From the vantage point of the CHC model, as applied to the KABC-II, the scales measure the following Broad Abilities (Rapid Reference 1.6 on page 14 describes how the scales are conceptualized by each theoretical perspective).

The names of the KABC-II scales reflect both the Luria process it is believed to measure and its CHC Broad Ability, as indicated in Rapid Reference 1.6: Learning/*Glr,* Sequential/*Gsm,* Simultaneous/*Gv,* and Planning/*Gf.* However, the Knowledge/*Gc* scale that measures crystallized ability reflects only CHC theory, as it is specifically excluded from the Luria system.

As stated, KABC-II yields two global scores that encompass the scales: the MPI and the FCI. The MPI provides a global overview of the KABC-II scales that make up the Luria model, and the FCI offers a global summary of the scales constituting the CHC model. The primary difference between the MPI and the FCI is the inclusion of the Knowledge/*Gc* scale in the FCI and its exclusion from the MPI (see the Don't Forget box). The inclusion of crystallized abilities in the global score yielded by the CHC model (FCI) offers an alternative way of view-

---

≡ Rapid Reference 1.5

Number of KABC-II Scales at Each Age Level

Age 3	Ages 4–6	Ages 7–18
MPI, FCI, or NVI *(only global scales are provided at age 3)*	MPI, FCI, or NVI Learning/*Glr* Sequential/*Gsm* Simultaneous/*Gv* Knowledge/*Gc*	MPI, FCI, or NVI Learning/*Glr* Sequential/*Gsm* Simultaneous/*Gv* Planning/*Gf* Knowledge/*Gc*

Note. The MPI from the Luria system *excludes* Knowledge/*Gc* subtests (age 3) and scale (ages 4–18). The FCI of the CHC system *includes* the Knowledge/*Gc* subtests (age 3) and scale (ages 4–18).

DON'T FORGET

Basic Information about the KABC-II

Author: Alan S. Kaufman and Nadeen L. Kaufman

Publication date: 2004

What the test measures: learning (long-term retrieval), sequential processing (short-term memory), simultaneous processing (visualization), planning (fluid ability), and verbal knowledge (crystallized ability)

Age range: 3 to 18 years

Administration time: Core battery: from 25–35 minutes at age 3 to 50–70 minutes at ages 13–18; Expanded battery: from 35–55 minutes at age 3 to 75–100 minutes at ages 13–18

Qualification of examiners: Graduate- or professional-level training in psychological assessment

Publisher: AGS Publishing
4201 Woodland Road
Circle Pines, Minnesota
55014-1796
Ordering phone: 800-328-2560
http://www.agsnet.com

Price (from 2004 catalog):
KABC-II Kit:
Includes four easels, one manual, all necessary stimulus and manipulative materials, 25 record forms, and soft-sided briefcase. $724.99
KABC-II Computer ASSIST ™ Scoring Software $199.99

ing children's cognitive abilities that is founded in a theory that has gained much popularity among assessment-oriented psychologists (Flanagan et al., 2000; McGrew & Flanagan, 1998) and is consistent with several other Kaufman tests (Kaufman & Kaufman, 1990, 1993, 2004a) and with traditional (Wechsler-Binet) views of cognitive ability.

In addition to the MPI and FCI, and the five scales, the KABC-II has a Nonverbal Scale, composed of subtests that may be administered in pan-

DON'T FORGET

Differences Between the KABC-II's Global Constructs

- The Mental Processing Index (MPI) measures general mental processing ability on the KABC-II from the Luria perspective and *excludes* measures of acquired knowledge.

- The Fluid-Crystallized Index (FCI) measures general cognitive ability on the KABC-II from the Cattell-Horn-Carroll (CHC) perspective and *includes* measures of acquired knowledge (crystallized ability).

≡Rapid Reference 1.6

Definitions of Luria and CHC Terms

KABC-II Scale	Luria Term	CHC Term
Learning/Glr	Learning Ability	Long-Term Storage and Retrieval (Glr)
	Reflects an integration of the processes associated with all three blocks, placing a premium on the attention-concentration processes that are in the domain of block 1, but also requiring block 2 coding processes and block 3 strategy generation to learn and retain the new information with efficiency. Sequential and simultaneous processing are associated primarily with Luria's block 2 and pertain to either a step-by-step (sequential) or holistic (simultaneous) processing of information.	Storing and efficiently retrieving newly learned, or previously learned, information.
Sequential/Gsm	Sequential Processing	Short-Term Memory (Gsm)
	Measures the kind of coding function that Luria labeled "successive" and involves arranging input in sequential or serial order to solve a problem, where each idea is linearly and temporally related to the preceding one.	Taking in and holding information, and then using it within a few seconds.
Simultaneous/Gv	Simultaneous Processing	Visual Processing (Gv)
	Measures the second type, or simultaneous, coding function associated with block 2. For its tasks, the input has to be integrated and synthesized simultaneously (holistically), usually spatially, to produce the appropriate solution. As mentioned earlier, the KABC-II measure of simultaneous processing deliberately blends Luria's block 2 and block 3 to enhance the complexity of the simultaneous syntheses that are required.	Perceiving, storing, manipulating, and thinking with visual patterns.

Planning/*Gf*	Planning Ability	Fluid Reasoning (*Gf*)
	Measures the high-level, decision-making, executive processes associated with block 3. However, as Reitan (1988) states, "block 3 is involved in no sensory, motor, perceptual, or speech functions and is devoted exclusively to analysis, planning, and organization of programs for behavior" (p. 335). Because any cognitive task involves perception of sensory input and either a motor or verbal response, the KABC-II measure of planning ability necessarily requires functions associated with the other two blocks as well.	Solving novel problems by using reasoning abilities such as induction and deduction.
Knowledge/*Gc*	(This scale is not included in the Luria model)	Crystallized Ability (*Gc*)
		Demonstrating the breadth and depth of knowledge acquired from one's culture.

Note: Knowledge/*Gc* is included in the CHC system for the computation of the FCI, but it is excluded from the Luria system for the computation of the MPI. The Planning/*Gf* scale is for ages 7–18 only. All other scales are for ages 4–18. Only the MPI and FCI are offered for three-year-olds.

tomime and responded to motorically. The Nonverbal Scale permits valid assessment of children who are hearing impaired, have limited English proficiency, have moderate to severe speech or language impairments, and have other disabilities that make the Core Battery unsuitable. Rapid Reference 1.7 lists the subtests that compose the Nonverbal scale. This special scale comprises a mixture of Core and supplementary subtests for all age groups.

The KABC-II includes two batteries: a Core and an Expanded. The Expanded battery offers supplementary subtests to increase the breadth of the constructs that are measured by the Core battery, to follow up hypotheses, and to provide a comparison of the child's initial learning and delayed recall of new learning. Scores earned on the supplementary subtests do *not* contribute to the child's standard scores on any KABC-II scale (except for the special Nonverbal scale). Rapid Reference 1.8 presents the Core and Expanded battery for each age group. The

≋Rapid Reference 1.7

Subtests Comprising the KABC-II Nonverbal Scale

	Ages 3–4	Age 5	Age 6	Ages 7–18
Hand Movements	X	X	X	X
Triangles	X	X	X	X
Conceptual Thinking	X	X	X	
Face Recognition	X	X		
Pattern Reasoning		X	X	X
Story Completion			X	X
Block Counting				X
Total number of subtests	4	5	5	5

Note. The Nonverbal subtests include both Core and Supplementary subtests.

scale structure of the KABC-II for age 3 and ages 4–6 differs from the structure for children between the ages of 7 and 18, and the subtest composition for ages 4, 5, and 6 differs slightly, reflecting the rapid developmental changes in cognition at about age 5. There is also a slight change for ages 7–12 versus 13–18. In both cases, the different subtest makeup concerns the Simultaneous/*Gv* scale. Descriptions of the 18 subtests are presented in Rapid Reference 1.9.

KABC-II Standard Scores and Scaled Scores

The KABC-II's two global scores, the MPI and FCI, both are standard scores with a mean of 100 and a standard deviation (SD) of 15. However, only *one* of these two global scores is computed and interpreted for any child or adolescent who is evaluated, based on the examiner's choice of the Luria or CHC model for that individual. Like the MPI and FCI, the KABC-II Nonverbal Index is also a standard score with a mean of 100 and SD of 15.

The five additional KABC-II scales offered for ages 4–18 each have a mean of 100 and SD of 15 (but only the MPI and FCI are offered at age 3). All KABC-II subtests have a mean of 10 and SD of 3. The Core subtest standard scores contribute to the scales, but the Supplementary scaled scores do not (except for the special Nonverbal scale).

≡Rapid Reference 1.8

Categorization of KABC-II Subtests as Core or Supplementary

Scale/Subtests	Age 3		Age 4		Age 5		Age 6		Ages 7–12		Ages 13–18	
	C	S	C	S	C	S	C	S	C	S	C	S
Sequential/Gsm												
Word Order	WO		WO		WO		WO		WO		WO	
Number Recall		NR	NR		NR		NR		NR		NR	
Hand Movements				HM		HM		HM		HM		HM
Simultaneous/Gv												
Rover							Ro		Ro		Ro	
Triangles	T		T		T		T		T			T
Conceptual Thinking	CT		CT		CT		CT					
Face Recognition	FR		FR			FR						
Gestalt Closure		GC		GC		GC		GC		GC		GC
Block Counting						BC		BC		BC	BC	
Planning/Gf												
Pattern Reasoning[a]					PR		PR		PR		PR	
Story Completion[a]								SC	SC		SC	
Learning/Glr												
Atlantis	A		A		A		A		A		A	
Atlantis Delayed						AD		AD		AD		AD
Rebus			R		R		R		R		R	
Rebus Delayed								RD		RD		RD
Knowledge/Gc												
Riddles	Ri		Ri		Ri		Ri		Ri		Ri	
Expressive Vocabulary	EV		EV		EV		EV			EV		EV
Verbal Knowledge		VK		VK		VK		VK	VK		VK	

Note. A subtest's abbreviation in the C column indicates that it is a Core subtest for that particular age, and a subtest's abbreviation in the S column indicates that it is a Supplementary subtest for that particular age.

[a]At ages 5–6, Pattern Reasoning and Story Completion are categorized as Simultaneous/Gv subtests.

≡Rapid Reference 1.9

Description of KABC-II Subtests

Scale/Subtests	Description
Sequential/*Gsm*	
Word Order	The child touches a series of silhouettes of common objects in the same order as the examiner said the names of the objects; more difficult items include an interference task (color naming) between the stimulus and response.
Number Recall	The child repeats a series of numbers in the same sequence as the examiner said them, with series ranging in length from two to nine numbers; the numbers are single digits, except that 10 is used instead of 7 to ensure that all numbers are one syllable.
Hand Movements	The child copies the examiner's precise sequence of taps on the table with the fist, palm, or side of the hand.
Simultaneous/Gv	
Rover	The child moves a toy dog to a bone on a checkerboard-like grid that contains obstacles (rocks and weeds) and tries to find the "quickest" path—the one that takes the fewest moves.
Triangles	For most items, the child assembles several identical rubber triangles (blue on one side, yellow on the other) to match a picture of an abstract design; for easier items, the child assembles a different set of colorful plastic shapes to match a model constructed by the examiner.
Conceptual Thinking	The child views a set of four or five pictures and identifies the one picture that does not belong with the others; some items present meaningful stimuli and others use abstract stimuli.
Face Recognition	The child attends closely to photographs of one or two faces that are exposed briefly and then selects the correct face or faces, shown in a different pose, from a group photograph.
Gestalt Closure	The child mentally fills in the gaps in a partially completed inkblot drawing and names (or describes) the object or action depicted in the drawing.
Block Counting	The child counts the exact number of blocks in various pictures of stacks of blocks; the stacks are configured

such that one or more blocks is hidden or partially hidden from view.

Planning/Gf

Pattern Reasoning[a]	The child is shown a series of stimuli that form a logical, linear pattern, but one stimulus is missing; the child completes the pattern by selecting the correct stimulus from an array of four to six options at the bottom of the page (most stimuli are abstract, geometric shapes, but some easy items use meaningful stimuli).
Story Completion[a]	The child is shown a row of pictures that tell a story, but some of the pictures are missing. The child is given a set of pictures, selects only the ones that are needed to complete the story, and places the missing pictures in their correct location.

Learning/Glr

Atlantis	The examiner teaches the child the nonsense names for fanciful pictures of fish, plants, and shells; the child demonstrates learning by pointing to each picture (out of an array of pictures) when it is named.
Atlantis Delayed	The child demonstrates delayed recall of paired associations learned about 15–25 minutes earlier during Atlantis by pointing to the picture of the fish, plant, or shell that is named by the examiner.
Rebus Learning	The examiner teaches the child the word or concept associated with each particular rebus (drawing), and the child then "reads" aloud phrases and sentences composed of these rebuses.
Rebus Learning Delayed	The child demonstrates delayed recall of paired associations learned about 15–25 minutes earlier during Rebus by "reading" phrases and sentences composed of those same rebuses.

Knowledge/Gc

Riddles	The examiner provides several characteristics of a concrete or abstract verbal concept, and the child has to point to it (early items) or name it (later items).
Expressive Vocabulary	The child provides the name of a pictured object.
Verbal Knowledge	The child selects from an array of six pictures the one that corresponds to a vocabulary word or answers a general information question.

Note. Descriptions are adapted from the *KABC-II Manual* (Kaufman & Kaufman, 2004a).

[a]At ages 5–6, Pattern Reasoning and Story Completion are categorized as Simultaneous/*Gv* subtests.

CHANGES FROM K-ABC TO KABC-II

The K-ABC underwent major revision—structurally and conceptually. The K-ABC's theoretical foundation in Luria's (1966) sequential-simultaneous processing theory and cerebral specialization theory was modified and supplemented in the second edition. Unlike the K-ABC, the KABC-II was founded in Luria's *three* blocks and added a second theory to its foundation—CHC—giving examiners more flexibility in interpretation. To create the dual theoretical basis, 10 new subtests were created and 8 old ones were removed, while 8 original K-ABC subtests were retained. Because of the extension of the KABC-II age range to 18 years 11 months, virtually all retained subtests include many new difficult items to ensure adequate ceilings for bright adolescents. The strong ceilings are evident at all ages: The MPI, FCI, and Nonverbal Index (NVI) all yield high scores of 160, which is 4 SDs above the normative mean of 100. The five individual indexes also have extremely high ceilings, yielding high scores ranging from 154 to 160 across all age groups. Table 1.1 shows the ceilings for the KABC-II indexes. Rapid Reference 1.10 lists the subtest changes from the K-ABC to KABC-II, and Rapid Reference 1.11 lists the correlations between the KABC-II and the K-ABC subtests of the same name. The Don't Forget box lists some of the other specific changes made in the revision of the K-ABC.

DON'T FORGET

Changes from the K-ABC to the KABC-II

- The KABC-II features dual theoretical foundations, including both Luria and CHC theories.
- Age range was expanded to 3–18 years.
- Directions to some retained subtests were improved for clarity.
- New concrete stimuli and easy items were added to improve the floor of Triangles for young children.
- New easy picture items were added to improve the floor of Riddles for young children.
- Many new Face Recognition items were added, and some distracting background details were removed from retained items to help ensure that the task focuses specifically on recognition of the face.
- Hand Movements and Gestalt Closure were retained from the K-ABC but only as supplementary KABC-II subtests.
- Expressive Vocabulary was a preschool-level subtest on the K-ABC and was expanded to span the entire 3–18 age range on the KABC-II.
- On Word Order, explanation of the color interference task was improved, and an additional sample item was added to avoid penalizing a child who does not catch on immediately to the notion of interference.

Table 1.1   KABC-II Index Ceilings (highest possible standard score)

Age	Gsm	Gv	Glr	Gf	Gc	FCI and MPI	NVI
13–18	158	160	160	160	160	160	160
10–12	158	160	160	160	160	160	160
7–9	158	157	160	160	160	160	160
6	158	158	160		154	160	159
5	158	159	160		154	160	160
4	158	160	160		154	160	160
3						160	160

Note. Data are from the *KABC-II manual* (Kaufman & Kaufman, 2004a), Table D.2.

≡ *Rapid Reference 1.10*

Subtest Changes from the K-ABC to KABC-II

Subtests Retained from the K-ABC	Subtests New to the KABC-II	Subtests Eliminated from the K-ABC
Word Order	Atlantis	Magic Window
Number Recall	Rebus	Spatial Memory
Triangles	Atlantis Delayed	Matrix Analogies
Face Recognition	Rebus Delayed	Photo Series
Riddles	Pattern Reasoning	Faces and Places
Hand Movements	Story Completion	Arithmetic
Gestalt Closure	Block Counting	Reading/Decoding
Expressive Vocabulary	Rover	Reading/Understanding
	Conceptual Thinking	
	Verbal Knowledge	

Note. Adapted from Table 1.1 of the *KABC-II technical manual* (Kaufman & Kaufman, 2004).

STANDARDIZATION AND PSYCHOMETRIC PROPERTIES OF KABC-II

The following sections discuss the standardization, reliability, and validity of the KABC-II.

Standardization

The KABC-II was standardized on a sample of 3,025 children who were chosen to match closely the 2001 U.S. Census data on the variables of age, gender, geographic region, ethnicity, and parental education. The standardization sample was

Rapid Reference 1.11

Correlations between KABC-II and the K-ABC Subtests of the Same Name

Subtest	Corrected r	
	Ages 3–5	Ages 8–12
Word Order	.65	.70
Number Recall	.69	.85
Triangles[a]	.55	.73
Face Recognition[b]	.45	
Riddles[c]	.80	.85
Hand Movements[d]	.58	.52
Gestalt Closure	.69	.66
Expressive Vocabulary[e]	.78	

Note. Ten subtests are new to the KABC-II, and eight of the original K-ABC subtests were eliminated in the KABC-II. All values were corrected for the variability of the norm group, based on the standard deviation obtained on the KABC-II, using the variability correction of Cohen, Cohen, West, and Aiken (2003, p. 58). Ns varied across individual subtests and ranged from 55 to 74 for ages 3–5, and the N was 48 for ages 8–12. Coefficients are from the KABC-II technical manual (Tables 8.15 and 8.16).

[a]New concrete stimuli and easy items were added to improve the floor of Triangles for young children.

[b]Face Recognition is only administered up to age 5 on the KABC-II and K-ABC.

[c]New easy picture items were added to improve the floor of Riddles for young children.

[d]Hand Movements and Gestalt Closure were retained from the K-ABC but only as supplementary KABC-II subtests.

[e]Expressive Vocabulary was a preschool-level subtest on the K-ABC and was expanded to span the entire 3–18 age range on the KABC-II.

divided into 18 age groups, each composed of 100–200 children. The sample was split approximately equally between boys and girls.

Reliability

The reliability and validity information are presented in the KABC-II manual (Kaufman & Kaufman, 2004a) and are summarized in Rapid Reference 1.12. The average internal consistency coefficients are .95 for the MPI at both ages 3–6 and ages 7–18, and for the FCI they are .96 for ages 3–6 and .97 for ages 7–18. Internal

≡Rapid Reference 1.12

KABC-II Reliability

Scale/Subtest	Internal Reliability		Test-Retest Reliability	
	Ages 3–6	Ages 7–18	Ages 3–6	Ages 7–18
Sequential/*Gsm*	**.91**	**.89**	**.79**	**.80**
Number Recall	.85	.79	.69	.82
Word Order	.87	.87	.72	.72
Hand Movements	.69	.78	.50	.60
Simultaneous/*Gv*	**.92**	**.88**	**.74**	**.77**
Block Counting	.90	.87		.63
Conceptual Thinking	.80		.55	
Face Recognition	.75		.56	
Rover	.83	.80		.64
Triangles	.86	.87	.79	.83
Gestalt Closure	.74	.74	.70	.81
Learning/*Glr*	**.91**	**.93**	**.79**	**.79**
Atlantis	.83	.86	.73	.70
Rebus	.92	.93	.70	.79
Delayed Recall	.82	.90		.80
Planning/*Gf*		**.88**		**.81**
Pattern Reasoning[c]	.89	.90		.74
Story Completion[c]	.82	.77		.72
Knowledge/*Gc*	**.91**	**.92**	**.93**	**.92**
Expressive Vocabulary	.84	.86	.86	.89
Riddles	.85	.86	.80	.89
Verbal Knowledge	.85	.89	.81	.83
MPI	**.95**	**.95**	**.86**	**.90**
FCI	**.96**	**.97**	**.90**	**.93**
NVI	**.90**	**.92**	**.72**	**.87**

Note. Scale reliabilities are in bold.

[a]Reliabilities for scales and global scales were computed using the formula provided by Nunnally (1978, p. 248).

[b]Using Fisher's *z* transformation.

[c]On Simultaneous/*Gv* scale at ages 5–6.

consistency values for individual subtests ranged from .69 for Hand Movements to .92 on Rebus (for ages 3–6), and for the 7–18 age group internal consistency values ranged from .74 on Gestalt Closure to .93 on Rebus. The median internal consistency value for the individual subtests was .84 for ages 3–6 and .86 for ages 7–18.

The KABC-II is a fairly stable instrument with average test-retest coefficients of .86, .89, and .91 for the MPI at ages 3–5, 7–12, and 13–18, respectively. Average test-retest coefficients for the FCI were .90, .91, and .94 at ages 3–5, 7–12, and 13–18, respectively (see Rapid Reference 1.12 for a reliability summary that includes internal consistency and stability values). Across the three broad age groups, the ranges of the stability values of Learning/*Glr* (.76–.81), Sequential/*Gsm* (.79–.80), Simultaneous/*Gv* (.74–.78), Planning/*Gf* (.80–.82), and Knowledge/*Gc* (.88–.95) denote adequate stability. The Simultaneous/*Gv* emerged as the least stable of all the composite scores.

The largest practice effects (i.e., score increases from first testing to second) were about 14–15 points for the Learning/*Glr* scale at ages 7–18. The large gains on this scale are not surprising given that the nature of the tasks demands that children learn new material, so if children are tested again once they have learned the material, they have a distinct advantage over the first time they were tested. Indeed, the practice effect of about 1 SD over a month's time strongly suggests that the children really learned the material in the first place and are reflecting a certain amount of retention over time. That kind of long-term retention is consistent with the notion of delayed recall that was introduced with the original WJ (Woodcock & Johnson, 1977). Children and adults were expected to retain the paired associate learning over time; to measure delayed recall on the original WJ, examiners were instructed to administer the pertinent subtests 1–8 days later (on the WJ III, examiners are told to give the delayed tasks 30 minutes to 8 days later).

At ages 7–18, Planning/*Gf* also had a relatively large practice effect (10–11 points), whereas Simultaneous/*Gv* showed a moderate effect (7–9 points), and both Sequential/*Gsm* (–1 to 1 point) and Knowledge/*Gc* (3 to 3.5 points) had small effects. These results are entirely consistent with the differential practice effects known for decades about Wechsler's Performance IQ versus Verbal IQ (Kaufman, 1994b). On the WISC-III, for example, Performance IQ gains averaged 12.5 points as opposed to 2.5 points for Verbal IQ. The KABC-II Planning/*Gf* and Simultaneous/*Gv* tasks—like Wechsler's Performance subtests—are novel tasks. However, they only retain their novelty the first time around; even several months later, the tasks have lost their novelty and children will perform markedly better.

At ages 3–5, practice effects for all scales tended to be small to moderate (2–6 points), but the same pattern observed for older children on the KABC-II (and on

≡Rapid Reference 1.13

**Practice Effects for the Separate KABC-II Scaled Scores:
Subtests with Relatively Large Gains from Test to Retest**

Subtest	Ages 3–5	Ages 7–12	Ages 13–18
Face Recognition	1.0	—	—
Rover	—	1.8	1.6
Triangles	0.8	1.2	1.1
Gestalt Closure	1.1	1.6	1.5
Atlantis	1.2	3.4	3.3
Rebus	0.8	1.7	1.4
Story Completion	—	2.6	2.8

Note. Relatively large gains are defined as at least 0.3 SD (a gain of at least 0.9 scaled-score points from test to retest). Data are from the *KABC-II Technical Manual* (Table 8.3). Intervals ranged from 12 to 56 days with a mean of 27 days.

Wechsler's scales for children and adults) was observed for the preschool sample: Largest practice effects were on Learning/*Glr* and Simultaneous/*Gv* (5–6 points), and smallest effects were on Sequential/*Gsm* and Knowledge/*Gc* (2–4 points).

Overall practice effects on the FCI and MPI were 10–11 points for ages 7–18 and 5–6 points for ages 3–5. These results need to be internalized by examiners, especially when testing children ages 7 and older, for whom practice effects are substantial. The advice given by Kaufman (1994a) for the Wechsler scales generalizes to the KABC-II: "Robert DeNiro said to Christopher Walken, in *The Deer Hunter,* that you just get 'one shot.' What applies to deer hunting applies to Wechsler profiles. You get one shot" (p. 31).

Rapid Reference 1.13 extends the findings on practice effects to subtest scaled scores, and the results for separate tasks are entirely consistent with the data reported for the scales in Rapid Reference 1.14. Like the Learning/*Glr* Index, the individual subtests of this scale generally had relatively large gains in scaled scores on retesting, as did the Simultaneous/*Gv* subtests. However, the largest gain was seen in Story Completion (a Planning/*Gf* subtest), which had gains of 2.6 to 2.8 points on retest. In Rapid Reference 1.13, subtests that produced relatively large gains from test to retest are featured (with large gains defined as at least 0.9 scaled score points, which equals 0.3 SD).

≡Rapid Reference 1.14

Practice Effects for the KABC-II Global Scales

Scale	Ages 3–5	Ages 7–12	Ages 13–18
Sequential/Gsm[a]	2.2	−0.8	1.1
Simultaneous/Gv[a]	5.0	9.2	6.6
Learning/Glr[a]	5.9	14.6	13.9
Planning/Gf	—	10.4	10.8
Knowledge/Gc[a]	3.9	3.3	3.4
MPI	5.9	11.9	11.3
FCI	5.3	10.3	10.3
NVI	4.8	7.9	7.8

Note. Data are from the KABC-II technical manual (Table 8.3). Intervals ranged from 12 to 56 days with a mean of 27 days.

[a]Ages 4–18 only.

Validity

Construct validity of the KABC-II is supported by the factor-analytic studies described in the KABC-II manual (Kaufman & Kaufman, 2004a). Results of confirmatory factor analyses (CFAs) across age levels supported different batteries at different age levels. At age 3 a single factor model is the basis for the KABC-II (although CFA did yield a distinction between the Sequential/*Gsm* subtests and the rest of the battery). At age 4 the Concept Formation subtest loaded substantially on both Knowledge/*Gc* and Simultaneous/*Gv*. This dual-loading led to a nonsignificant distinction between Knowledge/*Gc* and Simultaneous/*Gv*. Despite the findings of the CFA, the final battery separates Knowledge/*Gc* and Simultaneous/*Gv* into distinct scales on the basis of the distinct content in each of the scales. The other two factors measured at age 4, Sequential/*Gsm* and Learning/*Glr*, were well supported and distinct.

At ages 7 to 18 distinguishing Simultaneous/*Gv* and Planning/*Gf* was critical. Thus, CFA helped determine which subtests to place on Simultaneous/*Gv* and Planning/*Gf* to yield the best distinction between the factors. Combining Rover and Triangles at ages 7–12 and Rover and Block Counting at ages 13–18 produced a Simultaneous/*Gv* factor that was distinct from Planning/*Gf*. The KABC-II manual suggests that at ages 7–12 Block Counting is a more cognitively complex task and at ages 13–18 it is more purely visual. In addition, the older children, who were administered the most difficult Triangles items, required more reasoning ability than visualization to complete the task.

The main CFA statistics for evaluating how well a test's data fit a theoretical model are the *comparative fit index* (CFI) and the *root mean square error of approximation* (RMSEA). According to Hu and Bentler (1999), CFI values should be greater than .95 and RMSEA values should be less than .06 to provide evidence of good fit. For the KABC-II, values of CFI were well above the suggested cutoff of .95, with all values exceeding .99. These results were obtained for each separate age group: 4, 5–6, 7–12, and 13–18. Values above .99 were obtained in analyses that included only Core subtests and also in analyses that comprised all KABC-II subtests (Core and supplementary). Similarly, values of RMSEA were at or below cutoff of .06 for each age group, averaging about .04 to .05 (Kaufman & Kaufman, 2004a, Figures 8.1 & 8.2). Overall results of the CFA are very strongly supportive of the theory-based scale structure of the KABC-II.

In addition to factor analyses, validity of the KABC-II is further supported by correlations with the following instruments (Kaufman & Kaufman, 2004): the Wechsler Intelligence Scale for Children (third and fourth editions), the Wechsler Preschool and Primary Scale of Intelligence—third edition, the KAIT, and the WJ III. Each of the global scales of these instruments correlated strongly with the KABC-II MPI and FCI. Correlations ranged from .71 to .91 (see Rapid Reference 1.15). Rapid Reference 1.16 also shows that the KABC-II Knowledge/*Gc* scale correlated substantially higher with the verbal scales of the WJ III and

≡*Rapid Reference 1.15*

Correlations of KABC-II Full Scale IQ with Other Global Measures

Measure	KABC-II MPI	KABC-II FCI
WISC-III Full Scale IQ (N = 119)	.71	.77
WISC-IV Full Scale IQ (N = 56)	.88	.89
WPPSI-III Full Scale IQ (N = 36)	.76	.81
KAIT Composite (N = 29)	.85	.91
WJ III GIA (N = 86)	.77	.78

Note. All values are corrected for the variability of the standardization sample. Coefficients are from the *KABC-II technical manual* (Tables 8.17, 8.18, 8.19, 8.21, and 8.22).

Rapid Reference 1.16

Convergent/Discriminant Validity of the KABC-II: Correlations with other Cognitive Scales

	Sequential/Gsm	Simultaneous/Gv	Learning/Glr	Planning/Gf	Knowledge/Gc
WJ III					
Comprehension-Knowledge (Gc)	.46	.53	.53	.57	(.84)
Visual Spatial (Gv)	.35	(.51)	.46	.43	.46
Fluid Reasoning (Gf)	.45	.59	.50	(.64)	.60
Processing Speed (Gs)	.15	.28	.21	.35	.25
Working Memory (Gsm)	(.55)	.39	.51	.44	.56
WISC-IV					
Verbal Comprehension Index (VCI)	.44	.53	.63	.57	.85
Perceptual Reasoning Index (PRI)	.22	(.66)	.56	(.69)	.60
Working Memory Index (WMI)	(.71)	.49	.46	.50	.65
Perceptual Speed Index (PSI)	.16	.46	.58	.56	.53

Note. All values are corrected for the variability of the standardization sample. Most values are from the *KABC-II Technical Manual* (Tables 8.17 and 8.22). Convergent validity correlations are circled.

WISC-IV than it did with the reasoning, visual spatial, and memory scales of each instrument. These patterns of correlations support the convergent and discriminant validity of the KABC-II. Chapter 5 presents a more detailed review of some validity issues, and Chapter 6 touches on the validity of the KABC-II in special populations.

To evaluate the relationship of the KABC-II scores to the key criterion of academic achievement, the KABC-II was correlated with the KTEA-II for 2,475 students between prekindergarten and grade 12 (Kaufman & Kaufman, 2004b) and with a total of 401 children on the WJ III Achievement battery, the Wechsler Individual Achievement Test—Second Edition (WIAT-II), and the Peabody Individual Achievement Test—Revised (PIAT-R; Kaufman & Kaufman, 2004a). Rapid Reference 1.17 summarizes these results for different grade levels, focusing on global scores: FCI, MPI, and total achievement standard score. For the KTEA-II, FCI correlated .79, on the average, with KTEA-II Achievement Composite, with the MPI correlating slightly lower (.75). These coefficients with the conormed KTEA-II are similar in magnitude to the mean values of .75 (FCI) and .71 (MPI) with the other achievement batteries. Values in the .70s are comparable to the *best* coefficients reported by Naglieri and Bornstein (2003) in their summary of a vast number of correlational studies between diverse cognitive and achievement batteries: "For the large studies, the ability/achievement composite correlations for the K-ABC (.74) followed by the CAS and WJ III (both .70) were top ranked" (Naglieri & Bornstein, p. 244). The WISC-III coefficients were lower (.63) in that study, although a recent correlation between WISC-IV Full Scale IQ and WIAT-II Total Achievement was substantial (.87; The Psychological Corporation, 2003, Table 5.15).

In Rapid Reference 1.18, correlations are shown between KABC-II global scores (including the NVI) and the major composites yielded by the KTEA-II Comprehensive Form for ages 4.5–6 and 7–18 years. For the younger group, the MPI was equivalent to the FCI as a correlate of KTEA-II achievement composites. For 4.5–6-year-olds, MPI correlated a bit higher with Written Language, FCI correlated a bit higher with Oral Language, and they correlated about the same with Reading, Math, and the Comprehensive Achievement Composite. For ages 7–18, FCI was consistently a higher correlate than MPI of each academic domain, as reflected in the coefficient with Comprehensive Achievement (.80 vs. 74).

For both age groups, FCI and MPI correlated lowest with Oral Language (.57–.67) and highest with Reading and Math (.67–.74). The NVI correlated with Math at almost the same level as the MPI and FCI (.65–.67 vs. .68–.71) but otherwise correlated substantially lower than MPI and FCI with other academic areas. For example, NVI correlated about .60 with Reading, whereas the other two global

≡ Rapid Reference 1.17

Correlations between KABC-II Global Standard Scores (FCI and MPI) and Global Standard Scores on Four Major Achievement Batteries, by Grade Level

Achievement Test Global Standard Score	N	FCI	MPI
KTEA-II			
Pre-K to K	370	.74	.72
Grade 1	198	.78	.77
Grade 2	202	.79	.77
Grades 3–4	361	.82	.78
Grades 5–6	381	.77	.71
Grades 7–8	397	.82	.75
Grades 9–12	566	.80	.73
WJ III			
Grades 2–5	79	.70	.63
Grades 6–10	88	.79	.77
WIAT-II			
Grades 2–5	82	.72	.65
Grades 7–10	84	.87	.83
PIAT-R			
Grades 1–4	32	.67	.69
Grades 5–9	36	.73	.67
Mean r for KTEA-II	**2,475**	**.79**	**.75**
Mean r for WJ III, WIAT-II, and PIAT-R	**401**	**.75**	**.71**

Note. KTEA-II correlations are from Kaufman and Kaufman (2004b, Table 7.18). WJ-III, WIAT-II, and PIAT-R correlations are from Kaufman and Kaufman (2004a, Tables 8.23, 8.24, 8.26, 8.28, 8.29, and 8.30). All correlations are adjusted for the variability of the norms sample (SD = 15).

scores correlated about .70. Therefore, KABC-II examiners who opt to administer the Nonverbal scale need to be aware that prediction of the child's academic achievement will suffer (except for prediction of mathematics).

Nonetheless, despite the lower correlations of NVI with Achievement (relative to MPI and FCI), and correlations in the .50s and .60s with Oral Language, all of the coefficients for the KABC-II global scores shown in Rapid References

≋*Rapid Reference 1.18*

KABC-II Global Scale Correlations (including NVI) with KTEA-II Composites (ages 4.5–18 years)

KTEA-II Composite	FCI	MPI	NVI
Reading			
Ages 4.5–6	.67	.68	.57
Ages 7–18	.74	.68	.61
Math			
Ages 4.5–6	.70	.71	.65
Ages 7–18	.71	.68	.67
Written Language			
Ages 4.5–6	.67	.70	.56
Ages 7–18	.66	.62	.56
Oral Language			
Ages 4.5–6	.62	.57	.52
Ages 7–18	.67	.61	.56
Comprehensive Achievement			
Ages 4.5–6	.75	.73	.65
Ages 7–18	.80	.74	.70

Note. All correlations were corrected for the variability of the norm group, based on the standard deviation obtained on the KTEA-II, using the variability correction of Cohen et al. (2003, p. 58). Data are adapted from Kaufman and Kaufman (2004b).

1.7 and 1.8 on pages 16 and 17 compare favorably with the values yielded by global scores on other tests (Naglieri & Bornstein, 2003) and reflect strong support for the KABC-II's criterion-related validity.

Additional discussion of the interface between the KABC-II and KTEA-II is provided in Chapter 6 in the section "Integrating the KABC-II and KTEA-II," including correlations between the KABC-II Scale Indexes and KTEA-II Composites.

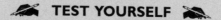

TEST YOURSELF

1. The key difference between the KABC-II's two global scores is that the MPI (Luria's theory) *excludes* measures of acquired knowledge, whereas the FCI (CHC theory) *includes* measures of acquired knowledge. True or False?

2. The KABC-II includes all of the following scales except _____.
   (a) Sequential/*Gsm*
   (b) Simultaneous/*Gv*
   (c) Learning/*Glr*
   (d) Knowledge/*Gc*
   (e) Processing Speed/*Gs*
   (f) Planning/*Gf*

3. At ages 7–18 the KABC-II yields five Broad Ability scales for the CHC model; at ages 4–6 it yields four Broad Ability scales for the CHC model. How many Broad Ability scales does the KABC-II yield for the CHC model at age 3?

4. Scores earned on the supplementary subtests do *not* contribute to the child's standard scores on any KABC-II scale (except for the special Nonverbal scale). True or False?

5. At ages 7–18, the largest practice effects (i.e., score increases from first testing to second) were about 14–15 points for what scale?
   (a) Simultaneous/*Gv*
   (b) Knowledge/*Gc*
   (c) Learning/*Glr*
   (d) Sequential/*Gsm*

6. For ages 7–18, MPI (without Knowledge/*Gc*) was consistently a higher correlate than FCI (with Knowledge/*Gc*) of each KTEA-II academic domain. True or False?

7. The KABC-II Knowledge/*Gc* scale correlated the highest with which scales of the WJ III and WISC-IV?
   (a) Reasoning scales
   (b) Visual spatial scales
   (c) Memory scales
   (d) Verbal scales

Answers: 1. True; 2. e; 3. None—only a global score (FCI, MPI, or NV!) is produced; 4. True; 5. c; 6. False; 7. d

Two

HOW TO ADMINISTER AND SCORE THE KABC-II

INTRODUCTION

The advantages of standardized cognitive ability tests are numerous: They create predictable conditions in which to observe a child using his or her abilities and resources to solve problems; they provide a comparison of individual cognitive skills with a group of same-aged children; they permit observation of naturally occurring developmental changes in cognitive ability; and they allow us to determine hypotheses about individual cognitive strengths and weaknesses. The prior statements are only valid, however, if the test is administered in a standardized fashion.

Experienced examiners know how to balance a formal administration of each subtest with informal ways of obtaining the child's best performance. Experienced examiners also balance attention to the administration of the test with observations about how the child is responding to the test. Test administration balancing skills develop with experience. The more times you administer the KABC-II, the more automatic the instructions become, allowing you to spend more of your time paying attention to the child's behavior and manipulation of the cognitive tasks as opposed to thinking about what words to say or which way to lay out test materials. The more familiar you are with the words and instructions of the KABC-II, the more likely that you will be relaxed and create a friendly and enjoyable rapport with the child. To make the KABC-II results reliable, valid, and meaningful, learn how to administer the test battery in a standardized format with a positive and encouraging manner.

TEST PREPARATION

The following sections cover different ways in which you should prepare for the administration of the test.

Testing Room

Make every effort to administer the KABC-II in a testing room that is quiet, clean, and comfortable. The reality is that, whether we like it or not, the results of cognitive ability tests have the potential to stay with a child for a very long time and change others' expectations of that child. Therefore, we need to be advocates for the child even before testing begins. You have an obligation to provide an appropriate testing room. Many of us have been presented with storage closets, cafeterias, and other odd places to conduct an assessment, and many of us have amusing tales of the unusual places where we have been finally forced to test. However, our ethical duty is to conduct assessments in an environment that will maximize success. Sometimes you will just have to become creative in performing that duty!

There are obvious elements to the ideal testing room. The room should be clean, friendly, comfortable, relatively quiet, and free from too many distracting toys, materials, and clutter. The tables and chairs should be of appropriate height and proportion and large enough to lay out test materials comfortably. Create a seating arrangement that will allow you to see both sides of the easel and that will give the child enough room to manipulate materials. Most often, this can be accomplished if you and the child are seated on adjacent sides of a table, as shown in Figure 2.1. You can also sit opposite the child, as long as you can see both sides of the easel.

Try to keep unused portions of the test materials out of the child's view but within reach so that you can maintain an easy flow of presentation. In addition, keep the record form either behind the easel or on a clipboard that prevents the child from seeing the answers or scoring.

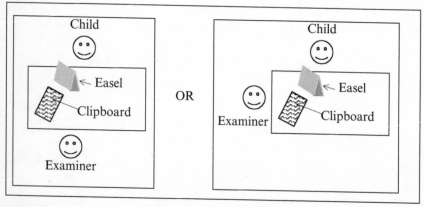

Figure 2.1 Alternative seating arrangements for testing.

Materials

The KABC-II materials are designed to provide minimal interference with the measurement of the cognitive process being assessed. The ultimate goal is for the examiner to pay attention to the child, not necessarily to the materials.

Easels

The materials for the KABC-II are mostly contained in easels that are sturdy and easy to handle. The pictures used on the easels are novel, colorful, and easy to understand. One of the most user-friendly aspects of the easels is that administration instructions are always on the same side of the easel as well as being color coded and easy to read, and correct answer pictures are oriented so that you can recognize them instantly.

The examiner pages for each subtest contain a title page that shows the subtest name, the ages for administration, and whether it is a Core or Supplementary subtest for each age group. The next two pages for each subtest contain a statement of what the subtest measures, a description of the task, information about giving the subtest, information on sample items and teaching the task, scoring instructions, start points, and basal and discontinue rules. The next page in the subtest section contains the sample items along with notes about administration and examiner actions (in black ink) and words to be spoken by the examiner (in red ink). The item pages for each subtest provide detailed directions and illustrations of correct responses on the right-hand side of the page.

The KABC-II easels also have text that facilitates the examination of children who speak both Spanish and English. Correct answers are printed on the easel pages in English and Spanish for the Expressive Vocabulary, Gestalt Closure, and Riddles subtests. The Spanish instructions and teaching prompts for each subtest are placed on a foldout flap at the end of the subtest. This flap can be left out during the administration in case the examiner needs to refer to it during the subtest administration.

Protocols

There is only one protocol required for the entire administration of the KABC-II. The record form layout is somewhat different from other forms in that the summary recording of scores for 7- to 18-year-olds is on the front of the form, and the summary recording of scores for 3- to 6-year-olds is on the back. In addition, white space has been left on nearly every page of the record form for you to write notes about qualitative indicators and observations about test-taking behaviors. These observations and notes can be summarized on a special page devoted to documenting background question responses, behavioral observations,

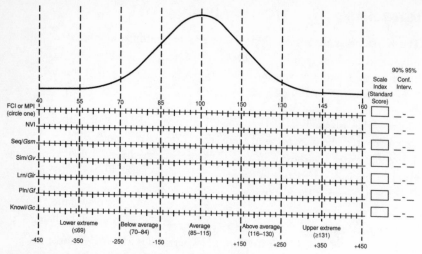

Figure 2.2 Graphing KABC-II scale indexes.

Source: This chart is from page 3 of the KABC-II record form. Reproduced with permission of AGS.

and any considerations that would bring the validity of the test results into question. There is also a page in the record form that is devoted to graphing the child's numerical scores (Figure 2.2) and analyzing scale indexes.

Other new additions to the record form are color-coded response and scoring items; the symbol of an apple by items that can be taught by the examiner; ages for core and supplementary subtests at the top of each page; timing, basal, and discontinue rules for each subtest; and Spanish as well as English responses on the Riddles scoring page.

Manipulatives

Three KABC-II subtests have additional materials: Triangles has two sets of pieces, one for younger children and one for older examinees, that are used to make designs; Rover has a stimulus book and a small plastic dog; and Story Completion has a stimulus booklet and picture cards. There are also a few blocks included that are only used as teaching items on the Block Counting subtest. The manipulatives for these subtests are easy to handle and are appropriate for children of all ages. We suggest keeping the test materials out of sight because some children may find them interesting enough to be distracting. It is also a good idea to check that the test kit is complete before you start so that there are no unnecessary delays during administration. We recommend that you place the unused easels and materials on a chair or table next to you for easy access.

ESTABLISHING AND MAINTAINING RAPPORT

The following sections discuss how to build rapport with examinees.

Rapport with Very Young Children

Establishing rapport with preschool-age children can be very tricky and requires a great deal of flexibility and creativity on your part. Before a young child ever enters the examination room, the child's preconception about what will take place is determined by how the parents present the testing to the child. We advise parents to explain the assessment procedure to a young child in terms that they can clearly understand: "You are going to do some things with Dr. X like play games, look at pictures, and other things. Some things will be easy, and some will be hard." Because the word *test* often makes young children become anxious (or may not even convey any meaning to children who have not been in a school setting), we advise parents to avoid using it in their description of the upcoming evaluation.

Separation from parents can be a significant issue for many young children. For this reason, it is best to ask the parents ahead of time about how their child typically gets along in situations that require separation from them. If a child is typically shy or easily upset, then ask the parents to accompany him or her in the testing room until the child is comfortable with you and the testing situation. You can also help a child ease into the testing situation by playing with him or her in the waiting room or the examination room prior to beginning the structured testing.

Your manner of speaking to a very young child may make the child feel comfortable or threatened. Try to speak with a tone that isn't too loud or formal, but also don't talk down to a young child or use baby talk. Adjust your vocabulary to a level that is appropriate to the child's developmental level. However, note that although you should be friendly in your manner of speaking, you may need to become firm in redirecting a child who has behavioral difficulties.

Once rapport has been established, you may need to work even harder to keep a young child motivated and attentive during the assessment. Consider asking the parents what they use to motivate their child outside of the testing situation. Some children may require external rewards such as stickers, tokens, food, or candy (if it is acceptable to the parent). Other children will respond well to verbal reinforcement (e.g., "You're working so hard") or nonverbal praise (e.g., giving a thumbs-up or a high five).

Young children typically have more motor activity than older children and are not used to sitting for long periods of time in a structured setting. For that reason, expect more frequent breaks when assessing young children. Be flexible and consider letting a youngster stand or sit on the floor with you if he or she is more comfortable (this would be most appropriate for subtests that don't require manipulatives). Most important, keep the testing moving at a steady, smooth pace and create rapid transitions between subtests.

Rapport with Elementary- and Secondary-Aged Children and Adolescents

The best approach for establishing rapport with older children and adolescents is to be honest and straightforward about the purpose of testing and the activities that the child will be engaging in. A simple explanation that you will be spending some time working on puzzles and guessing games that will help you figure out how the child learns and what things the child is "good at and not so good at" will probably suffice. You should also explain that some of the questions might be easy and some hard and that it is important for the child to do his or her best.

Positive Feedback

During the test, be warm and supportive. It is very easy to inadvertently give away nonverbal and verbal hints as to the correctness of answers. Be aware of this pitfall and try to keep track of exactly what feedback you may be providing. Phrases like "way to go," "fine," or "nice job" are all appropriate statements when the child is obviously trying hard. These are process comments, and they provide less implied feedback on the correctness of answers. Statements like "You are trying really hard, nice job!" and "I can see that this is fun for you!" are comments about the child's effort and motivation, not about the correctness of any item. Process comments also say something supportive and valuable about the child rather than the product of correct or incorrect answers. Even if the child is not doing very well, at least he or she is being complimented for tenacity or acknowledged for trying harder items.

On the other hand, you can also overdo support and even process feedback. It is important to sound sincere and natural, and profuse feedback can sometimes backfire and lose its value. Therefore, the pacing and timing of supportive feedback is important and should be tailored to the individual child to maintain the appropriate rapport.

Limit Setting

The counterpart to positive feedback is limit setting. Just as you need to create a warm, supportive, and caring environment, you should also provide a clear expectation of age-appropriate behavior for the examinee. A good rule of thumb is to be polite and respectful but also firm. If a child does not respond to gentle limit setting, you have some choices about how to proceed. Those choices depend on whether the child's behavior is interfering with the administration of the test or the child's performance. If the behaviors are not really getting in the way of a valid performance, then consistent prompts and nonverbal reinforcement may suffice. Perhaps a break and then reiteration of the limits before beginning again may help. You can also remind the student about how classroom rules also apply when you are testing.

On the other hand, if the behaviors are getting in the way of administration and performance, then it is best to stop the administration and explain to the child that the limits are fixed and describe the logical consequences if the behavior continues. Of course, if it gets to the latter point, you will have rich clinical information about how the child perceives authority figures, how the child perceives cognitive challenges, and how the child responds to an examiner who sets and sticks to a limit.

In any case, try to leave the testing session on a positive note. It may be necessary to break up the testing session into smaller sessions so the child doesn't become frustrated. You could also spend some time playing or doing a pleasant activity at the end of the smaller test sessions so the child will have a positive orientation toward test sessions. Try to remain flexible (and sometimes imaginative) and meet the needs of the child. All information, whether a test score in a session or information about the venue of the test session, is important and useful, and it will contribute to the comprehensive assessment.

Breaks

It is all right to take breaks during the administration of the KABC-II, but it is very important to time the break so as not to spoil the opportunity for administration of the optional Delayed Atlantis and Delayed Rebus subtest. Reminders of when to administer the delayed time sequence are on the easels, on the back of the Rover booklet, in the manual, and in the subtest-by-subtest analysis in this book. The specific instructions are given on the easel. The minimum allowable interval between initial and delayed subtests is 10 minutes, and the maximum is 45 minutes. Based on standardization administrations, the typical interval is about 20 minutes.

Also consider taking breaks when you think that the child is overloaded, fatigued, or becoming oppositional. Of course, use your judgment to time the break appropriately (i.e., don't let the child manipulate when breaks are taken). Maintain small talk and friendly banter between subtests, which will help the flow of the test move along and reduce the time that the child is not engaged and occupied.

TESTING INDIVIDUALS WITH SPECIAL NEEDS

Children with specific sensory or motor difficulties may need special accommodations when they take the KABC-II. Difficulties like visual impairment, hearing impairment, severe expressive language problems, physical handicaps, Mental Retardation, neurological impairments, and behavior disorders may require you to adapt ways that the child can respond to test items. If you suspect a need for accommodation, then create a plan adapting the materials before you begin the KABC-II. You can talk with teachers and parents to find out if there are adaptive methods already in use in the classroom or at home that are successful and can be employed during testing. There is no need to reinvent the wheel when trying to accommodate a child's special needs.

Many times children with special needs experience fatigue due to the extra effort required for them to take the test and work with the impairment. Children with motoric issues may need extra time to manipulate the materials in Triangles; they may need to go slower when pointing at the pictures in Word Order; or they may simply need to have rests between items on Hand Movements. Other acceptable modifications are listed in Rapid Reference 2.1. Your flexibility and ex-

---

≡Rapid Reference 2.1

Acceptable Administration Modifications

- American Sign Language interpretation, lip reading, and writing of answers for children who are deaf or hard of hearing
- Written responses and nodding for children with severe expressive language problems
- Frequent breaks and reinforcers for children with low frustration tolerance and behavior disorders
- Frequent breaks for children who may fatigue easily due to medication side effects or neurological conditions such as traumatic brain injury
- Using the nontimed scoring on the Triangles, Pattern Reasoning, and Story Completion subtests for older examinees
- Teaching sample and teaching items in a language other than English and/or accepting predominantly Spanish or other language responses for any subtest, but especially Riddles, Verbal Knowledge, and Expressive Vocabulary

Note. These and other modifications must be explained or factored in when you are interpreting results.

pertise are critical here because the further the test administration strays from standardization, the higher the likelihood of results that have to be explained in light of the deviation from standardization. However, sometimes the best that you and the child can do is to take your time and be creative and flexible about how the test is completed.

Again, the issue with deviating from standardized procedures is not that it is forbidden or that it automatically renders the scores invalid. A well-planned scheme of accommodations to make possible the testing of children with unique special needs is an appropriate and desirable course of action. This course should be well documented and interpreted appropriately.

GENERAL TEST CONSIDERATIONS

The following sections cover a number of considerations that may affect test administration.

Use of Sample and Teaching Items

In designing their tests, the Kaufmans wanted to ensure that each child understands the task prior to obtaining a score on a task. Sample and teaching items provide the mechanism by which children are given fair opportunity to adequately learn a task during administration. Thus, when a child responds incorrectly on a sample item or a teaching item, you demonstrate the correct response, give a second trial, and teach the task, if necessary. All subtests, except the Knowledge/*Gc* subtests and the Delayed Recall subtests, include teaching items. The specific teaching instructions are printed on the pages of the easel.

Although the instructions for teaching the task are clearly articulated in the easel, sometimes a child may still not understand a task after the teaching is complete. This lack of understanding is evident if a child fails a second trial. In such a situation, the administration rules allow you to use your own words to restate the directions or to describe the task more generally using additional examples, easy words, or gestures. If necessary you may use a different language to communicate the directions to the child (e.g., American Sign Language or Spanish), or you may write the directions for the child to read. However, you should be careful to avoid giving the child a strategy for solving items during your teaching of the task.

Out-of-Level Norms

Children ages 4 to 7 who are very low functioning may benefit from the administration of a battery designed for children of a younger chronological age. For example, if a 5-year-old is very low functioning, the 5-year-old battery may be too frustrating (and may not have an adequate floor), but the Core battery for 4- or 3-year-olds may be at an appropriate level of difficulty. On the opposite end of the spectrum, very high-functioning children ages 3 to 6 may benefit from the administration of a battery designed from chronologically older children. For example, a high-functioning 6-year-old may be bored during administration of the 6-year-old battery (and may not achieve a ceiling) but will be appropriately challenged by the battery for children ages 7–12. For these reasons, the KABC-II provides the opportunity for out-of-level testing.

The decision to do out-of-level testing must be made with caution. The KABC-II Core batteries were designed to be appropriate for most children in the specific age groups. In general, for an average child, an out-of-level subtest will usually not have an adequate floor or ceiling. Thus, you must have a strong expectation that a child will perform below average when administering a Core battery that is below the child's chronological age or that a child will perform above average when administering a Core battery that is above the child's chronological age. Rapid Reference 2.2 lists the options for out-of-level administration.

The out-of-level battery yields scores based on norms for the child's own age group. For example, if a 6-year-old is administered the age 5 out-of-level battery, then the scores are based on how other 6-year-olds performed on those same subtests. The battery administered determines the scores that are possible: If a 3-year-old battery is administered, then only the FCI or MPI can be calculated, but if a 4-year-old battery is administered then the full complement of indexes is yielded.

≡ Rapid Reference 2.2

Options for Administering an Out-of-Level Battery to Children Who are Low or High Functioning

Children Who Are Low Functioning: Administer Core Battery for Age	Child's Chronological Age	Children Who Are High Functioning: Administer Core Battery for Age
—	3	4
3	4	—
3, 4	5	6, 7–12
5	6	7–12
5, 6	7	—

All of the subtests that are out of level are denoted in the subtest norm tables through the use of dark shading and labels. Even if you do not administer an entire out-of-level battery, you may administer certain out-of-level subtests (while using appropriate caution). For example, useful information may be gleaned by administering Hand Movements to a precocious 3-year-old, although Hand Movements is too difficult for children who are low functioning. If you choose to administer such an out-of-level subtest, you should clearly mark on the record form and in your case report that the subtest was out of level.

To calculate the standard scores when conducting out-of-level testing, you first enter the subtest scaled score tables to obtain children's scaled scores on the out-of-level subtests. Consequently, all scaled scores (and, hence, sums of scaled scores) are based on one's age mates. However, to obtain the index profile, you enter the norms tables for the age group of the scale that you administered. For example, if you have administered the 4-year-old battery to a gifted 3-year-old, first obtain the scaled scores from Table D.1 for children ages 3-0 (Rebus and Hand Movements are out-of-level subtests in this case), then go to Table D.2 and obtain the index scores from the table for children aged 4-0 (which is the battery that was administered). Because scaled scores and sums of scaled scores are based on age mates, the out-of-level indexes are ultimately compared to age mates, even though you obtain the index scores from a table that is based on the battery administered.

Timing

Historically, timed subtests have not been a central feature of the K-ABC or other Kaufman tests. Only three subtests on the KABC-II require precision timing on later items: Triangles, Pattern Reasoning, and Story Completion. Children and adolescents aged 7 to 18 have the possibility of obtaining one or two extra points on each item that they complete in a rapid time frame. Timing for this age group on these activities was how accurate measurement of high-functioning adolescents was achieved in developing the subtests. The directions for timing are on the record form and in the manual.

It is preferable to use a stopwatch for timing; for ideal conditions, select one that does not make noise. Some children become anxious when they see a stopwatch or figure out that they are being timed. You should practice using the stopwatch in an unobtrusive way, so that you don't fumble with it during administration. Do not be excessively secretive; try to be casual and matter-of-fact about the stopwatch. If a child asks questions about being timed be truthful and try to say something reassuring to allay any discomfort. For example, you could say, "Yes, I am timing you, but that's not what is important—it is more important that you try hard and do a good job" or "Yes, I am supposed to time you, but I want you to pay attention to what you are doing, not the watch."

You will need to have the stopwatch ready to go at the beginning of the subtest items because some children are very quick at understanding the task demand and proceeding with the items. Be alert during the subtest because an item ends when the examinee communicates, either verbally or nonverbally, that he or she has finished. Sometimes children will complete an item and not indicate that they are finished. In this case, it is all right for you to ask, "Are you done?" and stop recording the time as soon as possible.

On the three timed subtests, you can ultimately decide to score the subtest without using time points. That is, if in your professional judgment it would be inappropriate to assign extra points for rapid responding to a child (perhaps because of a motor impairment), then you can score the subtest without using the time points. Simply use the norms for "no time points" listed in Table D.1. However, whenever possible, the standard scoring method (using time points for ages 7–18) is preferred.

Querying

Querying an answer only occurs on the Riddles, Expressive Vocabulary, and Gestalt Closure subtests of the KABC-II. In these instances, ask for more information or clarification in a neutral kind of way such as "Tell me more about that" or "Explain that for me a bit more." Incorrect answers are never queried.

Note a query on the record form with a "Q" or some other notation that marks the item. This procedure will allow you to go back and see how many items were answered spontaneously and how many were vague, unintelligible, or unusual. Also note if the quality of the response improved after you queried. Did the response improve or deteriorate? Or did the child run out of ideas and respond with "I don't know"? Sometimes a child will respond to a query with a great number of words, and it is a good idea to determine if this helps the overall score or not. Using a system of abbreviations will help you note interactions quickly at the time they are happening (Rapid Reference 2.3 provides a list of abbreviations).

Repeating Items

Most subtests on the KABC-II allow a question or stimulus to be repeated as often as the child requires. The nature of the Story Completion, Triangles, Block Counting, Pattern Reasoning, Gestalt Closure, Atlantis Delayed, and Rebus Delayed subtests requires that the stimuli page remain in front of the child as long as he or she needs. In the case of Riddles, Expressive Vocabulary, and Verbal Knowledge, which have verbal or auditory stimuli, you are allowed to repeat the verbal stimulus if needed because the subtests measure language-based knowledge rather than memory.

However, there are some subtest responses that have a memory component and therefore do not allow repetition of a stimulus because it would interfere with performance. These subtests are Atlantis, Rebus, Number Recall, Word Order, Hand Movements, and Face Recognition. On these subtests, the child must remember the stimulus the first time it is presented because there is no other opportunity to see or hear the information.

In any event, whenever a child asks you to repeat a direction or stimulus mark "R" or "Rep" or some other code on the record form just after it happens. Mark the request for repetition right from the start of the test; otherwise, you may only become aware that it is excessive when many instances have gone by already and it is too late to remember exactly when and where the undocumented repetitions occurred.

When a child makes excessive requests for repetitions you should investigate further. There are many reasons why a child might ask for excessive repetitions (see Rapid Reference 2.4 for examples). However, the only way to know the reason for

≡Rapid Reference 2.3

Abbreviations for Recording Responses

@	at
DK	don't know
INC	incomplete
IMP	impulsive
NR	no response
OT	overtime
PC	points correctly
PI	points incorrectly
↑	increase
↓	decrease
R	reflects before responding
SC	self-corrects
ST	invents strategies
V	verbalizes (talks his or her way through task)

≡Rapid Reference 2.4

Reasons a Child Might Ask for Excessive Repetitions

- Cannot hear the examiner's voice
- Is distracted by excessive sudden noises or events
- Has an auditory processing deficit
- Has a significant problem with auditory short-term memory
- Does not understand the rules of the subtest
- Has a significant attentional problem
- Is very young and has a developmentally appropriate short attention span
- Is nervous and needs reassurance

Note. This list is not exhaustive.

requests for repetitions is to look at the cumulative data of the comprehensive assessment. It is not advisable to simply report the number of times a child asks for repetition of stimulus items or directives during a subtest or battery. In this instance, associate quantitative with qualitative data. Look at multiple requests in context—any one of the possible reasons for excessive requests for repetitions cited in Rapid Reference 2.4 could be true, and also several reasons could be true at the same time. One thing is certain, however: The fact that the child is asking you to repeat directions or items excessively is an indicator of something that should be checked out with objective data and with reports from teachers, parents, and others who know the child well.

Recording Responses

The record form clearly delineates the correct responses and scoring that should be marked on the record form. Spanish responses to certain subtests are given in a different color on the record form. As mentioned before, requests for repetition of stimulus items, or any other behaviors and verbalizations that may enhance or detract from performance, should be noted on the record form as they happen. You can decide at a later time whether the behaviors contribute to the interpretation of the results. The Don't Forget box suggests other important notations to make on the record form.

DON'T FORGET

Additional Important Notations to Make on the Record Form

- Note *your* verbal responses during the test administration.
- Note which items you had to teach.
- Note if you had to teach the items in a special way.
- Note if the child needed verbal encouragement from you during difficult items.
- Note any interaction that was above and beyond the usual feedback and directions.

SUBTEST-BY-SUBTEST ADMINISTRATION AND QUALITATIVE INDICATORS

In this section, only important reminders about the materials and administration are presented. The administration of the KABC-II Core and Supplementary subtests is described in detail in the manuals, on the easels, and on the record form; therefore, this section focuses more on helpful summaries and reminders for experienced examiners and important focus points for new examiners.

Information about administration

for each subtest is in the sections that follow. (Specific details on starting points, basal rules, and discontinue rules are in Rapid Reference 2.5.) In addition, notes about qualitative indicators (QIs) have been placed in each subtest's section because observations about behaviors that can enhance or detract from performance are noted on the record form after each subtest. The subtests are presented in the order in which they appear in the easels. At the end of this chapter, a Don't Forget box summarizes helpful reminders about administration.

Atlantis

This is a Core subtest for the MPI and FCI at ages 3-0 to 3-11 and is a Core Learning/*Glr* subtest for ages 4-0 to 18-11.

Administration

Only the easel and the record form are needed to administer Atlantis. Basically, you teach the name of a new fish, shell, or plant, then turn the page (after 2 seconds) and ask the child to point to the fish, shell, or plant that was named. If the child points to the wrong picture, you point to the picture and state the correct name. It is important to pronounce the names slowly and clearly and to emphasize the syllable of the name that is capitalized; for example, the name "DAB-lee" has the emphasis on "DAB." The ability to correct the child's incorrect responses is marked on the record form by an apple sign next to every item on the easel. This is a subtest that is part of the Learning/*Glr* scale, and so the correction of every incorrect item is the interactive learning part of the subtest.

Remember that if you plan to administer the Atlantis Delayed subtest you will have to follow the standard subtest sequence for the child's age in order to have the right amount of time between the initial and delayed portions of Atlantis. At age 5, Gestalt Closure has to be given as a supplementary subtest so that there is the right amount of time between the initial and delayed portions of the subtest.

Qualitative Indicators (Optional)

Before you move on from Atlantis, check any of the QIs that are mentioned on the record form that apply. Even if you intend not to include the QIs when you are scoring the results of the battery as a whole, you may change your mind during later subtests and may then have a hard time remembering which QIs were displayed on various subtests. Thus, it is good practice to note with a check mark, or notes and words of your own, behaviors that could enhance or detract from performance.

There are four QIs that are on the record form that may detract from performance:

≡ Rapid Reference 2.5

Summary of KABC-II Start Points, Basal Rules, and Discontinue Rules

Subtest	Start Point	Basal	Discontinue
Atlantis[a]	Item 1 for all ages		Cumulative raw score must be below any of the 5 stopping points clearly marked on the record form.
Conceptual Thinking	Sample 1 for ages 3–5 Sample 6 for age 6	If child scores 0 on any of the first 3 items (not counting the sample item), drop back one start point.	4 scores of 0 in 5 consecutive items
Face Recognition	Sample 1 for all ages		4 consecutive scores of 0
Story Completion	Sample for all ages, then age-based start: Item 1 for ages 6–8 Item 4 for ages 9–13 Item 8 for ages 14–18	If the child scores 0 on any of the first 3 items given (not counting the sample item), drop back one start point.	3 consecutive scores of 0
Number Recall	Sample for all ages, then age-based start: Item 1 for ages 3–6 Item 4 for ages 7–18	If the child scores 0 on any of the first 3 items (not counting the sample item), drop back one start point.	3 consecutive scores of 0
Gestalt Closure	Sample for all ages, then age-based start: Item 5 for ages 6–7 Item 9 for ages 8–10 Item 14 for ages 11–18	If child scores 0 on any of the first 3 items given, (not counting the sample item), drop back one start point.	4 consecutive scores of 0

Subtest	Start Point	Item Rule	Discontinue Rule
Rover	Sample for all ages, then Item 1		5 consecutive scores of less than 2
Atlantis Delayed	Item 1 for all ages		Stop at the last item administered on Atlantis using the table shown on the record form or after 4 consecutive scores of less than 2.
Expressive Vocabulary	Item 1 for ages 3–4 Item 7 for age 5 Item 11 for ages 6–11 Item 18 for ages 12–18	If child scores 0 on any of the first 3 items, drop back one start point.	4 consecutive scores of 0
Verbal Knowledge	Item 1 for ages 3–6 Item 11 for age 7 Item 21 for ages 8–10 Item 28 for ages 11–13 Item 34 for ages 14–18	If child scores 0 on any of the first 3 items given, drop back one start point.	5 scores of 0 in 6 consecutive items
Rebus[a]	Item 1 for all ages		Cumulative raw score must be below any of the 5 stopping points clearly marked on the record form.
Triangles	Sample A for ages 3–7, sample B for ages 8–18, then age-based start: Item 1 for ages 3–5 Item 5 for ages 6–7 Item 11 for ages 8–9 Item 15 for ages 10–18	If child scores 0 on any of the first 3 items given (not counting Sample Items), drop back one start point.	3 consecutive scores of 0
Block Counting	Sample A for all ages, then age-based start: Item 1 for ages 5–11 Item 7 for ages 11–18	If child scores 0 on any of the first 3 items given (not counting Sample Items), drop back one start point.	4 consecutive scores of 0

(continued)

Subtest	Start Point	Basal	Discontinue
Word Order	Item 1 for ages 3–5, Sample A for item 6–18, then age-based start: Item 4 for ages 6–7 Item 7 for ages 8–18	If starting at Item 4, the child must score 1 or 2 on both 4 and 5. If starting at Item 7, the examinee must pass first 3 items or drop back to Item 4 and continue testing forward until discontinue is reached.	3 consecutive scores of 0
Pattern Reasoning	Sample for all ages, then age-based start: Item 1 for ages 5–8 Item 6 for ages 9–18	If child scores 0 on any of the first 3 items given (not counting Sample Items), drop back one start point.	4 scores of 0 in 5 consecutive items
Hand Movements	Sample for all ages		3 consecutive scores of 0
Rebus Delayed	Item 1 for all ages		Stop at the last item administered on Rebus using the table shown on the record form or after 4 consecutive scores of less than 2.
Riddles	Item 1 for ages 3–6 Item 9 for ages 7–8 Item 12 for ages 9–10 Item 16 for ages 11–13 Item 21 for ages 14–15 Item 26 for ages 16–18	If child scores 0 on any of the first 3 items given, drop back one start point.	4 consecutive scores of 0

- Fails to sustain attention
- Impulsively responds incorrectly
- Reluctant to respond when uncertain
- Responds negatively to correction

This list of QIs is not exhaustive: It is quite possible that you may observe other behaviors that detract from performance, and it is important for you to make a note of your own impressions before moving on to the next subtest.

On the other hand, you may notice behaviors that really helped the child's performance. Two behaviors that may enhance performance are noted on the record form:

- Unusually focused
- Verbalizes a strategy for remembering

Again, you may see many other behaviors that also enhanced performance on Atlantis, and they can be noted on the record form as well. Performance QIs on Atlantis may also be compared with those on the Rebus subtest, which is also on the Learning/*Glr* Scale.

Conceptual Thinking

This is a Core subtest for the MPI and FCI at ages 3-0 to 3-11, a Core Simultaneous/*Gv* subtest for ages 4-0 to 6-11, and a Nonverbal scale subtest for ages 3-0 to 6-11.

Administration

Conceptual Thinking is a nonverbal measure of reasoning about classifications of things and objects in the world. The child must point to a picture that does not go with the others around it. You introduce the subtest with a sample item by saying, "Look at these pictures [gesture to the pictures]. One doesn't go with the others. Point to the one that doesn't belong." You get to teach the sample and Items 1 and 2 before the child has to respond without assistance. Only the easel and record form are needed for this subtest.

Qualitative Indicators (Optional)

There are three QIs suggested for behaviors that may detract from performance:

- Fails to sustain attention
- Impulsively responds incorrectly
- Reluctant to respond when uncertain

Remember that this subtest is for younger children, and therefore other behaviors that detract from performance may also be present.

A positive QI for this subtest is "perseveres." Younger children naturally have a tendency toward a shorter attention span; therefore, a child who really studies all of the pictures and does not give up when items get difficult may well be able to persevere when others give up. This is worth noting for a young child.

Face Recognition

This is a Core subtest for the MPI and FCI at ages 3-0 to 3-11, a Core Simultaneous/*Gv* subtest for ages 4-0 to 4-11, a Supplementary Simultaneous/*Gv* subtest for ages 5-0 to 5-11, and a Nonverbal scale subtest for ages 3-0 to 5-11.

Administration

The easel and record form are needed for the administration of Face Recognition. This is another subtest that is only used with younger examinees and is a measure of short-term memory and visual processing. You will show a picture of one or two faces and allow the child to look at the picture for 5 seconds. You then turn the page, and the child has to pick out the face(s) from a group of people shown on the response page. This subtest is timed in that you will need to time the 5-second exposure of the stimulus face(s). The sample items and Items 1 and 2 can be taught if the child is having difficulty.

Qualitative Indicators (Optional)

QIs for this subtest are based on attention. It is important to note if the child has to be prompted to pay attention or if the child is good at paying attention and really studies the response page. Look for any unusual positive or negative behaviors that reflect attention. It may also be helpful to study any pattern of unusual responses: Does the child respond to the same faces, similar faces, or similar descriptives? Note down any analyses that you observe because the information can be compared to other visual processing subtests.

Story Completion

This subtest is part of the Supplementary Simultaneous/*Gv* scale for ages 5-0 to 6-11, the Core Planning/*Gf* scale for ages 7-0 to 18-11, and the Nonverbal scale for ages 5-0 to 18-11.

Administration

Story Completion is a subtest that requires the easel for the first few items and the response booklet, cards, stopwatch, and record form for all items. The administration of this subtest requires a standardized way of laying out the cards:

- Place the booklet in front of the child (pictures facing the child).
- Place the cards
    face up
    in alphabetical order
    in a single row *below* the booklet
    starting at the child's *left.*
- Begin timing as soon as the cards have been laid out.
- Pick up cards that have been placed
    on the booklet first
    beginning on the child's *left*
    stacking the *leftmost* card on top.

Make sure that the child is done with an item, especially if there is a card missing. In this case, it is permissible to say "Each space needs a picture" before collecting the cards. Otherwise, after you are sure that the child is finished, or when the time limit has elapsed, pick up the cards and turn them over in your hand to read the word at the top of each card to score the item. There are diagrams on the easel for each item to show you the correct answer, and the words are also printed on the record form.

Following this procedure is the easiest and most accurate way of organizing the layout and eventual scoring of the items for this subtest, and you need to practice it before formally administering it. Once you have mastered it, the administration flows smoothly and frees up your attention for observations about how the child is taking the subtest and processing information.

Qualitative Indicators (Optional)
There are quite a few QIs for Story Completion because it is a test that taps complex information and planning processes. These are the potential QIs that may detract from performance:

- Does not sustain attention
- Does not monitor accuracy
- Impulsively responds incorrectly
- Reluctant to commit to a response
- Reluctant to respond when uncertain
- Worries about time limits

You must pay attention to many events during this subtest, looking for strategies that the child may employ, listening to verbalizations about the stories, watching to see if the child is attracted to distracter cards, and noting the cognitive style of reflection or impulsivity. Positive indicators, on the other hand, may center on

- Perseverance
- Trying out options
- Being unusually focused
- Verbalizing story ideas
- Working quickly but carefully

Take time to note any positive or negative QIs about this informative subtest before moving on to the next subtest. In addition, you may want to compare these QIs with those that you may find on Pattern Reasoning, the other subtest on the Planning/*Gf* scale.

Number Recall

This is a Supplementary subtest for the MPI and FCI at ages 3-0 to 3-11 and a Core Sequential/*Gsm* subtest for ages 4-0 to 18-11.

Administration

This subtest can be administered from the record form once the directions are familiar to you. However, the detailed directions are on the easel and in the manual for initial administrations. You need to simply say "I am going to say some numbers. Say them just as I do"; then you say the numbers at a steady rate of one per second. It is permissible to teach the sample item and Items 1 and 2 if necessary.

Do not drop your voice at the end of the number sequence, and say the numbers at a steady rate. Many times a younger child will begin to say the numbers before you are finished. In this case, make a nonverbal gesture to stop the child (e.g., putting your hand up in a "stop" gesture or putting your finger to your lips) and then complete the sequence. You are not allowed to repeat a sequence of numbers except when teaching an item.

Qualitative Indicators (Optional)

This is a short and straightforward subtest. Therefore, attention is often an indicator of success. Failure to pay attention will hurt performance, and having the capacity to hold attention will help performance. One interesting line of observation for you is to see if any strategies that the child shows really do help or hurt performance. For example, if the child places long strings of numbers into chunks, that strategy may help performance, but if the child tries to write the numbers as he or she is hearing them, this may slow things down and hurt performance. It is important for you to note any strategies that the child employs on the record form. It may also be helpful to compare these strategies with those that the child may use on Word Order, the other subtest on the Sequential/*Gsm* scale.

Gestalt Closure

This is a Supplementary subtest for the MPI and FCI at ages 3-0 to 3-11 and a Supplementary Simultaneous/*Gv* subtest for ages 4-0 to 18-11.

Administration

Only the record form and easel are needed for this subtest. It may be given at all ages if you want supplementary information (apart from the Core subtests) or if you want to increase time between Atlantis and Atlantis Delayed for 5-year-olds. The task demand is simple, and most children catch on quickly. The stimulus pictures are presented at a brisk but not rushed pace, and the child is given a prompt ("Make a guess") if he or she does not respond in 30 seconds.

All items have a variety of correct responses printed on the right side of the examiner's side of the easel. There are also examples of responses that you should query (and only score as correct if the queried response is correct) and examples of incorrect responses. Each type of response also has the Spanish counterpart printed next to it, and you can score the responses as correct even if they are only in Spanish.

Qualitative Indicators (Optional)

The Gestalt Closure subtest has several positive and negative QIs mentioned on the record form. The negative QIs on the record form center on attention, impulsivity, and perseveration:

- Fails to sustain attention
- Impulsively responds incorrectly
- Reluctant to respond when uncertain
- Perseverates

The positive QIs, on the other hand, are similar to other subtests:

- Perseveres
- Unusually focused
- Verbalizes ideas

It may be a good idea to compare the QIs on Gestalt Closure to other Simultaneous/*Gv* subtests to see if there are any similarities or contrasts.

Rover

This is a Core Simultaneous/*Gv* subtest for ages 6-0 to 18-11.

Administration

You will need the Rover stimulus booklet, the Rover plastic dog, a stopwatch, the easel pages, and the record form to administer Rover. Rover primarily measures Simultaneous/*Gv* processing, but it also measures problem solving and adherence to rules. Therefore, it takes some practice to administer, score, and note QIs during the subtest, but the information gleaned is rich and helpful. Generally, you will be teaching the examinee the rules step by step, and you are allowed to correct examinees when they forget or do not understand a procedure.

You generally do the following:

- Place the booklet before the child so that the item numbers are upside down to the child.
- Place Rover on the dot and demonstrate how Rover moves, how to count when Rover is moving, and where Rover can and cannot move.
- Instruct the child to get Rover to the bone in the smallest number of moves.
- Correct the child if he or she breaks a rule.
- Correct the child if he or she does not count aloud.
- Time the child after telling him or her to begin.

The detailed directions for you are on the easel and in the manual and are easy to follow. There are also pictures on the right-hand side of the examiner's side of the easel that depict the correct route(s) for each item.

Samples A and B and Items 1 through 5 can be taught, and you should give the examinee time to recover if you correct him or her as soon as they break a rule. After the child finishes the item you should also remind him or her about the rule that was broken.

Qualitative Indicators (Optional)

Again, Rover is a very information-rich test. Not only does the test measure visual and simultaneous processes, but you also get to observe how a child responds to instructions and rules during an activity. The QIs that may interfere with performance on this subtest are listed on the record form:

- Fails to sustain attention
- Impulsively responds incorrectly
- Repeatedly breaks rules
- Worries about time limits

On the other hand, Rover is also a subtest that allows you to observe whether a child tries out response options before giving a final answer and if he or she has an unusual capacity to pay attention and figure things out. Therefore, the positive QIs for this subtest are as follows:

- Tries out options
- Unusually focused

Atlantis Delayed

This is a Supplementary Learning/*Glr* subtest for ages 5-0 to 18-11.

Administration

Atlantis Delayed is not a part of the Core battery, but it can provide some invaluable information about memory and information storage and retrieval. The initial subtest, Atlantis, should have been given anywhere between 10 and 45 minutes before Atlantis Delayed. The average amount of time between these subtests is usually 20 minutes.

Before you start administration of Atlantis Delayed you must refer to the record form and circle the highest item reached on Atlantis. This circle will tell you where to stop on Atlantis Delayed. The circle is very important because it will mark the line between the items that the examinee was exposed to on Atlantis and the items that the examinee was not exposed to on Atlantis. Do not administer this subtest if the child did not reach Item 4 on Atlantis.

Qualitative Indicators (Optional)

The QIs for Atlantis Delayed are on page 8 of the record form—not after the subtest, as with the other subtests. The examinee is not expecting to see the Atlantis pictures again, and so it might be interesting to see how the child responds to the idea of having to recall information. The QIs for Atlantis Delayed are listed thus:

- Fails to sustain attention
- Impulsively responds incorrectly
- Reacts negatively to unexpected task
- Reluctant to respond when uncertain

A QI that might help performance is listed on the record form as "unusually focused."

Expressive Vocabulary

This is a Core subtest for the FCI at ages 3-0 to 3-11, a Core Knowledge/*Gc* subtest for ages 4-0 to 6-11, a Supplementary Knowledge/*Gc* subtest for ages 7-0 to 18-11, and a Supplementary subtest for ages 3-0 to 18-11.

Administration

Expressive Vocabulary draws on the child's expressive language skills to measure knowledge or crystallized ability. Therefore, this subtest is not given (or is given only as a supplementary subtest) if you are using the Luria approach. It is, however, a Core subtest for the CHC method. The materials needed for administration are the easel and record form. Expressive Vocabulary is one of the few subtests on the KABC-II that allow you to query vague or ambiguous answers. You should query answers if the child does any of the following things:

- Says something true about the object or gives one of its properties
- Says a name that is not specific enough or is overly general
- Names an irrelevant part of the picture
- Names a specific part instead of the whole object

Answers to Expressive Vocabulary can be given in any language, and the easel has correct and incorrect responses and query prompts for answers in English and Spanish.

Qualitative Indicators (Optional)

There are just a few QIs for Expressive Vocabulary. The main QI that could interfere with performance is a reluctance, for whatever reason, to respond. If you observe a reluctance to respond you may want to make a note of it and compare response patterns on other subtests or the battery in general.

Two positive QIs are mentioned on the record form:

- Perseveres
- Verbalizes related knowledge

You may wish to see if these QIs are also present on the child's responses to other verbal subtests as well to see if there is a pattern of responding to language-based tasks.

Verbal Knowledge

This is a Supplementary subtest for the FCI at ages 3-0 to 3-11, a Supplementary Knowledge/Gc subtest for ages 4-0 to 6-11, a Core Knowledge/Gc subtest for ages 7-0 to 18-11, and a Supplementary subtest for ages 3-0 to 18-11, for the Luria model.

Administration

Verbal Knowledge draws on the child's receptive language skills to measure knowledge or crystallized ability. Therefore, this subtest is not given (or is given as a supplementary subtest) if you are using the Luria approach. It is, however, a Core subtest for the CHC method.

The administration of Verbal Knowledge is simple, and you will need just the easel and the record form to administer the subtest. In fact, after initial instructions, you will read the prompts from the record form. The directions and item prompts are written in green ink on the record form and should be read aloud and verbatim. There are no teaching items on this subtest.

Qualitative Indicators (Optional)

This subtest is sensitive to an examinee's paying attention to all of the options before responding. It is important that he or she looks at all of the six pictures and deliberates between options if necessary. The QIs that might negatively affect performance are mentioned on the record form:

- Fails to sustain attention
- Frequently asks for repetition
- Impulsively responds incorrectly
- Reluctant to respond when uncertain

An examinee who takes his or her time and surveys all of the pictures has a distinct advantage on this subtest. Therefore, these QIs may enhance performance:

- Surveys pictures before responding
- Unusually focused

You may want to compare or contrast the QIs on this subtest with those of the other subtests on the Knowledge/Gc scale to get a picture of behaviors that may influence performance on language subtests.

Rebus

This is a Core Learning/Glr subtest for ages 4-0 to 18-11.

Administration

All that is needed for the administration of the Rebus subtest is the easel and record form. Rebus measures the ability to learn new information in the form of symbols and words. It is an activity that requires quite a bit of concentration, memory, attention, and language processes all at the same time. Hence, Rebus places on the Learning Scale along with Atlantis. A fundamental difference between Rebus and Atlantis is that you teach the words and symbols to the child but do *not* give corrective feedback as with Atlantis.

Item 1 is the only item that can be taught if the child makes a mistake. After Item 1, the general sequence of administration is the same for the rest of the items. Basically, you teach new rebuses, rehearse the rebuses with the child, turn the page, and ask the child to read the rebus sentences. After a few items the child usually becomes comfortable with the sequence and you and the examinee form a rhythm together. It quickly becomes apparent to the child that the sentences need to make logical sense, and it is interesting to see how examinees handle missing key words when trying to comprehend the rebus sentences at the same time.

Rebus requires a little rehearsal and practice to learn how to administer it in a smooth fashion. Once you learn the basic rhythm, the administration is easy and allows you to spend more time watching how the child manages the learning experience.

Qualitative Indicators (Optional)

The QIs for Rebus are numerous because the subtest measures complex processes and takes a lot of concentration, coordination, and flexibility. These QIs may negatively affect performance:

- Fails to sustain attention
- Impulsively responds incorrectly
- Perseverates
- Refuses to engage in task
- Reluctant to respond when uncertain

The behaviors that may enhance performance are about attention and the capacity to use context cues about the sentence meaning.

Triangles

This is a Core subtest for the MPI and FCI at ages 3-0 to 3-11, a Core Simultaneous/*Gv* subtest for ages 4-0 to 12-11, a Supplementary Simultaneous/*Gv* subtest for ages 13-0 to 18-11, and a Nonverbal scale subtest for ages 3-0 to 18-11.

Administration

You will need the easel, record form, plastic and rubber shapes, and stopwatch for administration of this subtest. There are ample teaching and sample items at each age level on Triangles, and you will need to practice laying out pieces and become familiar with scoring criteria and prompts before administration. The pieces that you will need for each item are conveniently pictured in the lower right-hand corner of the examiner's pages. Remember to put the pieces in a random array in front of the examinee before you expose the stimulus page. For the yellow-and-blue foam pieces, try to place half with the yellow side up and half with the blue side facing up. Many younger children try to match the pieces with the easel picture and lift the piece to the actual page. If this happens, say "Please keep the pieces on the table."

Qualitative Indicators (Optional)

As with other timed subtests, it is important to note if the examinee mentions any worry about time limits or about being timed. Sometimes worrying about time gets in the way of processing information on a subtest and negatively affects performance. There are other negative QIs:

- Fails to sustain attention
- Moves pieces haphazardly
- Does not monitor accuracy (is satisfied with incorrect response)

Performance-enhancing QIs deal with concentration and consistent checking of work before going ahead. Flexibility also helps on Triangles because trying different solutions and strategies helps when faced with a difficult problem. Positive QIs include:

- Perseveres
- Tries out options
- Unusually focused
- Works quickly but carefully

Block Counting

This is a Supplementary Simultaneous/*Gv* subtest for ages 5-0 to 12-11, a Core Simultaneous/*Gv* subtest for ages 13-0 to 18-11, and a Nonverbal scale subtest for ages 7-0 to 18-11.

Administration

Block Counting taps similar information processes to Triangles. Remember that Block Counting is only a Core subtest for ages 13–18, but it can be given to children as young as 5 years.

You will, for the most part, need the easel, stopwatch, and record form to administer Block Counting. There are wooden blocks present in the test kit, but they are only used on teaching items if necessary. It is all right for the examinee to touch the pictures on this subtest. If the child asks whether there are any gaps in the pile, you are to say "The pile is solid—there are no gaps." Items 20–35 have time limits that require you to start timing when you turn the page to expose the picture.

Qualitative Indicators (Optional)

The record form shows general negative and positive indicators about performance for Block Counting. The following behaviors might detract from performance:

- Fails to sustain attention
- Impulsively responds incorrectly
- Reluctant to respond when uncertain
- Worries about time limits

These are the positive QIs for this subtest:

- Perseveres
- Unusually focused
- Verbalizes a strategy

Many times, children and adolescents will start to think aloud during the more challenging items, and you may hear them talking their way through a problem. Sometimes the child who perseveres and will not give up reaches a higher ceiling item just because of endurance.

Word Order

This is a Core subtest for the MPI and FCI at ages 3-0 to 3-11 and a Core Sequential/*Gsm* subtest for ages 4-0 to 18-11.

Administration

Word Order requires the easel, the record form, the Word Order object card, and the cover card for administration. You say a series of words, and the child then points to pictures of those words in the same order. Say the stimulus words at a steady rate of one per second. Try not to group the words rhythmically, and do not drop your voice at the end of a sequence. You are also not allowed to repeat any stimulus words unless you are teaching the task. On later items, you cover up the pictures while the child names colors rapidly, then you uncover the pictures and the child has to point to the pictures that were named.

Qualitative Indicators (Optional)

Sometimes the color interference task can distress the child. It is a good idea to make note of how the examinee adjusts to the change from one task to a new task during a single subtest. This subtest is sensitive to attention and impulsivity; therefore the negative QIs are listed thus:

- Distressed by color interference task
- Fails to sustain attention
- Impulsively responds incorrectly

On the other hand, a child who can develop strategies like verbalizing or who can sustain attention can enhance his or her performance on Word Order. These are the enhancing QIs:

- Unusually focused
- Verbalizes stimulus

Pattern Reasoning

This is a Core Simultaneous/*Gv* subtest for ages 5-0 to 6-11, a Core Planning/*Gf* subtest for ages 7-0 to 18-11, and a Nonverbal scale subtest for ages 5-0 to 18-11.

Administration

The Pattern Reasoning subtest is administered with the easel, the record form, and a stopwatch. The examinee sees a row of images with one image missing and selects an image that can be placed in the gap to complete the pattern. The child can either say or point to the correct response. If the child spends a great deal of time on one item, it is all right for you to move him or her along by saying "Make a guess." Start timing when you turn the page to expose the stimulus problem. All examinees start with Sample 1.

Qualitative Indicators (Optional)

Pattern Reasoning requires quite a bit of concentration and attention and a willingness to take time to look at all of the response options. As with any subtest that requires timing, the presence of a stopwatch can distract some children from performing to the best of their ability. The QIs that detract from performance are mentioned on the record form:

- Fails to sustain attention
- Impulsively responds incorrectly

- Reluctant to respond when uncertain
- Worries about time limits

The positive QIs mentioned on the record form focus on the ability to sustain attention and not give up even when the problems become more difficult. Some children may also solve the item from looking at the stem of the problem as opposed to trying out different options. These are the positive QIs for Pattern Reasoning:

- Perseveres
- Unusually focused
- Tries to solve problem without looking at options

Hand Movements

This is a Supplementary subtest for the MPI and FCI at ages 3-0 to 3-11, a Supplementary Sequential/*Gsm* subtest for ages 4-0 to 18-11, and a Nonverbal scale subtest for ages 3-0 to 18-11.

Administration

Hand Movements requires the easel and record form for administration. You present a series of movements with your hand (palm down, fist, and side) and then wait for the child to copy the sequence with his or her hand. It is important to make sure that the child is paying attention before you start the sequence with your hand. Also, move your hand at a steady rate of one movement per second and just touch the table lightly. If a child starts to respond before you are done with an item, tell the child "Wait" and then complete the sequence.

Qualitative Indicators (Optional)

It is interesting to see how younger children choose which hand to use for this subtest. Some children try one hand and then the other, and sometimes the child might even try to alternate hands for the same item. It is also interesting to see if the child invents a strategy to help remember the movements. The child may try to move along with you and rehearse as he or she sees the movements; some children verbalize names for the movements.

These are the negative QIs for Hand Movements that are on the record form:

- Fails to sustain attention
- Hesitates over which hand to use

The positive QIs are as follows:

- Unusually focused
- Verbalizes a strategy

Rebus Delayed

This subtest is part of the Supplementary Learning/*Glr* scale for ages 5-0 to 18-11.

Administration

Rebus Delayed measures long-term storage and retrieval of information learned earlier in the testing session. Therefore, it is important that the standard subtest sequence for the child's age is followed in order to have the appropriate time interval between Rebus and Rebus Delayed. At ages 13–18, Gestalt Closure should be given as a supplementary subtest immediately before Rebus Delayed. The minimal allowable interval is 10 minutes, and the maximum is 60 minutes.

Rebus Delayed is not given if the examinee's raw score on Rebus was 4 or less. It is also important not to administer items above the stopping point shown on the record form. The items after the stopping point have no relevance for the child because they were not taught on the initial subtest.

Qualitative Indicators (Optional)

Rebus Delayed demands that previous learning be brought up and reworked. The Rebus task also demands that the sentences make sense, and this need for comprehension of the whole sentence can confound performance with some children. The negative indicators for Rebus Delayed are stated on the record form:

- Fails to sustain attention
- Impulsively responds incorrectly
- Perseverates
- Reacts negatively to unexpected task
- Reluctant to respond when uncertain

The positive QIs for Rebus Delayed are cited as follows:

- Unusually focused
- Uses context cues (i.e., sentence meaning)

The child that can be flexible and use sentence meaning to help with decoding the rebuses does well on this subtest.

Riddles

This is a Core subtest for the FCI at ages 3-0 to 3-11, a Core Knowledge/*Gc* subtest for ages 4-0 to 18-11, and a Supplementary subtest in the Luria Model for all ages.

Administration

Riddles draws on the child's receptive language skills to measure knowledge or crystallized ability. Therefore, this subtest is not given (or is given only as a supplementary subtest) if you are using the Luria approach. It is, however, a Core subtest for the CHC method.

Riddles is a measure of verbal comprehension, verbal reasoning, and word retrieval, and therefore it is permissible to receive answers in English, Spanish, or another language (just as long as you know if the answer is correct). The items are read verbatim from the record form. Both English and Spanish answers are written on the record form as well. You will also need the easel picture items if you will be administering Items 1–8 to younger children.

Qualitative Indicators (Optional)

The QIs that might detract from performance are mentioned on the record form:

- Fails to sustain attention
- Frequently asks for repetition
- Frequently responds based on the first one or two clues

The positive QIs for this subtest are as follows:

- Unusually focused
- Verbalizes stimulus

As with the other subtests that go to make up the Crystallized Knowledge/*Gc* scale, it is a good idea to compare positive and negative QIs on Riddles with those of the other language subtests. The Don't Forget box lists helpful reminders for the administration of all of the KABC-II subtests.

GENERAL CONSIDERATIONS FOR SCORING

The following sections discuss considerations that may affect the scoring of subtests.

Substitutions

During the development of the KABC-II, certain subtests were chosen to be Core subtests because they best represent the construct of the scale being measured. Therefore, always administer the Core subtests unless disruptive events beyond your control occur (e.g., loud, disruptive noises). These types of events

DON'T FORGET

Helpful Administration Reminders

Atlantis

- Do not forget to introduce the whole battery and explain the variety of tasks and the easy and difficult aspects *before* starting this subtest. This is the first subtest for all ages, and the examinee must be eased into the activity and feel comfortable with the process before jumping into items on which he or she will be graded.
- Make sure that your tone is neutral when correcting an incorrect response— do not impart a critical or negative tone when you are correcting. If you have to teach items, try to make it a pleasant learning experience for the examinee.
- Take your time when pointing out corrections to the child. Give the child a few moments to recode the name of the picture.
- It is all right to repeat the name of the stimulus. However, take note if a child repeatedly asks for you to repronounce the names of the pictures: Is he or she having problems with discriminating sounds, or just having trouble remembering the names? Note down excessive requests for repetition of the stimulus names and try to check this observation with other data from the rest of the battery.
- Note how the child responds to being redirected when he or she gives a wrong answer. Does he or she become defensive? Does rapport with you or the test change? Does he or she verbalize any negative feelings or thoughts?

Conceptual Thinking

- Make sure that the child is looking at the page before you give the prompt.
- Fade out the prompts when the child is used to the subtest format procedures.
- If the child asks a question about an item, respond with something like "Just pick the one that you think is best" or "Pick the best answer that you can think of."
- Note if the child looks at all of the stimulus options before responding.
- Note if you have to help the child orient to the stimulus every time the page is turned.

Face Recognition

- Practice timing 5-second intervals before administering the subtest.
- Make sure the child is looking at the stimulus page before proceeding with an item.
- Do not allow the child to turn the pages.
- Remember if the child only points to one face (on a two-face item) to say "Remember, you have to point to two people."
- Remember that you cannot repeat exposure to a stimulus page even if the child asks for another look.
- Note how the child responds to more difficult items.
- Note if the child verbalizes how he or she is discriminating between faces.

(continued)

Story Completion

- Make sure you have enough room to lay out the stimulus booklet with both pages open.
- Make sure that the stimulus cards are in the right order in the box.
- Practice saying the instructions while laying out the cards before administering the subtest.
- Do not forget that you only informally time the first seven items.
- Remember to time Items 8–18 for ages 7–18 for 1 or 2 extra points.
- Note if the child talks his or her way through the story.
- Note if the child impulsively picks any card or cards to fill in the blanks.
- Note if the child thinks first and then places cards.
- Note if the child places cards and tries out different scenarios as he or she goes along.

Number Recall

- Practice saying the numbers 1 second apart in front of the second hand of a clock or watch.
- Make sure you do not raise or lower your voice at the end of the series of digits.
- Try not to give feedback after each item (most of the time the child will know if he or she got the item correct or incorrect), but give encouragement where appropriate.
- Note any observable strategies that the child may use to help with remembering, such as saying the numbers back quickly, chunking, or writing the numbers on the table or in the air.

Gestalt Closure

- Be careful not to give verbal or nonverbal cues about the correctness of any answer.
- Remember, if the child gives the name of only part of the picture, say "Yes, but tell me the name of the whole thing."
- Remember, if the child gives a response that is vague, ask a clarifying question, such as "Yes, and what is it called?" or "Tell me more."
- Remember that it is not necessary for the child to give the precise name. It is all right for him or her to indicate recognition of the correct object.
- Remember to give credit if the child points to something in the room that is the same as the correct response.
- Note if the child spends too little time looking at the picture.
- Note if the child takes a long time to respond.
- Note any bizarre answers.

Rover

- Practice the rules and especially responses to practice or sample items (correct and incorrect answers).

- Try out the items for yourself, working out each item and becoming familiar with the different routes. This will make later administration much easier for you.
- Remember to time *all* items, but be informal on the first six items. On Item 7 you will inform the examinee that he or she is going to be timed by saying, "I'm going to keep track of how long this takes us. Don't rush; the most important thing is to give the correct answer."
- Be patient with children who have a hard time remembering the rules or remembering your directions—most children will eventually catch on.

Atlantis Delayed

- Give the examinee a few moments to get used to the idea that he or she is going to have to recall names and pictures.
- Remain neutral in your responses to correct or incorrect answers—remember that no feedback should be given during the delayed part of Atlantis.
- Note if the child takes a long time to recall each name.
- Note whether the child blurts out answers and then self-corrects.

Expressive Vocabulary

- Turn the pages at steady pace.
- Accept Spanish answers with the same criteria as English answers.
- Do not forget that the illustrations that have an arrow or a magnified section mean you have to call attention to a particular part of the picture.

Verbal Knowledge

- It is all right for the child to point to the response or to say the name of the letter underneath the picture.
- Turn the easel around after Item 46 to continue.
- Do not tell the child the correct response, but do encourage effort.
- Note whether the child looks at all of the response options before answering.
- Note if the child impulsively points to a picture without taking time to think about it.
- Query a response if it is clear that the child misunderstood your stimulus word or phrase.

Rebus

- Make sure that the child says the word right *after* you say it (not at the same time or a long time after you say it).
- Practice pointing and saying the stimulus words at the same time before giving the test.
- Do not repeat the stimulus words unless a major interruption stops you from being heard or from speaking.
- If the child pauses for 5 seconds on the response page, say "Go on to the next one."

(continued)

- Do not score *the* after Item 7.
- Accept either *is* or *are* when that rebus appears.
- Remember to follow the standard subtest sequence for the child's age in order to have the appropriate time interval between Rebus and Rebus Delayed (10–60 minutes).
- Gestalt Closure should be given as a supplementary subtest immediately *before* Rebus Delayed for 13- to 18-year-olds.

Triangles

- Practice laying out the puzzle pieces before administering the subtest—it is important to lay out each item in a confident manner because the examinee will be watching and encoding information at the same time.
- Practice saying the directions as you are laying out the pieces.
- Note any strategies that the child uses in manipulating the pieces (e.g., chunking, color coding, trial and error, inventing new approaches).
- Stop timing when it is clear that the child is done (ask if you are not sure).
- An examinee aged 7–18 may be scored with the untimed procedure if timing would be inappropriate (e.g., if the child has motor-skill problems). In this case, use the scoring procedure for ages 3–6.
- Do not name any of the designs (e.g., *truck* for Item 4).

Block Counting

- Make sure that the examinee sees the sample block on the picture.
- Note if the examinee is impulsive or reflective.
- Remember, you can build a three-dimensional teaching model with the blocks if you need to.
- All examinees start at Sample A.
- Remember that it is all right for the examinee to touch the picture.
- Notice if the child's response style changes when the items get more difficult.

Word Order

- Practice saying the names of the picture with an even pace 1 second apart.
- Practice sliding the covering card with your nonwriting hand holding the tab.
- Practice the interference movements with the color card, sliding the cover card back and forth and checking to see which color row needs to be exposed.
- Remember to slide the covering card *away* from the child to expose the colors and *toward* the child to expose the pictures.
- Remember that the color row changes with every item.
- Note if the child says the names of the pictures as he or she points.
- Note if the color interference test makes the child forget the stimulus words.
- Note if the child guesses.

Pattern Reasoning

- Remember there are no time limits, just bonus points for quick performance on upper items.
- Remember that a child aged 7–18 may be scored with the untimed procedure if timing would be inappropriate (e.g., if the child has a motor impairment). In this case, score 1 point for a correct response for *all* items.
- Try not to give verbal or nonverbal feedback about the correctness of items, but do praise effort.
- Note where the child's eyes go on the stimulus page—does he or she look at all of the response options? Does he or she check back and forth between the stimulus and the response options?

Hand Movements

- Remove any loose or noisy jewelry on the hand that you will use to administer the items.
- Remove your hand from view as soon as you finish an item.
- Note how the child responds (any changes) when the item sequence gets longer.

Rebus Delayed

- Remember that *the* is not scored after Item 2.
- You can accept *is* or *are* when that rebus appears.
- Remember there is no penalty for extra words.
- Note how the child responds to seeing Rebus come up again.
- Don't forget after discontinuing to refer to the table in the record form to convert the cumulative raw score to the total raw score for the subtest.

Riddles

- You can repeat an item if the child asks you to or if you think the child did not hear it.
- If the child describes the object or concept, say "Yes, but what do we call it?"
- If the child gives an overly general response, say "Yes, but tell me a better name for it."
- If the child gives a response with two or more words, say "Remember, the answer has to be just one word. Tell me the best word."
- Remember that you can accept responses in Spanish (or other languages), but you cannot administer any item in Spanish (or another language).
- Responses scored under "query" are scored incorrect unless the child gives a correct response after being queried.
- Try not to give verbal or nonverbal feedback about the correctness of responses.
- Note if the child asks for excessive repetitions of the stimulus problem.
- Note how the child self-monitors progress. For example, does the child respond if he or she gets several items wrong?

should only occur rarely (otherwise you should probably review the appropriateness of the testing location).

In the event that a substitution must be made, it is permissible to substitute *one* Supplementary subtest for a Core subtest. Figure 2.3 shows the permitted substitutions for Core subtests.

Prorating

If there is a subtest that is spoiled or omitted, you may prorate to obtain a global scale index or the Nonverbal index. However, there are two conditions that should be met:

1. There is at least one valid subtest on each scale that is included in the global scale index.
2. There are at least two usable subtests if you are prorating for the Simultaneous/*Gv* index or the Nonverbal index.

To prorate, compute the rounded mean of the usable scaled scores and substitute the mean number for the subtest scaled score. The authors caution that you should not perform any interpretive analysis with any scores obtained by prorating.

Raw Scores of Zero

There are two rules to follow to decide whether to interpret a scale that has subtest raw scores of zero:

1. If three or more subtests on the core battery have raw scores of zero, do not interpret either global scale.
2. If there are not at least two subtests with raw scores greater than zero on a scale or the Nonverbal scale, do not interpret that scale index.

Raw Scores

Computing the raw scores for each subtest is relatively easy because the scoring is objective and does not require interpretation by the examiner. Rapid Reference 2.6 lists the subtests that are scored with simple binary (0/1) scoring. There are some tricky areas in scoring in some places, however, and these areas are reviewed in the Caution box. Once all of the raw scores are calculated, transfer them to the front or back page (depending on the age of the examinee).

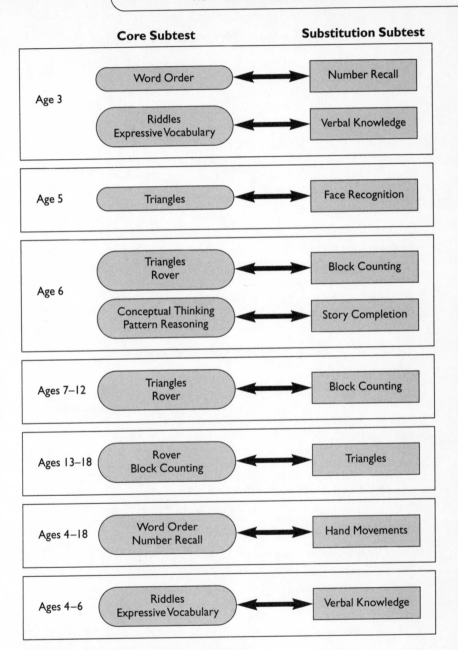

Figure 2.3 Acceptable subtest substitutions.

KABC-II Subtests with Simple 1 or 0 Scoring

For each item, an examinee is scored either 1 or 0 points for the following subtests:

Conceptual Thinking

Face Recognition

Number Recall

Gestalt Closure

Expressive Vocabulary

Verbal Knowledge

Word Order[a]

Hand Movements

Riddles

[a]Word Order is scored 1 or 0 for Items 6–27, but for Items 1–5 examinees earn 2 points if they get the item correct on the first trial and 1 point if they get the item correct on the second trial.

CAUTION

Subtests with Multipoint Scoring

Atlantis Scoring Rules

- Score 2 points for a correct response, 1 point for an incorrect response in the same category (fish, shell, or plant), and 0 points for an incorrect response in a different category.
- For example, if you present Zuke and the child points to Zuke, then he or she receives 2 points. However, if the child points to Lops, then you would mark 1 point because Lops is a fish but not the right fish. In this example, if you present Zuke and the child points to a plant or shell, then you would score the response as 0 because the plant and shell are different categories.
- If the child stops at any of the stopping points (as opposed to going to the end of the entire subtest) you need to convert the cumulative score to a raw score using the table on the record form.

Story Completion Scoring Rules

- Items 1–7 are scored 1 or 0.
- However, for ages 7–18, scoring also relies on time points. An examinee can gain up to 2 extra points on these items for quick completion, as indicated on the record form.
- If the examinee goes over the time limit, the score is 0.

Rover Scoring Rules

- Scoring is based only on the path that the child takes as the shortest route. Oral counting errors or failure to count aloud do not affect scores.

- However, on Items 4 and 5, failure to orally count two moves on the rock results in a score of 0 (this is prompted in the appropriate easel pages and is there only to make sure that the child knows to count 2 for a rock).
- The correct number of moves is stated on the record form, and if the child gets Rover to the bone in this number of legal moves, then the score is 2.
- The record form tells you whether to give a 1 or 0 score depending on how many moves the child makes above the correct amount.
- By Item 6 the examinee should understand the rules, and therefore the presence of any illegal move shifts the score to 0 automatically.

Atlantis Delayed Scoring Rules

- If the examinee stops before Item 12 on Atlantis Delayed, use the table on the record form to convert the cumulative score to a raw score.

Rebus Scoring Rules

- Each word in a Rebus sentence has a check box on the record form. Mark the number of correct words and locate the score above that number.
- Responses have to be completely correct to get credit (e.g., *girls* is incorrect for *girl*).
- There is also *no* penalty for extra words.
- After discontinuing, refer to the table in the record form to convert the cumulative raw score to the total raw score.

Triangles Scoring Rules

- The scoring of easier items on Triangles is clearly itemized on the record form, and all of the criteria for an individual item must be met for a score of 1.
- At ages 7–18 record the time with a stopwatch because scoring is dependent on the amount of seconds it takes for the child to complete the item.
- Any orientation of the design is acceptable, but there can be no gaps greater than one quarter of an inch between pieces, and alignment should be no more than one quarter of an inch off.

Block Counting Scoring Rules

- Items 1–26 are scored with 1 point for a correct response.
- Items 27–35 are scored 2 points for a correct response and 1 point for a response that is 1 block greater or less than the correct response.
- On Items 20–35, score 0 for a response that exceeds the time limit.

Pattern Reasoning Scoring Rules

- At ages 5–6 score 1 point for a correct response.
- At ages 7–18 record the response time for Items 10–36 and award bonus points for quick responses.

Rebus Delayed Scoring Rules

- Record responses the same way that you did on Rebus. A response must be completely correct to be given credit.
- If the examinee stops before Item 11 on Rebus Delayed, use the table on the record form to convert the cumulative score to a raw score.

OBTAINING AND RECORDING SCALED SCORES AND INDEX SCORES

The front cover of the record form is for recording scores for ages 7–18, and the back cover of the record form is for recording scores for 3- to 6-year-olds. Make sure that you have the correct cover before proceeding. Also remember that the front *inside* cover is for documenting scale index analyses and graphing scale indexes for 7- to 18-year-olds. The front *inside* cover of the record form is for documenting scale index analyses and graphing scale indexes for 3- to 6-year-olds.

Step-by-Step Procedure for Recording Scores

The steps in Rapid Reference 2.7 are included to help you collate the scores and indexes needed for basic interpretation. The steps are somewhat abbreviated, and therefore you should refer to the manual for expanded information. This list of steps is presented to illuminate the main procedural steps needed for filling out the front or back cover pages for ages 4–18. The scoring steps are similar for 3-year-olds, but there is a special place for cumulative scores and indexes for this age group on the back cover page. Remember that the Nonverbal index cumulative score section is separate and is on both the front and back score pages.

≡ Rapid Reference 2.7

Procedures for Recording Scores

Step 1

Write the subtest raw scores in the first column of the table labeled Subtest Scores.

Designate if Story Completion, Triangles, or Pattern Reasoning was scored without time points by checking the box next to the subtest name.

Step 2

Convert subtest raw scores to scaled scores using Table D.1 in the manual.

Step 3

Record the percentile rank and/or the age equivalent for each subtest score. Refer to Tables D.4 and D.5, respectively, in the columns next to the scaled scores.

Step 4

Transfer the subtest scaled scores to the area beneath the name of the scale to which the subtest belongs. *The subtest names and scale names are color coded to help this transfer.*

Step 5

Write the sum of the subtest scaled scores in the designated oval.

Step 6

Transfer each sum to the appropriate oval in the section below, labeled Scale Indexes.

Step 7

Convert the sums of scaled scores for the scales and the global scale to standard scores by referring to Table D.2.

Step 8

Write the converted scores in the rectangles to the right of the ovals, in the column headed Standard Scores.

Step 9

Write the 90% or 95% confidence interval for each standard score (also in Table D.2) in the indicated spaces.

Step 10

Circle the confidence interval used.

Step 11

Obtain percentile ranks corresponding to the scaled scores in Table D.4.

Analysis of Scale Indexes

Pages 3 and 23 of the record form continue with analyses and interpretation of results (see Chapters 3 and 4).

🐦 TEST YOURSELF 🐦

1. **On all subtests on the KABC-II, an examiner can accept a correct answer in any language.** True or False?

2. **Instructions as to which subtests to administer at any given age are available where?**

   (a) Record form

   (b) Manual

   (c) Back of the Rover booklet

   (d) All of the above

3. **The stimulus exposure for Atlantis is _____ seconds.**

4. **The Spanish instructions and teaching prompts for each subtest are placed on a foldout flap at the beginning of the subtest.** True or False?

5. **The maximum amount of minutes allowed between the initial Atlantis and Atlantis Delayed is**

   (a) 20 minutes.

   (b) 15 minutes.

   (c) 45 minutes.

   (d) 30 minutes.

6. **The front of the KABC-II protocol provides scores for 7- to 18-year-olds, and the back of the protocol provides scoring for 3- to 6-year-olds.** True or False?

7. **The best time to record qualitative indicators is**

   (a) after the entire administration of the KABC-II.

   (b) during a break.

   (c) during the subtest.

   (d) when you are writing the report.

   (e) at the beginning of the subtest.

Answers: 1. True; 2. d; 3. Two; 4. False; 5. c; 6. True; 7. c

Three

HOW TO INTERPRET THE KABC-II: STEP BY STEP

I nterpretation of the KABC-II focuses on the *scale profile,* which has its roots in two separate theories: the CHC theory of cognitive abilities and Luria's neuropsychological theory. Although the first interpretive step requires interpretation of the global score (MPI for the Luria model and FCI for the CHC model), neither the global scores nor the subtest scores are considered particularly important for KABC-II interpretation. A global score provides a reliable norms-based overviews of the child's overall test performance and offers an approximate midpoint to assess the child's relative strengths and weaknesses on the KABC-II scales. In isolation, however, a global score tells nothing about a child's strengths and weaknesses; for that type of picture of a child's cognitive functioning, you need to interpret the scale profile. Similarly, scores on specific subtests are of little value. The primary function of subtests is to complement each other, so that each scale provides thorough measurement of their theoretical constructs it is intended to measure. When subtest scaled scores differ substantially from other subtests on the same scale, those deviations are useful for helping you generate hypotheses that require verification with additional data from other tests, clinical observations of behaviors, and integration of pertinent background information.

The main goal of the KABC-II interpretive steps provided in this chapter is to identify and promote understanding of the child's strong and weak areas of cognitive functioning and mental processing, from both *normative* (age-based) and *ipsative* (person-based) perspectives. The system in this chapter includes the four steps described in the KABC-II manual (Kaufman & Kaufman, 2004a, Chapter 5) but expands this system to include two additional steps. In the next section, the KABC-II scales are interpreted from the vantage point of the two theories on which the KABC-II is based. Then the six interpretive steps are presented and illustrated with data obtained from an administration of the KABC-II to a child who has reading problems.

What the Scales Measure

Each of the five KABC-II scales can be interpreted from both a CHC and Luria perspective. Even the Knowledge/*Gc* scale, though excluded from the Luria model, is interpretable through Luria's neuropsychological theory. Interpretations of the five scales from the vantage point of the dual theoretical model that underlies the KABC-II appear in the KABC-II manual (Kaufman & Kaufman, 2004a, pp. 43–45). At age 3, as noted previously, only global scores are provided. The scale profile is yielded for children ages 4–18, although Planning/*Gf* is included only for ages 7–18.

Overview of the KABC-II Step-by-Step Interpretive Approach

The interpretive system described in this book comprises *six* steps, two more than the system included in the KABC-II manual (Kaufman & Kaufman, 2004a, Chapter 5). The first four steps of the system described here are identical to the four steps in the manual; steps 5 and 6 are new, but they represent a logical continuation of steps 1–4. Rapid Reference 3.1 summarizes the six interpretive steps, and the KABC-II Interpretive Worksheet (Appendix A) provides a place to work through and summarize each of the steps for your clients' profiles. Only the first two steps, which focus on the global score (step 1) and the profile of scale indexes (step 2), are considered *essential*. These two steps require administration only of the Core battery and are applicable to both the CHC and Luria model and for all children aged 3 to 18 years (see the Don't Forget box).

≡ *Rapid Reference 3.1*

Summary of KABC-II Interpretive Steps

Essential Steps

Step 1. Interpret the global scale index, whether the FCI (CHC model), MPI (Luria model), or Nonverbal index (NVI) (ages 3–18).

Step 2. Interpret the child's profile of scale indexes to identify strengths and weaknesses, both personal (relative to the child's overall ability) and normative (compared to children about the same age) (ages 4–18).

Optional Steps

Step 3. Planned scale comparisons
   Step 3A: Initial learning versus delayed recall—Learning/*Glr* (initial) versus delayed recall (ages 5–18)
   Step 3B: Learning versus acquired knowledge—Learning/*Glr* versus Knowledge/*Gc* (ages 4–18)

Step 4. Supplementary subtest analysis

Step 5. Planned clinical comparisons
      Step 5A: Nonverbal ability (NVI) versus verbal ability (ages 3–18)
      Step 5B: Problem-solving ability versus memory and learning (ages 3–18)
      Step 5C: Visual perception of meaningful stimuli versus abstract stimuli
            (ages 4–18)
      Step 5D: Verbal response versus pointing response (ages 4–18)
      Step 5E: Little or no motor response versus gross-motor response (ages
            4–18)

Step 6. Generating hypotheses to explain fluctuations in two circumstances
      Step 6A: Scales that are not interpretable (ages 4–18)
      Step 6B: Supplementary subtests that are inconsistent with pertinent
            Core subtests (ages 3–18)

DON'T FORGET

Administration Requirements for Conducting the Interpretive Steps

Interpretive Step	Administration Requirement	Supplementary Subtests Required
1	Core subtests	None
2	Core subtests	None
3A	Core and Supplementary subtests	Rebus Delayed and Atlantis Delayed (ages 5–18)
3B	Core subtests	None
4	Core and Supplementary subtests	Any Supplementary subtest
5A	Core and Supplementary subtests	Hand Movements (ages 3–18) Expressive Vocabulary (ages 7–18) Verbal Knowledge (ages 4–6)
5B	Core subtests	None
5C	Core subtests	None
5D	Core and Supplementary subtests	Verbal Knowledge (age 4)
5E	Core and Supplementary subtests	Block Counting (ages 7–12) Hand Movements (age 4)
6A	Core and Supplementary subtests	Same as step 5
6B	Core and Supplementary subtests	Any Supplementary subtests

Optional steps 3 to 6 incorporate Supplementary subtests and explore some alternative groupings of KABC-II subtests into clinically relevant clusters. The main goal of the optional steps is to generate hypotheses to be verified with other data (background information, clinical observations, and other test scores). With verification, these hypotheses may prove useful for developing educational strategies when used alongside the results of the scale index analyses conducted in step 2. None of the six steps involves interpretation of subtest-specific abilities.

The process of developing hypotheses about cognitive abilities via profile interpretation has drawn criticism by some. Kaufman (1994b) summarizes some of the critics' reviews of profile interpretation as well as IQ tests in general, and Kaufman and Lichtenberger (2002; Lichtenberger & Kaufman, 2004) address similar concerns about profile interpretation that have been raised by critics. For example, McDermott, Fantuzzo, and Glutting (1990) have leveled severe criticisms against any type of profile interpretive system. Critics have been especially vocal about interpretive systems developed for the profiles of Wechsler instruments. For example, Schaefer (2002) said the following about the system advocated in his review of *Essentials of WISC-III and WPPSI-R Assessment* (Kaufman & Lichtenberger, 2000): "Were readers of this book to fully embrace its contents, they might fall prey to delusions of profile overinterpretation" (p. 395).

In contrast to the severe criticisms of McDermott, Glutting, and colleagues, Flanagan and Alfonso (2000) have more moderate criticism of the psychometric profile approaches advocated by Kaufman and Lichtenberger (1999, 2002, Lichtenberger & Kaufman, 2004). The main criticisms stem from the fact that the Kaufman-Lichtenberger profile approach includes clinical categorizations and theoretical categorizations of subtests that do not have empirical support. Thus, Flanagan and Alfonso are not critical of the notion of profile interpretation per se but advocate the interpretation of alternate groupings of subtests only if those groupings are construct valid—for example, the Broad and Narrow Abilities from the perspective of CHC theory (e.g., Flanagan, McGrew, & Ortiz, 2000). Indeed, CHC theory is one of the KABC-II's founding theories.

In spite of our personal belief in the value of the complete profile interpretation approach outlined in this book, we do recognize that some examiners may be comfortable only with interpreting KABC-II scores that are specifically yielded by the battery (i.e., the global indexes and the scale indexes). For that reason, we have made only the first two interpretive steps essential; the remaining steps, which typically involve alternate groupings of KABC-II subtests and hypothesis generation, are considered optional.

In addition, the interpretive system proposed in the KABC-II manual and expanded in this book reflects a substantial modification of previous systems associated with Kaufman (1979) and his colleagues (e.g., Kaufman & Kaufman,

1983b; Kaufman & Lichtenberger, 2002; Lichtenberger & Kaufman, 2004). The new KABC-II approach, is similar to a new approach for WISC-IV interpretation (Flanagan & Kaufman, 2004) in that it (1) limits the number of alternate groupings of subtests to a small number of carefully chosen clusters; (2) does not advocate the interpretation of subtest-specific abilities under any circumstances; and (3) blends ipsative assessment (strengths and weaknesses relative to the person's own level of ability) with normative assessment (strengths and weaknesses relative to one's age mates) instead of focusing only on ipsative comparisons.

These conceptual modifications in both the KABC-II and WISC-IV interpretive systems reflect our response to critics of earlier systems and our careful evaluation of the points raised by critics. Nonetheless, no aspect of our interpretive approach—past or present—advocates interpreting the KABC-II profile, or any other cognitive test profile, *in isolation*. Certainly, such a practice would be of questionable validity and of questionable ethical practice. Our interpretive approach stresses the importance of finding multiple sources of data to support a hypothesis that is based on a pattern of index or clinical composite scores. That has always been our approach. We probably cannot find a better support for our system than the following comments made by Anastasi and Urbina (1997) in a footnote to a McDermott-Glutting study: "One problem with several of the negative reviews of Kaufman's approach is that they seem to assume that clinicians will use it to make decisions based solely on the magnitude of scores and score differences. While it is true that the mechanical application of profile analysis techniques can be very misleading, this assumption is quite contrary to what Kaufman recommends, as well as to the principles of sound assessment practice" (p. 513).

Descriptive Categories

Table 3.1 presents the descriptive categories that the test authors selected for KABC-II global scores and scale indexes. These verbal descriptions correspond to commonly used standard score ranges. The categories shown in this table are

Table 3.1   Descriptive Category System

Range of Standard Scores	Name of Category	SD from Mean
131–160	Upper Extreme	+2 to +4
116–130	Above Average	+1 to +2
85–115	Average Range	−1 to +1
70–84	Below Average	−1 to −2
40–69	Lower Extreme	−2 to −4

intended to reflect in words the approximate distance of each range of scores from the group mean—a verbal translation of the normal curve. This system differs from the system used for the original K-ABC and from many other classification systems, such as Wechsler's (2002, 2003).

The KABC-II system depends on the standard deviation of 15 to define its categories, with the Average range of 85–115 corresponding to ± 1 SD from the mean (100 ± 15), Below Average defined as 1 to 2 SDs below the mean (70–84), and so forth. You should use these categories to describe standard scores on the global scales and scale indexes. This system avoids the narrow 10-point categories (e.g., 70–79, 110–119) that appear frequently in other systems (including the one used previously for the original K-ABC). One problem with 10-point categories is that when confidence intervals are used to provide a reasonable band of error it is common for the confidence interval to span three different categories. That broad span of ability levels can be confusing, for example, when explaining a child's test performance to a parent.

It is inappropriate to overwhelm readers of a case report by providing descriptive categories for each standard score. These labels serve best when they either summarize an individual's performance on all scales via a global score or highlight significant discrepancies among the scales. Generally, the use of descriptive labels with scale indexes should be reserved for standard scores that are significantly above or below the child's own mean values, or for standard scores that are high or low relative to other children of the same age.

Step-by-Step Guide to the Interpretive Approach

This section describes the six steps of the KABC-II interpretive system. Specific tables and clerical procedures for conducting essential steps 1 and 2 for each child tested on the KABC-II are detailed on pages 38–41 of the KABC-II manual (Kaufman & Kaufman, 2004a) and are recorded on pages 3 and 23 of the record form. Guidelines for completing all six steps are included in this section and may be used in conjunction with the KABC-II Interpretive Worksheet in Appendix A (this worksheet may be reproduced for your personal use).

The interpretive steps are illustrated with data from 11-year-old Vanessa J., who was referred for testing by her father. Mr. J. was concerned about Vanessa's great difficulties in school, most notably with reading. Referral and background information and pertinent behaviors during the evaluation are listed below. The complete case report for Vanessa is presented in Chapter 7.

- Age 11-2, grade 4
- Referred for a reading disability

- African American father, mother born in Dominican Republic (moved to United States at age 16)
- Father is doorman in a Brooklyn, New York, apartment building
- Mother performs semiskilled work at a local dry cleaner
- Father is high school graduate, Mother completed 10th grade
- Has an older sister (age 14) who is an excellent student
- Lives in Brooklyn in a largely African American neighborhood

Vanessa displayed the following pertinent test behaviors:

- High frustration tolerance
- Eagerness to please
- Perseverance
- Use of many body gestures and nonverbal communication techniques to supplement sparse verbalizations
- Speech and language problems (articulation, auditory discrimination, dysnomia)
- Visual-perceptual problems

Step 1 (essential for ages 3–18): Interpret the global scale index, whether the FCI (CHC model), MPI (Luria model), or Nonverbal Index (NVI).

Regardless of the global scale index that is interpreted for a child tested on the KABC-II, step 1 requires you to obtain a percentile rank (Table D.4 in the KABC-II manual), confidence interval (90% or 95%, reported for each global score in Table D.2 in the KABC-II manual), and descriptive category (see Table 3.1). If the Nonverbal scale is administered, do not conduct any other interpretive steps.

Whereas both the FCI and MPI are theory-based global scores, the NVI is not. Instead, the NVI serves the practical function of permitting evaluation of children who cannot be validly assessed with either the CHC or Luria model (e.g., individuals with hearing impairment or moderate to severe speech and language problems; see Chapter 6). The KABC-II manual (Kaufman & Kaufman, 2004a, p. 45) describes the interpretations of the FCI and MPI.

Based solely on the reason that Vanessa was referred for evaluation (possible reading disability), the CHC model would be the model of choice. However, based on her background (bilingual home, non-mainstream environment), the Luria model would be a reasonable option. Vanessa's mother is from the Dominican Republic, and Vanessa has learned some Spanish; however, her father (Mr. J.) explained that English is Vanessa's primary language. Mr. J., an African American doorman in Brooklyn, New York, also stated that he has tried hard to expose both his daughters to all aspects of American society and culture. Based on an informal interview with Vanessa, the examiner agreed with Mr. J.'s assessment that English is Vanessa's primary language and that she is acculturated to American society. Consequently, Vanessa was administered the CHC model of the KABC-II, which yields the FCI as the global measure of general cognitive ability.

Whether the FCI or MPI is used, before evaluating the global score you need to determine whether the global scale is interpretable. With the FCI and MPI, calculate the difference between the child's highest and lowest index (ages 4–18). If the difference between the two extreme standard scores is equal to or greater than 1.5 SDs (23 points), then you should not interpret the global score. This rule is straightforward and easy to remember. The same rule has been applied to the interpretation of the WISC-IV Full Scale IQ (Flanagan & Kaufman, 2004). If the variability between the indexes on the KABC-II is 23 points or greater, then the meaningfulness of the global score is diminished. In such cases, we encourage examiners to focus the interpretation on the profile of scale indexes and not to interpret the global score. The Don't Forget box reminds you to examine the difference between the highest and lowest index scores before interpreting the FCI or MPI.

For age 3, unlike ages 4–18, we do not recommend evaluating the interpretability of the MPI or FCI during step 1. A profile of scale indexes is not offered until age 4, rendering the global score the only standard score to interpret for 3-year-olds. Nonetheless, if informal examination of the 3-year-old's array of scaled scores suggests considerable variability across the subtests, then the MPI and FCI are less useful in describing global performance. Examiners should supplement the KABC-II with other tasks whenever a 3-year-old's global score appears to be the midpoint of diverse cognitive strengths and weaknesses.

For our illustrative case of Vanessa, age 11, the highest index is the Sequential/*Gsm* standard score of 127 and the lowest is the Simultaneous/*Gv* score of 80. Thus, the difference between these indexes is a substantial 47 points. Clearly, this

DON'T FORGET

Calculate Range of All Index Scores before Interpreting FCI or MPI

- Subtract the highest from the lowest index standard scores.
- If the difference is greater than or equal to 23 points (1.5 SD), then do not interpret the FCI or MPI.
- Rather, focus interpretation on the four or five indexes.

Table 3.2   Vanessa J.'s Global Score (FCI) Based on an Administration of the CHC Model of the KABC-II

	Standard Score	90% Confidence Interval	Percentile Rank	Descriptive Category
FCI	93	88–98	32nd	Average Range

Note. Because of the extreme variability between Vanessa's Sequential/*Gsm* scale (127) and her Simultaneous/*Gv* scale (80), which is a 47-point discrepancy, the global FCI does not provide a meaningful summary of her overall abilities. The interpretive focus will be on her five index scores.

discrepancy meets the criterion of 23 points, and it is in fact more than 3 SDs. The size of this discrepancy therefore indicates that the FCI should not be the focus of interpretation, and instead Vanessa's five indexes will provide the most useful interpretive information.

Had there not been such a large discrepancy between Vanessa's Sequential/*Gsm* and Simultaneous/*Gv* indexes, then Vanessa's FCI (Table 3.2) would have adequately summarized her overall performance on the test battery. The 90% confidence interval was selected as the band of error by Vanessa's examiner, based on her personal preference, but you also have the option of using 95% confidence. Both the 90% and 95% confidence intervals are provided in the norms table (Table D.2 in the KABC-II manual) and are equally appropriate for providing a suitable band of error around a person's obtained test scores.

Overall, Vanessa's FCI classifies her global ability within the Average range, using the KABC-II Descriptive Category system (see Table 3.1). The chances are good (90%) that her true FCI is somewhere within the range of 88 to 98. Vanessa scored higher than 32 percent of other 11-year-olds. However, these global descriptions of the FCI do not meaningfully reflect Vanessa's cognitive abilities, because of the 47-point discrepancy between two of the KABC-II indexes. Thus, we will turn to the next step to obtain more meaningful interpretive information.

Step 2 (essential for ages 4–18): Interpret the child's profile of scale indexes to identify strengths and weaknesses, both personal (relative to the child's overall ability) and normative (compared to children about the same age).

As indicated previously, interpretation of the KABC-II profile of scale indexes emphasizes both *ipsative* analysis (strengths and weaknesses relative to the per-

DON'T FORGET

Ground Rules for Step 2 of the Interpretive System (ages 4–18)

The approach to interpretation of the profile of scale indexes described in step 2 of the interpretive system is predicated on several ground rules, listed here. This step is excluded for children age 3 because an index profile is not provided at that age.

1. Interpret a scale index only if the child performed *consistently* on the subtests that compose the scale. To determine whether a child performed consistently, apply the base rate rule of <10% to define uncommon variability. Do not interpret a child's standard score on a scale if the difference between the child's highest and lowest scaled scores on its component subtests is so large that it occurred less than 10% of the time for children in the norm sample.

2. When determining Personal (relative) Strengths and Weaknesses in the child's scale profile, use the .05 level of statistical significance.

3. Each time a significant difference is found, apply the <10% base rate criterion to determine whether the difference is not only statistically significant but also uncommonly large in its magnitude.

4. In order for a difference to be considered potentially valuable for diagnostic and educational purposes, it must be both statistically significant and uncommonly large.

5. A difference between a scale index and the mean index that is statistically significant but not uncommonly large should be treated as a hypothesis to be verified with other data.

6. In addition to ipsative (within-child) strengths and weaknesses on the scales, Normative Strengths (indexes greater than 115) and Normative Weaknesses (indexes below 85) are considered potentially valuable for diagnostic and educational purposes.

7. Even if none of the analyses in steps 1–5 yield significant results, you are urged not to interpret scaled scores on individual subtests. Even very high or low subtest scaled scores should be used only to generate hypotheses (step 6) to be verified with other data.

son's own mean score) and *normative* analysis (strengths and weaknesses relative to the Average range of 85–115). To conduct step 2, apply both types of analysis to interpret the child's index profile. The Don't Forget box summarizes the ground rules that apply to the profile analysis that is conducted in step 2.

In accordance with these ground rules, the following decisions need to be made, in sequence, to identify areas of strength and weakness in a child's index profile. Again, Vanessa's KABC-II profile (see Figure 3.1) is used to illustrate each stage of the analysis.

Scale Indexes				
	Standard Scores	**Confidence Interval** 90% / 95% (circle one)		**Percentile Rank**
Sequential/*Gsm*	127	(117 – 133)		96
Simultaneous/*Gv*	80	(73 – 89)		9
Learning/*Glr*	94	(87 – 101)		34
Planning/*Gf*	90	(82 – 100)		25
Knowledge/*Gc*	87	(81 – 93)		19

Figure 3.1 Scale Index Profile for Vanessa J. based on an administration of the CHC model of the KABC-II.

Step 2A: Determine whether each scale is interpretable, using a base rate criterion of <10%.

Interpret an index only if the child performed consistently on the Core subtests that compose the scale. To determine whether a child performed consistently, apply a base rate rule of <10% to define uncommon variability in the subtest scores. Using the Analysis of Scale Indexes worksheet on page 3 or 23 of the KABC-II record form, subtract the child's lowest scaled score on a scale from his or her highest score. How large a scaled-score range occurred less than 10% of the time in standardization for children of a similar age? That critical value is given in Table D.6 of the KABC-II manual and on the record form (the critical values are also listed in the KABC-II Interpretive Worksheet in Appendix A of this book). Do not interpret a child's standard score on a scale if the difference between the child's highest and lowest scaled scores on its component subtests is so large that it occurred less than 10% of the time for children in the norm sample.

Vanessa's scaled scores on the Core subtests included on each of the five CHC scales are shown in Figure 3.2. Figure 3.3 shows the calculation of the interpretability of each of Vanessa's scale indexes.

By referring to the table on page 3 of the record form and using the values for ages 7–12, the examiner determined that all five scales are interpretable. (Page 23

DON'T FORGET

What to Do with an Uninterpretable Index

An uninterpretable index simply indicates that the index does not meaningfully represent the child's ability in that domain. It does not mean that the index is invalid. An uninterpretable index results because the child's scores on the subtests that compose that scale vary greatly. Consequently, there is no sense in combining them to yield an index—that index would reflect the midpoint of different levels of ability on the component subtests, nothing more. Finding an uninterpretable index in a child's profile (or even more than one) will impel some examiners to try to understand why the child's scores varied so much on subtests that usually go together for most children. Examiners who enjoy the kind of detective work that helps explain unexpected fluctuations in a child's profile of scores should conduct the optional steps of the interpretive system. Optional step 6 provides examiners with guidelines to generate hypotheses about why the child's subtest scores varied so much that his or her index could not be meaningfully interpreted.

Ages 7–18 Calculation of Scale Indexes

Sequential/*Gsm*		
Scaled Scores		
15		5. Number Recall
14		14. Word Order
29	**Sum**	

Planning/*Gf*		
Scaled Scores		
7		4. Story Completion
10		15. Pattern Reasoning
17	**Sum**	

Learning/*Glr*		
Scaled Scores		
8		1. Atlantis
10		11. Rebus
18	**Sum**	

Simultaneous/*Gv*		
Scaled Scores		
7-12	13-18	
7		7. Rover
6		12. Triangles
		13. Block Counting
13		**Sum**

Knowledge/*Gc*		
Scaled Scores		
8		10. Verbal Knowledge
7		18. Riddles
15		**Sum**

Figure 3.2 Vanessa J.'s Subtest scaled scores grouped by scale to determine whether each scale is interpretable.

of the record form provides these critical values for ages 4–6 to evaluate whether scales are interpretable or noninterpretable. Table D.6 in the KABC-II manual provides critical values for ages 4–18.) Vanessa's range of scaled scores for Sequential/*Gsm* of 1 point (15 minus 14) is smaller than the range of 5 or more points needed to denote a noninterpretable Sequential/*Gsm* scale for ages 7–12.

Scale	Scale Index (Standard Score)	Subtest Scaled Scores				Range Occurring < 10%[a]
		High	Low	Range	Interpretable?	
Sequential/*Gsm*	127	15	14	1	Ⓨ N	5
Simultaneous/*Gv*	80	7	6	1	Ⓨ N	6
Learning/*Glr*	94	10	8	2	Ⓨ N	6
Planning/*Gf*	90	10	7	3	Ⓨ N	6
Knowledge/*Gc*	87	8	7	1	Ⓨ N	5

[a] Minimum subtest scaled score range that occurs in < 10% of the population for children ages 7–12.

Figure 3.3 Analysis of the interpretability of Vanessa J.'s scale indexes.

Even the largest range of scaled scores for Vanessa (3 points on Planning/*Gf*) is considerably smaller than the critical value of 6 for that scale. (Noninterpretable scales have so much variability that these scaled-score ranges occurred less than 10% of the time in the normative population.)

Because all five scales are "unitary" (each one has relatively small variability from Core subtest to subtest), the abilities that underlie each one can be meaningfully interpreted when conducting the remaining aspects of profile analysis in the next several parts of step 2. Had one or more of Vanessa's scales contained too much variability in its Core subtest scores, then that scale (or scales) would not be interpretable (see the Caution box). No strengths or weaknesses on such scales can be interpreted, even if the child's indexes are extremely high or low. Optional step 6 in the interpretive system provides guidelines for generating hypotheses to explain the variability in the Core subtests on scales that are not interpretable.

> ### CAUTION
> Do not interpret a scale index if the range of its subtest scaled scores is unusually large, i.e., if ranges that great (or greater) occurred less than 10% of the time in the normative population.

Step 2B: Identify Normative Weaknesses (standard scores lower than 85) and Normative Strengths (standard scores greater than 115) in the scale profile.
Figure 3.4 shows the filled-out section of the record form (Analysis of Scale Indexes on page 3) that is used for determining and recording Vanessa's strengths and weaknesses on the KABC-II, both Normative and Personal. Two of Vanessa's indexes are outside the Average range of 85–115.

Scale	Scale Index (Standard Score)	Subtest Scaled Scores					Normative Weakness (NW) or Normative Strength (NS)		Personal Weakness (PW) or Personal Strength (PS)		
		High	Low	Range	Interpretable?		<85	>115	Diff from Mean	PW or PS (p<.05)	Infrequent (<10%)
Sequential/*Gsm*	127	15	14	1	Ⓨ	N	NW	(NS)	+31	PW (PS)	✓
Simultaneous/*Gv*	80	7	6	1	Ⓨ	N	(NW)	NS	-16	(PW) PS	✓
Learning/*Glr*	94	10	8	2	Ⓨ	N	NW	NS	-2	PW PS	
Planning/*Gf*	90	10	7	3	Ⓨ	N	NW	NS	-6	PW PS	
Knowledge/*Gc*	87	8	7	1	Ⓨ	N	NW	NS	-9	(PW) PS	

Mean (rounded) 96   ☒ CHC model (include Knowledge/*Gc*)
☐ Luria model (omit Knowledge/*Gc*)

Figure 3.4 Vanessa J.'s scale index analysis to demonstrate computation of Personal Strengths and Weaknesses.

Sequential/*Gsm* (index = 127, 96th percentile) is in the Above Average range and is a Normative Strength for her. Simultaneous/*Gv* (index = 80, 9th percentile) is in the Below Average range and is a Normative Weakness. Note that Vanessa's Knowledge/*Gc* index of 87 does not qualify as a Normative Weakness because it is between 85 and 115 (100 ± 1 SD) and is in the Average range.

Vanessa's Normative Strength on the Sequential/*Gsm* scale and her Normative Weakness on the Simultaneous/*Gv* scale are considered valuable for diagnostic and educational purposes. However, no one score or test should ever be used in isolation to make clinical diagnoses or develop individual educational plans (IEPs).

When the Luria model is administered, the Knowledge/*Gc* scale is excluded from the MPI. The Knowledge/*Gc* may be administered as a supplementary scale. When the Knowledge/*Gc* scale yields an index below 85 or above 115 in that circumstance, label it as a Normative Weakness or Normative Strength (as long as it is interpretable), but clearly label the fact that it is a supplementary scale as well.

Step 2C: Identify Personal (relative) Weaknesses and Personal Strengths in the scale profile.

The main purpose of this part of step 2 is to generate hypotheses about the child's relatively strong or weak areas of cognitive functioning.

Determine Personal Weaknesses and Personal Strengths in the scale profile, based on the child's own mean scale index. For the CHC model, use the mean of all indexes (four indexes for ages 4–6 and five for ages 7–18). For the Luria model, exclude Knowledge/*Gc* from computation of the mean for all ages (4–18) even if this scale was administered as a supplement. However, in such instances, it is still appropriate to compare the Knowledge/*Gc* index to the mean of the other scales in the Luria model to determine whether it qualifies as a Personal Strength or Weakness.

Include noninterpretable indexes in the computation of the mean. However, do not interpret a noninterpretable index as a Personal Strength or Personal Weakness even if it deviates significantly from the mean. (Noninterpretable indexes are included in the computation of the mean for practical reasons. Had they been excluded, the mean index would potentially be based on different numbers of indexes for each child tested—for example, two or three—which would produce an unwieldy number of tables for determining statistical significance.)

For simplicity, mean indexes are rounded to whole numbers. Because the main purpose of identifying Personal Strengths and Weaknesses is to generate hypotheses about the child's cognitive functioning, the liberal .05 level of statistical significance is applied, and no correction (such as the Bonferroni procedure) is made to adjust the significance values to account for the multiple comparisons that are made. Table D.7 in the KABC-II manual (reproduced on the record form on page 23 for ages 4–6 and on page 3 for ages 7–18) provides the size of the difference from the child's own mean index that is needed for significance. These values are provided separately for the CHC and Luria models and are computed separately for different age groups within each model.

Figure 3.4 shows that Vanessa's mean index on the five scales that constitute the CHC model is 95.6, which rounds to 96. Three of Vanessa's indexes deviate significantly ($p < .05$) from her mean of 96. Vanessa's Sequential/*Gsm* index of 127 is significantly (31 points) above her mean index of 96, denoting a Personal Strength in her cognitive profile. Vanessa's Simultaneous/*Gv* index of 80 and Knowledge/*Gc* index of 87 are both significantly below her own mean, indicating Personal Weaknesses in these two aspects of cognitive functioning. Note that in step 2B Sequential/*Gsm* was also identified as a Normative Strength for Vanessa, and Simultaneous/*Gv* was identified as a Normative Weakness.

Had any of Vanessa's indexes been noninterpretable (based on step 2A), then the "Difference from Mean" box for each noninterpretable index would have been left blank (see Kaufman & Kaufman, 2004a, Figure 5.4, for an illustration of a noninterpretable index).

Step 2D: Determine whether any of the scales that are Personal Strengths or Personal Weaknesses differ to an unusually great extent from the child's mean scale index, using the <10% base rate criterion.

Differences that are statistically significant are real, not artifacts of test score fluctuations that occur by chance. However, statistical significance alone is not sufficient to understand the potential importance of a child's Personal Strengths and Personal Weaknesses. It is essential also to consider how unusual the child's discrepancies are in the normal population of children. To be potentially important for diagnostic and educational purposes, it is important for deviations from the child's own mean to be *both* statistically significant *and* unusually large.

To determine how many points an index must deviate from the child's own mean to denote an unusual occurrence, consult the KABC-II manual or record form. Values for the KABC-II indexes are presented in Tables D.7a (CHC model) and D.7b (Luria model) in the manual, and at the bottom of pages 3 and 23 of the record form.

For the purposes of KABC-II interpretation, a base rate of <10% is used consistently to denote infrequency of occurrence. Tables D.7a and D.7b also provide values for more stringent base rates (<5% and <1%) for interested clinicians.

Figure 3.4 shows that Vanessa's Personal Strength or Weakness on the Sequential/*Gsm* scale is not only statistically significant but also unusually large, occurring less than 10% of the time in 10- to 12-year-old children. Similarly, her Personal Weakness on the Simultaneous/*Gv* scale is both significant and infrequent. Her deviation of 16 points below her mean was exactly equal to the critical value for ages 10–12 on Simultaneous/*Gv;* hence it just qualified as uncommonly large. However, Vanessa's Personal Weakness on Knowledge/*Gc,* though statistically significant, is not large enough to be labeled infrequent (her deviation from the mean of 7 points was substantially below the critical value of 14 points that was needed to meet the <10% criterion). It is noteworthy that Vanessa's 31-point deviation above the mean on the Sequential/*Gsm* scale was so large that it occurred less than 1% of the time in the normal population of 10- to 12-year-olds (Kaufman & Kaufman, 2004a, Table D.7a).

Strengths and Weaknesses, both Personal and Normative, are useful to the extent that they can provide useful information for diagnostic and educational purposes. Normative Strengths and Normative Weaknesses are noteworthy in and of themselves and potentially valuable for these purposes. Personal Strengths and Personal Weaknesses, however, should be both statistically significant and infrequent to be of potential diagnostic and educational value. Otherwise, Personal Strengths or Personal Weaknesses that occur commonly in the normal population should ordinarily be treated as hypotheses to be verified with other data.

There are, however, some exceptions to this general rule. Most notably, Normative Strengths and Normative Weaknesses—even if they do not qualify as Personal Strengths or Personal Weaknesses—are nonetheless of concern and of potential diagnostic and educational value (see step 2B).

Vanessa's Personal Strength on Sequential/*Gsm* and Personal Weakness on

Simultaneous/*Gv*, by virtue of being both significant and infrequent, provide valuable information for any possible diagnosis of a reading disability and for formulating scientifically based interventions. Sequential/*Gsm,* as an area of strength, can be capitalized on when selecting pertinent interventions, as can Vanessa's weakness on the Simultaneous/*Gv* scale.

The KABC-II test authors encourage the use of the term *Key Asset* for indexes that meet all three of the criteria outlined in step 2 of the interpretive system: Normative Strength, Personal Strength, and infrequent (<10%) occurrence. Analogously, they recommended the term *High-Priority Concern* for indexes that qualify as Normative Weaknesses, Personal Weaknesses, and infrequent (see the Don't Forget box). Vanessa's Sequential/*Gsm* index of 127 qualifies as a Key Asset (see Table 3.3), which will enable the examiner to provide useful information to teachers for identifying the most appropriate scientifically based interventions for Vanessa.

Her Simultaneous/*Gv* index of 80 qualifies as a High-Priority Concern (see Table 3.5), which demands special attention when translating her test profile to diagnostic and educational considerations. That index might reflect a disorder in a basic psychological process when considering a possible diagnosis of a Specific Learning Disability in reading (a processing disorder in one or more basic psychological processes is a prerequisite for diagnosing an individual with a Specific Learning Disability). Vanessa's possible processing disorder might pertain to visual processing (*Gv*) or simultaneous processing.

Even though the CHC model was administered to Vanessa, the examiner's interpretation of Vanessa's index profile depends on theoretical orientation. If you prefer Luria's approach to interpretation, you may favor considering the possibility that Vanessa has a disorder in simultaneous processing, whereas if you are more comfortable with CHC theory, you may focus on a possible visual processing disorder.

DON'T FORGET

Definitions of Indexes That Are Key Assets and High-Priority Concerns

Three Conditions Needed for Key Assets	**Three Conditions Needed for High-Priority Concerns**
1. Normative Strength	1. Normative Weakness
2. Personal Strength	2. Personal Weakness
3. Infrequent (<10%) occurrence	3. Infrequent (<10%) occurrence

Table 3.3   Overview of Vanessa's Strengths and Weaknesses on the KABC-II

Index	Standard Score	NS or NW	PS or PW	Uncommonly Large (<10%)	Label
Learning/*Glr*	94				
Sequential/*Gsm*	127	NS	PS	Yes	Key Asset
Simultaneous/*Gv*	80	NW	PW	Yes	High-Priority Concern
Planning/*Gf*	90				
Knowledge/*Gc*	87		PW	No	

Notes. NS = Normative Strength. NW = Normative Weakness. PS = Personal Strength. PW = Personal Weakness.

Key Assets and High-Priority Concerns demand immediate attention. Personal Strengths and Personal Weaknesses that are neither unusually large nor extreme in their magnitude relative to the normative population should be treated as nothing more than hypotheses to be verified with other data. Nonetheless, all test scores, no matter how reliable or extreme, are always enhanced when interpreted within multiple sources of data about the individual. These data may be other test scores obtained during the evaluation (including KABC-II Supplementary scaled scores); test scores from previous evaluations or school records; data from health records; background or referral information (including behavior checklists filled out by parents or teachers); clinical observations of behaviors during the evaluation; and behavioral observations made in alternative settings (e.g., the classroom, auditorium, or home). Integration of data from multiple sources is always essential when interpreting the scores obtained on any test, no matter how comprehensive.

Optional Steps 3–6

The two essential steps permit you to interpret the global score (step 1) and the profile of scale indexes (step 2). Standard scores on all of those scales represent the most important scores yielded by the KABC-II, and therefore their systematic interpretation is the most crucial aspect of this stepwise system. Optional steps 3 through 6 are provided if you wish to go beyond the global score and the scale index profile to try to uncover additional potentially meaningful hypotheses about the child's functioning.

Because the two planned comparisons that are made in step 3 involve scale indexes (Learning/*Glr*, Knowledge/*Gc*, and the supplementary Delayed Recall standard score), rather than alternate groupings of KABC-II subtests, we recommend that you routinely conduct this step. The administration of the Delayed Recall scale provides rich information in a few extra minutes of testing time. The planned comparison between initial learning (Learning/*Glr* index) and delayed recall (step 3A) yields an estimate of how well children are able to retain newly learned information over an interval of about 20 minutes. The planned comparison made in step 3B gives you an opportunity to contrast children's ability to learn new information (Learning/*Glr* index) with their previous learning of facts, words, and concepts (Knowledge/*Gc*)—that is, new versus old learning.

Both step 3 planned comparisons translate directly to the classroom and provide pertinent data to help develop educationally relevant interventions. If you select the CHC model, give the Knowledge/*Gc* scale as part of the standard KABC-II administration. If you select the Luria model, then strongly consider administering the Knowledge/*Gc* scale as a supplementary scale (one that won't contribute to the child's global score) so that you can make the step 3B comparison between new and old learning.

In step 4, supplementary subtests are compared to scaled scores on pertinent Core subtests. Conduct this step if you administer one or more supplementary KABC-II subtests. It will enable you to determine whether or not the child's scaled scores are consistent with Core subtests on the same scale. For example, if you administer Hand Movements, you can determine whether the child's scaled score on that supplementary subtest is consistent with his or her mean scaled score on the two Core Sequential/*Gsm* subtests (Word Order and Number Recall). This step can be conducted for all ages, 3 to 18 years. Even though no separate scales are offered at age 3, you can compare these young children's scaled scores on supplementary subtests to the mean of all Core subtests administered to them.

Like step 3, step 5 requires you to make planned comparisons between pairs of standard scores. However, unlike the two planned comparisons in step 3—which involve standard scores on *actual* KABC-II scales—four of the five planned comparisons in step 5 involve *alternate groupings* of KABC-II into clinically relevant clusters (the one exception is the Nonverbal Ability versus Verbal Ability planned comparison, which compares the NVI to all three Knowledge/*Gc* subtests). Because the step 5 planned comparisons tend to involve clusters that are clinically derived but have no theoretical foundation, we recommend this step only if you are comfortable with in-depth profile analysis and with exploring a variety of hypotheses to explain fluctuations in the child's profile of test scores. If you adhere to the points raised by some researchers (e.g., McDermott,

Fantuzzo, & Glutting, 1990; Schaefer, 2002) *against* a more thorough examination of fluctuations in subtest profiles, then do not conduct step 5.

The step 5 planned comparisons are especially useful when one or more of the child's scale indexes cannot be interpreted because of too much inter-subtest variability. In those cases, alternative explanations might help explain the fluctuations within a scale. But, once again, even if the child has several noninterpretable indexes, only conduct step 5 if you are comfortable with a hypothesis generation approach to test interpretation.

Step 6 offers guidelines for a variety of hypotheses that might explain noninterpretable scale indexes (step 6A) or supplementary subtest scaled scores that are inconsistent with pertinent Core subtests (step 6B). The recommendations made for step 5 regarding who should conduct the planned comparisons and who should not apply as well to step 6.

In general, all of the optional steps are intended primarily to generate hypotheses to be verified with other data. If you are interested in this optional portion of the interpretive system, you do not need to feel compelled to conduct all comparisons. Only some may be clinically relevant for a given child. Steps 4 and 6B are only pertinent if you administer at least one supplementary subtest. Most planned comparisons in step 5 require the administration of supplementary subtests and cannot be made unless the appropriate supplementary tasks are given. Flexibility and hypothesis generation are the keys to making optimal use of optional steps 3–6. In all cases, the greatest emphasis is on essential steps 1 and 2, which explore standard scores on theory-based scales that have strong empirical support from CFA (see Kaufman & Kaufman, 2004a, Chapter 8).

The Don't Forget box provides the ground rules for conducting the planned comparisons in optional steps 3 and 5 and for comparing scaled scores on Supplementary subtests to pertinent Core subtests (step 4). These guidelines are similar to the ones for step 2, but they differ in one important way: *Regardless of the results of the comparisons—even if some statistical differences prove to be unusually large—all findings should be verified with other data to be considered potentially valuable for diagnostic or educational purposes.* The Caution box reminds readers of this important fact.

Optional Step 3: Planned Scale Comparisons

This step includes two planned comparisons: (1) Initial Learning versus Delayed Recall, and (2) Learning Ability versus Acquired Knowledge. For the first planned comparison (step 3A), the Learning/*Glr* index is compared to the child's standard score on the supplementary Delayed Recall scale; for the second (step 3B), the child's indexes on the Learning/*Glr* and Knowledge/*Gc* scales are compared. The Learning/*Glr* scale is included in both the CHC and Luria models, but the Knowledge/*Gc* scale is included only in the CHC model. If you administer the Luria

DON'T FORGET

Ground Rules for Optional Steps 3, 4, and 5 of the Interpretive System

Analysis of the planned comparisons conducted in step 3 (involving actual scales, both Core and Supplementary), step 4 (involving scaled scores on Supplementary subtests) and step 5 (involving clinically derived clusters) is predicated on several ground rules:

1. Interpret a standard score on a scale (step 3) or cluster (step 5) only if the child performed *consistently* on the subtests that compose the scale or cluster. To determine whether a child performed consistently, apply the base rate rule of <10% to define uncommon variability. Do not interpret a child's standard score on a scale or cluster if the difference between the child's highest and lowest scaled scores on its component subtests is so large that it occurred less than 10% of the time for children in the norm sample. *Only conduct a planned comparison if both standard scores being compared are interpretable.* For step 4, follow an analogous guideline: Only compare Supplementary scaled scores to the mean of pertinent Core subtests *if that scale is interpretable* (as determined in step 2A).

2. When comparing pairs of scales or clusters, use the .05 level of statistical significance. The same level is used for step 4 comparisons involving Supplementary subtests.

3. Each time a significant difference is found in steps 3–5, apply the <10% base rate criterion to determine whether the difference is not only statistically significant but also uncommonly large in its magnitude.

No significant difference between pairs of standard scores—even if it is unusually large—is considered potentially valuable for diagnostic and educational purposes unless the finding is verified with other data. The same guideline holds for the comparisons between Supplementary scaled scores and pertinent Core subtests.

model but also want to make the step 3B planned comparison, then administer that scale as a Supplementary scale. The step 3A comparison requires you to administer the Supplementary Delayed Recall scale (i.e., the Atlantis Delayed and Rebus Delayed subtests).

Step 3A: Initial Learning versus Delayed Recall—Learning/Glr (initial) versus Delayed Recall (ages 5–18). To conduct the comparison in step 3A, administer the supplementary Delayed Recall scale (the Atlantis Delayed and Rebus Delayed subtests). The data obtained from the Delayed Recall scale will al-

CAUTION

Even if some statistical differences prove to be unusually large, *all findings* from steps 3 and 5 should be verified with other data to be considered potentially valuable for diagnostic or educational purposes.

low you to contrast children's initial learning of new information with their ability to retain that information about 20 minutes later. When the Delayed Recall scale is administered, children must retain information over time, despite the interference of intervening cognitive tasks, and without warning that they need to remember the paired associations. Together, the Learning/*Glr* and Delayed Recall scales yield a broader assessment of children's ability to store and retrieve newly learned material.

Significantly lower performance on delayed memory tasks relative to immediate learning may indicate deficits in a child's ability to retain previously learned material. A child with such deficits may need more repetition to learn than most peers, as he or she is likely poor or inconsistent in remembering previously learned material. The opposite pattern of lower immediate learning relative to delayed learning (or equally depressed scores) may indicate poor initial learning but not rapid forgetting (Lichtenberger, Kaufman, & Lai, 2002).

Many of the task demands of Atlantis, Atlantis Delayed, Rebus, and Rebus Delayed may affect a child's performance and therefore impact the pattern of Initial Learning > Delayed Recall or Initial Learning < Delayed Recall. For example, Atlantis requires children to auditorily process the nonsense name of each picture (of a fish, plant, or shell), pair it with the visual stimulus, and then retrieve it. Thus, the learning of Atlantis's auditory-visual associations may be problematic, or the ability of a child to recognize the visual stimulus may be problematic. Similarly, for Rebus, children are required to visually process each abstract rebus symbol, pair it with the word that it represents, and then recall it. The learning of Rebus's auditory-visual association may be problematic, or a child may have difficulty with the free recall demands of the task.

To conduct the step 3A planned comparison for Vanessa, the examiner first had to determine whether both Delayed Recall and Learning/*Glr* scales were interpretable (see Figure 3.5) and then had to calculate the standard score for the Delayed Recall Scale (Table D.3 of the KABC-II Manual provides conversion scores). Several tables list the size of subtests' scaled score range that occurs in less than 10% of the population (e.g., Table D.8 in the KABC-II Manual and the "Critical Values for Steps 2A and 3A" in the KABC-II Interpretive Worksheet in this book). Thus, Vanessa's Learning/*Glr* index was found to be interpretable, as was her Delayed Recall supplementary scale (a difference of 6 or more points between Atlantis Delay and Rebus Delay is needed to identify noninterpretable Delayed Recall standard scores).

Table D.9 in the KABC-II manual provides data on whether differences between Learning/*Glr* and Delayed Recall scales are statistically significant and, if so, whether the difference occurred infrequently in the normative sample. Rules for making these comparisons are delineated in Rapid Reference 3.2 and in the

≡ Rapid Reference 3.2

Critical Values for Steps 3A and 3B:
Differences between Cluster Scores That Are Statistically Significant or Infrequent

Clusters	Age 4		Age 5		Age 6		Ages 7–9		Ages 10–12		Ages 13–18	
	Sig.	10%	Sig.	10%	Sig.	10%	Sig.	10%	Sig.	10%	Sig.	<10%
Learning/Glr (initial) vs. Delayed Recall			15	16	14	16	13	16	12	16	12	16
Learning/Glr (initial) vs. Knowledge/Gc	13	25	12	25	12	25	12	24	11	24	11	24

KABC-II Interpretive Worksheet. As noted, scales must be interpretable (using the <10% base rate) or the comparison cannot be made, and all findings must be verified with other data (even unusually large differences). Without verification, none of these comparisons should be used for diagnostic or educational purposes.

Figure 3.5 shows that Vanessa's Learning/*Glr* index of 94 does not differ significantly from her Delayed Recall standard score of 92, indicating that her abilities in learning new information and storing and retrieving that information are equally developed.

Sometimes examiners will not be able to conduct step 3A because either the Learning/*Glr* index or the Delayed Recall standard score (or both) is not interpretable. For example, some children may perform relatively well on both Atlantis tasks (initial and delayed) and perform less well on both Rebus subtests (or they may display the reverse pattern). For example, Atlantis and Atlantis Delayed demand that a child *recognize and point to* the correct stimulus choice, whereas Rebus and Rebus Delayed demand that a child *recall and name* the word that corresponds to each stimulus. One of the planned comparisons included in step 5 evaluates whether the child performed better on subtests requiring a *pointing response* versus a *verbal response,* permitting clinicians to follow up on variability that might be observed in the child's scores on the learning tasks. Similarly, a step 5 compar-

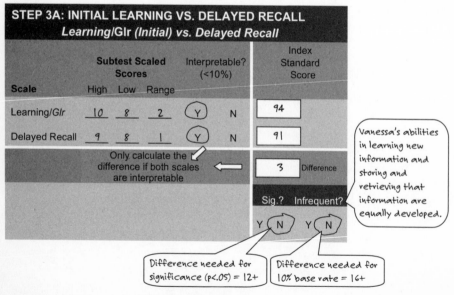

Figure 3.5 Vanessa J.'s step 3A comparisons.

ison involves how well a child performs on tasks that incorporate *abstract* visual stimuli (like Rebus) versus *meaningful* visual stimuli (like Atlantis).

Step 3B: Learning versus Acquired Knowledge—Learning/*Glr* versus Knowledge/*Gc* (ages 4–18). This comparison involves two scale indexes. As mentioned, if you administer the Luria model, you need to give Knowledge/*Gc* as a supplementary scale if you want to make this comparison. This pairwise contrast of indexes provides potentially crucial information about children's ability to learn new material during the test session versus their ability to learn verbal facts and concepts over time at home and in school. When children score significantly higher on Learning/*Glr* than Knowledge/*Gc*, one might hypothesize that they have not learned as much within their home and school environments as they are capable of learning. The reasons for these differences need to be explored, and the finding requires verification.

Indeed, mean scores by different ethnic groups on the Learning/*Glr* scale are close to the normative mean of 100. At ages 4–6, African American children averaged 99.3 on the Learning/*Glr* index after adjustment for gender and socioeconomic status (mother's education), and at ages 7–18 their adjusted index was 98.3 (Kaufman & Kaufman, 2004a, Tables 8.7 and 8.8). For Hispanic children, the corresponding adjusted values are 98.9 (ages 4–6) and 97.0 (ages 7–18). The sample sizes at ages 4–6 were too small to interpret mean Learning/*Glr* indexes for American Indians and Asians, but at ages 7–18 the adjusted means were 96.7 and 102.8, respectively (Kaufman & Kaufman, 2004a, Table 8.8). For each of these ethnic groups, the Learning/*Glr* index provides a fair appraisal of children's learning abilities.

In contrast to a discrepancy in which Learning/*Glr* is higher than Knowledge/*Gc*, some children display the opposite pattern: crystallized ability (acquired knowledge) greater than learning ability. There are several reasons why such a pattern may appear. For example, the Learning/*Glr* subtests, Rebus and Atlantis, both require attention and memory skills. A child with attentional difficulties or memory deficits may perform poorly on these subtests and the Learning/*Glr* score may be depressed. In addition, stronger Knowledge/*Gc* indexes may be present for children who are in cultures or backgrounds that place a high value on achievement and push children to overachieve (see, for example, the case of Allisonbeth, age 3-10, in Chapter 7). Furthermore, a school-age child who reads a great deal and is alert to the environment—regardless of parental pushing—is likely to acquire an abundance of facts and develop a strong vocabulary, thereby leading to exceptionally strong performance on the Knowledge/*Gc* subtests.

Figure 3.6 shows that Vanessa's Learning/*Glr* index of 94 does not differ significantly from her Knowledge/*Gc* index of 87, suggesting that Vanessa's ability

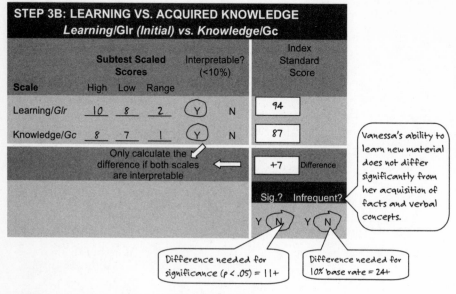

Figure 3.6 Vanessa J.'s step 3B comparisons.

Table 3.4   Supplementary Subtests by Age

Supplementary Subtest	Age 3	Age 4	Age 5	Age 6	Ages 7–12	Ages 13–18
Number Recall	X					
Gestalt Closure	X	X	X	X	X	X
Hand Movements		X	X	X	X	X
Verbal Knowledge		X	X	X		
Face Recognition			X			
Block Counting			X	X	X	
Story Completion				X		
Expressive Vocabulary					X	X
Triangles						X

to learn new material does not differ significantly from her acquisition of facts and verbal concepts.

Optional Step 4: Supplementary Subtest Analysis (ages 3–18)

For this optional step, you can compare each Supplementary subtest that was administered with the mean scaled score of the Core subtests on that scale, *if the scale is interpretable* (see Table 3.4). If a scale is not interpretable (as determined in step

2A), do not make any comparisons involving supplementary subtests for that scale.

There are no Supplementary subtests for the Learning/*Glr* or Planning/*Gf* scales. Hand Movements is supplementary on the Sequential/*Gsm* scale at every age from 4 to 18, as is either Verbal Knowledge or Expressive Vocabulary on the Knowledge/*Gc* scale (depending on the child's age). There are several Supplementary Simultaneous/*Gv* subtests at each age from 4 to 18.

At age 3, compare the Supplementary subtest score with the mean scaled score (rounded to the nearest 0.1) on all subtests included in the global scale index (FCI or MPI). Compute the difference between the Supplementary subtest scaled score and the mean scaled score, and compare this difference with the values shown in Table 3.5 to see if the difference is statistically significant ($p < .05$) or uncommonly large (<10%).

The difference scores listed in Table 3.5 provide base rates at the <10% level (discrepancies that are uncommonly large—occurring in less than 10% of the sample). However, if you are interested in applying more stringent base rates to these comparisons, refer to table D.10 in the KABC-II manual. This table in the manual lists base rates at the <5% and <1% levels.

Vanessa's scaled scores on Core subtests are shown in Figure 3.2, and the comparison between her Supplementary subtests and the mean of her Core subtests is shown in Figure 3.7 (which is an excerpt from the KABC-II Interpretive Worksheet). The difference between Vanessa's score of 10 on Hand Movements and her mean score on the two Core Sequential/*Gsm* subtests (14.5) equals 4.5. This value is statistically significant at $p < .05$, but it falls just short of the value of 5.0 that is needed to denote an unusually large discrepancy (<10%), as indicated in Table 3.7. Therefore, Vanessa performed significantly lower more on Hand Movements than on the Core Sequential/*Gsm* subtests, although this difference was not large enough to be considered unusually large. Nonetheless, all significant differences should be treated as hypotheses to be verified with other data. Possible hypotheses are explored in step 6B.

Vanessa earned scaled scores of 10 on Block Counting and 5 on Gestalt Closure, the two Supplementary Simultaneous/*Gv* subtests. Her mean scaled score on the two Simultaneous/*Gv* subtests was 6.5. From Table 3.5, we learn that the 3.5 difference between her Block Counting scaled score and the mean is significant but not unusually large; for 7- to 12-year-old children, 3.2 points is required for statistical significance and 5.5 points is the critical value to determine if a difference is unusually large. In contrast, the difference of 1.5 between Gestalt Closure and her mean is too small to be significant. Hence, Vanessa performed significantly better on Block Counting than on the Core

Table 3.5 Differences between Supplementary Subtest Scaled Scores and the Mean Scaled Score of a Scale That Are Statistically Significant or Infrequent

Supplementary Subtest	Age 3		Age 4		Age 5		Age 6		Ages 7–12		Ages 13–18	
	Sig. <.05	<10%	Sig. <.05	<10%	Sig. <.05	<10%	Sig. <.05	<10%	Sig. <.05	<10%	Sig. <.05	<10%
Gestalt Closure vs. Simultaneous/Gv			3.8	5.0	3.6	5.0	3.9	5.3	3.7	5.5	3.7	6.0
Hand Movements vs. Sequential/Gsm			3.5	5.0	3.5	5.0	3.5	5.0	3.5	5.0	3.5	5.0
Verbal Knowledge vs. Knowledge/Gc			3.1	4.0	3.1	4.0	3.1	4.0				
Face Recognition vs. Simultaneous/Gv					4.0	6.0						
Block Counting vs. Simultaneous/Gv					2.7	5.0	2.9	5.0	3.2	5.5		
Story Completion vs. Simultaneous/Gv							3.1	7.0				
Expressive Vocabulary vs. Knowledge/Gc									3.1	3.5	3.1	3.5
Triangles vs. Simultaneous/Gv									3.1		3.1	5.0
Number Recall vs. MPI	3.2	5.8										
Number Recall vs. FCI	3.1	4.9										
Gestalt Closure vs. MPI	3.8	4.6										
Gestalt Closure vs. FCI	3.7	4.4										

Source: Data are from Table D.10 of the KABC-II Manual (Kaufman & Kaufman, 2004a).

Note: Sig. = statistically significant. <10% = values that great (or greater) occurred less than 10% of the time in the normative population.

Scale	Scale Interpretable in Step 2?	Sum of Scaled cores	Mean Scaled Score	Supplementary Subtest	Scaled Score	Diff. from Mean	Differences between supplementary subtest & mean scaled score that are significant or infrequent			
							Sig. (p<.05)	Sig?	Infrequent (<10%)	Infreq?
Sequential/Gsm	(Y) N	29	/2 = 14.5	Hand Movements	10	4.5	3.5	(Y) N	5.0	Y (N)
Simultaneous/Gv	(Y) N	13	/2 = 6.5	Gestalt Closure	5	1.5	3.7	Y (N)	5.5	Y (N)
				Block Counting	10	3.5	3.2	(Y) N	5.5	Y (N)
Knowledge/Gc	(Y) N	15	/2 = 7.5	Expressive Vocab.	4	3.5	3.1	(Y) N	3.5	(Y) N

STEP 4: SUPPLEMENTARY SUBTEST ANALYSIS FOR AGES 7–12

Step 6B will help develop and verify hypotheses to explain the difference between the Core and Supplementary Knowledge/Gc subtests

Figure 3.7 Vanessa J.'s step 4 comparisons between Supplementary subtests and the mean of Core subtests.

Simultaneous/*Gv* subtests, a hypothesis that requires verification and exploration (step 6B).

On the Knowledge/*Gc* scale, Vanessa earned a scaled score of 4 on the supplementary Expressive Vocabulary subtest, 3.5 points less than her mean of 7.5 on the two Core subtests. This difference is both statistically significant and unusually large (the critical value for the base rate of <10% is exactly 3.5 points). However, all significant findings that occur during the optional steps need to be verified with other data—even findings that are unusually large in magnitude relative to the normative population. Possible hypotheses to verify are considered in step 6B.

Optional Step 5: Planned Clinical Comparisons
The following five planned clinical comparisons comprise step 5:

Step 5A: Nonverbal Ability (NVI) versus Verbal Ability (ages 3–18)
Step 5B: Problem-Solving Ability versus Memory and Learning (ages 3–18)
Step 5C: Visual Perception of Meaningful Stimuli versus Abstract Stimuli (ages 4–18)
Step 5D: Verbal Response versus Pointing Response (ages 4–18)
Step 5E: Little or No Motor Response versus Gross-Motor Response (ages 4–18)

These planned clinical comparisons tap two different domains of information processing. Steps 5A and 5B involve integration and storage, whereas steps 5C, 5D, and 5E involve input and output. Conducting the two comparisons that involve integration and storage will help you develop and analyze hypotheses about the child's verbal versus nonverbal ability (step 5A) and problem-solving ability versus memory and learning (step 5B). Hypotheses about the input and output of information involve the child's ability to process meaningful versus abstract visual stimuli (step 5C), to answer questions with a verbal versus a pointing response (step 5D), and to respond to problems that demand little or no motor response as opposed to a gross motor response (step 5E).

When conducting these comparisons, the same general guidelines that were applied to earlier optional steps also apply to step 5—the Don't Forget box on page 99 reviewed these guidelines for conducting the step 5 planned comparisons. The KABC-II Interpretive Worksheet (Appendix A) provides a format for walking through each of step 5's comparisons while applying the general interpretive guidelines. Appendix B provides tables to calculate standard scores corresponding to sums of subtest scaled scores for the following planned comparison clusters: Delayed Recall, Verbal Ability, Meaningful Stimuli, and Abstract Stimuli. Appendix C provides the necessary data to calculate standard scores for the Problem-Solving and Memory and Learning clusters. Appendix D provides the necessary data to calculate standard scores for the Verbal Response, Pointing Response, Little Motor, and Gross-Motor clusters.

The subtests that compose each pair of clusters in the planned clinical comparisons for step 5 are shown in Figure 3.8 separately by age group. Most of the comparisons conducted in this step do *not* require administration of Supplementary subtests. The principle exceptions are step 5A (Nonverbal Ability vs. Verbal Ability) and step 5D (Verbal Response vs. Pointing Response), which requires Luria examiners to administer the Knowledge/*Gc* scale as a supplement (and Verbal Knowledge is supplemental for the CHC Model at ages 4–6). For step 5E (Little Motor Response vs. Gross-Motor) examiners must administer Block Counting at ages 7–12 (although it is only a core subtest for ages 13–18). In addition, at age 5, two out-of-level tests must be administered to conduct step 5C (Story Completion) and step 5E (Rover). At age 3, Hand Movements must be administered to conduct step 3A, although it is an out-of-level test at this age. Table 3.6 lists the critical values for each of the planned clinical comparisons. Vanessa J.'s KABC-II scores are used to illustrate each of these comparisons (see Figures 3.9–3.13).

Step 5A: Nonverbal Ability (NVI) versus Verbal Ability (ages 3–18). This comparison requires the administration of the entire Nonverbal Scale and all three Knowledge/*Gc* subtests. The NVI serves as the measure of Nonverbal Ability and requires the administration of one or more Supplementary subtests at each age; Hand Movements, for example, must be administered to all age groups (includ-

STEP 5A: PLANNED CLINICAL COMPARISONS

VERBAL ABILITY vs. **NONVERBAL ABILITY**

Verbal Ability — Scaled Scores 3-18:

Scaled Scores 3-18	Subtest
___	Riddles
___	Expressive Vocabulary
___	Verbal Knowledge

Nonverbal Ability — Scaled Scores:

Subtest	3-4	5	6	7-18
Conceptual Thinking	___	___	___	
Face Recognition				___
Story Completion			___	___
Triangles	___	___	___	___
Pattern Reasoning	___	___	___	___
Hand Movements	___	___	___	___
Block Counting				___

STEP 5B: PLANNED CLINICAL COMPARISONS

MEMORY & LEARNING vs. **PROBLEM-SOLVING ABILITY**

Memory & Learning — Scaled Scores:

Subtest	3	4	5-18
Word Order	___	___	___
Face Recognition	___	___	
Atlantis			___
Number Recall	___	___	
Rebus	___	___	

Problem-Solving Ability — Scaled Scores:

Subtest	3-4	5	6	7-12	13-18
Conceptual Thinking	___	___	___		
Triangles					___
Pattern Reasoning	___	___	___	___	
Rover				___	
Story Completion				___	___
Block Counting					___

STEP 5C: PLANNED CLINICAL COMPARISONS

MEANINGFUL STIMULI vs. **ABSTRACT STIMULI**

Meaningful Stimuli — Scaled Scores:

Subtest	4	5-18
Atlantis	___	___
Face Recognition	___	___
Story Completion		___

Abstract Stimuli — Scaled Scores:

Subtest	4	5-12	13-18
Triangles	___	___	
Rebus	___	___	___
Pattern Reasoning			___

STEP 5D: PLANNED CLINICAL COMPARISONS

VERBAL RESPONSE vs. **POINTING RESPONSE**

Verbal Response — Scaled Scores:

Subtest	4-6	7-18
Number Recall	___	___
Rebus	___	___
Expressive Vocabulary	___	
Riddles		___

Pointing Response — Scaled Scores:

Subtest	4	5-18
Word Order	___	___
Face Recognition	___	
Atlantis		___
Verbal Knowledge		___

STEP 5E: PLANNED CLINICAL COMPARISONS

LITTLE MOTOR RESPONSE vs. **GROSS MOTOR RESPONSE**

Little Motor Response — Scaled Scores:

Subtest	4	5-6	7-18
Conceptual Thinking	___		
Face Recognition	___		
Pattern Reasoning		___	___
Block Counting			___

Gross Motor Response — Scaled Scores:

Subtest	4	5-6	7-12	13-18
Hand Movements	___			
Triangles		___	___	
Rover			___	___
Story Completion			___	___

Figure 3.8 Subtests comprising each of the clusters in step 5's planned clinical comparisons.

ing age 3, even though it is an out-of-level subtest for that age). Verbal Ability corresponds to the standard score that is obtained from the child's scaled scores on *all three* Knowledge/*Gc* subtests (i.e., the two Core subtests, plus the one Supplementary, at each age).

The Nonverbal Ability versus Verbal Ability comparison corresponds to the

Table 3.6 Differences[a] Between Cluster Scores That Are Statistically Significant or Infrequent

Clusters	Age 3		Age 4		Age 5		Age 6		Ages 7–9		Ages 10–12		Ages 13–18	
	Sig. .05	Freq. <10%	Sig. .05	Freq. <10%	Sig. .05	Freq. <10%	Sig. .05	Freq. <10%	Sig. .05	Freq. <10%	Sig. .05	Freq. <10%	Sig. .05	Freq. <10%
Learning/Glr (initial) vs. Delayed Recall					15	16	14	16	13	16	12	16	12	16
Learning/Glr (initial) vs. Knowledge/Gc			13	25	12	25	12	25	12	24	11	24	11	24
Nonverbal Index (NVI) vs. Verbal Ability	12	24	12	24	11	21	9	21	9	23	9	23	9	21
Problem-Solving Ability vs. Memory and Learning	16	26	14	28	11	22	10	24	11	25	11	23	11	24
Meaningful Stimuli vs. Abstract Stimuli			15	27	12	24	12	24	12	22	13	22	14	22
Verbal Response vs. Pointing Response			12	20	12	20	12	20	12	18	12	18	11	18
Little Motor Response vs. Gross-Motor Response			17	29	13	25	13	25	12	22	13	22	15	25

[a]Absolute values (regardless of direction)

familiar discrepancy between Wechsler's Performance and Verbal Scales on his various test batteries. On the WPPSI-III the most pertinent contrast is Performance IQ versus Verbal IQ, but on the WISC-IV—which does not yield Verbal and Performance IQs—it is the Perceptual Reasoning Index (PRI) vs. the Verbal Comprehension Index (VCI). For the WAIS-III, examiners can use either the Verbal and Performance IQs or the relevant indexes. Thus, hypotheses that are developed from a significant discrepancy between the Nonverbal and Verbal Ability clusters may be supported or refuted with data from other tests such as the IQs or indexes on the Wechsler instruments.

The literature on intellectual functioning has provided a wealth of data on verbal versus nonverbal comparisons. Kaufman and Lichtenberger (1999, 2000, 2002) review and summarize much of this literature, which suggests many possible explanations for various cognitive patterns. For example, individuals who obtain a significantly higher nonverbal than verbal profile might do so because of strengths in visualization and fluid reasoning compared to weaknesses in short-term memory. Better-developed simultaneous-holistic than analytic-sequential processing may be another viable explanation for this pattern. Some clinical groups also typically show greater nonverbal than verbal performance on IQ tests. For example, children and adolescents with learning disabilities often show nonverbal abilities to be greater than verbal ones because of their poor school achievement (Kaufman & Lichtenberger, 2002). Not surprisingly, bilingual individuals also often show a nonverbal > verbal pattern, which is why the authors of the KABC-II recommend administration of the Luria model (excluding Knowledge/Gc from the global score). Individuals with autism have been shown to have a nonverbal > verbal pattern (see Chapter 6 of this book); however, this pattern does not hold for high-functioning individuals with autism or those with Asperger's Disorder.

The opposite pattern of higher verbal than nonverbal performance has been noted in some clinical samples, such as depression (Kaufman & Lichtenberger, 2002). Impaired concentration, psychomotor retardation, anxiety, or low motivation may be the key factors in lowered performance on nonverbal tasks for individuals with depression (Gregory, 1987; Pernicano, 1986). Children with motor coordination problems, such as those with cerebral palsy, may also demonstrate a verbal > nonverbal pattern of performance. Clearly, the physical demands of some of the KABC-II nonverbal tasks (although not all require a motor response) will potentially lower a child's score if he or she has motor coordination problems.

Vanessa's step 5A clinical comparison is demonstrated in Figure 3.9. First, the range of scaled scores in the Verbal Ability cluster is evaluated. The range of scaled scores is 4 points, which is not uncommonly large, and indicates that the

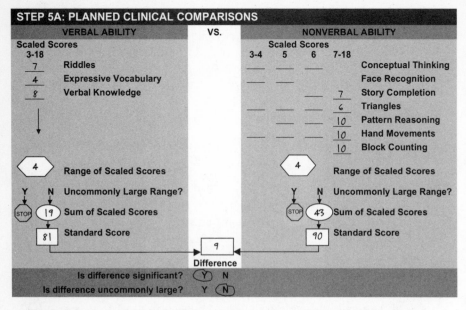

Figure 3.9 Vanessa J.'s step 5A comparison between Verbal and Nonverbal Ability.

Verbal Ability cluster is interpretable. The range of scaled scores in the Nonverbal Ability cluster is evaluated next. The range of scaled scores for this cluster is also 4 points, which is not uncommonly large and indicates that the Nonverbal Ability cluster is also interpretable. Since both clusters are interpretable, the standard score for each of the clusters is calculated. Appendix B provides the conversion of sum of scaled scores to standard scores for the Verbal Ability cluster (and the KABC-II manual lists the scores for the NVI). Vanessa's NVI is 90, and her Verbal Ability standard score is 81. The 9-point discrepancy between the clusters is significant at the .05 level, but it is not uncommonly large (23 or more points are needed for the 10% base rate). *Vanessa's nonverbal ability is significantly better than her verbal ability (acquisition of facts and verbal concepts). This difference is statistically significant but not uncommon.*

Step 5B: Problem-Solving Ability versus Memory and Learning (ages 3–18). Both the Simultaneous/*Gv* and the Planning/*Gf* scales measure children's ability to solve problems. Simultaneous/*Gv* subtests tend to emphasize visualization as the key element for solving problems, whereas Planning/*Gf* subtests tend to be highly dependent on verbal mediation. Both types of tasks require children to solve problems, however, which makes their combination meaningful in a conceptual sense. The Sequential/*Gsm* and Learning/*Glr* scales both involve memory, either short term or long term. In addition, Carroll's (1993) theory groups both types of abilities together as a broad factor called Memory and Learning. For all ages, this planned comparison is composed only of Core subtests. At ages 5–6, the Simultaneous/*Gv* subtests are contrasted with the combination of Sequential/*Gsm* + Learning/*Glr*. At ages 7–18, the combination of Simultaneous/*Gv* + Planning/*Gf* is contrasted with the combination of Sequential/*Gsm* + Learning/*Glr*.

For age 4, the clusters for this comparison do not correspond neatly to the scales. Face Recognition, though included on the Simultaneous/*Gv* scale, is grouped with the Memory and Learning cluster because it requires visual memory but little or no problem solving. At age 3, Conceptual Thinking and Triangles both assess a young child's problem-solving abilities, and these are therefore contrasted with the cluster of Atlantis, Word Order, and Face Recognition.

Many clinical groups may display differences in their performance on the Memory and Learning Cluster (containing *Gsm* and *Glr* subtests) and the Problem-Solving Cluster (containing *Gv* and *Gf* subtests). For example, there is strong evidence that children with attentional problems (such as those with Attention-Deficit/Hyperactivity Disorder [ADHD]) have deficits in working memory (Seidman, Biederman, Faraone, & Milberger, 1995; Seidman, Biederman, Faraone, Weber, & Oullette, 1997). Children experiencing symptoms of anxiety or depression may also show depressed performance on tasks requiring short-term memory (Hong, 1999; Kellogg, Hopko, & Ashcraft, 1999). Thus, there is evidence that would predict lower scores on the Memory and Learning cluster for these clinical groups.

However, in addition to problems with attention, deficits in hindsight, forethought, and planning ability have also been noted for children with ADHD (Pennington, Grossier, & Welsh, 1993; Weyandt & Willis, 1994). Thus, these types of deficits may depress scores on tasks tapping fluid ability (*Gf*), such as those in the Problem-Solving Ability cluster. Children that have brain injuries affecting their frontal or executive functioning (Perugini, Harvery, Lovejoy, Sandstrom, & Webb, 2000) may also do poorly on the *Gf* tasks of the Problem-Solving cluster. It is important to note that the functions of attention and executive cognitive processes (e.g., *Gf*) are intertwined and difficult to isolate for assessment (Barkley, 2003). Much of the research literature examining the neurological explanations for these two processes focuses on deficits or damage in the same prefrontal cortex of the brain (Boliek & Obrzut, 1997; Zelazo, Carter, Reznick, & Frye, 1997). Therefore, it is difficult to predict whether a specific pattern of performance will exist in the Memory and Learning versus Problem-Solving Ability cluster for children with ADHD and related disorders.

In addition to the clinical groups mentioned, children with reading disabilities have historically displayed patterns of performance on cognitive tests that are related to the Memory and Learning versus Problem-Solving Ability clusters. Children with reading disabilities have shown depressed scores on the K-ABC Sequential Processing scale in comparison to the Simultaneous scale (e.g., Hooper & Hynd, 1982, 1985; Kamphaus & Reynolds, 1987; Lichtenberger, 2001), and also show associated deficits in left-hemispheric processing (James & Selz, 1997; Lyon, Fletcher, & Barnes, 2003; Reynolds, Kamphaus, Rosenthal, & Hiemenz, 1997). Thus, a pattern of Memory and Learning < Problem-Solving Ability may be present for children with reading disabilities.

Vanessa's step 5B clinical comparison is demonstrated in Figure 3.10. First, the range of scaled scores in the Memory and Learning cluster is evaluated. The range of scaled scores is 7 points, which is not uncommonly large and indicates that the Memory and Learning cluster is interpretable. The range of scaled scores in the Problem-Solving cluster is evaluated next. The range of scaled scores for this cluster is only 4 points, which is not uncommonly large and indicates that the Problem-Solving cluster is also interpretable. Since both clusters are interpretable, then the standard score for each of the clusters is calculated. Appendix C provides the conversion of the sum of scaled scores to standard scores for both the Memory and Learning cluster and the Problem-Solving cluster. Vanessa's Memory and Learning cluster standard score is 112, and her Problem-Solving

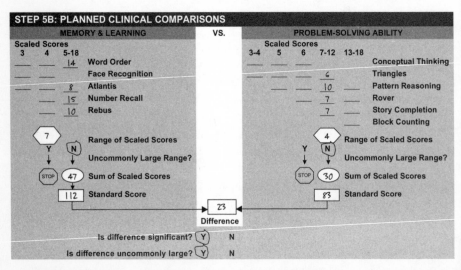

Figure 3.10 Vanessa J.'s step 5B comparison between Memory and Learning and Problem-Solving Ability.

standard score is 83. The 23-point discrepancy between the clusters is significant at the .05 level and is also uncommonly large (23 or more points are needed for the 10% base rate). *Vanessa's memory and learning abilities are significantly better than her problem-solving ability, and this difference is large enough to be labeled uncommon within the normal population of children about her age.*

Although Vanessa's scores on these clusters revealed an uncommonly large difference between Problem-Solving and Memory and Learning, this difference needs to be investigated further and supported with other data (see the previous Don't Forget box for the interpretive guidelines). A closer examination of these clusters with a clinical eye helps us to see that her strength in Sequential processing and weakness in Simultaneous processing is probably the key finding. Vanessa's Planning/*Gf* and Learning/*Glr* scales did not really differ very much. Therefore, this difference between Problem-Solving Ability (comprised of Simultaneous/*Gv* + Planning/*Gf* subtests) and Memory and Learning (Comprised of Sequential/*Gsm* + Learning/*Glr* subtests) is probably just a reflection of the most important difference found in her profile—the *Gv* < *Gsm* noted in the step 2 analysis. This point highlights the need to be a clinician, not just a number cruncher, during the evaluation of the KABC-II profile. Despite the fact that step 5B produced an uncommonly large discrepancy for Vanessa, the results of this comparison are not even included in Vanessa's case report (see Chapter 7) because they lacked clinical value for diagnostic or educational purposes.

Step 5C: Visual Perception of Meaningful Stimuli versus Abstract Stimuli (ages 4–18). Both the Meaningful Stimuli and the Abstract Stimuli clusters are composed of visual subtests from three indexes: Learning/*Glr,* Simultaneous/*Gv,* and Planning/*Gf.* From the Learning/*Glr* scale, Atlantis contributes to the Meaningful stimuli cluster, as the fish, shells, and plants are all meaningful, concrete stimuli; in contrast, Rebus contributes to the Abstract Stimuli cluster because the stimuli are symbolic (although many of the abstract stimuli deliberately offer clues to help the child remember the association—for example, two intersecting diamonds for "and" and a rain cloud for "rain"). From the Simultaneous/*Gv* scale, Face Recognition is part of the Meaningful Stimuli cluster, as pictures of people are clearly meaningful, but, in contrast, Triangles includes abstract designs. On the Planning/*Gf* scale, Story Completion—which depicts interpersonal scenes—is included in the Meaningful Stimuli grouping, whereas Pattern Reasoning contributes to the Abstract Stimuli cluster because most of its stimuli are symbolic.

Thus, the Meaningful Stimuli and Abstract Stimuli clusters are nicely balanced. The cognitive abilities measured by the Meaningful Stimuli grouping are essentially the same as the abilities measured by the Abstract Stimuli cluster. That deliberate balance permits an especially useful comparison of the child's ability to manipulate meaningful versus abstract visual stimuli—as long as each cluster is unitary and does not display too much inter-subtest variability.

The clinical literature suggests that individuals with brain damage may have difficulty with tasks that involve abstract stimuli. For example, much research has been conducted with Wechsler's Block Design (similar to the KABC-II's Triangles), which uses abstract block models as stimuli. Block Design has been shown to be vulnerable to any kind of cerebral brain damage, and it is especially sensitive to posterior lesions in the right hemisphere (Lezak, 1995). In addition to Triangles, other subtests from the Abstract Stimuli cluster on the KABC-II have been linked to research related to abilities on tasks with abstract content. For example, on tests similar to Pattern Reasoning (e.g., WAIS-III Matrix Reasoning) poor performance has been shown to be linked to poor nonverbal abstract reasoning (Groth-Marnat, Gallagher, Hale, & Kaplan, 2000).

Vanessa's step 5C clinical comparison is demonstrated in Figure 3.11. First, the range of scaled scores in the Meaningful Stimuli cluster is evaluated. The range of scaled scores is 1 point, which is not uncommonly large and indicates that the Meaningful Stimuli cluster is interpretable. The range of scaled scores in the Abstract Stimuli cluster is evaluated next. The range of scaled scores for this cluster is 4 points, which is not uncommonly large and indicates that the Abstract Stimuli cluster is also interpretable. Since both clusters are interpretable, the standard

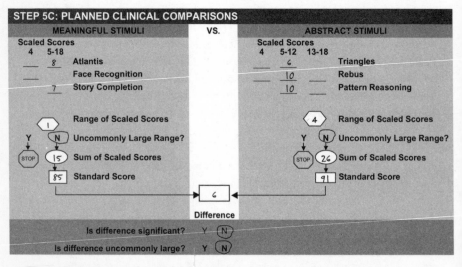

Figure 3.11 Vanessa J.'s step 5C comparison between Meaningful and Abstract Stimuli.

score for each of the clusters is calculated. Appendix B provides the conversion of sum of scaled scores to standard scores for both the Meaningful and Abstract Stimuli Clusters. Vanessa's Meaningful cluster standard score is 85, and her Abstract Stimuli standard score is 91. The 6-point discrepancy between the clusters is neither significant nor uncommonly large (13 points are needed for significance, and 23 or more points are needed for the 10% base rate). *Vanessa's ability to process abstract stimuli does not differ significantly from her ability to process meaningful stimuli.*

Step 5D: Verbal Response versus Pointing Response (ages 4–18). Similar to the comparison made in step 5C, the Verbal Response cluster and Pointing Response cluster are matched on cognitive ability at ages 5–18. That is to say, one Learning/*Glr* subtest contributes to each cluster (Rebus requires a verbal response, while Atlantis demands a pointing response). Similarly, the Sequential/*Gsm* and Knowledge/*Gc* scales each contribute one subtest to the Verbal Response category and one subtest to the Pointing Response category. From the Sequential/*Gsm* scale, Number Recall and Word Order require verbal responses and pointing responses, respectively. At ages 7–18, the Knowledge/*Gc* subtests are classified as Pointing Response (Verbal Knowledge) and Verbal Response (Riddles). For children below age 7, Expressive Vocabulary replaces Riddles as a Verbal Response task because the early Riddles items, designed for very young children, require pointing to the correct picture.

At age 4 the subtests are fairly matched on cognitive ability as well, but there is one extra Simultaneous/*Gv* subtest that contributes to the Pointing Response cluster—Face Recognition. In addition, note that some subtests are excluded from the Pointing versus Verbal comparison because children may respond *either* by pointing to the correct response or by naming the letter that corresponds to the right answer: Pattern Reasoning and Conceptual Thinking.

Various clinical groups may perform better on the Verbal Response cluster than the Pointing Response cluster. For example, children who have motor impairment may be more comfortable with a verbal response. However the physical demands of the pointing response are minimal, so this effect will likely only be noted for those individuals with severe motor impairment. In contrast, the pattern of Verbal Response < Pointing Response may be seen in a variety of instances. For example, children who are bilingual will likely be more challenged by the verbal response than the pointing response. Children and adolescents with learning disabilities often show poorer performance on tasks requiring verbal responses because of their poor school achievement (Kaufman & Lichtenberger, 2002). Specifically, children with expressive language disorders may perform sig-

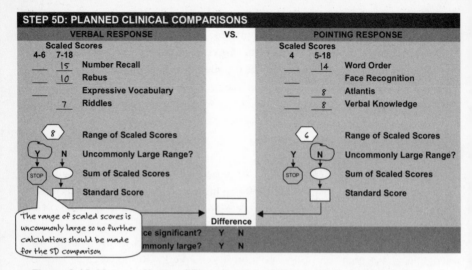

STEP 5D: PLANNED CLINICAL COMPARISONS

| VERBAL RESPONSE | VS. | POINTING RESPONSE |

Verbal Response — Scaled Scores (4-6 / 7-18):
- Number Recall — 15
- Rebus — 10
- Expressive Vocabulary
- Riddles — 7

Range of Scaled Scores — 8
Uncommonly Large Range? — Y / N (Y circled)
STOP — Sum of Scaled Scores
Standard Score

Pointing Response — Scaled Scores (4 / 5-18):
- Word Order — 14
- Face Recognition
- Atlantis — 8
- Verbal Knowledge — 8

Range of Scaled Scores — 6
Uncommonly Large Range? — Y / N (N circled)
STOP — Sum of Scaled Scores
Standard Score

Difference

Difference significant?   Y   N
...uncommonly large?   Y   N

The range of scaled scores is uncommonly large so no further calculations should be made for the 5D comparison

Figure 3.12 Vanessa J.'s step 5D comparison between Verbal and Pointing Responses.

nificantly worse on tasks demanding verbal responses than pointing responses. Generally, individuals with communicative difficulties, such as those with autism, have shown depressed performance on tasks requiring verbal expression (see Chapter 6 of this book).

Vanessa's step 5D clinical comparison is demonstrated in Figure 3.12. First, the range of scaled scores in the Verbal Response stimuli cluster is evaluated. The range of scaled scores is 8 points, which is uncommonly large and indicates that the Verbal Response cluster is *not* interpretable. Consequently, we can stop evaluating the planned comparison. *Both* clusters must be interpretable to calculate the difference between them. Although the range of scaled scores (6 points) for the Pointing Response cluster is not uncommonly large and indicates that the cluster is interpretable, it is not even necessary to calculate the standard score for either cluster. *The Verbal Response–Pointing Response clinical comparison cannot be made because both groupings must be interpretable.*

Step 5E: Little or No Motor Response versus Gross-Motor Response (ages 4–18). The Little or No Motor Response cluster is composed of subtests that require a simple pointing response (such as Face Recognition), a simple verbal response (Block Counting), or either (Pattern Reasoning). In contrast, the Gross-Motor Response cluster comprises subtests that all demand the motor manipulation of objects (or, in the case of Hand Movements, the child's own hands).

When evaluating the discrepancy between these two clusters, examiners should integrate the results with their clinical observations of the child's motor coordination during the pertinent KABC-II subtests as well as observations of motor behavior on other tasks (e.g., how they held a pencil during informal or standardized drawing tests). The level of gross-motor ability demanded by each subtest in the Gross-Motor cluster varies and should also be considered. For example, Hand Movements and Triangles probably demand the most gross-motor skill, and Rover demands the least. Children who are observed to display coordination problems during the evaluation may obtain their lowest scores on the subtests that place the greatest premium on good coordination for successful performance.

Children who are referred for evaluation because of suspected brain dysfunction with motor involvement might perform much better on the Little or No Motor cluster than on the Gross-Motor cluster. On the WISC-IV, for example, a small sample of children diagnosed with motor impairment performed better on visual perceptual tasks requiring little or no motor coordination, such as Matrix Reasoning and Picture Completion (23rd percentile), than on subtests requiring gross-motor responses, such as Block Design and Coding (10th percentile). Similar findings were reported for small samples of children diagnosed with closed head injury (39th vs. 22nd percentile) and with open head injury (38th vs. 20th percentile; The Psychological Corporation, 2003, tables 5.33, 5.34, and 5.37).

For children with motor impairments and brain injuries, the KABC-II subtests in the Gross-Motor cluster might seriously underestimate their cognitive ability. For children ages 7–18 who have a known or suspected motor problem or head injury, it is usually a good idea to use the special subtest norms for Pattern Reasoning, Triangles, and Story Completion that are based only on correct responses (without time points for quick perfect performance; see Chapter 2).

Vanessa's step 5E clinical comparison is demonstrated in Figure 3.13. First, the range of scaled scores in the Little Motor Response cluster is evaluated. The range of scaled scores is 0 points, which is clearly not uncommonly large and indicates that the Little Motor Response cluster is interpretable. The range of scaled scores in the Gross-Motor Response cluster is evaluated next. The range of scaled scores for this cluster is 1 point, which is not uncommonly large and indicates that the Gross-Motor Response cluster is also interpretable. Since both clusters are interpretable, the standard score for each of the clusters is calculated. Appendix D provides the conversion of sum of scaled scores to standard scores for both the Little and Gross-Motor Response Clusters. Vanessa's Little Motor Response cluster standard score is 100, and her Gross-Motor standard score is 78. The 22-point discrepancy between the clusters is significant and uncommonly large (13 points are needed for significance, and 22 or more points are needed for the 10%

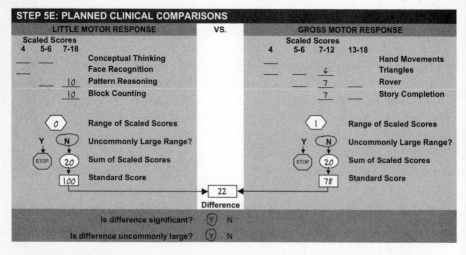

Figure 3.13 Vanessa J.'s step 5E comparison between Little Motor Response and Gross-Motor Response.

base rate). *Vanessa's ability to solve problems that require little or no motor response is significantly better than her ability to solve problems that require gross motor coordination, and the difference is uncommonly large within the normal population.*

Step 6: Generate Hypotheses to Explain Fluctuations in Two Circumstances

Step 6 evaluates two specific circumstances:

Step 6A: Scales that are not interpretable (ages 4–18)

Step 6B: Supplementary subtests that are inconsistent with pertinent Core
subtests (ages 3–18)

Step 6 has two parallel parts: One evaluates scales that are not interpretable, and the other evaluates supplementary subtests that are not consistent with the core subtests. Whether you are trying to identify hypotheses to explain scale indexes that are not interpretable or to explain why Supplementary subtests differ significantly from pertinent Core subtests, you must seek out corroborating data or observations to support your hypotheses. During this optional step of profile interpretation, it is fine to generate more than one hypothesis to explain a noninterpretable index or inconsistent supplementary subtest. Sometimes the effort to identify meaningful hypotheses will prove fruitless unless additional testing is conducted. The main guidelines are to be flexible, to seek multiple pieces of corroborating evidence, to be a vigilant clinician during the administration of all tasks, and to be knowledgeable in pertinent theory and research.

Step 6A: Generate Hypotheses to Explain Fluctuations in Scales That Are Not Interpretable (ages 4–18). To determine if step 6A needs to be conducted, review the findings in step 2A, in which you determined whether each of the scales was interpretable. If all scales are interpretable, proceed directly to step 6B. However, if one or more of the scale indexes were found to be uninterpretable in step 2A (i.e., uncommonly large subtest variability within the scale), then proceed with step 6A. This step offers three approaches for developing hypotheses to explain the substantial intrascale variability:

- *First line of attack.* Examine the results of Step 5—planned clinical comparisons—to identify possible hypotheses.
- *Second line of attack.* Determine how the Core subtests in each scale complement each other (e.g., if they measure different CHC narrow abilities, that might help explain why the child scored at different levels on them)
- *Third line of attack.* Examine QIs, behavioral observations in general, and pertinent background information to generate possible hypotheses.

First line of attack—planned clinical comparisons. With the first line of attack, examine the results of step 5's relevant planned clinical comparisons. Consider, for example, the Sequential/*Gsm* scale, which is composed of Word Order and Number Recall for ages 4–18. If that index was found to be uninterpretable, one specific planned comparison is relevant for generating a hypothesis to explain the subtest variability: Verbal Response versus Pointing Response. A child who performed substantially better on Word Order than Number Recall (rendering the Sequential/*Gsm* index uninterpretable) might be better—in general—when responding by pointing (e.g., touching the pictures named by the examiner during Word Order) than by verbalizing the response (i.e., the numbers spoken by the examiner during Number Recall). Examine this planned comparison. Did the child have a significant difference in Verbal Response versus Pointing Response? Presuming that this difference is consistent with the direction of the child's discrepancy between Word Order and Number Recall, then one hypothesis to possibly explain that discrepancy (and, hence, to explain the uninterpretable Sequential/*Gsm* index) concerns the child's ability to respond to tasks by pointing to versus naming the correct answers. Note that a significant difference in a planned comparison is enough to generate a hypothesis—it doesn't have to be unusually large. However, one would have more confidence in a hypothesis that is based on an unusually large difference than on a difference that is significant but not uncommonly large.

The planned comparison involving Verbal versus Pointing Responses is also useful for generating hypotheses to explain (1) an uninterpretable Learning/*Glr* index for ages 4–18 (Atlantis = Pointing, Rebus = Verbal) and (2) an uninterpretable Knowledge/*Gc* index for ages 7–18 (Verbal Knowledge = Pointing, Riddles = Verbal).

Similarly, visual perception of Abstract versus Meaningful Stimuli provides a useful vehicle for generating hypotheses to explain (1) an uninterpretable Learning/*Glr* index for ages 4–18 (Atlantis = Meaningful, Rebus = Abstract), (2) an uninterpretable Planning/*Gf* index for ages 7–18 (Story Completion = Meaningful, Pattern Reasoning = Abstract), and (3) an uninterpretable Simultaneous/*Gv* index for age 4 (Face Recognition = Meaningful, Triangles = Abstract). The Memory and Learning versus Problem-Solving planned comparison is useful for explaining an uninterpretable Simultaneous/*Gv* index, but only for very young children (ages 3 and 4): Face Recognition (Memory and Learning) versus Triangles and Conceptual Thinking (Problem-Solving).

Finally, the planned comparison concerning the degree to which coordination plays a role in successful performance (Little or No Motor vs. Gross-Motor) is useful for generating hypotheses to explain uninterpretable Planning/*Gf* and Simultaneous/*Gv* indexes. For the Planning/*Gf* index at ages 7–18, Pattern Reasoning requires Little or No Motor coordination in contrast to the Gross-Motor coordination needed to respond to Story Completion. For the Simultaneous/*Gv* scale, this planned comparison can generate hypotheses at a variety of ages. These hypotheses, along with all of the others discussed in the text from step 6A, are summarized in Figure 3.14 (which is an excerpt from the Interpretive Worksheet).

In Vanessa's case, all of her five indexes were interpretable, so we would not proceed with step 6A. For illustrative purposes, we will review the case of 13-year-old Aiden, whose Learning/*Glr* index was uninterpretable due to the extreme discrepancy between Rebus (12) and Atlantis (6). Thus, we check the KABC-II Interpretive Worksheet for how to proceed with step 6A (see also Figure 3.14). Looking under the row containing the Learning/*Glr* index, we see that two planned clinical comparisons may provide hypotheses for the Atlantis-Rebus variability: (1) Meaningful versus Abstract Stimuli and (2) Verbal Response versus Pointing Response. The Meaningful Stimulus cluster comprises Atlantis and Story Completion, whereas the Abstract Stimulus cluster comprises Rebus and Pattern Reasoning. The results of this comparison for Aiden reveal that he performed significantly better on Abstract Stimuli than on Meaningful Stimuli (a difference that is also uncommonly large). Then we examine the second clinical comparison to further develop hypotheses for Aiden's Rebus-Atlantis variabil-

STEP 6A: GENERATE HYPOTHESES TO EXPLAIN FLUCTUATIONS IN SCALES THAT ARE NOT INTERPRETABLE.

First Line of Attack: Examine Planned Clinical Comparisons (from Step 5) to identify possible hypotheses.

Was Index found uninterpretable in step 2? (check box if yes)	Cluster that may provide hypotheses for the subtest variability in the index	Age	Core Subtests Relevant to the Clusters
Sequential/*Gsm* ☐	Verbal Response vs. Pointing Response	4–18	Number Recall (*Verbal*) vs. Word Order (*Pointing*)
Simultaneous/*Gv* ☐	Abstract vs. Meaningful Stimuli	4	Face Recognition (*Meaningful*) vs. Triangles (*Abstract*)
	Memory and Learning vs. Problem Solving Ability	3–4	Face Rec. (*Mem. & Learn.*) vs. Triangles/Concep. Th. (*Prob. Slv.*)
	Little Motor vs. Gross Motor Response	4	Face Recognition/Concept. Thinkg. (*Little*) vs. Triangles (*Gross*)
	Little Motor vs. Gross Motor Response	5	Concept Thinking/Pattern Reason. (*Little*) vs. Triangles (*Gross*)
	Little Motor vs. Gross Motor Response	6	Concept Th./Pattern Reason. (*Little*) vs. Triangles/Rover (*Gross*)
	Little Motor vs. Gross Motor Response	13–18	Block Counting (*Little*) vs. Rover (*Gross*)
Learning/*Glr* ☐	Verbal Response vs. Pointing Response	4–18	Rebus (*Verbal*) vs. Atlantis (*Pointing*)
	Abstract vs. Meaningful Stimuli	4–18	Rebus (*Abstract*) vs Atlantis (*Meaningful*)
Planning/*Gf* ☐	Abstract vs. Meaningful Stimuli	7–18	Pattern Reasoning (*Abstract*) vs. Story Completion (*Meaningful*)
	Little Motor vs. Gross Motor Response		Pattern Reasoning (*Little*) vs. Story Completion (*Gross*)
Knowledge/*Gc* ☐	Verbal Response vs. Pointing Response	7–18	Riddles (*Verbal*) vs. Verbal Knowledge (*Pointing*)

Second Line of Attack: Examine how the Core subtests within each scale complement each other.

Consult Rapid References 3.3 through 3.7 to develop hypotheses.

Third Line of Attack: Examine Qualitative Indicators (QIs), behavioral observations, and background information.

Follow up hypotheses derived from QIs, behavioral observations, and background information by collecting supplemental data if necessary (e.g., administer additional subtests, contact further sources for collateral information).

Figure 3.14 Excerpt from the KABC-II Interpretive Worksheet for Step 6A.

ity—the Verbal Response versus Pointing Response comparison. Rebus, Number Recall, and Riddles comprise the Verbal Response cluster, and Atlantis, Word Order, and Verbal Knowledge comprise the Pointing Response cluster. However, in Aiden's case, this planned comparison cannot be conducted because of uncommon variability within the cluster's subtests. Therefore we are left with the hypothesis that Aiden performed better with abstract than meaningful stimuli, and we will search for further data to support it.

Second line of attack—how the Core subtests within each scale complement each other. To determine how the subtests that constitute each KABC-II scale complement each other, we have dissected what we feel are the critical distinguishing features of the subtests in each scale and have listed them in easy-to-access Rapid References. These distinguishing features include global areas such as input, output, integration, and storage, and the theoretical CHC narrow abilities (see Table 3.17) that underlie each subtest.

Complementary aspects of the subtests that compose each KABC-II scale are summarized in Rapid Reference 3.3 (Learning/*Glr*), 3.4 (Sequential/*Gsm*), 3.5 (Simultaneous/*Gv*), 3.6 (Planning/*Gf*), and 3.7 (Knowledge/*Gc*).

To exemplify how we would proceed with developing hypotheses for Aiden's uninterpretable Learning/*Glr* scale, look at Rapid Reference 3.3. We can see that Atlantis, which was the lower of Aiden's two *Glr* scaled scores, gives feedback for errors, but Rebus does not. We know that Aiden performed better with abstract

≡Rapid Reference 3.3

How the Learning/*Glr* Subtests Complement Each Other

	Atlantis	Rebus
Provides feedback for errors?	Yes	No
Uses meaningful auditory stimuli?	No	Yes
Context important for success?	No	Yes
Does sequence of stimuli matter?	No	Yes
CHC narrow abilities		
Associative Memory (Glr)	✓	✓

Notes. Core Learning/*Glr* subtests for ages 4–18 are Atlantis and Rebus. The Supplementary Delayed Recall scale for ages 5–18 includes the Atlantis Delayed and Rebus Delayed subtests. The Delayed Recall scale measures *both* Associative Memory and Learning Abilities.

≡ *Rapid Reference 3.4*

How the Sequential/*Gsm* Subtests (Core + Supplementary) Complement Each Other

	Word Order	Number Recall	Hand Movements
Nature of content?	Words	Numbers	Hand position
How achieves difficulty?	Interference task	Long number series	Long sequences of hand positions
Integration of auditory and visual stimuli?	Yes	No	No
Channel of communication?	Auditory-motor	Auditory-vocal	Visual-motor
Requires flexibility to shift tasks?	Yes	No	No
CHC narrow abilities			
Memory Span (*Gsm*)	✓	✓	✓
Working Memory (*Gsm*)	✓		
Visual Memory (*Gv*)			✓

Notes. Core Sequential/*Gsm* subtests for ages 4–18 are Word Order and Number Recall. Hand Movements is a Supplementary Sequential/*Gsm* subtest for ages 4–18.

than with meaningful *visual* stimuli from our examination of the step 5C planned clinical comparison (Meaningful Stimuli vs. Abstract Stimuli). However, Rebus uses meaningful *auditory* stimuli, but Atlantis does not. In Rebus (Aiden's better performance) the context is important for success, but there is no context in Atlantis. Also, the sequence of the stimuli in Rebus matters, but it does not in Atlantis. Thus, many of the points presented in Rapid Reference 3.3 may be developed into hypotheses to explain the variability in his Learning/*Glr* scale (which need to be supported with other data). However, the CHC narrow abilities are the same for Atlantis and Rebus—they are both measures of Associative Memory—so CHC theory will not provide any useful hypotheses for explaining Aiden's uninterpretable Learning/*Glr* index.

However, CHC narrow abilities can often offer much insight into why a child might obtain an uninterpretable Index on a KABC-II scale other than Learning/*Glr*. On the Sequential/*Gsm* scale, Word Order (by virtue of its color inter-

≡ Rapid Reference 3.5

How the Simultaneous/Gv Subtests Complement Each Other

CHC Narrow Abilities	Triangles	Conceptual Thinking	Face Recognition	Pattern Reasoning	Rover	Block Counting	Gestalt Closure
Visualization (Gv)	✓	✓		✓		✓	
Spatial Relations (Gv)	✓						
Visual Memory (Gv)			✓				
Spatial Scanning (Gv)					✓		
Closure Speed (Gv)							✓
Induction (Gf)		✓		✓			
General Sequential Reasoning (Gf)					✓		
Math Achievement (Gq)					✓	✓	

Notes. Core Simultaneous/Gv subtests for age 4 are Triangles, Conceptual Thinking, and Face Recognition. Gestalt Closure is a Supplementary Simultaneous/Gv subtest at age 4. Core Simultaneous/Gv subtests for age 5 are Triangles, Conceptual Thinking, and Pattern Reasoning. Gestalt Closure, Face Recognition, and Block Counting are Supplementary Simultaneous/Gv subtests at age 5. Core Simultaneous/Gv subtests for age 6 are Triangles, Conceptual Thinking, Pattern Reasoning, and Rover. Gestalt Closure, Face Recognition, Block Counting, and Story Completion are Supplementary Simultaneous/Gv subtests at age 6. Core Simultaneous/Gv subtests for age 7–12 are Rover and Triangles. Gestalt Closure and Block Counting are Supplementary Simultaneous/Gv subtests at age 7–12. Core Simultaneous/Gv subtests for age 13–18 are Rover and Block Counting. Gestalt Closure and Triangles are Supplementary Simultaneous/Gv subtests at age 13–18.

≡Rapid Reference 3.6

How the Planning/*Gf* Subtests Complement Each Other

CHC Narrow Abilities	Pattern Reasoning	Story Completion
Visualization (*Gv*)	✓	✓
Induction (*Gf*)	✓	✓
General Sequential Reasoning (*Gf*)		✓
General Information (*Gc*)		✓

Notes. Planning/*Gf* subtests are only administered at ages 7–18. There are no Supplementary Planning/*Gf* subtests.

≡Rapid Reference 3.7

How the Knowledge/*Gc* Subtests Complement Each Other

	Riddles	Verbal Knowledge	Expressive Vocabulary
Type of stimuli?	Auditory	Visual + Auditory	Visual
Measures auditory-visual integration?	No	Yes	Yes
CHC narrow abilities			
Lexical Knowledge (*Gc*)	✓	✓	✓
Language Development (*Gc*)	✓		
General Knowledge (*Gc*)		✓	
General Sequential Reasoning (*Gf*)	✓		

Notes. Riddles uses both auditory and visual stimuli for its easiest items. Riddles and Expressive Vocabulary are Core Knowledge/*Gc* subtests for ages 4–6. Verbal Knowledge is a Supplementary Knowledge/*Gc* test for ages 4–6. Riddles and Verbal Knowledge are Core Knowledge/*Gc* subtests for ages 7–18, and Expressive Vocabulary is a Supplementary subtest for this age group.

ference task) measures the narrow ability of Working Memory, but Number Recall does not (see Rapid Reference 3.4). A child who performs substantially more poorly on Word Order than on Number Recall might have difficulties with working memory. That hypothesis can be checked out with clinical observations during KABC-II subtests that are dependent on working memory for successful performance (e.g., to be able to retain and "juggle" pertinent information during

Story Completion items while performing the executive functions needed for decision making and hypothesis generation).

From Rapid Reference 3.5, it is clear that the Simultaneous/Gv scale comprises an array of CHC narrow abilities, an array that changes with age as a function of the scale's precise subtest composition. Rover, for example, measures the CHC narrow abilities of Spatial Scanning (Gv), General Sequential Reasoning (Gf), and Math Achievement (Gq), whereas Triangles measures two different narrow abilities: Visualization (Gv) and Spatial Relations (Gv). Both subtests measure at least one narrow ability that is subsumed under the broad ability of Visual Processing (Gv), justifying the pairing of Rover and Triangles as the Core Simultaneous/Gv subtests for ages 7–12 years. Yet if a child of 7–12 has an uninterpretable index on that scale with Rover > Triangles, it may be that the child has a relative strength on the Gv narrow ability of Spatial Scanning compared to a relative weakness on either or both of the two Gv narrow abilities measures by Triangles. Or the child might have a relative strength on the Gf narrow ability measured by Rover (General Sequential—or Deductive—Reasoning).

These hypotheses can immediately be tested out by considering the child's performance on other KABC-II subtests that measure the same narrow ability (see table 3.7). For example, General Sequential Reasoning is measured not only by Rover but also by Story Completion and Riddles. When KABC-II Core or Supplementary subtests do not measure the pertinent narrow abilities, examiners might consider administering additional tasks that measure the specific narrow abilities that are desired (see Flanagan & Ortiz, 2000, for lists of subtests that measure many of the 70 or so narrow abilities).

This methodology for applying CHC analysis to an uninterpretable Simultaneous/Gv index at ages 7–12 applies to that scale at other ages as well and also to the Planning/Gf index for ages 7–18 (see Rapid Reference 3.6) and the Knowledge/Gc index at ages 4–18 (Rapid Reference 3.7).

We are deliberately not providing a specific set of rules for using Rapid References 3.3–3.7 during the second line of attack. Steps 4 and 5 include step-by-step empirical analyses to determine the significance of differences and to evaluate whether the differences are uncommonly large. As stated, both significant and uncommonly large differences in the planned comparisons enhance the degree to which one can have confidence in various hypotheses that are generated. But always keep in mind that step 6 (including both 6A and 6B) relies mostly on detective work, observational skills, and theoretical understanding of what the scales measure. The generation of hypotheses and the process of finding support for these hypotheses from multiple sources of data, therefore, are necessarily

Table 3.7 Narrow CHC Abilities Measured by KABC-II

CHC Narrow Ability	KABC-II Subtests that Measure the Ability
Gf narrow abilities	
Induction	Conceptual Thinking, Pattern Reasoning, and Story Completion
General Sequential Reasoning	Story Completion, Rover, and Riddles
Gc narrow abilities	
General Information	Verbal Knowledge and Story Completion
Language Development	Riddles
Lexical Knowledge	Riddles, Verbal Knowledge, Expressive Vocabulary
Gsm narrow abilities	
Memory Span	Word Order (without color interference), Number Recall, and Hand Movements
Working Memory	Word Order (with color interference)
Gv narrow abilities	
Visual Memory	Face Recognition and Hand Movements
Spatial Relations	Triangles
Visualization	Triangles, Conceptual Thinking, Block Counting, Pattern Reasoning, and Story Completion
Spatial Scanning	Rover
Closure Speed	Gestalt Closure
Glr narrow abilities	
Associative Memory	Atlantis, Rebus, Delayed Recall scale
Learning Abilities	Delayed Recall scale
Gq narrow ability	
Math Achievement	Rover, Block Counting

Notes. Gf = Fluid Reasoning; Gc = Crystallized Ability; Gsm = Short-Term Memory; Gv = Visual Processing; Glr = Long-Term Storage and Retrieval; Gq = Quantitative Ability. CHC narrow ability categorizations are courtesy of D. P. Flanagan (personal communications, October 2, 2003; February 12, 2004; February 19, 2004).

more clinical than empirical. This emphasis on the clinician's skills is the essence of the third line of attack.

Third line of attack—QIs, behavioral observations, and background information. If the first two lines of attack provide little or no insight to explain an uninterpretable index, then the third line of attack offers a variety of additional strategies to generate hypotheses. Suppose a child performed much better on Pattern Reasoning than on

Story Completion, producing an uninterpretable Planning/Gf index. Hypotheses can be generated to explain the subtest variability from all three lines of attack.

From the first line of attack, Pattern Reasoning includes abstract visual stimuli and requires little or no motor coordination, whereas Story Completion utilizes meaningful visual stimuli and demands gross-motor coordination to respond to the items (see Figure 3.14). It is possible that the child had an uninterpretable Planning/Gf index because of better ability to respond to abstract than meaningful visual stimuli or difficulties responding via gross-motor coordination (hence, Pattern Reasoning > Story Completion). Both of these possible hypotheses can be either supported or refuted by the results of pertinent planned comparisons conducted in step 5.

From the second line of attack, consider Rapid Reference 3.6, which lists the CHC narrow abilities measured by both Core Planning/Gf subtests. They both measure Induction, a Gf narrow ability, and Visualization, a Gv narrow ability. Quite clearly, narrow abilities that are common to both Core subtests cannot offer hypotheses to explain why the child performed differently on the subtests. However, note that Story Completion measures two additional CHC narrow abilities: General Sequential Reasoning (Gf) and General Information (Gc). The child's low scaled score on Story Completion, relative to his or her Pattern Reasoning scaled score, may reflect the child's weakness in the Gf ability of deductive reasoning (which can be checked out by examining the child's scores on Rover and Riddles), or the child may have had difficulty with the general information needed to understand the social content of the items (which can be checked out by examining the child's scaled score on the other KABC-II subtest that measures the Gc narrow ability of General Information—Verbal Knowledge).

From the third line of attack, the examiner needs to consider all pertinent information about the child that was gained from background and referral information or by carefully observing the child during the evaluation. For example, both of the Planning/Gf subtests are extremely susceptible to impulsivity; consequently, "impulsivity" is a QI that is listed on the KABC-II record form for Pattern Reasoning and Story Completion. Suppose that for the child in question—whose uninterpretable Planning/Gf index was due to Pattern Reasoning > Story Completion—impulsivity was listed as a QI for Story Completion but *not* for Pattern Reasoning. The child may have started placing picture cards to complete each story with no reflection whatsoever but may have taken more care before selecting the correct response on Pattern Reasoning items. That QI of impulsivity would be sufficient to generate the hypothesis that the uninterpretable Planning/Gf index was largely due to the impulsivity that was noted on only one of the two Core subtests.

But the behavioral hypotheses do not have to come only from the QIs. Any disruptive behavior that the examiner might have detected during the Story Completion subtest (but *not* during Pattern Reasoning) provides a plausible hypothesis for possibly explaining the uninterpretable Planning/*Gf* index—for example, the child might have been distractible during Story Completion, or anxious, or intolerant of frustration, or bored.

Similarly, background information often provides useful hypotheses to explain uninterpretable indexes. Continuing with the same example, a child whose list of referral concerns includes interacting inappropriately with other children and social immaturity might have performed relatively low on Story Completion at least in part because of the social content of its items. Also, this third line of attack is often useful for providing data to corroborate data from the first two lines of attack. For example, suppose the child in question was observed to have motor coordination difficulties during the evaluation (or was referred for a possible motor impairment). That observation (or bit of referral information) can provide independent corroboration of a significant planned comparison in step 5 that revealed a significant coordination discrepancy (Little or No Motor > Gross-Motor).

In general, when conducing the third line of attack to help explain an uninterpretable index, review the QIs for the highest and lowest subtests in the scale to see if there is evidence that noncognitive or extraneous behaviors differentially influenced performance on the two subtests. Also, carefully go over all of your notes in the margins of the record form to identify any disruptive behaviors that were evident during the administration of the subtests that yielded the lowest scaled scores, and to identify any enhancing behaviors (such as perseverance or extremely focused attention) during the subtests on which the child performed well. However, with all three lines of attack, the goal is to generate as many hypotheses as possible to explain uninterpretable indexes. After generating numerous hypotheses, try to identify the best ones based on multiple pieces of corroborating data. When necessary, administer additional tests or subtests.

Following up with the case of Aiden (who had an uninterpretable Learning/*Glr* index), we examine his QIs, but these do not help reveal any noticeable explanations for the differences between Rebus and Atlantis. Aiden's QIs help us to see that, for both subtests, he was very focused and didn't hesitate to respond when uncertain. He wasn't impulsive during either test, and he seemed to sustain his attention. However, some of the other behavioral observations help reveal other hypotheses. Aiden appeared to enjoy Rebus, making comments such as "This is cool, it's like cracking a code." One of his comments helped examiners to discern that he used the context in the Rebus items as part of his strategy for solving the problems: "If I can't remember the word, is it okay if I guess from the other words?" Interestingly, Aiden's background information also reveals further hypotheses for the Rebus-Atlantis discrepancy. Because of a recent family trip to China, Aiden had developed an intense interest in the Chinese language, which uses symbolic characters. Thus, perhaps this interest may have aided his performance on Rebus as well as his motivation to persevere on difficult Rebus items.

Step 6B: Generate hypotheses to explain Supplementary subtests that are inconsistent with pertinent Core subtests (ages 3–18). The process of conducting step 6B is similar to that of conducting step 6A. To determine if step 6B needs be conducted, review the findings in step 4, which determined whether each of the Supplementary subtests was significantly different from the mean of the Core subtests. You may check off the boxes in the step 6B portion of the KABC-II Interpretive Worksheet to summarize which Supplementary subtests are relevant for this step (see Rapid Reference 3.7). If none of the Supplementary subtests differ from the Core subtests, then do not proceed with step 6B. However, if a Supplementary subtest does differ from the Core subtests (i.e., if step 4 revealed that the difference between Supplementary subtest scaled score and mean of Core subtests is significant— the difference does not need to be unusually large), then proceed to try to identify possible hypotheses about why the Supplementary subtest was either significantly higher or lower than the Core subtests on its scale.

The first line of attack described in the previous section—involving planned comparisons—is not typically very useful for generating hypotheses for step 6B. Indeed, Supplementary subtests are typically excluded from the planned comparisons. Occasionally, the step 5 clusters can provide the examiner with some insights. For example, consider the Supplementary Gestalt Closure subtest. It is excluded from all clusters in the step 5 planned comparisons, but, conceptually, Gestalt Closure belongs to several clusters: Verbal (as opposed to Pointing) Response, Little or No Motor (as opposed to Gross-Motor) coordination, and Meaningful (as opposed to Abstract) Visual Stimuli. Consequently, the results of planned comparisons might sometimes prove useful for generating hypotheses to explain uninterpretable results.

More generally, however, it is the second and third lines of attack that are of primary importance for generating hypotheses to explain why a Supplementary subtest differs significantly from its Core subtests. Rapid References 3.4, 3.5, and 3.7 are especially useful for implementing the second line of attack. (Rapid References 3.3 and 3.6 are not needed for this step because Learning/*Glr* and Planning/*Gf* do not have any Supplementary subtests.) Sometimes hypotheses generated during the second line of investigation will be able to be corroborated by one or more of the planned comparisons conducted during step 5. An illustration of reliance on the results of a planned comparison to corroborate a "second line" hypothesis is shown in the next example.

Consider Hand Movements, the Supplementary Sequential/*Gsm* subtest for ages 4–18. Suppose the child scored significantly higher on Hand Movements than on the Core Sequential/*Gsm* subtests. From Rapid Reference 3.4, Hand Movements is shown to differ from both Core subtests by (1) using visual stimuli (hand positions) instead of verbal stimuli (words or numbers spoken by the examiner), (2) involving the visual-motor channel of communication, and (3) measuring the CHC narrow ability of Visual Memory, which is a *Gv* ability. The child's better performance on Hand Movements than the Core Sequential/*Gsm* subtests might be due to any or all of the hypotheses generated from Rapid Reference 3.4. These hypotheses can be supported or refuted by other profile findings. Regarding the fact that Hand Movements uses nonverbal stimuli, did the child tend to perform better on nonverbal than verbal subtests (specifically, did the child perform significantly better on the Nonverbal Ability vs. Verbal Ability planned comparison)? Concerning the hypothesis about the visual-motor channel of communication, how well did the child perform on other visual-motor subtests (such as Triangles and Story Completion)? And for the third hypothesis about the *Gv* narrow ability of Visual Memory, how did the child perform on other *Gv* subtests (most notably, on the Simultaneous/*Gv* scale)? How about on Face Recognition, which also measures Visual Memory (for young children)? How about on tests that are dependent on visual memory even if they primarily assess other abilities (such as Atlantis, Rebus, and the supplementary Delayed Recall scale)?

Rapid References 3.5 and 3.7 can be used to generate analogous kinds of hypotheses for the Supplementary Simultaneous/*Gv* and Knowledge/*Gc* subtests, respectively. And for the third line of attack, the same approach described for step 6A is applied to 6B. For the Hand Movements example, on which the child performed better on Hand Movements than on the two Core Sequential/*Gsm* subtests, was the child more focused, attentive, or motivated on Hand Movements than on Word Order and Number Recall? Did the child display unusually coordinated behavior that might have facilitated performance on Hand Movements? And so forth.

Figure 3.15 shows an excerpt from the KABC-II worksheet of step 6B. The information in the worksheet provides a summary of what is discussed here in the text.

In Vanessa's case, when we review the results of step 4, we see that three of the Supplementary subtests were significantly different from their Core counterparts. Her Hand Movements scaled score of 10 was significantly lower than the

STEP 6B: GENERATE HYPOTHESES TO EXPLAIN SUPPLEMENTARY SUBTESTS THAT ARE INCONSISTENT WITH THE MEAN OF CORE SUBTESTS.

First Line of Attack: Determine which Supplementary subtests are significantly different from the Core Subtests.

a. Check box if Supplementary subtest is significantly different from mean of core subtests (see step 4 results)

Supplementary Subtest	3	4	5	Age 6	7–12	13–18
Number Recall						
Gestalt Closure						
Hand Movements						
Verbal Knowledge						
Face Recognition						
Block Counting						
Story Completion						
Expressive Vocabulary						
Triangles						

b. Conduct only an informal examination of the Planned Clinical comparisons, as most Supplementary subtests are excluded from the planned comparisons

The following Supplementary tests are included in step 5's clusters:

• Expressive Vocabulary (Gc subtest) is in the Verbal Ability cluster.

• Verbal Knowledge (Gc subtest) is in the Verbal Ability and Pointing Response clusters.

• Hand Movements (Gsm Subtest) is in the Gross motor response and nonverbal ability clusters.

• Block Counting (Gv subtest) is in the Little Motor cluster.

Second Line of Attack: Examine how Supplementary and Core subtests within each scale complement each other.

Consult Rapid References 3.4, 3.5, and 3.7 to develop hypotheses.

Third Line of Attack: Examine Qualitative Indicators (QIs), behavioral observations, and background information.

Follow up hypotheses derived from QIs, behavioral observations, and background information by collecting supplemental data if necessary (e.g., administer additional subtests, contact further sources for collateral information).

Figure 3.15 Excerpt from the KABC-II Interpretive Worksheet for step 6B.

mean of the two Core Sequential/*Gsm* subtests (14.5), Block Counting (10) was significantly higher than the mean of the two Core Simultaneous/*Gv* subtests (6.5), and Expressive Vocabulary (4) was significantly lower than the mean of the two Core Knowledge/*Gc* subtests (7.5). Her scaled score on Gestalt Closure (5), though indicative of weak performance relative to other 11-year-olds, was not significantly lower than the mean of the Simultaneous/*Gv* Core subtests.

First consider Vanessa's Hand Movements scaled score of 10. That level of performance is within the Average range and emerges as significantly below pertinent Core subtests because her Sequential/*Gsm* index of 127 was a Key Asset for her. When we consider that she had a High-Priority Concern in visual processing, as evidenced by her Simultaneous/*Gv* index of 80, a clear-cut hypothesis for Hand Movements emerges. From Rapid Reference 3.4, Hand Movements measures the *Gv* narrow ability of Visual Memory. Vanessa probably scored significantly lower on Hand Movements than on other short-term memory tasks because her deficit in visual processing prevented her from performing at an Above Average level in her area of strength.

It is interesting that Vanessa scored significantly higher on Block Counting than on Core Simultaneous/*Gv* subtests. This Supplementary subtest (for 7- to 12-year-olds) places a great premium on visual processing. During the administration of this task, the examiner noted several positive QIs: high level of focused attention, concentration, and especially her perseverance. The examiner also observed that Vanessa used her hands to cover up blocks she had already counted (an apparent self-monitored compensation for visual perceptual problems) and tried each item numerous times before she was satisfied enough to respond. These observed behaviors seemed to have facilitated her test score in an area of general weakness for her.

Finally, Vanessa's relatively low score on Expressive Vocabulary relative to other Knowledge/*Gc* subtests is entirely consistent with her word retrieval problems when trying to find the precise name for many of the objects depicted in Expressive Vocabulary. She was able to describe many objects with great specificity but often could not think of their names. This behavior was not observed to any marked degree on Riddles, and it was not relevant for Verbal Knowledge (which demands no verbal expression). The word retrieval problem was evident during Gestalt Closure as well, and it probably impacted her scaled score on that subtest as well.

Vanessa's performance and behaviors on additional cognitive measures (selected WISC-IV subtests) and achievement tests (KTEA-II Comprehensive) also supported several of these hypotheses. To see how all of these clinical observations and empirical data come together into a cohesive picture, read Vanessa's comprehensive report in Chapter 7 of this book.

🐿 TEST YOURSELF 🐿

1. **The approach of test interpretation for the KABC-II advocated in this chapter requires examiners to focus on**

    (a) unique abilities of subtests.

    (b) the child's overall ability as indicated by the MPI or FCI.

    (c) abilities represented by the four or five indexes, even if an index is uninterpretable.

    (d) abilities represented by the four or five indexes plus behavioral observations, background information, and scores on other tasks.

2. **You have been analyzing Annie's profile and have found that the FCI is not interpretable due to scatter among the indexes (they range from 135 on Knowledge/Gc to 95 on Learning/Glr). What should you do?**

    (a) Interpret the MPI from the Luria model instead

    (b) Throw the entire assessment out

    (c) Focus your interpretation on the KABC-II indexes

    (d) Interpret the NVI instead

3. **The KABC-II authors consider which steps of the interpretive process essential?**

    (a) Steps 1 and 2

    (b) Steps 3 and 4

    (c) Steps 5 and 6

    (d) All six steps

4. **In completing step 2C of the KABC-II Interpretive Worksheet (Appendix A), you find that there is a 22-point discrepancy between Jose's (age 13) Sequential/Gsm index and his mean of all scale indexes. Since this is a statistically significantly difference ($p < .05$),**

    (a) you can assume that this is a meaningful difference that should be considered potentially valuable for diagnostic and educational purposes, regardless of whether it is also an uncommonly large difference.

    (b) Jose's profile should be considered invalid.

    (c) you can identify Jose's Sequential/Gsm index as a Key Asset.

    (d) you must complete step 2D to determine whether a discrepancy of that size occurred in less than 10% of the population.

5. **A High-Priority Concern is one that**

    (a) is a Normative Weakness.

    (b) is a Personal Weakness.

    (c) is an infrequent (<10%) occurrence.

    (d) is all of the above.

6. **A Normative Strength is an index that is more than 1 standard deviation above the mean (116 or above).** True or False?

7. **If an index is not interpretable, it should not be used to calculate the mean of the scale indexes.** True or False?

8. **Karin's Simultaneous/Gv scale could not be interpreted because of too much variability between the subtests that comprise that index. In her case, the step 5 planned comparisons**

   (a) will determine which unique subtests can be interpreted.

   (b) will develop alternative explanations for the fluctuations within the scale.

   (c) will contrast the Simultaneous/Gv index to the Sequential/Gsm index.

   (d) will lead you through special psychometric conversions that allow the Sequential/Gv index to become meaningfully interpreted.

9. **Which of the step 5 Planned Clinical Comparisons tap the integration and storage domain of information processing?**

   (a) Nonverbal Ability versus Verbal Ability (step 5A)

   (b) Problem-Solving Ability versus Memory and Learning (step 5B)

   (c) Visual Perception of Meaningful Stimuli versus Abstract Stimuli (step 5C)

   (d) Verbal Response versus Pointing Response (step 5D)

10. **Even if none of the analyses in steps 1–5 yield significant results, you are urged not to interpret scaled scores on the individual subtests.** True or False?

Answers: 1. d; 2. c; 3. a; 4. d; 5. d; 6. True; 7. False; 8. b; 9. a & b; 10. True.

Four

HOW TO INTERPRET THE KABC-II: QUALITATIVE INDICATORS

INTRODUCTION

KABC-II Qualitative Indicators (QIs) are test-taking behaviors that may exert a negative or positive influence on test performance. They are behavioral factors that have the potential to affect the reliability and validity of test-scores, although they are essentially unrelated to the test construct being measured (Sattler, 2001). Glutting and Oakland (1989, 1993) suggest that observations of test-taking behaviors help explain individual variation in the ways children approach and react to cognitive tasks and that they are "ethnologically relevant expressions of the children's attitudes and conduct" (p. 25).

A large part of the qualitative observations research implies that test performance is sensitive to context and that test performance is an evaluation of the child in *relation* to a specific activity (Polkinghorne & Gibbons, 1999). The study of process and contextual activity has been researched in the Vygotskian and Lurian venue for many years (Minnick, 2000) but not specifically linked to activity during the administration of cognitive ability batteries. However, in the Lurian tradition, we have emphasized that the process and the contextual understanding of how a child obtains a score is just as important as the score itself. This child-centered approach has been advocated in more than a quarter-century of publications on a diversity of test instruments, including the original K-ABC, the KABC-II, Wechsler's various scales, the WJ III, and other tests (Kaufman, 1979, 1994a; Kaufman & Kaufman, 1977, 1983, 1993; Kaufman & Lichtenberger, 1999, 2002; Lichtenberger & Kaufman, 2004; Lichtenberger, Mather, Kaufman, & Kaufman, 2004).

HISTORY OF FORMAL AND INFORMAL ASSESSMENT OF TEST SESSION BEHAVIORS

Historically, in terms of specific instruments to assess test session behaviors, the first measure that was developed was called the *Test Behavior Observation Guide*

(Watson, 1951). The next measure, the *Stanford-Binet Observation Schedule,* was presented on the record form of the *Stanford-Binet Intelligence Scale* in 1960. These measures were joined by the *Test Behavior Checklist* (Aylward & MacGruder, 1996) and others, such as the *Behavior and Attitude Checklist* (Sattler, 1988, 2001). All of these instruments contained 30 or fewer items, usually measured on a Likert scale to be filled out immediately after administering a test or battery of tests. Most of the items centered on motivation, attitudes toward testing, attitudes toward examiners, and the like. However, a specific theoretical model for constructs included in these instruments was lacking.

Glutting and Oakland (1993) developed the first standardized instrument that measured test-session behaviors, the *Guide to Assessment of Test Session Behavior* (GATSB). The GATSB was conormed with the WISC-III (Wechsler, 1991). Glutting and Oakland included types of behavior "that reflect a child's temperament and personality, including attention, interest, cooperation, avoidance, motivation, effort, persistence, and the ability to shift perceptual sets or to shift task focus and remain flexible" (p. 25). Many research studies with the GATSB confirmed its reliability and validity with different populations and brought issues about test session behaviors into a new light. Indeed, although the GATSB had some psychometric shortcomings (Kaufman & Kaufman, 1995), it proved to be useful in gaining information about the relative severity of children's inattentive, avoidant, and uncooperative behaviors during test administrations and helped demonstrate that these factors can affect the magnitude of children's cognitive ability scores (Daleiden, Drabman, & Benton, 2002; Glutting, Oakland, & McDermott, 1989; Glutting, Robins, & de Lancey, 1997; Glutting, Youngstrom, Oakland, & Marley, 1996).

Recently, McConaughy and Achenbach (2004) have published the *Test Observation Form* (TOF). The TOF "is a standardized form for rating observations of behavior, affect, and test-taking style during testing sessions for children aged 2 to 18" (p. 1). The TOF was standardized on the same norm sample as the Stanford-Binet Intelligence Scale, fifth edition (Binet-5; Roid, 2003) and yields scores on five syndrome scales, internalizing and externalizing scales, and an Attention-Deficit/Hyperactivity Scale oriented toward the *Diagnostic and Statistical Manual of Mental Disorders,* fourth edition, text revision (*DSM-IV-TR*). The TOF can also be a part of the Achenbach System of Empirically Based Assessment (ASEBA; Achenbach & McConaughy, 2004) system that measures parent and teacher observations of child behavior.

The five syndrome scales of the TOF are factor analytically based and are labeled Withdrawn/Depressed, Language/Thought Problems, Anxious, Oppositional, and Attention Problems. The authors state that the TOF can be used with any individual cognitive ability test or achievement test. How the TOF and the KABC-II interface has not been studied, but such investigations will help provide validation of the QIs.

Much more work needs to be done to define the constructs that underlie qualitative assessment of test session behaviors. For example, when most of the previously mentioned test behavior checklists were published, less was known about the formal measurement of executive functions in younger children than is known today. Ironically, today it is difficult to find a cohesive and accepted definition of executive functions (Zelazo, Carter, Reznick, & Frye, 1997), but a simple and effective starting point would be that executive functions are higher-level cognitive abilities that "draw upon the individual's more fundamental or primary cognitive skills, such as attention, language, and perception, to generate higher levels of creative and abstract thought" (Delis, Kaplan, & Kramer, 2003, p. 1).

Traditionally, cognitive ability batteries had very little overlap with measures of executive function (Ardila, 2002), although this failure to assess executive functions probably does not characterize the latest measures such as the KABC-II, the CAS (Naglieri & Das, 1997), the WJ III (Woodcock, McGrew, & Mather, 2001), and the WISC-IV (Wechsler, 2003). These tests provide new subtests and scales that probably tap executive or frontal lobe functions more than ever before. However, only the usual and extensive postpublication research studies in the field will document this possibility as a fact.

Neuropsychological test developers have long instructed examiners to note qualitative information in the test session to assist with differential diagnosis. The Luria-Nebraska has a qualitative system on the record form (Golden, 1997). The authors of the NEPSY (Korkman, Kirk, & Kemp, 1998) provide base rates for some qualitative observations specific to their test that focus on Attention/Executive Behaviors, Rate Change, Visual Behaviors, Oral/Verbal Behaviors, Pencil Grip, Visuomotor Precision, and Motor Behaviors.

Knowledge and experience are necessary to see the unique factors that influence test performance for each child. Again, the nature of the qualitative assessment of test-taking behaviors rests on a case study approach that melds background information with quantitative results that support differential diagnosis. In addition, the qualitative assessment results must then be validated across settings. Verifying test behaviors to see if they are present in other settings, such as the classroom, is important regardless of the differential diagnosis because learning behaviors account for much of the variance in grades assigned by teachers (Schaefer & McDermott, 1999).

INTERPRETATION OF QUALITATIVE DATA FROM THE KABC-II

In the original K-ABC, information about how to use qualitative observations of test-taking behaviors was provided in the manual. Similar kinds of explanations have also appeared in manuals and related publications for other Kaufman tests—for example, the KAIT (Kaufman & Kaufman, 1993)—and are common elsewhere (Korkman, Kirk, & Kemp, 1998; Naglieri, 1999; Schrank, Flanagan, Woodcock, & Mascolo, 2002).

However, for the KABC-II, the QIs have been conveniently placed on the record form to remind examiners of behaviors that they may observe during the administration of specific subtests and to assist examiners in organizing observations about how the child is performing over the duration of the test itself. To illustrate, consider the QIs for the KABC-II Number Recall subtest shown in Rapid Reference 4.1 (QIs listed on the record form with a minus sign [−1] may detract from performance, whereas QIs listed with a plus sign [+] may positively affect performance). Most children understand the task demands of Number Recall easily, but the subtest has a very short response window before the memory trace dissipates. The short response time, coupled with the fact that there are no options for repetition, makes this subtest subject to the negative effects of anxiety, depression, and inattention. Children who are anxious may have thoughts that get in the way of their encoding and may also block the flexibility of thought that is necessary for strategy development on more difficult items (Hong, 1999; Kellogg, Hopko, & Ashcraft, 1999). In addition, studies have linked lower scores on subtests such as Number Recall with elevated scores on the Children's Depression Inventory (Tramontana & Hooper, 1997). There is also considerable evidence to support poor performance of children with ADHD on subtests similar to Number Recall (e.g., Assesmany, McIntosh, Phelps, & Rizza, 2001; Loge, Staton, & Beatty, 1990; Mayes, Calhoun, & Crowell, 1998). Thus, the QI that may negatively affect performance on Number Recall is "Fails to sustain attention."

On the other hand, a child who can sustain focused attention and also create strategies to help keep the memory trace from dissipating will do well on this subtest. Thus the QIs written on the record form that are likely to enhance performance on Number Recall are "Displays chunking or other strategy" and "Unusually focused."

Consider also the QIs for Atlantis Delayed (see Rapid Reference 4.2).

≡ Rapid Reference 4.1

QIs for Number Recall

+ Displays chunking or other strategy

− Fails to sustain attention

+ Unusually focused

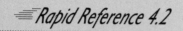

QIs for Atlantis Delayed

+ Perseveres

− Reluctant to respond when uncertain

+ Verbalized related knowledge

This subtest (like Rebus Delayed) is included in the KABC-II to permit examiners to study the child's retention of information learned about 20 minutes earlier in the evaluation. Consequently, the QIs for Atlantis Delayed focus on the *difference* between Atlantis and Atlantis Delayed. Studies support the notion that certain children will perform better on the initial versus the delayed portion of these tests for a variety of reasons (Grossman, Kaufman, Mednitsky, Scharff, & Dennis, 1994).

The record form for the KABC-II not only has space on the subtest pages for recording QIs but also has a summary page on the inside front cover (see Figure 4.1). You can use the Summary of Qualitative Indicators table on page 2 of the

Subtests	Disruptive QIs					Enhancing QIs			
	Fails to sustain attention	Impulsively responds incorrectly	Perseverates	Is reluctant to respond when uncertain	Worries about time limits	Perseveres	Tries out options	Is usually focused	Verbalizes a strategy, ideas, etc.
Atlantis									
Conceptual Thinking									
Face Recognition									
Story Completion									
Number Recall									
Gestalt Closure									
Rover									
Atlantis Delayed									
Expressive Vocabulary									
Verbal Knowledge									
Rebus									
Triangles									
Block Counting									
Word Order									
Pattern Reasoning									
Hand Movements									
Rebus Delayed									
Riddles									
Totals									

Figure 4.1 Summary of qualitative indicators from KABC-II Record Form (page 2).

Note. Examiners check off behaviors that were observed during each subtest and then total the behaviors at the bottom of the chart. These observed behaviors will help determine the validity of the results as well as helping develop hypotheses about children's performance.

record form to check off the types of QIs that were observed from subtest to sub-test. Note that there is a section for QIs that disrupt performance and a section for QIs that enhance performance. You can also use page 2 of the record form to write pertinent comments about background information, behavioral observations, and the validity of results.

To use this table, simply check off the QIs that you observed on each subtest and then total the columns of the table. There is also space below the Summary table to document any unique QIs. After you analyze the QI table and your own notes, answer the question: "Are there any considerations that would bring the validity of the test results into question?" There are many possible responses to this question, which are too numerous to list here. However, the goal of tallying QIs is to develop a measure of qualitative observations about test session behaviors, which will allow you to make a well-supported statement about the effect on the quantitative results of the test. During this process, your ability as a skilled examiner marries professional judgment about the tools that you use to assess children.

The general considerations about QIs for each KABC-II subtest, as well as each task's specific QIs, are given later in this chapter in the section "Subtest-by-Subtest Analysis of the 18 Subtests." Additionally, as indicated, some subtest-specific QIs are also listed on the actual record form.

Judging whether the QIs are stable "learning traits" that generalize to other settings requires you to use other data for validation. Instruments like the Student Observation System (SOS), an aspect of the Behavior Assessment System for Children, Second Edition (BASC-2; Reynolds & Kamphaus, 2004), can further assist the examiner not only in initial observations of classroom qualitative behaviors but also in direct follow-up evaluations of the effectiveness of interventions. The TOF (McConaughy & Achenbach, 2004) is also a vehicle for hypothesis testing because the TOF is linked not only to clinical syndromes but also to other Achenbach measures such as the Child Behavior Checklist (Achenbach & McConaughy, 2004).

FUNCTIONS OF QUALITATIVE INDICATORS

Qualitative indicators serve several functions during the course of the administration and interpretation of the KABC-II (see the Don't Forget box for a summary of these functions).

1. Qualitative indicators provide a cross-check for you to evaluate the *reliability* of the child's test scores obtained during any test sessions. Therefore, if the reliability of test behavior is called into question in the initial session, you may want to schedule additional sessions at different times and

---

DON'T FORGET

Summary of the Functions of the QIs

- QIs provide a cross-check for you to evaluate the reliability of the child's test scores obtained during test sessions.
- QIs provide a cross-check of the validity of the test scores obtained during test sessions.
- QIs help determine definitions of standards of test performance.
- QIs provide supplemental information for interpreting scores when test-taking behaviors systematically interfere with performance.
- QIs help ensure that the positive as well as the negative influences of various test-taking behaviors are observed.
- QIs may assist with making decisions about abilities or constructs that should be investigated further.

---

places to see if maladaptive test-taking behaviors are consistently present. If the behaviors are present during other testing sessions, then the examiner will need to check for the same behaviors across settings (Glutting & McDermott, 1988, 1996; Oakland & McDermott, 1990). Reliability, in this sense, focuses on the importance of establishing whether the QIs are *consistently present* during test sessions and settings. The Caution box lists the types of questions that concern the reliability of QIs.

A common example of the examiner's having to establish the reliability of QIs is when a child exhibits different test session behaviors in subtests common to a given modality. For example, some children display poor attention and distractibility when subtests are presented with only auditory stimuli (e.g., Number Recall items and most Riddles items) but are able to sustain attention and exhibit less distractibility with subtests that measure similar constructs with visual cues (e.g., Word

---

CAUTION

Types of Questions That Concern the Reliability of QIs

- Does the child act this way every time he or she is tested?
- Does the child act this way only when being tested in a standardized fashion, or in any testing situation?
- Does the child act this way when taking tests in the classroom?
- Does the child exhibit these test session behaviors with other examiners?

Order and Pattern Reasoning). If you notice such a pattern on these KABC-II subtests, then you may want to verify the observation of the QIs with other tests and with other personnel to see if the inattentive and distractible behaviors are consistently present. If the behaviors are indeed consistently present, then determine the validity of the QI as it relates to the impact on test performance.

2. Qualitative indicators provide a cross-check of the *validity* of the test scores obtained during test sessions. If you determine that the QI is reliably present, then determine the impact of the QI. For a QI to be valid, it must exert a moderate to severe impact on test performance in a consistent way. One of the implicit goals of any cognitive ability battery is to obtain results that are not unduly affected by a child's conduct during the test session (Glutting & Oakland, 1993). In other words, QIs help determine if the child's obtained (*quantitative*) scores reflect the intended cognitive constructs as opposed to the constructs within the context of other extraneous behavioral (*qualitative*) variables.

Most examiners will comment in the assessment report about the validity of the test scores and the behaviors of the examinee during the test session. Many times observations about poor test session behaviors will be made even though the results are not reliable or verified; typically, they are accepted with a caveat that the scores may not represent the child's true ability. Hebben and Milberg (2002) suggest that examiners "should try to document any behaviors that seems unusual or rare within his or her own typical experience, and then decide whether this information is relevant to clinical decision making" (p. 77). Validity, in this sense, is concerned with the *relevance* of the QI. Relevance is associated with the determination of the QIs in the test session that *interfered* with test performance. The specific questions that concern the validity of QIs are addressed in the Caution box.

As when considering reliability, after determining that a child consistently behaves in an inattentive and distractible way on tests with auditory-only stimuli, establish if the QIs had a mild, moderate, or severe impact on the test scores. In this case, if the child's scores on Number Recall and Riddles were

CAUTION

Questions That Concern the Validity of QIs

- Did the test session behavior help or hurt the child's performance on a specific item or subtest?
- Did the test session behavior appear to have a mild, moderate, or severe impact on test performance?

much lower than scores on subtests that have visual stimuli, then a hypothesis is formed and needs to be verified. Then consider administering auditory-only stimuli subtests from other comparable test batteries. You may conduct a BASC-SOS observation in the classroom to evaluate the child's levels of attention and distractibility during auditory directions from the teacher versus auditory directions with visual cues. All of this information will help you determine if a suspected QI is having a detrimental effect not only on the subtests of the KABC-II but in the classroom as well.

3. Qualitative indicators help determine definitions of standards of test performance. Glutting and Oakland (1993) have made a distinction between examiners who prefer to focus on the child's *typical* performance and those who prefer to emphasize the child's *optimal* performance. They suggest that examiners who favor *typical* performance as a standard are inclined to accept most test results as valid because they view test session behaviors as being common to the test session *and* to the child's everyday functioning. Other examiners favor *optimal* performance as a standard; they see inappropriate test session behaviors as compromising a clear understanding of the child's academic abilities. For example, consider the child who is distracted by noises outside the testing room during the subtests on the KABC-II Sequential/*Gsm* scale and who earns a below average index on that scale. Examiners who believe in the typical standard of performance will interpret that low index to be accurate and representative of everyday sequential processing. In contrast, examiners from the optimal-standard point of view would view the scores and QIs as impeding clear judgments about the child's sequential processing abilities. The optimal examiner would also entertain the possibility of the child's abilities changing at a later date (Glutting & Oakland, 1993).

4. Qualitative indicators provide supplemental information for interpreting scores when test-taking behaviors systematically interfere with performance. When a child's performance on other assessment instruments confirms the interference noted in the QIs, then your decision about how to interpret a particular subtest is well founded. For example, the KABC-II manual directs you not to interpret scales that do not have integrity (where scores on the subtests that constitute a scale have too much variability; see the appropriate Don't Forget box in Chapter 3). However, you may analyze the different subtests and seek possible hypotheses about why the scores are different and then seek verification with further data (see step 6 outlined in Chapter 3). Sometimes, test-taking behaviors affect scores on one subtest but not on another. For example, Atlantis and Rebus compose the

Learning/*Glr* scale for ages 4–18. Suppose this scale has too much variability to be interpreted for a given child, with the Rebus scaled score much higher than the Atlantis scaled score. If you note QIs during the test administration that reveal distractibility for Atlantis but no disruptive behaviors during Rebus, then the child's distractibility might be an explanation for the nonmeaningful Learning/*Glr* index. The QIs, therefore, provide valuable information in the forming and testing of hypotheses about individual strengths and weaknesses and in making sense out of unexpected fluctuations in the child's test score profile.

5. Qualitative indicators help ensure that the positive as well as negative influences of various test-taking behaviors are observed. They also aid in understanding the *process* of the test situation as well as the *products*. As the KABC-II quantitative and qualitative data are assimilated into the comprehensive assessment, you have to differentially decide what information is extraneous to the whole diagnostic picture. In addition, decide what information is cohesive, is verified, and leads to interventions that not only remediate deficits but also cement the child's strengths to maximize success. If you prefer a strength model of remediation, the notation of positive test-taking behaviors that contribute to scores may help with intervention design. For example, many children who have poor visual-spatial skills will encounter great difficulty on the Triangles subtest of the KABC-II. Some children will become frustrated and give up easily, others will verbally mediate their way through the test, and still others will simply stay with the task until it is finished regardless of how long it takes. All three of these approaches to working the designs on Triangles give valuable clues about what behaviors sustain eventual success for a given child. The luxury of large batteries like the KABC-II is that they provide multiple opportunities to observe the basic strengths of the child that contribute to good test scores and, hopefully, to success in other environments as well.

6. Qualitative indicators may assist with making decisions about abilities or constructs that should be investigated further, including those that are not generally measured by a cognitive ability battery such as the KABC-II. Children who demonstrate any of the following difficulties may have weaknesses in executive functioning: (1) independently orienting and sustaining attention, (2) demonstrating impulsivity when reflection is needed, (3) staying still and orienting to test materials, (4) entertaining competing answers, (5) demonstrating rigidity when flexibility is needed, and (6) checking answers. If you note that these behaviors are qualitatively interfering with scores on the KABC-II, then investigate further or recommend further

testing in the area of executive functioning. However, the same behaviors might be associated with excessive anxiety or depression rather than a problem with executive functioning. None of these conditions is directly assessed by the KABC-II, in terms of being a single construct or focus of a scale, but they may be major influences on test performance and should be differentially diagnosed.

The QIs that are mentioned on the record form of the KABC-II are the factors that we believe are most likely to affect subtest performance, but they are not exhaustive. Indeed, the lists are minimal and are intended only to alert you to the possible behaviors. It is most important to look at the observations in context, as suggested in the interpretive system for the KABC-II, and confine the qualitative results to a planned comparison with quantitative results and with verification of hypotheses from different sources. In addition, you should make decisions about qualitative observations that are specific to the child being examined. The information must make sense in light of the child's background information, observations made by other professionals who work with the child on a daily basis, and other tests administered in the comprehensive assessment. The determination of the validity of test scores in this context relies on your skillful clinical interpretation of qualitative reliability and validity factors in the child's performance as well as your willingness to form hypotheses about test-taking behaviors and to test those hypotheses.

QUALITATIVE INDICATORS THAT INFLUENCE PERFORMANCE

The QIs mentioned on the record form are a *short* list of possible behaviors that we hope will alert you to the possibilities of influence that could be present during the subtest. However, there is a body of growing evidence to support the notion that many QIs can be representative of clinical issues not directly measured by cognitive ability tests (McConaughy & Achenbach, 2004). There are several threads of research in different clinical categories that might provide you with a background for observations of behaviors that enhance or detract from test performance. It is important to note that these clinical categories are not diagnosed simply by observations of test-taking behavior during a standardized assessment. However, the skilled clinician takes every opportunity during a comprehensive assessment to direct observations and qualitative information to places where it will do most good. The differential diagnosis part of any assessment consists of a flow of hypotheses that are constantly being assessed and reassessed. Therefore, the information in this section is presented to give you an evidence-based background for the types of behaviors (and QIs) that can be observed during test-taking sessions in a variety of clinical situations.

Anxiety

Anxiety in the context of formal testing has long been known to have disruptive effects on performance and may well have frequently contributed to false positive diagnoses in neuropsychological evaluations (Tramontana & Hooper, 1997). Probably the most commonly known effect of anxiety on test performance is that of decreased performance on tests like Wechsler's Digit Span (Ialongo, Edelsohn, Werthamer-Larsson, Crockett, & Sheppard, 1996; Kusche, Cook, & Greenberg, 1993; Prins, Groot, & Hanewald, 1994). Recently, the effects of anxiety on cognitive ability test scores have generally pointed to the negative effects of anxiety on working memory, in that extraneous thoughts about performance and correctness interfere with simple working memory, strategy formation, and response sets (Hong, 1999; Kellogg, Hopko, & Ashcraft, 1999). These findings probably also pertain to several subtests on the KABC-II that feature short-term memory and working memory such as Number Recall, Hand Movements, Word Order, Atlantis, and Rebus. (The Don't Forget box reminds you of the potential effects of anxiety.)

Anxiety is especially apparent in children with Obsessive-Compulsive Disorder. Neuropsychological studies of children with Obsessive-Compulsive Disorder suggest findings of visual-spatial deficits along with frontal and basal ganglia dysfunctions (Cox, 1997; Tramontana & Hooper, 1997). Pay special attention to

---

DON'T FORGET

Effects of Anxiety

Cognitive Domain Affected	KABC-II Subtests Affected
Working memory	Number Recall
Short-term memory	Hand Movements
Strategy formation	Word Order
	Atlantis
	Rebus

Note. Although anxiety may affect these KABC-II subtests, poor performance on these subtests is not necessarily indicative of problems with anxiety.

the subtests Triangles, Gestalt Closure, and Rover on the KABC-II with these children.

Executive Functioning and Attention

The complexity and heterogeneity of executive functions make it difficult to delineate a clear consensus in the research literature regarding what actual cognitive processes are involved. It is widely accepted that they encompass a numerous set of higher-order cognitive functions (Wecker, Kramer, Wisniewski, Delis, & Kaplan, 2000). Executive functions are multifarious in nature and are synergetic cognitive processes. The components of executive functions are measured on the Delis-Kaplan Executive Function System as flexibility of thinking, inhibition, problem solving, planning, impulse control, concept formation, abstract thinking, and creativity (Delis, Kaplan, & Kramer, 2003). However, other tests of executive functions measure numerous other functions such as establishing, maintaining, and changing set; initiation; planning and organization; judgment; reasoning and abstraction; self-regulation; visual attention; auditory attention; off-task behavior; and rule-violating behaviors (Hebben & Milberg, 2002; Korkman, Kirk, & Kemp, 1998).

Attention is also a multidimensional construct and, in a broad sense, is woven into the definition and tests of executive functions because it is a central and constant variable that provides the basis for successful higher-level functioning. Attention is one of the more basic cognitive skills—along with memory, language, and perception—that allows for the generation of higher cortical processing skills such as planning and organization (Delis et al., 2003). The definition of attention encompasses the ability to stay on task, resist distractions, follow through with tasks, persist with tasks, visually attend to tasks, return to tasks after being interrupted, and shift attention across tasks (Barkley, 2003). These functions are intertwined with the executive cognitive processes and are very difficult to isolate for specific assessment. Indeed, much of the literature on executive functions and attention focuses on neurological explanations of deficits or damage in the same prefrontal cortex of the brain (Boliek & Obrzut, 1997; Zelazo, Carter, Reznick, & Frye, 1997). In addition, distinctions between executive functions and attention are not made in the commonly used *DSM-IV-TR* diagnostic criteria for Attention-Deficit/Hyperactivity Disorder American Psychiatric Association, 2000). Symptoms in the *DSM-IV-TR* that mark "difficulty with organizing tasks and activities," which are executive functions, are also placed in the category of "inattentive behaviors." To further impede the differential diagnosis, executive and attentional deficits are known to be highly comorbid with depression, anxiety, and conduct disorders (Tramontana & Hooper, 1997). There is no doubt that the differential diagnosis of attention, executive functioning, and psychopathology is difficult at best, but it must be attempted if negative attentional and executive QIs are suspected.

Some subtests on the KABC-II may be sensitive to different aspects of attention and executive functions. For example, distractibility during the administration of a Number Recall item, the inability to sustain attention during the rule-giving instructions of Rover, and failure to examine all of the picture options in Concept Formation or Pattern Reasoning are all different aspects of attention that have a negative effect on performance. The subtests that require planning, such as Story Completion and Pattern Reasoning, may be particularly difficult for children with attentional problems (Barkley, 2003; Naglieri, Goldstein, Iseman & Schweback, 2003). On the other hand, poor attention resulted in lower scores on all WISC-III factor indexes and Full Scale IQ, not just the factors that are often associated with attention (Konold, Maller, & Glutting, 1998). Whether this finding applies to the KABC-II remains to be seen.

Barkley (2003) suggests that apart from planning deficits, children with attentional problems also exhibit poor sense of time, decreased verbal and nonverbal working memory, reduced sensitivity to errors, and possible impairment in goal-directed creativity. These cognitive impairments may translate to KABC-II subtest performance in many ways. Processing speed is not specifically measured on the KABC-II, so a poor sense of time would probably not affect scores on most subtests; the three subtests that offer bonus points for speed, however, might be affected to some extent. Riddles requires verbal working memory, as does Word Order, Rebus, and Atlantis. Pattern Completion, Rover, and Hand Movements, on the other hand, probably have a higher demand for nonverbal than for verbal working memory (although both are probably present).

Barkley's notion of a "reduced sensitivity to errors" may well play out in KABC-II subtests such as Rover, which requires strict rule adherence; Pattern Reasoning, which requires the deduction of a rule or comparison; and Rebus, which requires a heavy loading of metacognition to keep checking the correctness of interpretations. As for the "possible impairment in goal-directed creativity," this may be observed especially on Rover, where there is a clear spatially oriented goal that can only be achieved by paying attention to rules and competing answers. This possible impairment also may be observed on Triangles, where the goal is observable but the examinee has to be flexible and creative, especially around ceiling items. (The Don't Forget box reminds you of the potential effects of executive functioning and attention.)

Behaviors indicating difficulties with anxiety or inattention are frequently also

DON'T FORGET

Effects of Executive Functioning and Attention

Cognitive Domain Affected	KABC-II Subtests Affected
Attention	Number Recall
Executive functioning	Rover
Working memory	Concept Formation
	Pattern Reasoning
	Story Completion
	Riddles
	Word Order
	Rebus
	Atlantis
	Hand Movements

Note. Although problems with executive functioning and attention may affect these KABC-II subtests, poor performance on these subtests is not necessarily indicative of disorders associated with poor executive functioning and attention.

observed in children with depression. Although the KABC-II is not used to make the clinical diagnosis of depression, the research relevant to the behaviors seen in depression are pertinent to QIs on the KABC-II. For example, Tramontana and Hooper (1997) state that children who score higher on the Children's Depression Inventory tend to have lower scores on Wechsler subtests that are very similar in construct and design to subtests like Triangles and Number Recall on the KABC-II. Deficits in abstract reasoning are also noted in tests similar to the KABC-II Pattern Reasoning subtest (Staton, Wilson, & Brumbac, 1981). On the other hand, verbal abilities for children with depression tend to remain in the average range (Semrud-Clikeman, Kamphaus, Teeter, & Vaughn, 1997) or experience mild declines in verbal performance over time (Kovacs & Goldston, 1991).

Children who are depressed tend to do quite well on types of tests like Atlantis Delayed and Rebus Delayed; in fact, their scores on the delayed subtests may be better than the initial learning subtest scores (Reynolds & Bigler, 1997). This phenomenon was examined with the KAIT (Kaufman & Kaufman, 1993). A sample of patients with clinical depression, most of whom were hospitalized with major depression, averaged about 102 on the three KAIT IQs and did not differ significantly from their matched control group on any subtest (Grossman, Kaufman,

Mednitsky, Scharff, & Dennis, 1994). One significant difference was noted, however, in a comparison of immediate and delayed memory. The discrepancy was significantly larger for the depressed than for the control group, with the depressed sample performing considerably higher on the delayed than on the immediate task.

The good performance by depressed patients on the KAIT is contrary to some research findings that have pinpointed deficiencies by depressed individuals in memory, both primary (Gruzelier, Seymour, Wilson, Jolley, & Hirsch, 1988) and secondary (Henry, Weingartner, & Murphy, 1973); in planning and sequential abilities (Burgess, 1991); in psychomotor tasks such as Wechsler's performance subtests (Blatt & Allison, 1968; Pernicano, 1986); and, more generally, in cognitive tests that demand sustained, effortful responding (Golinkoff & Sweeney, 1989).

The KABC-II subtests, like those on the KAIT, require good skills in planning ability and memory and clearly require effortful responding for success. The ability of children with depression to cope well with the demands of the various KABC-II subtests and to excel on measures of delayed recall suggests that some of the prior research may have reached premature conclusions about these patients' deficiencies—in part because of weaknesses in experimental design (such as poor control groups) and inappropriate applications of statistics (Grossman et al., 1994; Miller, Faustman, Moses, & Csernansky, 1991). That notion is given support by the results of other investigations of patients with depression that have shown their intact performance on the Luria-Nebraska Neuropsychological Battery (Miller et al., 1991) and on a set of tasks that differed in its cognitive complexity (Kaufman, Grossman, & Kaufman, 1994).

An interesting point to keep in mind is that some studies have linked depression in children to a lower self-perception of cognitive competence (Hammen & Rudolph, 2003). How this self-perception affects scores on the KABC-II is unknown at this point in time, but children's effort, motivation, persistence, and perception of how they are performing are all important factors for the examiner to try to assess.

Disruptive Behaviors

Disruptive behaviors are common in children across a variety of settings and are often noted in children with Conduct Disorder and ADHD. Again, although the QIs in and of themselves would not be used to diagnose such disorders, certain behaviors (and QIs) may be frequently observed in such cases. Children with Conduct Disorder tend to have generally lower scores on cognitive ability batteries, and attention deficits are frequently present (Hinshaw & Lee, 2003). Verbal reasoning subtests and tests that require inner speech or verbal mediation are sometimes problematic for children with Conduct Disorder (Semrud-Clikeman et al., 1997; Tramontana & Hooper, 1997). Subtests on the KABC-II that require complex strategy formation place heavy demands on executive functions and verbal mediation. Therefore, the Story Completion, Pattern Reasoning, and Rover subtests may be casualties of frustration tolerance in conduct-disordered children, based on research with similar kinds of tasks (e.g., Speltz, DeKlyen, Calderon, Greenberg, & Fisher, 1999). These children may reach early ceiling items and experience difficulty and frustration if they do not have the ability or coping skills to explore learning sets with verbal mediation.

Overall problems with verbal subtests, both in the receptive and expressive areas, are noted for children with Conduct Disorder (Semrud-Clikeman et al., 1997; Tramontana & Hooper, 1997). Examiners may want to pay special attention to the qualitative behaviors during the Knowledge/*Gc* subtests on the KABC-II to see if there are any compensatory strategies present or behaviors that clearly relate to conduct issues.

Cultural Issues

Cultural variables that may influence test performance are complex at best. Tests that tap directly into crystallized abilities, such as the Knowledge/*Gc* subtests, are likely to be influenced by the child's previous exposure to life experiences, quality education, linguistic background, and an overall enriched background. Glutting and Oakland have researched the cultural validity of the GATSB in terms of ethnic differences in observations by examiners and have found that observational systems of the test session tended to be free from significant cultural bias (Nandakumar, Glutting, & Oakland, 1993; Oakland & Glutting, 1990). A careful analysis of the child's background and approach to learning in the classroom will assist in the determination of any negative influences in the test session that are cultural in nature.

The QIs that are listed in the subtest analyses that follow are a part of the interpretive system of the KABC-II, and they are intended to add qualitative information about the child's test performance. They are not meant to be exhaustive. We hope the QIs will be of assistance in the formation of hypotheses about the child's possible learning strengths and weaknesses—hypotheses that should be verified externally with other tests and information. In this way, quantitative and qualitative information works together for the benefit of the child being assessed. (The Don't Forget box reminds you of the potential effects of cultural issues.)

DON'T FORGET

....

Effects of Cultural Issues

Cognitive Domain Affected	KABC-II Subtests Affected
Crystallized abilities	Verbal Knowledge
	Riddles
	Expressive Vocabulary

Note. Although cultural issues may affect these KABC-II subtests, poor performance on these subtests does not necessarily indicate that cultural issues have depressed scores on these subtests.

SUBTEST-BY-SUBTEST QUALITATIVE/PROCESS ANALYSIS OF THE 18 SUBTESTS

The following lists of abilities and processes are not intended to be limiting. Indeed, we hope that they stimulate original observations about the child you are assessing. Other plausible abilities can easily be enumerated for each subtest based on a variety of armchair, clinical, and empirical analyses of the original K-ABC tasks (Kaufman & Kaufman, 1983b), Wechsler subtests (Kaufman, 1994a; Kaufman & Lichtenberger, 2002; Lichtenberger & Kaufman, 2004; Sattler, 2001), and related cognitive tasks. However, the lists that follow for each subtest are geared toward the two theories—Luria and CHC—that form the foundation of the KABC-II, have empirical validation, or provide potentially valuable clinical information about the influence of behavior on test performance.

In Rapid Reference boxes 4.3–4.20, KABC-II Core and Supplementary subtests are described in the order in which they appear in the easels. We have also placed information about the abilities and processes being measured by the subtest in each section to act as a reminder for the examiner to meld the content *and* processes of each subtest. Remember, the QIs mentioned in this section are not exhaustive, and they may expand on those QIs written on the record form.

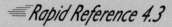

Atlantis: Processes and QIs

General Observations

Atlantis requires the child to sustain attention while learning numerous new associations between pairs of words and pictures that are continuously presented. In addition, the child will need to be flexible and change incorrect responses when the examiner prompts with correct responses. Atlantis is the first subtest in the battery for many ages, and the examiner should try to differentiate between those indicators that are specific to the newness or beginning of the test and those that are present throughout the battery.

Potential Influences on Performance:

- Attention span
- Ability to respond when uncertain
- Ability to benefit from or accommodate correction
- Distractibility
- Frustration tolerance
- Anxiety
- Ability to verbalize a strategy for remembering
- Tendency to impulsively respond incorrectly

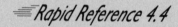

Conceptual Thinking: Processes and QIs

General Observations

Conceptual Thinking requires the child to take the time to look at several pictures, discern how most of them relate conceptually, and then look for one that does not fit the classification rule. Impulsivity may disrupt performance because the child must take in the whole set of stimuli to come to a final response. The ability to reflect and sustain attention until there is enough information to complete a response is a demanding executive process for young children.

Potential Influences on Performance:

- Cognitive style (reflective vs. impulse)
- Flexibility
- Perseverance
- Presence of sustained and divided attention for the duration of each individual item (vs. sustained for the whole subtest)
- Ability to check the answer and self-correct if necessary
- Tendency to impulsively respond incorrectly
- Reluctance to respond when uncertain

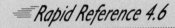

≡Rapid Reference 4.5

Face Recognition: Processes and QIs

General Observations

During Face Recognition the child must orient to the stimulus and sustain attention until the response page is presented. This subtest is also influenced by the child's ability to generate a way to discriminate and encode facial details when multiple faces are presented.

Potential Influences on Performance:

- Ability to sustain attention for each item set
- Distractibility
- Anxiety
- Cognitive style (reflective vs. impulsive)
- Tendency to impulsively respond incorrectly
- Reluctance to respond when uncertain

≡Rapid Reference 4.6

Story Completion: Processes and QIs

General Observations

Story Completion requires that a child be alert to real-life situations and the environment. This subtest is strongly influenced by the child's ability to sustain attention while selecting cards that fit in to partially formed stories or scenarios. The ability to organize and keep competing themes in mind at the same time places a high demand on executive functions. Impulsivity can interfere with this subtest because distractor cards are also present, which places a heavy burden on the child to make the right decision and then check that choice against alternatives.

Potential Influences on Performance:

- Sustained, selective, and divided attention
- Organizational skills or strategy formation for large sets of information
- Self-correction (metacognition)
- Cognitive style (reflectivity vs. impulsivity)
- Flexibility (tries out options)
- Frustration tolerance
- Reluctance to commit to a response
- Tendency to worry about time limits
- Tendency to work quickly but carefully
- Ability to verbalize story ideas

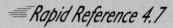

Number Recall: Processes and QIs

General Observations

The Number Recall task demand is relatively easy for the child to understand, and the task is executed quickly. However, Number Recall requires attention to auditory sequential details that can get quite difficult at ceiling items. Hence, many times the child tries to develop a strategy for remembering before the memory trace dissipates. Due to a very short response window, no chance for repetition of the stimulus, and very short rehearsal opportunity, anxiety and distractibility are common negative influences on performance.

Potential Influences on Performance:

- Distractibility
- Anxiety
- Depression
- Strategy formation for difficult items (e.g., chunking numbers)
- Ability to sustain attention
- Ability to stay focused

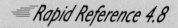
Rapid Reference 4.8

Gestalt Closure: Processes and QIs

General Observations

Gestalt Closure requires children to be flexible in their thinking. They must visually organize a stimulus picture and entertain possibilities of what the picture may be. Children who are alert to the environment and who are creative and flexible in their perception and thinking will do well. On the other hand, this subtest is sensitive to perseveration, the inability to respond when uncertain, and possibly a field-dependent cognitive style.

Potential Influences on Performance:

- Cognitive flexibility
- Perseveration
- Ability to respond when uncertain
- Field dependence
- Depression
- Ability to sustain attention
- Ability to verbalize ideas
- Reluctance to respond when uncertain
- Tendency to impulsively respond incorrectly

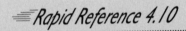

Rapid Reference 4.9

Rover: Processes and QIs

General Observations

Rover requires a great deal of working memory and executive skills in that many processes have to be organized at the same time for success on each item. First, the child must sustain attention and learn the rules of the task (which include visual, auditory, and haptic modalities), as well as accommodating reminders when a rule is broken. Second, the child must keep these rules in mind with competing possible answers and discriminate the correct answer by comparison.

Potential Influences on Performance:

- Sustained, divided, and selective attention for each item
- Organizational strategies for complex task demands
- Ability to remember rules, accommodate new rules, and adhere to rules
- Distractibility
- Anxiety
- Depression
- Impulsivity
- Tendency to worry about time limits
- Tendency to try out options

Rapid Reference 4.10

Atlantis Delayed: Processes and QIs

General Observations

The delayed aspect of Atlantis requires the child to access previously learned material and, of course, is dependent on how well the child learned the material during the initial learning phase. Any of the observations mentioned for the Atlantis subtest (attention span, ability to respond when uncertain, ability to benefit from correction, distractibility, frustration tolerance, and anxiety) could have interfered with the initial learning and storage of the material. In addition, children with brain injury or organicity tend to perform better on the initial than delayed test (due to characteristic storage/retrieval problems), and children who are depressed tend to perform just as well or surprisingly better on the delayed than the initial part of learning tasks.

Potential Influences on Performance:

- Negative reaction to an unexpected task demand for retrieval
- Brain injury–related storage and retrieval problems
- Depression (may enhance performance)
- Failure to sustain attention
- Reluctance to respond when uncertain
- Tendency to impulsively respond incorrectly

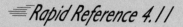

Expressive Vocabulary: Processes and QIs

General Observations

Expressive Vocabulary, like many other language- and achievement-oriented tests, is very much a function of environmental opportunity and cultural background. These tests are subject to the influences of the child's experiences and interaction with the world as well as language ability.

Potential Influences on Performance:

- Alertness to the environment
- Cultural preferences regarding expression of vocabulary (concrete/functional vs. abstract/lexical)
- Enrichment of early environment
- Availability of language-rich activities in the home
- Bilingual-related issues (e.g., word retrieval, inaccurate internal translation)
- Reluctance to respond when uncertain
- Perseverance
- Ability to verbalize related knowledge

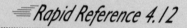

Verbal Knowledge: Processes and QIs

General Observations

Verbal Knowledge demands sustained attention and working memory while the picture response options are being considered. The child must match the word to its picture counterpart. Therefore, the child must hold the word or concept in mind as he or she peruses the answer options. Sustained attention for each item is an important process in this subtest, as are the usual cultural and environmental influences in subtests that require judgment and language about everyday situations and things.

Potential Influences on Performance:

- Presence of sustained attention and working memory
- Tendency to survey pictures before responding
- Reluctance to respond when uncertain
- Tendency to frequently ask for repetition
- Tendency to impulsively respond incorrectly
- Distractibility
- Alertness to the environment
- Cultural perceptions about word meanings
- Enrichment of early environment
- School learning
- Availability of media (books, magazines, quality television shows)

≡ Rapid Reference 4.13

Rebus: Processes and QIs

General Observations

Rebus requires the child to be actively involved with the examiner in the learning process. While the examiner does provide cued learning, there is no corrective feedback as in the case of Atlantis. The child, therefore, must pay attention to the cued learning and then immediately apply it to a response demand. As the items become more complex, so does the attention and executive function demand. Due to the complexity of the task, some children may experience anxiety or frustration when faced with symbols that they do not recognize. In turn, those unknown symbols may interfere with comprehension and the child's sense of success or task completion for each item.

Potential Influences on Performance:

- Presence of sustained or divided attention
- Anxiety
- Use of context cues (i.e., sentence meaning)
- Refusal to engage in task
- Distractibility
- Frustration tolerance
- Reluctance to respond when uncertain
- Tendency to check individual symbols with overall comprehension (metacognition)
- Ability to generate strategies for memory (mnemonic devices)

≡*Rapid Reference 4.14*

Triangles: Processes and QIs

General Observations

Performance on Triangles is impaired to some extent for children with a field-dependent cognitive style and for those who have difficulty working under time pressure. Performance is enhanced for those who know to frequently check for accuracy, can employ a systematic strategy for analyzing the model design into its component parts, and are flexible in their approach to problem solving. In addition, research has shown that children with depression tend to have lower scores on subtests like Triangles.

Potential Influences on Performance:

- Field dependence
- Field neglect
- Tendency to worry about time limits
- Tendency to move pieces haphazardly
- Perseverance
- Tendency to work quickly but carefully
- Tendency to self-correct (check and correct mistakes)
- Ability to formulate strategies for accommodating complex sets of information
- Ability to sustain attention during difficult items
- Depression

≡Rapid Reference 4.15

Block Counting: Processes and QIs

General Observations

Block Counting has process demands very similar to those of the Triangles subtest. The individual must maintain a flexible approach to the increasingly demanding items. Field dependence impairs the ability to understand components of a new task demand on this subtest, especially with more difficult items. The ability to sustain attention while investigating the unique task demand is important because intuitive or impulsive answers are salient but usually incorrect. This subtest may also be sensitive to impulsivity because, unlike Triangles, Block Counting does not have kinesthetic feedback in terms of putting the actual model together; the child simply responds to a visual presentation with a verbal answer (or nonverbal, using fingers or writing, if necessary).

Potential Influences on Performance:

- Field dependence
- Tendency to worry about time limits
- Ability to formulate strategies for accommodating complex sets of information
- Ability to sustain attention during difficult items
- Tendency to impulsively respond when uncertain
- Ability to verbalize a strategy
- Perseverance

≡Rapid Reference 4.16

Word Order: Processes and QIs

General Observations

Performance on Word Order is impaired for children who are distractible, anxious, or limited in their attention span. Success on items that employ color naming as a 5-second interference task is enhanced by good concentration, flexibility to shift quickly when the demands of the task change, ability to understand and follow directions, ability to generate a strategy for recalling stimuli without rehearsal, maturity to work productively despite distractions, and ability to tolerate frustration.

Potential Influences on Performance:

- Distractibility
- Divided attention or working memory
- Tendency to impulsively respond incorrectly
- Depression
- Anxiety
- Comprehension of task demand and accommodation as task demand shifts
- Frustration tolerance
- Ability to verbalize stimulus
- Distress at color interference task

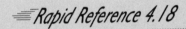

≡ Rapid Reference 4.17

Pattern Reasoning: Processes and QIs

General Observations

Pattern Reasoning places a great demand on executive functioning skills because the child must sustain attention while using several different cognitive processes at the same time. Scores on Pattern Reasoning may be depressed for children with an impulsive cognitive style because of the numerous response choices. Indeed, many children will self-correct at the last second because of their impulsivity. Children who are depressed may also experience difficulty on Pattern Reasoning. In general, children need flexibility to cope with the change in response style when the items shift from pictorial to abstract analogies. In addition, performance is enhanced for children who can spontaneously generate a systematic strategy for inferring the nature of the analogy for each abstract item.

Potential Influences on Performance:

- Presence of sustained and divided attention
- Tendency to impulsively respond incorrectly
- Ability to self-correct when mistake is made
- Cognitive flexibility when item sets change
- Depression
- Tendency to worry about time limits
- Tendency to try to solve problem before looking at options

≡ Rapid Reference 4.18

Hand Movements: Processes and QIs

General Observations

Scores on Hand Movements can be depressed by distractibility, perseveration, and anxiety. Success is usually contingent on a good attention span and concentration. While concentrating, it is beneficial to develop some type of mediating strategy (e.g., verbally labeling each of the three hand positions, finding a method for organizing the stimuli into a pattern) to aid performance. Some children may have difficulty determining which hand to use or may use different hands on different items. Therefore, lack of hand dominance may interfere with smooth reproductions of stimuli.

Potential Influences on Performance:

- Attention span
- Distractibility
- Ability to sustain attention during more difficult items
- Strategy formation for complex items
- Ability to verbalize a strategy
- Hesitancy over which hand to use

≡ Rapid Reference 4.19

Rebus Delayed: Processes and QIs

General Observations

Performance on the Rebus Delayed subtest, as with Atlantis Delayed, is subject to how well the child performed on the initial subtest. The initial task requires that the child sustain attention and maintain working memory while staying free from anxiety and distractibility and be able to respond when uncertain. Rebus also demands the ability to generate strategies for memory (e.g., mnemonic devices) to help storage and retrieval. Much like Atlantis Delayed, Rebus Delayed is probably sensitive to children with brain injury or organicity who characteristically have difficulty with storage and retrieval of newly learned information. In addition, children with depression may do just as well or, surprisingly, better on Rebus Delayed than on the initial Rebus.

Potential Influences on Performance:

- Ability to respond when uncertain
- Negative reaction to unexpected task
- Brain injury or organicity-related storage and retrieval problems
- Depression (may enhance performance)
- Tendency to impulsively respond incorrectly
- Ability to use context cues (i.e., sentence meaning)
- Perseveration

≡ Rapid Reference 4.20

Riddles: Processes and QIs

General Observations

Performance on Riddles is dependent to some extent on richness of early environment, alertness to the environment, cultural opportunities at home, outside reading (or being read to), and interests. Good attention and concentration facilitates success on Riddles, as does the ability to decenter, a Piagetian concept denoting skill at focusing on all pertinent attributes rather than attending only to a single feature. Distractibility, perseveration, and impulsivity all may hinder performance.

Potential Influences on Performance:

- Failure to sustain attention
- Lack of enriched background
- Lack of exposure to early activities that demand listening skills
- Alertness to the environment
- Frequent requests for repetition
- Tendency to respond based on first one or two clues
- Ability to verbalize stimulus

 **TEST YOURSELF**

1. **Qualitative indicators are test-taking behaviors that exert only a negative influence on test performance.** True or False?

2. **The following QIs may bring the validity of test results into question:**
   (a) Aggressive and oppositional behavior
   (b) Withdrawal and refusal to respond
   (c) Inattention and distractibility
   (d) All of the above

3. **The KABC-II QIs**
   (a) are relevant only to the KABC-II and therefore should be considered as isolated samples of behavior.
   (b) should be compared to behaviors noted outside of the testing situation.
   (c) are quantified and scored to obtain a standard score and percentile rank.
   (d) are observed only in children ages 3–6.

4. **Qualitative behaviors can be observed on every subtest of the KABC-II.** True or False?

5. **With regard to executive functions, QIs can**
   (a) diagnose executive function deficits.
   (b) suggest further investigation of executive functions.
   (c) discriminate deficits in different parts of the brain.
   (d) define frontal-lobe lesions.

6. **QIs diagnose clinical psychopathology.** True or False?

7. **The authors of the KABC-II support**
   (a) the use of qualitative as well as quantitative information in assessment.
   (b) the usefulness of QIs in the comprehensive assessment process.
   (c) the acknowledgment of the contribution of QIs to clinical judgment.
   (d) the documentation of QIs during the assessment process.
   (e) all of the above.

Answers: 1. False; 2. d; 3. b; 4. True; 5. b; 6. False; 7. e

Five

STRENGTHS AND WEAKNESSES OF THE KABC-II

Elaine Fletcher-Janzen and Elizabeth O. Lichtenberger

INTRODUCTION

All cognitive ability batteries have strengths and weaknesses: No one battery can answer all of the questions posed by any clinician. Indeed, cognitive ability batteries are only a part of what should be a comprehensive assessment that includes many tests to answer the referral question. Clinicians have to make decisions about how they view the definition and measurement of the cognitive abilities' part of a comprehensive assessment and then find tools to help them do this defining and measuring. Therefore, because there is a myriad of referral questions and needs with different ages and populations, it is highly unlikely that a single instrument will be the correct choice for all occasions. We, as clinicians, tend to specialize with certain age groups or special populations, and after some experience with different assessment tools we learn which tools help us do our job the best. Each clinician has to evaluate the tools available by deciding what the strengths and weaknesses of each test are and then evaluating the fit with the needs of the child being assessed. To that end, we present the strengths and weaknesses of the KABC-II in this chapter (Rapid References 5.1 through 5.5 list strengths and weaknesses in the following areas: test development, administration and scoring, reliability and validity, standardization, and interpretation).

Of course, many of the more detailed strengths and weaknesses of a cognitive ability test only come to light after there has been a period of time for researchers and practitioners to examine the everyday use of the battery. Therefore, because this chapter is being written at the same time the KABC-II is making its debut, most of the strengths and weaknesses mentioned here are based on insights gained from the examination of the original K-ABC for the past 20 years, projections about how the battery will perform given its extensive revision, the rules of psychometric design, and field practice with the tryout and standardization versions of the KABC-II.

Strengths and Weaknesses of KABC-II Test Development

Strengths	Weaknesses
• The test is based on a dual theoretical model: traditional Lurian theory and current CHC model of cognitive abilities.	• It measures five CHC broad abilities but does not measure two potentially important cognitive abilities: Auditory Processing (*Ga*) and Processing Speed (*Gs*). Consequently, examiners who want to measure *Ga* and *Gs* will need to apply the cross-battery approach to measure the whole model.
• It allows the examiner to choose theoretical framework for administration and interpretation.	
• It assesses a wide range of children and adolescents (ages 3–18).	
• It is conormed with the KTEA-II to allow for understanding of cognitive abilities in context of the child's academic strengths and weaknesses.	• The record form is complex.
	• Bonus points are used on three subtests.
• Approximately 66% of the tryout sample was from ethnic minority background—therefore the initial analyses of items for bias reflected a majority of non-Anglo responses.	• The test is heavy to carry, with numerous easels and parts.
	• Bonus points for Story Completion and Triangles confound the measurement of reasoning with visual/motor speed component.
• There are ample floors and ceilings on nearly all subtests.	
• It allows the examiner to accept a correct response regardless of the mode of the answer (signing, language other than English, writing), which allows for assessment of cognitive ability regardless of mode of communication.	
• Materials are well organized and clearly labeled.	
• Easels are sturdy and have all the necessary information on them, with pictures for easy reference.	
• Novel and stimulating artwork is included throughout the test.	
• It provides out-of-level norms for assessing young children who may meet floor and ceilings too soon for diagnostic utility.	
• Qualitative assessment during administration is supported by QIs on the record form.	

≡ *Rapid Reference 5.2*

Strengths and Weaknesses of KABC-II Administration and Scoring

Strengths	Weaknesses
• Sample and teaching items can be spoken in the child's native language.	• Scoring for the Atlantis, Rebus, and Delayed subtests requires careful attention to avoid clerical errors.
• If the child does not understand sample and teaching items, the examiner can explain in language appropriate to that specific child.	• Discontinue rules change from subtest to subtest, which may be confusing.
• It features very short and simple examiner instructions that reduce the chances that a child won't understand task demands.	• Lower-ability children have a hard time understanding grammar items on Rebus.
• Limited subjectivity in scoring is easier for the examiner.	• The record form does not include a place to record and calculate the Delayed Recall scale. However, the record form will be modified in the second printing to permit calculation of the Delayed Recall standard score (Mark Daniel, personal communication, May 3, 2004).
• The easel format simplifies the administration process.	
• Most subtests are presented in both visual and auditory formats, which increases understanding.	
• Record form is color coded for ease of administration and scoring.	
• Two sample items are included for the color interference part for Word Order to facilitate communication of the color interference task.	
• Computer scoring and interpretation will be available as soon as the KABC-II ASSIST becomes available.	

OVERVIEW OF STRENGTHS AND WEAKNESSES

The KABC-II has several major strengths: It was developed from insights from 35 years of experience and analyses with the McCarthy scales, the WISC-R, the K-ABC, and other Kaufman tests. In fact, several major changes were made directly due to feedback from clinicians in the field (e.g., better floors for younger children, better ceilings for gifted children, and more reasoning and less memory subtests). It was also developed from long-standing, evidence-based theoretical

≡ *Rapid Reference 5.3*

Strengths and Weaknesses of KABC-II Reliability and Validity

Strengths	Weaknesses
• Reliabilities for the global scale indexes are very high, averaging in the middle to upper .90s for the FCI and MPI and in the low .90s for the NVI.	• Some Supplementary subtests have low internal consistency reliabilities (Hand Movements at ages 3–6, $r = .69$; Gestalt Closure at ages 3–18, $r = .74$; and Face Recognition at age 5, $r = .65$).
• Subtests show good internal consistency at all ages. Median reliability (averaged across ages) for core subtests is .85 for ages 3–6 and .87 for ages 7–18.	• Seven of the 15 subtests for 7- to 18-year-olds have average adjusted test-retest coefficients below .80.
• Test-retest coefficients of global scales range from the mid-.80s to the mid-.90s for the FCI and MPI.	• Nine of the 12 subtests for 3- to 5-year-olds have adjusted test-retest coefficients below .80.
• Practice effects for the Learning/*Glr* scale are high, ratifying that the subtest is indeed measuring learning.	• Face Recognition has a low factor loading on the Simultaneous/*Gv* scale in the confirmatory factor analysis at age 4.
• Correlations among scale indexes show an appropriate level of independence but are high enough to indicate that they have a common underlying construct.	• Confirmatory factor analysis of Core subtests indicates correlation coefficients of about .9 between the *Gv* and *Gf* scales for ages 7–18 and between *Gc* and *Gv* at age 4.
• Loadings of the ability factors on the general factor tend to be high enough to indicate that the abilities are influenced by a general ability factor. This is consistent with CHC theory.	• No validity studies were reported in the manual for children diagnosed with traumatic brain injury or with speech and language impairment.
• Confirmatory factor analysis indicates extremely good fit to the data (CFI ranges from .993 to .999, and RMSEA ranges from .025 to .061) for analyses of Core subtests and also for analyses of *all* subtests (Core and Supplementary).	

(continued)

- Multiple clinical validity studies are presented in the manual (reading disability, learning disability, writing disability, mathematics disability, ADHD, emotional disturbance, hearing impaired, Mental Retardation, Autistic Disorder, gifted).

- The manual includes numerous correlation studies with a variety of cognitive and achievement tests (K-ABC, WISC-IV, WISC-III, WPPSI-III, KAIT, WJ-III Cognitive Battery, PIAT-R, WJ-III Achievement Battery, WIAT-II).

- The MPI and FCI correlated substantially with global scores on other cognitive test batteries such as the WISC-III and WISC-IV Full Scale IQ (adjusted rs of .88–.89 with WISC-IV and .71–.77 with WISC-III).

- The MPI and FCI correlated substantially with global scores on achievement test batteries such as the WJ-III and WIAT-2 (adjusted rs of .63–.79 for WJ-III and .65–.87 for WIAT-II). The KABC-II global scores also correlated substantially with overall scores on the KTEA-II Comprehensive Form (adjusted rs of .73–.80).

perspectives. Therefore, the theoretical and evidence base for the KABC-II redesign is very strong indeed.

There are also psychometric strengths that the field has now come to expect and demand: The KABC-II has excellent reliability, validity, and factor analytic properties as well as a large and well-stratified normative base.

Perhaps one of the most important attributes of the original K-ABC was that it consistently produced lower global score differences between ethnic groups than are yielded by traditional IQ tests, such as Wechsler's scales. This strength was due to much up-front development and was by design. The KABC-II has sustained this design by intentionally eliminating knowledge- or content-based subtests from the MPI, by including tasks that are interesting to children, by incorporating teaching items, and by continuing to include expert bias analyses, item response analyses, large representations of ethnic minority children in the

≡ Rapid Reference 5.4

Strengths and Weaknesses of KABC-II Standardization

Strengths	Weaknesses
• The standardization sample is well stratified.	• There are no major weaknesses.
• There is a large normative group (3,025).	
• Solid methodologies were used for eliminating test bias.	
• The KABC-II and KTEA-II were conormed, which provides valuable information for examiners wanting to compare ability and achievement.	
• Ten special group studies were conducted during standardization, enhancing the scale's clinical utility.	

tryout sample, nationally proportionate representation of ethnic minorities in the norm sample, and cultural validity studies. Indeed, the scale, subtest, and global scale mean scores and SDs for ethnic minorities in the norm sample are printed in the manual for examiners to study. Tables of this nature are not usually included in test manuals; however, the authors feel that this is important information for the test user and is just *one* of the many ways that an examiner can determine the validity of the KABC-II with different cultural groups. The cultural information included in the redesign of the K-ABC indicates that the KABC-II will continue to be strong in this area and provide clinicians with the psychometric strength to assess children in the most culturally fair way possible. As was true for the original K-ABC, the KABC-II yields smaller differences between ethnic groups than have been found for traditional measures of intelligence.

We feel that the KABC-II has no major weaknesses. However, there are some weaknesses that we consider minor. For example, there is emphasis on speed of processing for a few subtests, so differentiation occurs with older, bright examinees. However, the manual does allow examiners to calculate scores with the effect of speed removed, which compensates for this minor weakness. A few split-half internal consistency and test-retest coefficients are low for some subtests, but overall the KABC-II has very strong psychometric properties.

≣Rapid Reference 5.5

Strengths and Weaknesses of KABC-II Interpretation

Strengths	Weaknesses
• The KABC-II's theoretical foundations in the Luria and CHC models establish a framework for interpretation of the scales.	• The Knowledge/Gc subtests do not permit evaluation of the child's ability to express ideas in words because one of the subtests measures receptive language and the other two require only one-word answers.
• CHC model design makes the KABC-II work well with other tests for cross-battery assessment of broad and narrow abilities.	• The Meaningful Stimuli and Gross-Motor planned Clinical Comparisons from the interpretive system require administration of Story Completion and Rover, which are out-of-level subtests for age 5.
• Interpretation is dependent on global scales and scale indexes (avoiding negative effects of subtest profile analysis).	
• The interpretation system consistently prompts the examiner to verify hypotheses with other data.	
• The manual provides data on the mean MPI and FCI, scale index, and subtest scores for various ethnic groups along with validity data to assist with interpreting data for an individual from an ethnic minority group.	
• The KABC-II record form provides a place to record the basic analysis of the scale indexes, including strengths and weaknesses.	
• Out-of-level norms are available for bright 3-year-olds or lower-functioning 7-year-olds who have not yet developed the executive functioning needed for the Planning/Gf subtests. Out-of-level norms can also be given at the 6-year level or the 5-year level, neither of which includes a separate Planning/Gf scale. The 5-year level also does not include Rover, which might be difficult for them.	
• It allows examination of immediate versus delayed memory.	

- It allows examination of learning versus crystallized knowledge.
- A forthcoming computer scoring program will allow for other planned comparisons and narrative text for interpretation.
- The Nonverbal index may be calculated and interpreted for children for whom oral communication is difficult (e.g., children with hearing impairment, limited English proficiency, autism, speech or language impairments, and other impairments).

🐟 TEST YOURSELF 🐟

1. **The K-ABC and the KABC-II consistently produce lower global score differences between ethnic groups than Wechsler's scales.** True or False?

2. **The KABC-II measures five of the CHC global abilities. Additional measures need to be administered if examiners want to assess which other global CHC abilities?**

   (a) Fluid Reasoning (*Gf*) and Short-Term Memory (*Gsm*)

   (b) Processing Speed (*Gs*) and Auditory Processing (*Ga*)

   (c) Crystallized Ability (*Gc*) and Long-Term Retrieval (*Glr*)

   (d) Visual Processing (*Gv*) and Fluid Reasoning (*Gf*)

3. **There are _____ major weaknesses in the standardization of the KABC-II.**

4. **Reliabilities for the global scale indexes are high.** True or False?

5. **An examiner can teach any subtest item in**

   (a) sign language.

   (b) English only.

   (c) Spanish.

   (d) any language that is suitable for the context.

6. **Seven of the 15 subtests for 7- to 18-year-olds have average adjusted test-retest coefficients below .80.** True or False?

7. **Validity studies were reported in the manual for the following groups of children *except* those with**

   (a) traumatic brain injury and speech and language impairment.

   (b) autism and Mental Retardation.

   (c) giftedness.

   (d) learning disabilities and ADHD.

Answers: 1. True; 2. b; 3. No; 4. True; 5. d; 6. True; 7. a

Six

CLINICAL APPLICATIONS

In this chapter, we cover the following clinical applications of the KABC-II:

- The Nonverbal scale (including deaf and hard of hearing, autism, speech and language disorders)
- Assessment of mental retardation
- ADHD assessment
- Identifying learning disabilities
- Assessment of ethnic differences
- Socioeconomic status (SES) norms
- Integration of the KABC-II and the KTEA-II
- Cross-battery assessment with the KABC-II (by Dawn P. Flanagan)

The literature on each of these topics is immense, and we highlight what we feel are the major findings as they pertain to cognitive assessment and, specifically, to the K-ABC and KABC-II. As the KABC-II was just published when this book went to press, the only studies of clinical samples available to us are those presented in the KABC-II manual. Future clinically based studies on the KABC-II studies will enrich the clinical applications of this instrument.

CLINICAL APPLICATIONS OF THE NONVERBAL SCALE

The KABC-II Nonverbal Scale is composed of subtests that may be administered in pantomime and responded to motorically and is available for children and adolescents within the entire 3 to 18 year age range. This scale permits valid assessment of children for whom neither the FCI nor the MPI are appropriate, such as children with hearing impairment, limited English proficiency, moderate to severe speech or language disorders, autism, and related disorders that make oral communication difficult.

In this section on the KABC-II Nonverbal Scale, we review the literature available on the use of the original K-ABC's Nonverbal Scale, although note that the

═Rapid Reference 6.1

Comparison of the K-ABC and KABC-II Nonverbal Scales

Subtest	Original K-ABC Nonverbal Scale	KABC-II Nonverbal Scale			
		Ages 3–4	Age 5	Age 6	Ages 7–18
Hand Movements	✓ (ages 4–12.5)	✓	✓	✓	✓
Triangles	✓ (ages 4–12.5)	✓	✓	✓	✓
Face Recognition	✓ (age 4)	✓	✓		
Conceptual Thinking	Not on K-ABC	✓	✓	✓	
Pattern Reasoning	Not on K-ABC		✓	✓	✓
Story Completion	Not on K-ABC			✓	✓
Block Counting	Not on K-ABC				✓
Matrix Analogies	✓ (ages 5–12.5)	Eliminated from KABC-II			
Spatial Memory	✓ (ages 5–12.5)	Eliminated from KABC-II			
Photo Series	✓ (ages 6–12.5)	Eliminated from KABC-II			

composition of the Nonverbal scale has changed markedly from the K-ABC to KABC-II (see Rapid Reference 6.1). Although half of the subtests are new to the KABC-II Nonverbal Scale, the premise underlying its development was the same as for the first edition—to facilitate the valid assessment of children who have difficulty understanding verbal stimuli, responding orally, or both.

Hearing Impairment

In the United States, hearing impairment (broadly defined and inclusive of both deaf and hard-of-hearing populations) affects more than 20 million individuals, with approximately 500,000 people identified as deaf (National Center for Health Statistics, 1994). Of individuals 6- to 21-years-old, 70,767 had been served, as of 2002, under the Individuals with Disabilities Education Act (IDEA) because of hearing impairments (U.S. Department of Education, 2002). Children with hearing losses often face a variety of challenges, such as communication difficulties and deficient English skills (Bornstein, Wollward, & Tully, 1976; Schmelter-Davis, 1984), as well as experiencing gaps in their academic skills (Lane, 1976; Sherman & Robinson, 1982; Vernon & Andrews, 1990). A high percentage of these students, classified by their special education primary disability of a hearing impairment, also have other disabilities and educational needs (Gallaudet Research Institute, 2003).

Sattler and Hardy-Braz (2002) and Gordon, Stump, and Glaser (1996) list considerations when assessing individuals with hearing impairment. Many people who are deaf have relatively restricted English language skills (Gordon et al., 1996). Most standardized tests use a high level of English vocabulary and complex language structure and are standardized for administration through auditory-verbal means, often making them inappropriate for use with many individuals who are deaf and who have limited English skills. Unless the examiner or an interpreter uses sign language to administer the test, many tests cannot be understood (Stewart, 1986). However, using interpreters introduces additional variables and issues: Examiners must match their own communication skills with the characteristics of the individual child; whenever selecting instruments, examiners must consider both the targeted cognitive skills and the demands of the item, subtest, and battery, along with the communication modality (Hardy-Braz, 2003).

Notable exceptions to the dearth of multisubtest standardized tests appropriate for individuals with hearing impairment are the Nonverbal scales of the original K-ABC and the KABC-II, the Universal Nonverbal Intelligence Test (UNIT; Bracken & McCallum, 1998), the Leiter International Performance Scale—Revised (Roid & Miller, 1997), and a few other tests (see McCallum, Bracken, & Wasserman, 2001). In general, these scales were developed and normed with hearing-impaired (and non-English-speaking) individuals in mind; therefore, the use of signing or other alternate modes of communication is built into the standardization procedure and does not represent either a modification or violation of the norms.

While not every hearing-impaired child communicates via signs, American Sign Language (ASL) is the most prevalently used manual sign language in the United States. American Sign Language has grammar and syntax that are different from English idioms, grammar, and syntax (Valli & Lucas, 1995). In addition to differences in grammatical and syntactical usage, reading English is usually an area of significant weakness for persons who are deaf, so any testing procedure that involves reading may not provide an accurate measure for this population (Crichfield, 1986). Deaf and hard-of-hearing students who live in environments (e.g., home, school, society), which are not fully accessible, may also face challenges in accessing social, cultural, and historical knowledge and information that are often transmitted via audiological means. This inaccessibility may have significant negative impact on assessment batteries (Hardy-Braz, 2003).

Research on Use of Cognitive Tests with Deaf and Hard-of-Hearing Children

In some domains of cognitive ability, children who are deaf or hard of hearing perform differently than children who can hear clearly. When assessed nonverbally, children with hearing impairments generally perform within the Average range of cognitive ability, but mean verbal standard scores are typically on standard deviation below the mean (Braden, 1994). This typical pattern has been observed on a variety of Wechsler scales for individuals with hearing impairment, including the Wechsler Intelligence Scale for Children—Revised (WISC-R; Wechsler, 1974) and the third edition (WISC-III; Wechsler, 1991).

- Mean WISC-R and WISC-III Performance IQs are invariably between about 95 and 110, for example, 96.9 (Braden, 1985), 100.6 (Sullivan & Montoya, 1997), 102.3 (Braden, 1994), 105.8 (Wechsler, 1991), and 107.7 (Sullivan & Schulte, 1992).
- In contrast, mean Verbal IQs of 75.4 (Sullivan & Montoya, 1997), 81.1 (Wechsler, 1991), and 81.6 (Braden, 1994) have been reported.

The Performance (P) > Verbal (V) pattern is not surprising given that most deaf children have significant English language delays, deficits in acquired knowledge, or both. Although it was often administered in significantly modified and nonstandardized ways, the Wechsler Performance scale has traditionally been viewed as more fairly assessing cognitive abilities of deaf and hard-of-hearing children than the Verbal scale (although it did not assess the broad range of cognitive skills needed for academic success). For the WISC-IV, the Perceptual Reasoning index is more appropriate for assessing the abilities of individuals with hearing impairment than is the Verbal Reasoning index.

A few differences in Wechsler subtest scores have been noted in children who are deaf or hard of hearing. For example, Braden (1984) noted that WISC-R Coding and Picture Arrangement scaled scores were significantly lower for hearing-impaired children in his sample. These differences were attributed to more frequent deficits in temporal sequencing and a possibly greater incidence of neurological impairment among this population (Conrad & Weiskrantz, 1981). Findings from WISC-III Coding scores have been somewhat mixed, with some other hearing-impaired samples showing lower scores (e.g., Slate & Fawcett, 1995; Sullivan & Montoya, 1997) and others not showing depressed scores (e.g., Braden, 1994; Wechsler, 1991). The WISC-III Digit Span subtest, another task requiring sequential ability, is also consistently depressed in profiles of hearing-impaired children. Yet Digit Span is also a verbally loaded test that becomes significantly modified whenever administered in a visible fashion (e.g., sign language, cued speech), so it is difficult to tease apart the effects of verbal skill from sequential skill when interpreting this score as the subtest itself is substantially modified.

Factor analyses have provided evidence of some similarity and some dissimilarity between the cognitive abilities of hearing versus nonhearing children. For example, as in hearing samples, Sullivan and Schulte (1992) administered the entire test battery (Verbal and Performance scales) in a nonstandardized fashion and used the test publisher's normative sample and found that the factor structure for deaf and hard-of-hearing children on the WISC-R contained two main factors for deaf and hard-of-hearing children: Language Comprehension and Visual-Spatial Organization. However, unlike the hearing population, a Freedom from Distractibility factor was not identified on the WISC-R for the deaf and hard-of-hearing populations. When Braden (1985) factor analyzed just the Performance scale results from the large dataset collected from several different nonstandardized administrations of the WISC-R to hearing-impaired students (from Anderson & Sisco, 1977) with results compared with other hearing-impaired students, he found a single factor of Perceptual Organization.

Similar factor analyses have been conducted on the WISC-III. The WISC-III was administered in a nonstandardized format to 106 children ages 6 to 16 ($M =$ 11 years) with a pure-tone-average hearing loss of 45 dB HL or greater in the better ear (Sullivan & Montoya, 1997). Like the results on the WISC-R, two factors were derived from the deaf and hard-of-hearing sample on the WISC-III: Language Comprehension and Visual-Spatial Organization. Unlike the hearing standardization sample, Freedom from Distractibility and Processing Speed factors did not emerge for the deaf and hard-of-hearing sample.

Important clinically relevant findings were also reported in Sullivan and Montoya's (1997) WISC-III study. First, the preferred method of communication of the deaf and hard-of-hearing children, when matched by skilled examiners, did not appear to affect the children's overall IQs. That is, no differences in Verbal and Performance IQs were found between children who communicated via ASL versus Signed English (SE) versus oral means (i.e., lip reading and speech). Second, no significant differences were reported to result from directly signed administration versus the use of a skilled and trained sign language interpreter. Thus, Sullivan and Montoya concluded that nonstandardized test administration by a fluent ASL or SE psychologist or interpreter will not likely reduce the obtained scores, although the process modifies the cognitive demands of the tasks. However, compared to their hearing peers, deaf and hard-of-hearing children were likely to perform relatively poorly on the Verbal subtests of the WISC-III. The WISC-IV, however, no longer divides the test battery into Verbal and Performance scales yet provides greater administrative guidelines (manual pages 12 to 18) for use with these populations.

Use of the K-ABC with Deaf and Hard-of-Hearing Children

Research on the Nonverbal scale of the original K-ABC has supported its use with children who are deaf or hard of hearing. Studies have shown that children with hearing impairments have relatively normal intelligence as assessed by the K-ABC Nonverbal Scale, with mean Nonverbal standard scores in studies ranging from 96.8 to 100.7 (Ham, 1985; Porter & Kirby, 1986; Ulissi, Brice, & Gibbons, 1985). Researchers with samples of hearing impaired children have typically administered the K-ABC via pantomimed instructions. Porter and Kirby (1986) compared deaf children's performance on the K-ABC Nonverbal Scale when the test was administered in either pantomime or in sign language and found that the mean standard scores were not statistically different: 98.8 for pantomime and 96.8 for sign language.

Spragins (1998), who reviewed the K-ABC's Nonverbal Scale for use with deaf and hard-of-hearing individuals, praised the scale for including "teaching items," for providing tips to aid the examiner in pantomiming instructions, for producing good reliability coefficients, for its relationship to academic achievement for children who are deaf or hard of hearing (Phelps & Branyan, 1988; Ulissi et al., 1989), for keeping the role of language to a minimum, for correlating significantly with the WISC-R Performance Scale for deaf and hard-of-hearing children, and for including mostly untimed subtests. Spragins criticized the K-ABC Nonverbal Scale for comprising too few subtests at age 4 and for including a subtest that was difficult to score (Spatial Memory).

She concluded that the K-ABC Nonverbal Scale is a useful instrument for the evaluation of children who are deaf or hard of hearing. As noted, the KABC-II represents a substantial revision of the original K-ABC Nonverbal Scale. Nevertheless, several of the advantages noted by Spragins (1998) apply to the KABC-II Nonverbal Scale as well. The KABC-II includes teaching items, the manual offers tips for administering the subtests in pantomime, and the language load of the tasks continues to be reduced. Reliability coefficients remain good, averaging .90 for ages 3 to 6 and .92 for ages 7 to 18 (Kaufman & Kaufman, 2004a, Table 8.1).

The KABC-II Nonverbal Index (NVI) correlated substantially with achievement (median = .71 with KTEA-II overall achievement, see Rapid Reference 1.17; also see Kaufman & Kaufman, 2004a, pp. 118–126, for correlations with other achievement tests). In addition, the NVI correlated substantially with Wechsler's Performance IQ and Perceptual Reasoning index (mean = .67; Kaufman & Kaufman, 2004a, pp. 111–114). The KABC-II NVI also correlated .63

with K-ABC Nonverbal standard score at ages 3 to 5 and .76 at ages 8 to 12 (Kaufman & Kaufman, 2004a, Tables 8.15 and 8.16). Nonetheless, these validity studies are with normal children; to evaluate the validity of the NVI with deaf and hard-of-hearing children, studies with these populations must be conducted.

One advantage noted by Spragins (1998) for the original K-ABC Nonverbal Scale—the inclusion of subtests that were typically untimed—continues to be true for ages 3 to 6, but it is no longer true for the KABC-II NVI at the school-age level. However, the KABC-II offers an option for three Nonverbal subtests that helps reduce the role of speed on test performance. At ages 7 to 18, Triangles, Pattern Reasoning, and Story Completion all offer time points for children who solve the items relatively quickly. Examiners have the option of scoring these three subtests based *only* on correct responses (time points are excluded) whenever they believe that children would be unfairly penalized by an emphasis on response time. This alternative option is available not only for the FCI and MPI, but also for the NVI.

Regarding Spragins' (1998) criticisms of the original K-ABC Nonverbal Scale, the scale did include too few subtests (only three) for 4-year-olds, and the scale could not be administered at age 3. For the KABC-II, the NVI is composed of four subtests for ages 3 and 4. Also, Spatial Memory was eliminated from the KABC-II primarily because of its scoring difficulties, so it is not included on the NVI.

Use of the KABC-II with Deaf and Hard-of-Hearing Children

Several steps were conducted in the development of the KABC-II with these populations in mind. While the test instrument was being developed, an examiner experienced in working with deaf and hard-of-hearing children reviewed every item on the tryout edition of the KABC-II. Numerous items were altered or even eliminated from the standardization test battery based on their difficulty in communicating them via different communication modalities without significantly modifying the cognitive skill(s) targeted by each subtest. The KABC-II administration guidelines for deaf and hard-of-hearing students (Hardy-Braz, in press) were developed after interpretations and translations were made and accurately back translated for every test item in four different communication modalities or languages.

During the standardization process, three skilled school psychologists (fluent in direct communication skills and experienced in working with deaf and hard-of-hearing children) administered the KABC-II to 27 children who were classified in special education as hearing impaired. These children ranged in age from 6-8 to 17-7 (mean = 12.5 years) and were educated in either a state residential school for the deaf (California [CA]) or a local education program (Virginia [VA]). The scores of these children were compared to a nonclinical reference group that was matched for age, gender, parent education, and race or ethnicity. The hearing-impaired children earned an average standard score NVI of 95.7 (SD 17.1), which was 8.7 points lower than the reference group. The Nonverbal subtest scores ranged from 8.5 (Block Counting) to 9.6 (Hand Movements, Triangles, and Story Completion). Children with hearing impairment did not perform significantly differently from the reference group on either Hand Movements or Triangles but did perform significantly lower on Block Counting, Pattern Reasoning, and Story Completion (see Figure 6.1 for specific mean subtest scores).

Although the NVI is the most appropriate score to interpret when assessing deaf and hard-of-hearing children, this clinical sample was administered the full KABC-II battery during standardization for statistical analyses. Qualified and trained examiners may find other KABC-II subtests of use in assessments as well. As expected, hearing-impaired children performed most poorly on the Knowledge/*Gc* scale (mean standard score of 80.9). This scale is primarily verbally based and requires verbal expression and understanding as well as verbal reasoning, so for children who are hearing impaired, the requisite skills needed to succeed are often hindered by virtue of their disability. The Knowledge/*Gc* scale also contained the lowest subtest scaled score for this clinical group: Expressive Vocabu-

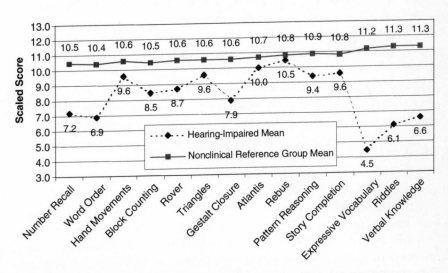

Figure 6.1 KABC-II scaled scores for children with hearing impairment.

Note. Hand Movements, Block Counting, Triangles, Pattern Reasoning, and Story Completion are included in the Nonverbal Index.

lary (the mean scaled score of 4.5 was more than 2 SDs below the average score for the reference group).

Similar to findings reported on the original K-ABC (Ullssi et al., 1985) and on Wechsler's tests (Braden, 1984; Slate & Fawcett, 1995; Sullivan & Montoya, 1997), children with hearing impairment also struggled on the Sequential/*Gsm* scale (with the exception of Hand Movements). Overall, children scored 20 points lower than the reference group on the Sequential/*Gsm* scale (mean index = 83.2). Apparently, the Low Average Sequential/*Gsm* index was primarily a function of the auditory stimuli (numbers and words spoken by the examiner) on the two Core Sequential/*Gsm* subtests. In contrast to the mean scaled scores of about 7 on the Core subtests, the sample of children with hearing loss earned a mean scaled score of 9.6 on the Supplementary Hand Movements subtest. That average performance suggests intact sequential processing and short-term memory for children with hearing loss when language is eliminated from the tasks.

In contrast to the Low Average Knowledge/*Gc* and Sequential/*Gsm* indexes, the sample of children with hearing loss scored solidly within the Average range on the Simultaneous/*Gv* index (mean = 94.6), the Planning/*Gf* index (mean = 97.6), and the Learning/*Glr* index (mean = 101.6). The latter result is extremely noteworthy because both Core Learning/*Glr* subtests require the child to understand words spoken by the examiner (that are paired with visual stimuli), and Rebus also requires verbal expression. Despite these considerable language demands, the Learning/*Glr* index indicates that the group of children with hearing loss were able to demonstrate intact learning ability—comparable to the normal control group—when faced with structured storage and retrieval tasks requiring integration of visual and auditory stimuli.

On the various Core and supplementary subtests that are included on the Simultaneous/*Gv* and Planning/*Gf* scales, only one subtest places demands on verbal expression—Gestalt Closure. That subtest yielded a mean scaled score of 7.9 for the children with hearing loss, undoubtedly a finding that is more related to the children's verbalizations than to their visual processing. Figure 6.2 shows the mean KABC-II Global scale scores for this clinical group.

As indicated, children with hearing impairments performed most similarly to the normative mean (and to the nonclinical reference group) on the Learning/*Glr* scale. Hearing-impaired children performed similarly on the two Learning/*Glr* subtests (Atlantis and Rebus) and also performed equally well on the Delayed Recall portion of the tests. Many hearing-impaired children have experience with visual languages (i.e., ASL or other signed languages), which may contribute to their ability to learn tasks like Rebus and Atlantis, which require mapping language onto a visual format.

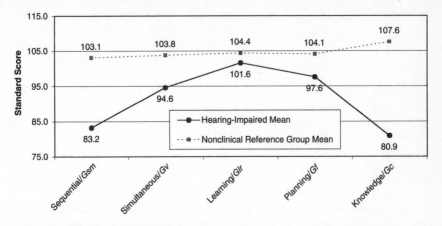

Figure 6.2 KABC-II Global Scale scores for the total sample of deaf and hard-of-hearing children (N = 27).

Note. Scores on all scales except Learning/*GLr* are significantly lower for children with hearing impairment than for the nonclinical reference group.

Further detailed analyses of the KABC-II data for a subsample of the 27 children with hearing loss were conducted by Hardy-Braz (in press; see also Kaufman & Kaufman, 2004a, pp. 130–131). This subsample of 21 children were identified as having (1) hereditary hearing loss, (2) minor or no comorbid conditions, and (3) at least one parent who communicated in ASL. Of the 21 students, 18 were reported to have a known hereditary etiology. This subsample of 21 hearing-impaired children scored slightly higher on all scale indexes and global scale indexes than the original sample of 27 hearing-impaired children. The mean NVI increased the most notably, from 95.7 to 101.5 (see Figure 6.3)—hereditary hearing loss, no comorbid conditions, a parent who communicated with ASL—likely contributed to the stronger performance on the NVI by the children with hearing loss.

The reasons for these differences may be related to the unique characteristics of this subsample—the presence of additional disabilities, the limited access to fluent communication and information in their home environments, the underlying genetic differences between the groups, the different educational programs, the larger sets of peers groups with whom they have direct communication, or some combination of each of these variables. Further research addressing these variables remains to be done. It does appear that the KABC-II is an instrument that can be of use in the assessment of deaf and hard-of-hearing individuals when appropriate accommodations are made by an experienced and qualified exam-

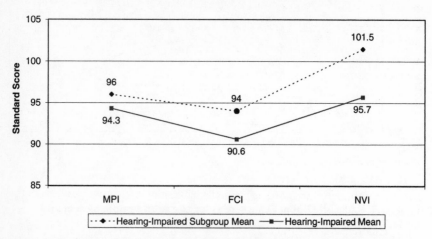

Figure 6.3 Performance on the MPI, FCI, and NVI for the total sample of 27 deaf and hard-of-hearing children and a subsample of 21 children.

Note. The most notable difference between the two samples was in the 5.8-point discrepancy on the NVI.

iner. When assessing these students, examiners should document what accommodations were made along with any modifications and their resulting impact upon the test results.

Autistic Disorder

The research on cognitive functioning of children with Autistic Disorder has focused on verbal versus nonverbal functioning and patterns of specific high and low subtests. Many studies have attempted to determine whether particular patterns of performance are helpful in differentially diagnosing Autistic Disorder from Asperger's Disorder. Before summarizing specific data on cognitive tests, we review the relevant controversy surrounding differentially diagnosing Asperger's Disorder and Autistic Disorder and how it impacts the research on cognitive assessment.

Controversy in the Literature on Autistic Disorder

The controversy surrounding the clinical diagnoses of Autistic Disorder and Asperger's Disorder has impacted the research on cognitive skills of children with these disorders. Numerous papers have questioned whether Asperger's Disorder and high-functioning autism are indeed separate and distinct disorders. Many authors agree that the symptoms of Asperger's Disorder only differ in degree from autism and thereby place Asperger's Disorder simply as another point on the autism spectrum (e.g., Manjiviona & Prior, 1995; Mayes, Calhoun, Crites, 2001; Miller & Ozonoff, 2000). However, other researchers support differentiating Asperger's Disorder and high-functioning autism as clearly distinct disorders (e.g., Klin, Volkmar, Sparrow, Cicchetti, & Rourke, 1995; McLaughlin-Cheng, 1998; Ozonoff, Rogers, & Pennington, 1991). On the other extreme are researchers who definitively state that the *DSM-IV* diagnosis of Asperger's Disorder is "unlikely or impossible" (e.g., Eisenmajer et al., 1996; Manjiviona & Prior, 1995; Mayes et al., 2001).

Key diagnostic differences exist between Asperger's Disorder and Autistic Disorder, although the disorders generally have similar diagnostic criteria in the *DSM-IV*. According to the *DSM-IV-TR* (American Psychiatric Association, 2000), children with Asperger's Disorder do not have communication deficits (including delay of language, inability to initiate or sustain a conversation, repetitive use of language, and symbolic play), and they do not show delays in cognitive development. Also, children with Asperger's Disorder are not attracted to inanimate objects, but typically children with autism are. The following symptoms are displayed in children with either autism or Asperger's Disorder:

- Impairment in social interaction (e.g., impaired nonverbal behavior, impaired ability to develop peer friendships, impaired ability to seek and share interests, lack of social and emotional reciprocity)
- Restricted, repetitive behaviors and interests (e.g., preoccupation with restricted interests; stereotypic, repetitive motor interests; restricted range of interests; interests in nonfunctional activities)

An overriding factor in making differential diagnosis for autistic-spectrum disorders is that Asperger's Disorder is not diagnosed if the criteria are met for Autistic Disorder or another pervasive developmental disorder (American Psychiatric Association, 2000).

Despite the large number of research studies derived from the Asperger's-autism controversy, a consensus about cognitive patterns has not been reached. A variety of methodological issues prevent an accurate comparison of the studies on this topic. For example, diagnostic criteria vary from study to study, some studies utilize subjects with only low cognitive ability whereas others focus on high-functioning individuals, age varies greatly across studies, and dependent measures vary across studies (e.g., WISC-III, K-ABC).

Verbal versus Nonverbal Performance

Recent research on autistic-spectrum disorders reveals extensive variability with regard to verbal-nonverbal discrepancies in IQ. Most of the available research analyzes the WISC-R and WAIS-R, with a handful of WISC-III studies available, along with other instruments such as the K-ABC, the Stanford Binet-Fourth Edition (Binet-4), or the Leiter-R. The recent variance noted in the literature is in contrast to research of a decade or so ago on children with autism (e.g., Lincoln, Courschesne, Kilman, Elmasian, & Allen, 1988; Rumsey, 1992; Yirmiya & Sigman, 1991) that typically reported a consistent pattern of higher nonverbal than verbal ability.

Researchers examine verbal-nonverbal discrepancies in two ways: (1) some studies report verbal-nonverbal IQ discrepancies based on the mean group performance and (2) others report the percentage of subjects that showed a verbal > nonverbal or nonverbal > verbal discrepancy. The size of a discrepancy needed to be considered significant is often based on normative data from a test's manual, but other times a verbal-nonverbal difference of *any* size is reported even if the difference is only 1 point.

The recent literature shows that the greatest proportion of autistic subjects appear to have verbal and nonverbal IQs that are not significantly different from one another (mainly examining high-functioning children with autism). For example, Mayes and Calhoun (2003) found no significant differences in WISC-III Verbal and Performance IQ scores in autistic subjects with either high or low IQs. This finding was further supported by Miller and Ozonoff's (2000) mean WISC-III data.

Other studies have found that about half to three-quarters of the individuals in autistic samples had nonsignificant verbal-nonverbal differences (Gilchrist et al., 2001; Manjiviona & Prior, 1995; Siegel, Minshew, & Goldstein, 1996). On Wechsler tests, Performance (P) > Verbal (V) pattern was the next most commonly reported pattern, ranging from 15% to 33% of the subjects with autism; however, the reverse V > P pattern was observed in 8% to 22% of the subjects (Gilchrist et al., 2001; Manjiviona & Prior, 1995; Siegel et al., 1996). Similar variability in verbal-nonverbal discrepancies has been reported for children with Asperger's Disorder (Barnhill, Hagiwara, Myles, & Simpson, 2000; Gilchrist et al., 2001; Manjiviona & Prior, 1995).

High and Low Subtests

Despite the failure of consistent P > V patterns to emerge in the literature on samples diagnosed with either Autistic or Asperger's Disorder, two Wechsler subtests repeatedly appear as the highest and lowest points in the profiles of these populations: Block Design versus Comprehension. A review of 20 studies with these populations found high Block Design present in 19 of them (Barnhill et al., 2000). In contrast, 18 of the 20 studies that Barnhill (2000) reviewed reported low Comprehension for these same populations. Subsequent studies have also validated the high Block Design—low Comprehension profile with autistic populations (e.g., Goldstein, Beers, Siegel, & Minshew, 2001; Goldstein, Minshew, Allen, & Seaton, 2002; The Psychological Corporation, 2003).

Strong performance on subtests requiring visualization, like Wechsler's Block Design, have been reported on other cognitive batteries. On the original K-ABC, children with Autistic Disorder scored highest on Triangles (Allen, Lincoln, & Kaufman, 1991); on the Leiter-R, the high points on the profiles of children with this disorder were subtests that draw primarily on visualization skills (e.g., Matching and Picture Context; Tsatsanis et al., 2003). In addition, on the Binet-4, the performance of children with Autistic Disorder was strongest on nonverbal subtests such as Pattern Analysis (analogous to Block Design) and Copying (requiring model reproduction with blocks and paper pencil; Mayes & Calhoun, 2003).

Examination of areas of strength and weakness beyond verbal-nonverbal discrepancies in the profiles of children with autism has included analysis of simultaneous and sequential processing. For example, Allen et al. (1991) found that on the original K-ABC, children with autism displayed a relative sequential processing weakness. In contrast, the results suggested that autistic children are more capable of performing effectively when tasks call for processing information in a simultaneous holistic fashion in nonverbal and visual-spatial realms.

KABC-II Findings for Individuals with Autistic Disorder

The KABC-II manual reports findings from a sample of 38 children with Autistic Disorder (not high-functioning autism or Asperger's Disorder). The mean age for the autistic group was 13-3 (ranging from 4-3 to 18-10). The sample was 84% male and 50% Caucasian. The cognitive functioning of the autistic group was in the Below Average to Lower Extreme range of functioning across all domains. Mean KABC-II global scores spanned the narrow range of 66.9 (FCI) to 68.6 (NVI). Their mean index profile ranged from a low of 66.1 on Knowledge/*Gc* to a high of 76.1 on Learning/*Glr*. The comparable mean standard scores on Knowledge/*Gc* and NVI indicate no difference in this sample performance on Verbal versus Nonverbal tasks. However, consistent with the research showing that children with autism perform relatively well on Wechsler's Block Design and K-ABC Triangles, the sample tested on the KABC-II earned their second highest mean scaled score on Triangles (6.1); only their mean score of 6.6 on the supplementary Gestalt Closure subtest was higher. These two areas of relative strength coincide with data on the original K-ABC (Allen et al., 1991).

Rapid Reference 6.2 summarizes the best and worst KABC-II scaled scores for the sample diagnosed with autism. Verbal Knowledge and Riddles were two of the three lowest average scaled scores. These low scores on two Knowledge/ *Gc* subtests is likely a reflection of this population's overall poor communicative and language abilities and general poor achievement in school. This finding is further supported by past research showing that children with Autistic Disorder perform poorly on subtests requiring verbal conceptualization, such as Wechsler's Comprehension (Barnhill et al., 2000; Ehlers, Nyden, & Gillberg, 1997). Unlike these two low Knowledge/*Gc* subtests, Expressive Vocabulary was not one of the lowest scores for the group, on average—perhaps because Expressive Vocabulary requires a simple naming of a pictured object and doesn't require a higher level of abstract thinking or verbal conceptualization.

Individuals diagnosed with Autistic Disorder performed very poorly on Rover, a Simultaneous/*Gv* subtest that requires children to find the quickest path for a toy dog to reach his bone on a checkerboardlike grid. Past research has shown that children with Autistic Disorder typically perform relatively well on tasks that require simultaneous processing and spatial visualization (Allen et al., 1991; Tsatsanis et al., 2003). Although Rover is a Simultaneous/*Gv* subtest, it also places heavy demands on executive functioning and deductive reasoning, abilities

≡ Rapid Reference 6.2

Children with Autistic Disorder: Lowest and Highest Mean KABC-II Subtest Scaled Scores

	Scaled Score
Lowest Subtests	
Rover	3.5
Verbal Knowledge	3.9
Riddles	4.0
Highest Subtests	
Atlantis	5.9
Triangles	6.1
Gestalt Closure	6.6

Source. Mean Fluid Crystallized Index (FCI) and scaled scores are from the *KABC-II manual* (Table 8.35).
Note. FCI = 66.9; Mental Processing Index (MPI) = 68.1; *N* = 38.

that may have not been as well developed as visualization in the KABC-II sample of individuals with autism.

Perhaps the most interesting finding in the KABC-II study with individuals diagnosed with autism is their relative strength on the Learning/*Glr* scale (index = 76.1). Indeed, the sample earned its highest standard score on the supplementary Delayed Recall scale (standard score = 82.8, a standard deviation higher than their mean MPI of 68.1). These scores indicate that the children with autism were able to learn new information that was taught by the examiner during the evaluation and that they were able to retain that information after an interval of about 20 minutes, despite the interference of being administered other cognitive tasks. There are four noteworthy aspects of this finding of relative strength in the learning and retention of newly learned information: (1) the component subtests involve language as well as visual stimuli, with Rebus requiring both verbalization and the learning of a new pictorial language; (2) most comprehensive batteries that have been administered to individuals with autism—such as Wechsler's scales, the Binet-4, and the original K-ABC—do not measure learning ability, so the present results are suggestive of a previously unknown cognitive strength for these children and adolescents; (3) the learning of new information ties directly to the classroom such that these results may provide specific ideas for the educational intervention of individuals with autism; and (4) another sample of children who traditionally perform relatively poorly on tests that emphasize language—those with hearing loss—also had relative strengths in learning (mean index = 101.6) and delayed recall (mean standard score = 101.3).

Previous research has shown a pattern of stronger simultaneous processing than sequential processing in children with Autistic Disorder (Allen et al., 1991), but that pattern was not found on the KABC-II. Autistic children earned similar mean indexes of about 70 on the Sequential/*Gsm* and Simultaneous/*Gv* scales. At least two differences in the studies may explain the difference in the findings: (1) the autistic group in the original K-ABC study was higher functioning than the KABC-II sample (Mental Processing Composite of 81.3 versus MPI of 68.1), and (2) the Simultaneous Processing subtests have changed considerably from the K-ABC to the KABC-II (Matrix Analogies, Spatial Memory, and Photo Series were removed; Rover and Block Counting were added). Indeed, the correlation between the K-ABC Simultaneous Processing scale and the KABC-II Simultaneous/*Gv* scale is .62.

Clinical Implications for Testing Children with Autistic Disorder

As our summary of previous cognitive research indicates, children with Autistic Disorder vary extensively with regard to their performance on Verbal, Nonverbal, Sequential, and Simultaneous tasks. Despite the fact that subtest patterns such as high Block Design/Triangles versus low Comprehension remain prevalent across samples of individuals with autistic-spectrum disorders, general patterns on tests measuring cognitive ability have not adequately been shown to differentially diagnose autistic-spectrum disorders. However, some children falling within the autistic spectrum by definition have more difficulties in communication than others (e.g., classic autism versus Asperger's Disorder or high-functioning autism). Such children with difficulties in the communication domain will benefit from an assessment instrument such as the Nonverbal scale of the KABC-II that evaluates abilities without demanding a significant amount of verbal skill. Yet even scales that require language abilities, such as the new Learning/*Glr* scale on the KABC-II, might help uncover hidden areas of strength in children with known or suspected autism.

The bottom line is that intellectual evaluations of individuals with Autistic Disorder are invaluable for educational planning (Kaufman & Lichtenberger, 2002). Thus, as clinicians, we can certainly use individuals' data from a measure such as the KABC-II Nonverbal Scale, Learning/*Glr* scale, and Delayed Recall scale to help develop the most appropriate interventions for treating the deficits of autism-spectrum disorders.

Speech and Language Disorders

Most often, children brought in for assessment of speech and language disorders are toddlers or preschoolers, the ages at which more complex language is emerging. In fact, about 3 to 10% of preschool children are estimated to have some form of developmental speech or language disorder (Ottem, 1999). Thus, preschool children that are brought in for an assessment are often referred because of concerns about their delayed speech or language skills (Field, 1987). By school age, however, a smaller number of children are estimated to have language impairment (only 3 to 5%; Aram & Hall, 1989).

Several terms are used to describe children who have difficulties with speech and language. For example, *specific language impairment* (SLI) is a term used to describe children who have age-appropriate nonverbal cognitive ability in combination with atypical expressive and receptive language development (Warner & Nelson, 2000). *Slow expressive language development* (SELD) and *specific language impairment—expressive* (SLI-E) are terms used to describe children who have age-appropriate cognitive and receptive language skills but whose production of words and word combinations are delayed or are especially marked. The DSM-IV-TR (American Psychiatric Association, 2000) requires the following for the diagnosis of language impairment: (1) significantly low scores on standardized language testing (i.e., below measures of their nonverbal intellectual capacity); (2) these low scores cannot be accounted for by other disabilities such as mental retardation; pervasive developmental disorders, such as autism; and physical disabilities, such as hearing impairment; and (3) the language difficulties must significantly interfere with academic functioning or communication ability. However, the operational definitions for diagnosing speech or language impairment differ according to local and state policies. Researchers and clinicians also vary in the labels and diagnostic criteria that they use for language impairments. Regardless of the specific diagnostic criteria or label used for a language impairment, individual examiners must select and interpret cognitive and assessment instruments to develop the most accurate understanding of a child's development.

Research Findings for Individuals with Speech and Language Disorders

Although it seems logical that children with speech and language disorders would perform significantly better on the Nonverbal portion of cognitive tests than the Verbal portion, a pattern of a strong dissociation between verbal and nonverbal skills is sometimes, but not always, evident in this population.

Some samples of children diagnosed with language impairment have demonstrated substantial (.5 to 1 SD) Nonverbal > Verbal discrepancies on the WISC-R (Allen et al., 1991; Doll & Boren, 1993; Rose et al., 1992), WISC-III (Doll & Boren, 1993; Phelps, Leguori, Nisewaner, & Parker, 1993) and WISC-IV (The Psychological Corporation, 2003). In contrast, a variety of other samples of children with language disorders have shown very small discrepancies (about 2 to 4 points) between Verbal and Nonverbal abilities on the Wechsler and Binet scales (e.g., Krassowski & Plante, 1997; Lichtenberger & Kaufman, 2004; Roid, 2003; Vig & Jedrysek, 1996).

Although the literature does not consistently show a pattern of large Nonverbal > Verbal discrepancy in the performance of children with language impairment on cognitive tests, there is a general consensus among clinicians that Nonverbal measures of cognitive ability more fairly assess the cognitive abilities of these children than do Verbal measures (Phelps, 1998; Warner & Nelson, 2000). However, the range of scores on Nonverbal tests varies widely from sample to sample and test to test. For example, some researchers have reported Nonverbal scores for this population that are more than 2 standard deviations below normal on the UNIT and Leiter-R (Farrell & Phelps, 2000), whereas others have reported standard scores in the 80 to 90 range on the original K-ABC Nonverbal Scale (Allen et al., 1991; Phelps et al., 1993), DAS Nonverbal Scale (Riccio, Ross, Boan, Jemison, & Houston, 1997), and Leiter (Cohen, Hall, & Riccio, 1997).

Here, too, however, the findings have not been consistent. Some samples of children with language impairment performed relatively well (standard scores of 94 to 103) on the original K-ABC Nonverbal Scale (Kennedy & Hiltonsmith, 1988; Swisher & Plante, 1993).

Because the original K-ABC deemphasized verbal knowledge and focused on mental processing, it gained popularity in assessing children with language disorders (Allen et al., 1991; Ricciardi, Voelker, Carter, & Shore, 1991). The K-ABC's subtests also minimally emphasize speed (using liberal time limits or no limits at all), which is valuable because children with language disorders typically have slower than normal reaction time and processing speed (Edwards & Lahey, 1996; Johnston & Ellis Weismer, 1983; Lahey, Edwards, & Munson, 2001).

Research on children with language impairments and the original K-ABC has demonstrated its usefulness for this population. The K-ABC and McCarthy Scales (McCarthy, 1972) were administered to a sample of 14 preschoolers identified as language impaired (Ricciardi et al., 1991). Unlike the K-ABC, the McCarthy's General Cognitive Index (GCI) emphasizes language competencies and acquired information. Because of the test content, the children with language impairment struggled more on the McCarthy GCI (mean = 64.8) than on the K-ABC Mental Processing Composite (mean = 79.2). This difference in performance is especially notable because the Flynn effect (Flynn, 1987) would have predicted that the K-ABC's more recent norms would have led to lower scores on the K-ABC than on the McCarthy.

Profiles of the K-ABC's scales have also been examined in language impaired samples to evaluate the difference between sequential and simultaneous processing. As with Nonverbal-Verbal discrepancies, the results of studies of mental processing of information yielded widely divergent findings. For example, Allen et al. (1991) found a 15-point discrepancy in favor of simultaneous over sequential processing in a sample of 20 children with language impairment (mean age 9-4), but Riccardi et al. (1991) revealed a negligible 1.5-point difference for their sample of children with language impairment.

Implications for Children with Language Impairment Tested on the KABC-II
The assets of the original K-ABC for assessing children with language impairments continue to be positive points for assessing this population with the KABC-II. The KABC-II deemphasizes language and acquired knowledge in the Luria model, the model that the Kaufmans recommend be administered to children with receptive, expressive, or mixed receptive-expressive language disorders. And if the examiner believes that the MPI yielded by the Luria model

unfairly penalizes children with moderate to severe language disorders, then the NVI provides an excellent way to assess these children's global cognitive functioning.

The Knowledge/*Gc* subtests (Riddles, Verbal Knowledge, and Expressive Vocabulary) are not likely to reflect the cognitive abilities of children with language impairments but are more likely to be a reflection of their areas of impairment. Nonetheless, when these subtests are administered as supplements to the MPI or NVI, examiners often will obtain beneficial additional information. For example, on tasks requiring simple verbal expression, such as naming a pictured object (Expressive Vocabulary) or requiring receptive understanding (Verbal Knowledge), children with language impairments do not always perform poorly (Lichtenberger & Kaufman, 2004). In contrast, on tasks that require more extensive processing of language and verbal reasoning (e.g., Riddles), children with language impairments may struggle. These differences in performance on the various verbally laden *Gc* tests may provide good behavioral observations and clinical information that will be useful for interpreting a wide range of the spectrum of abilities of children diagnosed with language disorders.

In addition to minimal focus on verbal knowledge in the Luria model, speed of processing is not emphasized in the KABC-II. Three subtests on the KABC-II require the recording of response time (Triangles, Pattern Reasoning, and Story Completion). On these three subtests, children and adolescents aged 7 to 18 can obtain one or two extra points on each item that they complete rapidly. For children with language impairments (who historically have struggled on tasks that require rapid processing), examiners should select the alternative option offered by the KABC-II, which permits scoring these three subtests based only on correct answers (with time points excluded). Scaled scores are then based on this special procedure, deemphasizing processing speed for children who might be unfairly penalized by the need to respond quickly.

Future research is needed to determine if a sequential < simultaneous pattern will emerge on the KABC-II for children with language impairment as it did on the K-ABC (Riccardi et al., 1991). Some of the subtests that are included on the KABC-II Simultaneous/*Gv* scale are different from those on the original K-ABC (e.g., Conceptual Thinking, Rover, and Block Counting are new, replacing subtests such as Matrix Analogies and Spatial Memory). In addition, verbal versus nonverbal discrepancies can be evaluated by conducting the Nonverbal Ability versus Verbal Ability planned comparison in Step 5 of the interpretive system (see Chapter 3). Validation studies are needed with samples of children and adolescents with diagnosed language disorders.

ASSESSMENT OF MENTAL RETARDATION

A variety of genetic syndromes have been identified that have Mental Retardation as part of their phenotype. For example, Down syndrome, Williams syndrome, Turner syndrome, Fragile X syndrome, Phenylketonuria (PKU), and autism are a few of the syndromes associated with Mental Retardation (Durkin & Stein, 1996). In addition to genetic causes, prenatal, perinatal, and postnatal infections can cause Mental Retardation (e.g., Rubella, toxoplasmosis, HIV, syphilis). Prenatal exposure to toxins such as alcohol or ionizing radiation can lead to mental retardation. In addition, traumatic brain injury or anoxia (lack of oxygen) during birth due to prolonged or obstructed labor can cause Mental Retardation. However, regardless of the etiology of the Mental Retardation, the key criteria for diagnosis of Mental Retardation are twofold: specific deficits in cognitive and impairment in adaptive functioning. Both the DSM-IV-TR (American Psychiatric Association, 2000) and the American Association on Mental Retardation (AAMR) (Luckasson et al., 2002) require that symptoms of Mental Retardation are present before age 18. The criterion of subaverage intellectual functioning is defined as an IQ of approximately 70 or below. The criterion of deficits in adaptive functioning requires impairment in two or more of the following areas: communication, self-care, home loving, social interaction, functioning academic skills, work, leisure, health, and safety. Both the DSM-IV-TR and the AAMR criteria emphasize that standardized tests include measurement error that should be considered in the diagnostic process, along with using careful clinical judgment.

Some research has shown correlations between specific causes of Mental Retardation and phenotypic expression (Durkin & Stein, 1996). For example, Hodapp, Leckman, Dykens, and Sparrow (1992) found distinctive cognitive profiles associated with Down syndrome and Fragile X syndrome. Bellugi and colleagues have found distinct cognitive profiles associated with Williams syndrome and Down syndrome (Bellugi, Lichtenberger, Jones, Lai, & St. George, 2000). However, the etiology of many cases of Mental Retardation is unknown. The cause of Severe or Profound Mental Retardation is more frequently known than the cause of Mild Mental Retardation (Durkin & Stein, 1996). Thus, many of the research studies on the cognitive patterns of individuals with Mental Retardation do not provide the etiology of the subjects' delays, and, indeed, lump together a variety of children diagnosed simply with Mental Retardation.

Research with children who are mentally retarded (generally groups with mixed etiology or unknown etiology) has revealed little variability between scales. For example, equally depressed performance on Wechsler Verbal and Performance scales is typical for this population (Slate, 1995; The Psychological Corporation, 2002; Spruill, 1998; Wechsler, 1991). On the Binet-4, Verbal Reasoning and Abstract/Visual Reasoning Area scores are often equally depressed (Bower & Hayes, 1995), and on the Binet-5, mean Verbal and Nonverbal IQs were virtually identical for individuals ages 3 to 25 with Mental Retardation (Roid, 2003, Table 4.12). The Cognitive Assessment System (CAS; Naglieri & Das, 1997) also revealed little variability in its scales for children with Mental Retardation. In addition, discrepancies between language and cognitive performance in young children with Mental Retardation do not usually add prognostic information beyond that contained in the global measure of cognitive ability (Vig, Kaminer, & Jedrysek, 1987).

Although characteristic Wechsler profiles for children with Mental Retardation (nonspecific etiology) have not been consistently reported (Spruill, 1998), an analysis of 10 WISC-R studies revealed that children with Mental Retardation had the most difficulty (i.e., scored the lowest) on tests of Crystallized Knowledge, including Vocabulary, Information, Arithmetic, and Similarities (Harrison, 1990). In contrast, these children tested with the WISC-R had the highest scores on Picture Completion and Object Assembly. However, that pattern reported on the older WISC-R did not consistently characterize samples of children with Mental Retardation assessed with the WISC-III or WPPSI-III (Bolen, 1998; Canivez & Watkins, 2001; Lichtenberger & Kaufman, 2004). Further, although the FSIQ has been shown to be adequately stable in mentally retarded populations, subtest stability, and stability of Verbal-Performance discrepancies has been reported as inadequate (Canivez & Watkins, 2001).

When examining etiology-specific groups with Mental Retardation, some patterns on cognitive tests have been reported. For example, on the K-ABC, small samples of children with Fragile X syndrome and Down syndrome were found to have higher Simultaneous Processing scores than Sequential Processing scores (Hodapp et al., 1992). Hand Movements was a relative strength for children with Down syndrome and a relative weakness for children with Fragile X. However, in groups with Mental Retardation with unknown or mixed etiology, K-ABC Simultaneous and Sequential scores have been approximately equal (Kaufman & Kaufman, 1983; Obrzut, Obrzut, & Shaw, 1984). Naglieri (1985) also reported that K-ABC Simultaneous-Sequential discrepancies for children with Mental Retardation are not significantly different from those found in the normative group.

KABC-II Findings on Mental Retardation

The *KABC-II Manual* (Kaufman & Kaufman, 2004a) reports the results of a study of 42 children diagnosed with Mild Mental Retardation. The mean age of the group was 11-2, and their mean FCI was 64.5 (SD = 13.6). This SD is larger than is typically found in samples diagnosed with Mental Retardation. In general, SDs for such samples are restricted in range in large part because strict cut-off scores (e.g., < 70) are used to make the diagnosis. All children in the KABC-II sample had a diagnosis of Mental Retardation when initially assessed (typically on a Wechsler scale). When previously diagnosed children are assessed again, their scores will tend to regress to the mean, especially when a different instrument is used from the one used for the diagnosis. Hence, the SDs on the FCI and other KABC-II indexes are larger than usual.

Like the group's mean FCI, their mean MPI (64.8) and NVI (65.6) were also in the mid-60s, consistent with expectations (see Figure 6.4). The group's scale profile showed some variability with mean indexes ranging from about 65 on the two problem-solving scales (Simultaneous/*Gv* and Planning/*Gf*) to 72.4 on the Learning/*Glr* scale. The group's mean NVI of 65.6 was slightly lower than its mean Knowledge/*Gc* Index (69.1), indicating about equal functioning on the traditional Nonverbal-Verbal comparison.

Although specific subtest patterns have not historically been able to characterize the performance of children with Mental Retardation, we examined the highest and lowest KABC-II subtests for these children (see Rapid Reference

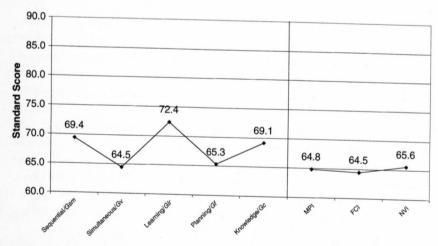

Figure 6.4 Mean KABC-II Global Scale scores for children with mild Mental Retardation (*N* = 42).

Note. Children with mental retardation perform substantially below nonclinical samples and have their worst performance on Simultaneous/*Gv* and Planning/*Gf*, but their best on Learning/*Glr*. Performances on the MPI, FCI, and NVI are approximately equal for this sample.

≡*Rapid Reference 6.3*

Children with Mild Mental Retardation: Lowest and Highest Mean KABC-II Subtest Scaled Scores

	Scaled Score
Lowest Subtests	
Rover	3.4
Pattern Reasoning	3.9
Triangles	4.1
Highest Subtests	
Expressive Vocabulary	5.6
Gestalt Closure	5.7
Atlantis	5.7

Source. Mean Fluid Crystallized Index (FCI) and scaled scores are from the *KABC-II manual* (Table 8.34).

Note. FCI = 64.5; Mental Processing Index (MPI) = 64.8; N = 42.

6.3). Two Simultaneous/*Gv* subtests were among the three lowest for this group: Rover and Triangles. Although both Rover and Triangles measure visual processing, Rover has distinct executive functioning and fluid reasoning components, exemplified by one of its CHC narrow abilities (General Sequential Reasoning, also referred to as deductive reasoning). Also among the three lowest subtests was Pattern Reasoning, a Planning/*Gf* subtest that also measures higher-level executive functioning and fluid reasoning abilities, and assesses the CHC narrow ability of Induction (or inductive reasoning).

In contrast, the three highest subtests for this group of children with Mental Retardation called on acquired knowledge, memory, and visual closure speed. The highest subtests came from three separate scales: Expressive Vocabulary (Knowledge/*Gc*), Gestalt Closure (Simultaneous/*Gv*), and Atlantis (Learning/ *Glr*).

Some of the limitations that were noted for using the first edition K-ABC with children who have Mental Retardation were addressed in the creation of the KABC-II. For example, Kamphaus and Reynolds (1987) noted that the K-ABC lacked enough easy items for developmentally delayed children, creating a poor floor for these children. Also, the K-ABC's Mental Processing Composite did not extend below a standard score of 55, which made the diagnosis of moderate (IQ range: 35 to 55) or severe (IQ range: 20 to 40) levels of Mental Retardation difficult. The KABC-II extended the floor on many subtests and allows out-of-level testing for children with known or suspected cognitive delays (see Chapter 2 for more information). The MPI, FCI, and NVI all yield scores that are 3 to 4 SDs below the normative mean of 100 (the lowest standard scores range from 40 to 49). The five indexes yield equally strong floors at all ages, with the lowest standard scores ranging from 40 to 51 (see Rapid Reference 6.4). These floors are lower than the original K-ABC, making it useful for diagnosing children with more extreme levels of Mental Retardation.

Another benefit of using the KABC-II in assessing children with Mental Retardation is the availability of sample and teaching items as well as the reduced emphasis on verbal expression and school-learned knowledge. In addition to ensuring that children understand a task, teaching items allow examiners to see how children respond to instruction, which is useful in developing educational recommendations. Response to feedback is also a built-in aspect of the Learning/ *Glr* subtests. During the administration of Atlantis, the child is corrected every time a mistake is made. On Rebus, although mistakes are not corrected, virtually all symbol-word associations are presented a second time to ensure that children are able to correct any mistakes they might have made.

≡ *Rapid Reference 6.4*

KABC-II Index Floors

Lowest Possible Standard Score

Age	Gsm	Gv	Glr	Gf	Gc	MPI	FCI	NVI
13–18	49	50	48	51	48	48	47	47
10–12	49	43	48	51	48	43	40	47
7–9	49	48	48	51	44	44	45	40
6	49	52	48	—	50	48	49	46
5	49	40	48	—	50	40	40	40
4	49	40	48	—	50	41	40	40
3	—	—	—	—	—	40	40	40

Source. Data are from the *KABC-II manual* (Kaufman & Kaufman, 2004a, Table D.2).

Note. Dashes indicate that standard scores are not available at that age for that index.

USE OF KABC-II FOR ATTENTION DEFICIT/HYPERACTIVITY DISORDER (ADHD) ASSESSMENT

The research published on children with Attention-Deficit/Hyperactivity Disorder (ADHD) has proliferated over the past couple of decades. Indeed, when we searched for ADHD just in the PsycInfo database, we found about 5,500 articles. The goal of this chapter is not to provide a critical review of all of the literature on this topic but to glean important facts relevant to assessing children with ADHD.

Prior to delving into assessment of children with ADHD, it is important to understand the primary symptoms of the disorder. The DSM-IV-TR (American Psychiatric Association, 2000) is used by many clinicians and researchers when differentially diagnosing ADHD from other clinical disorders. Two broad domains of symptoms exist for children with ADHD: inattention and hyperactivity-impulsivity. (The Don't Forget box lists the symptoms of these domains.) Inattention is described as difficulty persistently putting forth effort and difficulty sustaining attention. Being distracted by extraneous or extratask stimulation is less of a documented problem for children with ADHD (Barkley, 1998). Parents and teachers describe symptoms of inattention with terms or phrases such as *daydreams, can't concentrate, doesn't seem to listen,* and *fails to finish tasks* (Barkley, Du-Paul, & McMurray, 1990). *Impulsivity* is described as an undercontrol of behavior and an inability to delay a response or defer gratification (Barkley, 1997). *Hyperactivity* is described as excessive of developmentally inappropriate levels of activity, whether motor or vocal (e.g., restlessness, fidgeting, and unnecessary gross motor movements). Depending on the number and type of symptoms, ADHD may be subtyped into three categories: (1) predominantly inattentive type, (2) predominantly hyperactive-impulsive type, or (3) combined type.

The presentation of ADHD symptoms can vary across the age span, with some symptoms becoming more prominent at certain developmental levels (Conners & Jett, 2001). For example, normal three- and four-year-old children have some inattention and overactivity, but those with ADHD have much more severe symptoms that may cause an above average amount of conflict between the parent and child. (The Don't Forget box lists significant diagnostic signs at different age levels.) In middle childhood, children show perhaps the strongest signs of ADHD. The demands of school are stronger, and children with ADHD may begin to experience more academic and social failure during this time. In adolescence, overt hyperactivity decreases, but teens may experience more inner restlessness (Conners et al., 1997). In addition, although physical impulsivity decreases, poor attention and cognitive and verbal impulsivity may be problematic.

DON'T FORGET

Symptoms of Inattention and Hyperactivity-Impulsivity

Symptoms of Inattention	Symptoms of Hyperactivity-Impulsivity
• Often fails to give close attention to details or makes careless mistakes in schoolwork, work, or other activities • Often has difficulty sustaining attention in tasks or play activities • Often does not seem to listen when spoken to directly • Often does not follow through on instructions and fails to finish school work, chores, or duties in the workplace (not due to oppositional behavior or failure to understand instructions) • Often has difficulty organizing tasks and activities • Often avoids, dislikes, or is reluctant to engage in tasks that require sustained mental effort (such as schoolwork or homework) • Often loses things necessary for tasks or activities (e.g., toys, school assignments, pencils, books, or tools) • Is often easily distracted by extraneous stimuli • Is often forgetful in daily activities	**Hyperactivity** • Often fidgets with hands or feet or squirms in seat • Often leaves seat in classroom or in other situations in which remaining seated is expected • Often runs about or climbs excessively in situations in which it is inappropriate (in adolescents or adults, may be limited to subjective feelings of restlessness) • Often has difficulty playing or engaging in leisure activities quietly • Is often "on the go" or often acts as if "driven by a motor" • Often talks excessively **Impulsivity** • Often blurts out answers before questions have been completed • Often has difficulty awaiting turn • Often interrupts or intrudes on others (e.g., butts into conversations or games)

Source. From the Diagnostic and Statistical Manual of Mental Disorders—Fourth Edition—Text Revision (DSM-IV-TR; American Psychiatric Association, 2000).

DON'T FORGET

ADHD Presentation in Preschool, Middle Childhood, and Adolescence

Preschool Presentation	Middle Childhood Presentation	Adolescent Presentation
• Motor restlessness (climbs on and gets into things constantly)	• Easily distracted	• Discipline problems and family conflict
• Insatiable curiosity	• Engages in off-task behaviors	• Anger and quickly fluctuating emotions
• Vigorous and sometimes destructive play	• Unable to sustain attention	• Difficulty with authority
• Demanding of parental attention	• Impulsive	• Significant lags in academic performance
• Low-level of compliance	• Aggressive	• Poor peer relationships
• Excessive temper tantrums	• Acts like the "class clown"	• Poor self-esteem
• Difficulty completing developmental tasks (such as toilet training)	• Has increasing difficulties with peer relationships	• Hopelessness
• Decreased and/or restless sleep		• Lethargy; lack of motivation to achieve or exert effort
• Delays in motor or language development		• Driving mishaps, speeding, automobile damage
• Family difficulties		

Source: Information was adapted from Conners and Jett (2001).

Note. The symptoms listed for each age group are not necessary or sufficient for meeting diagnostic criteria, rather they are to give an understanding of how the clinical presentation of ADHD may change during development

In an assessment of a child with ADHD, the most important facets of the evaluation address the behavioral symptoms discussed in the preceding paragraphs. Typically a clinical interview and behavioral rating scales completed by parents, teachers, and the child are the main methods for collecting data about the ADHD symptoms. However, when possible, it is important to supplement these pieces of data with objective assessments of behavior and attention, such as those obtained from direct behavioral observations during testing. Such observations are not essential to making a definitive diagnosis, but they can yield further information about the presence and severity of cognitive impairments and can lead to additional treatment planning suggestions (Barkley, 1998).

In addition to determining the presence or absence of ADHD and differentially diagnosing ADHD from other psychiatric disorders, an evaluation will delineate the types of interventions needed to help ameliorate a child's psychological, academic, and social impairments. By identifying a child's strengths and weaknesses, you can consider how strengths and weaknesses may be used in developing a treatment plan.

Data from cognitive tests are central to an assessment of a child referred for an evaluation of ADHD, as it is useful in determining a child's strengths and weaknesses. However, cognitive tests have not reliably been able to discriminate groups of children with ADHD from normal children or children with reading disabilities (Barkley, 1998; Schwean & Saklofske, 1998). For example, although group differences have been found on Wechsler's Freedom from Distractibility factor, this factor has not consistently distinguished children with ADHD from those without (Anastopoulos, Spitso, & Maher, 1994; Barkley et al., 1990, Golden, 1996). While cognitive tests have not been shown to be of value in detecting ADHD characteristics (Barkley, 1998), data from these batteries can establish the severity of a child's impairment and can help rule in or rule out other possible explanations for presenting complaints.

Specific learning disabilities are often comorbid with ADHD, so cognitively oriented tests can help to identify when such disorders are coexisting. Generally, children with ADHD are more likely to be behind in their intellectual development than normal children, scoring an average of 7 to 15 points below control groups on standardized IQ tests (Faraone, Biederman, Lehman, and Spencer, 1993; Fischer, Barkley, Fletcher, & Smallish, 1990). However, children with ADHD represent the entire spectrum of intelligence, with IQs ranging from the Superior to those Well Below Average (Barkley, 1998; Kaplan, Crawford, Dewey, & Fisher, 2000). When children with ADHD perform poorly on a cognitive battery, you must try to factor in how much of their depressed scores were due to their inattentive-impulsive response style. In addition, because learning disabilities are often comorbid with

ADHD, lower IQs may be related as well to coexisting learning disorders (Bohline, 1985; Seidman, Biederman, Monuteaux, Doyle, & Faraone, 2001).

Estimates of the rates of learning disabilities coexisting with ADHD reveal that 8 to 39% of children with ADHD have a reading disability, 12 to 30% have a math disability, and 12 to 27% have a spelling disorder (Frick et al., 1991; Faraone et al., 1993; Barkley, 1990). Even when diagnosed learning disabilities are not present in children with ADHD, children with this disorder tend to struggle academically. Because of their inattentive, impulsive, and restless behavior in the classroom, their work productivity, accuracy, and level of mastery is depressed. Studies have shown that when the ADHD symptoms are treated with stimulant medication, significant improvements in academic productivity and accuracy occur (Barkley, 1997; Rapport, DuPaul, Stoner, & Jones, 1986). However, about 56% of children with ADHD may require academic tutoring to help improve classroom performance (Barkley, 1998).

In addition to the global constructs of intelligence and academic functioning, more specific cognitive abilities have been studied in children with ADHD. Working memory and planning are two that are of particular interest to clinicians and researchers that work with ADHD children. There is strong evidence that children with ADHD have deficits in working memory. These deficits are especially evident when large and complex amounts of verbal information must be held in mind (Seidman, Biederman, Faraone, & Milberger, 1995; Seidman, Biederman, Faraone, Weber, & Ouellette, 1997). Although the research is not as consistent as with verbal working memory, nonverbal working memory has been shown to be deficient in some studies of children with ADHD. For example on the K-ABC Hand Movements subtest, children with ADHD are less proficient at imitating the sequences of motor gestures than normal children (Breen, 1989; Grodzinsky & Diamond, 1992; Mariani & Barkley, 1997). Initially, the K-ABC Hand Movements subtest was found to be particularly useful for the assessment of children with ADHD in research conducted by Barkley's (1990) doctoral students: "Its sensitivity to ADHD may rest in the well-known fine motor coordination difficulties often seen in these children as well as in their inattention to the task itself, especially as sequences of movements become progressively longer" (p. 333). In Barkley's (1997) hybrid model of ADHD, low scores on Hand Movements were hypothesized to occur because of executive functioning deficits in working memory; research inspired by Barkley's theory has produced both positive results (Denny, 1997) and negative results (Cantrill, 2003; Perugini, 1999) on the discriminative value of Hand Movements for ADHD assessment. Ultimately, Barkley (1998) concluded that Hand Movements has not been able to reliably classify children with ADHD from those without.

Deficits in hindsight, forethought, and planning ability have also been noted for children with ADHD (Brady & Denckla, 1994; Pennington et al., 1993; Weyandt & Willis, 1994). Thus, these types of deficits have been examined to determine how well they can predict ADHD. For example, in a study using a battery of neuropsychological tests to assess frontal/executive functioning (Perugini, Harvery, Lovejoy, Sandstrom, & Webb, 2000), an impaired score on the battery of tests had an overall predictive power of .71 in positively identifying children with ADHD. However an unimpaired score could not reliably rule out the disorder, as was found in previous studies (Doyle, Biederman, Seidman, Weber, & Faraone, 2000; Grodzinsky & Barkley, 1999; Lovejoy et al., 1999; Matier-Sharma, Perachio, Newcorn, Sharma, & Halperin, 1995). Mahone and colleagues (2002) found that measures of executive functioning discriminated children with ADHD from those without at Average IQ levels, but the executive functioning measures poorly discriminated ADHD from control groups among children with Above Average IQ. Because of the relationship between executive functioning and intelligence, researchers have concluded that executive functioning should be considered relative to overall ability level, not in isolation, when studying ADHD (Denckla, 1994; Mahone et al., 2002; Murphy, Barkley, & Bush, 2001).

KABC-II FINDINGS ON ADHD

The KABC-II was administered to 56 children diagnosed with ADHD according to DSM-IV-TR criteria. The sample was 70% male and 73% Caucasian, with a mean age of 5-11. The ADHD sample was compared to a group of nonclinical children who were matched on sex, ethnicity, and parent education.

This sample of children with ADHD performed about equally well on all KABC-II indexes. They averaged about 93 on the MPI and FCI, with scale indexes spanning the narrow range from 92.5 on Simultaneous/Gv to 95.9 on both Learning/Glr and Knowledge/Gc. Children with ADHD scored significantly lower than nonclinical children on all scales. The Kaufmans' emphasis when revising the K-ABC and developing the second edition was to assess high-level cognitive ability on virtually all Core subtests, with an emphasis on working memory and executive functioning. Indeed, working memory is needed to succeed on the subtests that constitute each of the scales: It is needed to cope with the color interference task on Word Order (Sequential/Gsm); to code and store the paired associations on the Learning/Glr subtests; to permit children to generate and select hypotheses and perform other executive functions on the Simultaneous/Gv and Planning/Gf subtests (Rover, Pattern Reasoning, and Story Completion);

and to enable children to integrate different aspects of a construct to solve Riddles items (a Knowledge/*Gc* subtest).

Given the deficits in the areas of executive functioning and working memory for children with ADHD (Brady & Denckla, 1994; Mahone et al., 2002; Perugini et al., 2000; Seidman et al., 1995; Seidman et al., 1997), children with ADHD may experience difficulty on all of the KABC-II scales, leading to a pattern of uniform deficits (relative to the normal control group) on all of the KABC-II scales.

Similar to the small amount of variability on the five scales, the variability among the subtests was also minimal. Only 1.2 points separated the highest and lowest subtests for this sample (these are listed in Rapid Reference 6.5). Mean scaled scores for the children with ADHD ranged from a low of 8.4 on Block Counting to a high of 9.6 on Gestalt Closure. All of the Sequential/*Gsm* subtests were among the lowest scores for the group, along with Rover.

≣Rapid Reference 6.5

Children with Attention-Deficit Hyperactivity Disorder: Lowest and Highest Mean KABC-II Subtest Scaled Scores

	Scaled Score
Lowest Subtests	
Block Counting	8.4
Number Recall	8.8
Word Order	8.8
Hand Movements	8.8
Rover	8.8
Highest Subtests	
Triangles	9.3
Rebus	9.3
Pattern Reasoning	9.3
Expressive Vocabulary	9.3
Verbal Knowledge	9.4
Gestalt Closure	9.6

Source. Mean Fluid Crystallized Index (FCI) and scaled scores are from the *KABC-II manual* (Table 8.36).

Note. FCI = 93; Mental Processing Index (MPI) = 92.5; N = 56.

Whether future KABC-II studies of children and adolescents diagnosed with ADHD will display characteristic profiles or will continue to demonstrate flat profiles is unknown. However, as Barkley (1998) has emphasized, cognitive test profiles have not proven especially useful for ADHD diagnosis. What comprehensive test batteries offer most to clinicians are standardized observations of how children approach different tasks, especially if they have to cope with attentional problems.

The KABC-II, by virtue of its emphasis on executive functioning and working memory, offers clinicians a rich source of behavioral observations. In particular, Rover, the two Learning/*Glr* subtests, and the two Planning/*Gf* subtests put children with ADHD into sink or swim situations in which they must employ working memory and cope with a bombardment of stimuli while solving each item. The supplementary Delayed Recall scale affords the opportunity to assess how a child's attentional problems might interfere with retention of newly learned information about 20 minutes later in the evaluation (i.e., do the intervening tasks make it unusually difficult for individuals with attentional problems to retain the paired associations?). In addition, the KABC-II offers a structured method for observing behaviors (via the Qualitative Indicators, or QIs), which should be a useful tool for assessing children with ADHD.

All of these aspects of the KABC-II suggest its value for specific *individuals* referred for a known or suspected attentional disorder. Nonetheless, much additional *group* data based on samples of children diagnosed with ADHD are needed to facilitate and more fully understand the applications of the KABC-II in clinical practice. Especially valuable will be studies in which children with ADHD are assessed both on and off their therapeutic doses of medication. Test data obtained while the children are on medication will most accurately reflect their actual competence (rather than having results of questionable validity because of a significant amount of distractibility, hyperactivity, or impulsivity).

IDENTIFYING LEARNING DISABILITIES

In the United States, approximately 2.8 million students have specific learning disabilities (SLD), making up 51% of all individuals receiving special education services under IDEA (Office of Special Education Programs [OSEP], 2004). The identification of these individuals and the system designed to address their need are under regular revision, as in the scheduled reauthorization of IDEA and in the implementation of the No Child Left Behind Act (NICHCY, 2004).

As of the writing of this chapter, both the House and Senate versions of the IDEA Reauthorization Bill had been passed, and a committee was meeting to iron out differences between the two versions. The reauthorized IDEA and its ultimate state-by-state implementation will surely affect the way psychologists assess SLD because diagnosis will no longer stipulate that the child must have an ability-achievement discrepancy.

As noted, the reauthorized IDEA was in committee as this book went to press; the conference committee is made up of House and Senate members from both parties. There are a limited number of legislative days between the present writing and the end of this second session of the 108th Congress, so it is difficult to speculate about whether there will be a new law during this session. In any case, the operational guidelines at the state level will probably not be ready for some time.

In the meantime, several aspects of special education practice have recently received considerable criticism and are most likely to be radically changed with the new legislation or reauthorization. The fields of education, special education, and school psychology are preparing for the demise of the discrepancy formula currently used for the identification of children with SLD because both the Senate and House versions of the legislation state that such discrepancies are not necessary for diagnosing SLD, although a child's response to intervention may be used for diagnosis.

The reasons for the elimination of the discrepancy formula are described in depth elsewhere (Common Ground, 2000) and will not be reiterated here. However, some individuals (Stanovich, 1999; Velluntino, Scanlon, & Lyon, 2000) assign the failure of the discrepancy model mostly to the use of IQ tests. It is the position of the authors of this book on the KABC-II and other prominent leaders in the field of cognitive assessment that the value of the discrepancy model has always been questionable, *but the value of cognitive ability tests that measure information processing is not* (Flanagan & Kaufman, 2004; Kaufman & Kaufman, 2001; Lichtenberger, Mather, Kaufman, & Kaufman, 2004; Miller, 2004; Naglieri, 1999; Reynolds & Kamphaus, 2003). Indeed, the value of cognitive ability tests has been adequately established in school psychology and neuropsychological circles for some time (Bigler, Nussbaum, & Foley, 1997; Reynolds & Kamphaus, 2003; Rourke, 1989; Spreen, 2001). The prodigious body of research showing direct links between the brain and behavior will also increase as imaging and psychometric technology becomes more appreciated, affordable, and commonplace.

While there has been a change in thinking about the current method of determining SLD in children, it should be noted that the definition of SLD itself has *not* been under attack and will almost certainly remain intact (see Rapid Reference 6.6). Yet, even though the definition of SLD will remain the same in the newly reauthorized IDEA legislation—notably that children with SLD must have a dis-

≡Rapid Reference 6.6

Definition of Specific Learning Disability

Specific Learning Disability means a disorder in one or more of the basic psychological processes involved in understanding or in using language, spoken or written, that may manifest itself in an imperfect ability to listen, speak, read, write, spell, or do mathematical calculations. The term includes such conditions as perceptual disabilities, brain injury, minimal brain dysfunction, dyslexia, and developmental aphasia. The term does not apply to children who have learning problems that are primarily the result of visual, hearing, or motor disabilities, or mental retardation, or emotional disturbance, or of environmental, cultural, or economic disadvantage.

Source. From Federal Register 42 p. 60582.

order in one or more of the basic psychological processes—the methodology for diagnosing SLD (as described in the new IDEA guidelines) does not include specific recommendations either for identifying the processes that are disordered or the processes that are spared. Consequently, the implementation of the reauthorized IDEA within each state will take some time as state leaders attempt to deal with the disconnect between SLD definition and assessment methodology.

There continues to be a consensus of opinion that the assessment of a child's disability should be made in the context of a comprehensive assessment. Several organizations and agencies came together in 2002 (Common Ground, 2002) to review the assessment of learning disabilities and came to the following consensus:

Identification should include a student-centered, comprehensive evaluation and problem-solving approach that ensures students who have a specific learning disability are efficiently identified. Participants support existing IDEA requirements for a comprehensive evaluation that will use multiple measures, methods, sources of information, and clinical judgment to identify individual students with SLD. Important sources cited by the Roundtable participants include, but are not limited to, interviews with teachers and family members, standardized tests, teacher logs, student products, student records, observations, and continuous progress monitoring of performance. This statement is shaped by the guiding principle that no one particular measure or source is capable of providing sufficient information for accurately and reliably identifying individuals with SLD. A comprehensive evaluation will provide an accurate assessment of student strengths and weaknesses and should assist in identifying needed services and interventions. (p. 10)

There are many ways of determining the cognitive functioning of a child who is experiencing difficulties in the classroom, and a multifaceted approach seems most appropriate. There is much research evidence to prove that cognitive ability tests, in the past and on their own, simply cannot carry the burden of predicting how a child with an SLD responds to academic intervention. However, cognitive ability tests that measure processing strengths and weaknesses fit very well into the comprehensive assessment paradigm (Teeter, 1997) and those, like the KABC-II, that have a clear delineation of process from product will take a specific place in the comprehensive assessments of the future. Of course, the place for such batteries is already embedded in an extensive comprehensive psychological assessment.

Regardless of the form the final text of the current reauthorization of IDEA takes, we do know that there is a demand for the comprehensive assessment to drive intervention. This is the way it has always been, and this is the way it will always be because the referral questions for children with SLD have always asked, "What is wrong? And how can we help?" These questions demand differential diagnosis, a large part of which is determined by the cognitive abilities present in the individual child.

The comprehensive assessment is far more powerful in its sum than in its parts. For many years, SLDs have been determined by a part of the whole comprehensive assessment (the IQ score versus the achievement score). Now, many are calling for the reintegration of the comprehensive assessment—a practice that has been endorsed by the Kaufmans since the inception of the K-ABC and reflected again in the design and production of the KABC-II.

SLD Studies with the K-ABC

The original K-ABC was used in many research studies with SLD populations (for a detailed summary of these studies, consult Kaufman & Kaufman, 2001; Lichtenberger, 2001; and Lichtenberger, Broadbooks, & Kaufman, 2000). Overall, the evidence indicated that evidence for specific profiles for children with SLD on the K-ABC were equivocal. Some studies with SLD children suggested higher Sequential over Simultaneous Processing scores, indicating relative weaknesses in the sequential processing of information that tends also to be analytical and linguistic in nature. However, other studies indicated no differences in the Sequential and Simultaneous scales.

A 1999 study by Chow and Skuy may help account for equivocal results in different studies. Chow and Skuy (1999) studied the performance of children who had specific subtypes of learning disability. They included children with Nonverbal Learning Disability (NVLD), which is characterized by difficulties in simultaneous processing, relative strengths in auditory processing, and rote verbal abilities (Lichtenberger et al., 2000). Byron Rourke and colleagues conducted much of the definition and seminal research done on children with NVLD in the 1990s and found that the subtype parameters are quite definitive (e.g., Rourke, 1998). Chow and Skuy compared the NVLD children with children who have a language-based learning disability (LLD) characterized by the reverse profile to NVLD. The K-ABC results in this study found that children with NVLD performed with better scores on the Simultaneous scale than the Sequential scale. On the other hand, children with LLD performed in quite the opposite way, with higher Simultaneous than Sequential scale scores. Interestingly, both groups obtained similar Mental Processing Composite scores. The Chow and Skuy (1999) study indicates that investigating the performance of children with specific subtypes of learning disabilities on the K-ABC has some promise and may give support and credit to LD subtyping.

SLD Studies with the KABC-II

The following sections examine studies conducted on children with SLD using the KABC-II.

General Observations

There were three prepublication studies of children with learning disabilities conducted with the KABC-II: a reading disability study, a mathematics disability study, and a written expression disability study (Kaufman & Kaufman, 2004a). The results of the learning disability studies indicate some interesting similarities across groups. For example, all three groups had significantly different scores (p < .001) on *all* scales compared to the nonclinical reference sample. It would be reasonable to suspect that different disabilities would produce significant differences on some scales but not others. While some differences were greater than others, overall, all three groups were significantly different from the control sample for the entire set of KABC-II scales. Therefore, it would be appropriate to assume that children with learning disabilities, on the whole, will perform very differently on the KABC-II than their peers who do not have disabilities.

Another general observation for the three groups is that they all have mean Si-

≡Rapid Reference 6.7

**Simultaneous/*Gv*-Sequential/*Gsm* Discrepancies for
Three Groups with Learning Disabilities**

Math Disability	Reading Disability	Writing Disability
0.9	2.7	3.1

Source. Adapted from Kaufman and Kaufman (2004a, Tables 8.31, 8.32, 8.33).

multaneous/*Gv* Indexes that are slightly higher than all of the other mean indexes (see Rapid Reference 6.7). The phenomenon of the Sequential scale score being slightly lower than the Simultaneous scale score in children with SLD has been observed for years with the K-ABC, but the Learning/*Glr*, Planning/*Gf*, and Knowledge/*Gc* Scales are new, and it will be interesting to see if this relationship continues in future research studies.

Another salient overall comparison is that there was little difference in the MPI and FCI for the three groups, with standard scores ranging from 79.3 to 82.6 (see Figure 6.5). So we know that children with learning disabilities in these studies generally performed much lower than their control peers but not necessarily different from each other. One reason for the similarity in KABC-II profiles concerns the fact that the groups were in no way pure. Of the 96 students with math disabilities, 81% also had reading disabilities. Similarly, 34% of the students with written expression disabilities also had reading disabilities (M. H. Daniel, personal communication, May 26, 2004).

The performance of the three disability groups discussed in the preceding on the Learning/*Glr* scale of the KABC-II is of particular interest. The Learning/*Glr* scale was developed for the KABC-II for many reasons but primarily to assist in the investigation of a child's learning in a dynamic or interactive way. It was designed to provide the child with an opportunity to bring a learning experience together with the help of a teacher—in this case, the KABC-II examiner.

The Learning/*Glr* scale is a demanding scale because it requires that all of the cognitive processes work together. Children must use sequential abilities to listen and organize information in a serial manner and learn in a step by step fashion; they must use simultaneous processing to look, organize, and remember visual information; and they must use planning abilities to prioritize information pro-

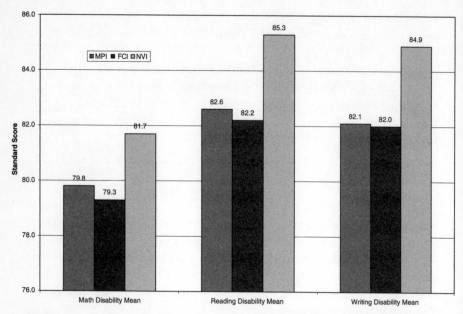

Figure 6.5 KABC-II MPI, FCI, and NVI for three learning-disabled groups.

cessing. The whole process utilized for the Learning/*Glr* scale is very much like a functional symphony where the first and second functional units of the brain (measured by the Sequential/*Gsm* and Simultaneous/*Gv* scales) must interact and take direction and sustain interest from the third functional unit (measured by the Planning/*Gf* scale). A disability in any of these areas can affect scores on the respective scales but may also affect the performance on the Learning/*Glr* scale where it all has to come together.

The KABC-II learning disability study groups demonstrated consistent difficulties in all of the scales, and the end product was commensurate performance difficulties on the Learning/*Glr* scale and its Delayed Recall counterpart. Of course, these results are group scores, and individual children with learning disabilities will inevitably show unique patterns of performance. Indeed, the research literature has not yet shown any definitive patterns of processing among all children with learning disabilities (Lichtenberger, 2001). Nonetheless, we would expect that a specific deficit would still show up in poor performance. It will be interesting to see in future research how different subtypes of learning disabilities may be evidenced on the Learning/*Glr* scale.

One point that should be mentioned is that each disability group had a Knowledge/*Gc* index that was very similar to the other KABC-II Indexes for that group.

Although the Knowledge/*Gc* scale is the closest in construct to the Achievement scale on the original K-ABC, there are notable differences. The KABC-II Knowledge/*Gc* index does not include the conventional achievement subtests (reading and math) that were on the K-ABC, and for ages 7 to 18 the Knowledge/*Gc* index is composed of one subtest that is entirely receptive in nature (Verbal Knowledge) and one that requires only one-word responses. Ordinarily, a discrepancy would be expected for samples of children diagnosed with learning disabilities (as in an ability-achievement discrepancy). Probably, the reason for this nondiscrepancy is that the Knowledge/*Gc* scale on the KABC-II is more receptive in nature and does not require complex verbal responses from the examinee as other verbal-achievement tests have done in the past. In addition, one of the Core Knowledge/*Gc* Core subtests (Riddles) demands good fluid reasoning ability (in addition to crystallized knowledge). Also, the Kaufmans deliberately tried to measure facts and verbal concepts on all three Knowledge/*Gc* subtests that are accessible within the everyday environment, as opposed to being specifically taught in school.

In summary, the three KABC-II learning disability studies showed performance in the Below Average range on all of the scales of the KABC-II for the children with learning disabilities, which was significantly lower than the scores earned by the nonclinical reference group. In addition, the groups showed slightly higher scores on the Simultaneous/*Gv* index versus the Sequential/*Gsm* index but generally performed similarly on all scales that constitute the KABC-II profile. As indicated, the similar profiles earned by the three subsamples of students with learning disabilities is undoubtedly related to the fact that all three groups included children who also had reading disabilities (34% of the written expression sample and 81% of the math sample).

KABC-II Reading Disability Study

The study conducted with children with reading disabilities had 141 participants who were selected based upon a significant discrepancy between performance on a measure of intellectual ability and a measure of reading achievement. The average age of the group was 13.2 (SD = 36 months). The study included 83 males and 58 females from a variety of SES and ethnic backgrounds (exact details can be found in the KABC-II manual).

Historically, many studies have shown that children with reading disabilities have problems with the Sequential Processing scale of the original K-ABC (e.g., Hooper & Hynd, 1982, 1985; Kamphaus & Reynolds, 1987; Lichtenberger, 2001; Lichtenberger et al., 2000) and associated left-hemispheric processing (James &

≡ Rapid Reference 6.8

Mean KABC-II Index Scores for Children with Reading, Mathematics, and Writing Disabilities

	Mean		
KABC-II Scale	**Math Disability**	**Reading Disability**	**Writing Disability**
Sequential/*Gsm*	83.7	85.4	84.6
Simultaneous/*Gv*	84.6	88.1	87.7
Learning/*Glr*	83.7	84.3	83.9
Planning/*Gf*	82.7	86.8	86.8
Knowledge/*Gc*	82.0	84.8	85.2

Source. Adapted from Kaufman and Kaufman (2004a, Tables 8.31, 8.32, 8.33).

Selz, 1997; Lyon, Fletcher, & Barnes, 2003; Reynolds, Kamphaus, Rosenthal, & Hiemenz, 1997). Although the sample with reading disabilities tested on the KABC-II scored almost 1 SD significantly below the nonclinical reference group on the Sequential/*Gsm* index, the reading-disabled sample showed similar depressions on all other indexes. Rapid Reference 6.8 shows the mean scores for the sample of children with reading disabilities as well as those with disabilities in the areas of mathematics and writing.

As documented, prior studies indicate that many times, especially for children with language-oriented disabilities, the Sequential score is lower than the Simultaneous score. This trend was also found for this particular sample, but the mean difference between the Simultaneous and Sequential scale was minimal (2.7 points; see Rapid Reference 6.7).

How do the depressed scores on all indexes translate into academic achievement? Rapid Reference 6.9 shows the scores on the Kaufman Test of Educational Achievement-II (KTEA-II), which was conormed with the KABC-II, for all the children with learning disabilities.

In general, all of the composite scores for the KTEA-II reading-disability sample show significant differences ($p < .001$) from the nonclinical reference group. The lowest composite scores for this group were, predictably, on the Decoding composite (76.7), followed closely by the Reading composite (76.9). Both composites indicated a 22-point difference between the reading disability and nonclinical groups. These scores are closely followed by composites that are

≋Rapid Reference 6.9

Mean KTEA-II Composite Scores for Children with Reading, Mathematics, and Writing Disabilities

	Mean		
KTEA-II Composite	**Math Disability**	**Writing Disability**	**Reading Disability**
Reading Composite	76.8	77.4	76.9
Mathematics Composite	77.2	81.1	81.2
Written Language Composite	77.2	77.5	77.5
Oral Language Composite	82.6	84.7	85.0
Sound-Symbol Composite	77.9	78.5	77.9
Reading Fluency Composite	77.7	77.5	77.4
Decoding Composite	76.8	77.3	76.7
Oral Fluency Composite	85.7	88.2	87.1
Comprehensive Achievement	**76.1**	**78.3**	**78.4**

Source. Adapted from Kaufman and Kaufman (2004b, Tables 7.32, 7.33, 7.34).

highly related to reading competency: the Reading Fluency composite (77.4) and the Written Language composite (77.5).

How does an examination of the KTEA-II reading subtests inform KABC-II test interpretation? Research in phonological awareness has been very popular in the past few years and has demonstrated that phonological awareness skills are highly related to decoding and fluency skills in reading (Teeter, 1997). In addition, neuroimaging and EEG studies have located specific parts of the brain that correlate with skills measured on the Sequential/*Gsm* scale and the component skills of phonological awareness (Harmony, 1997; Lyon et al., 2003). Therefore, it is very important for the examiner to look at scores relating to sequential processing skills on the KABC-II and see how they correlate with phonemic awareness and reading decoding skills on the KTEA-II for each child that is referred for reading problems. This analysis will help the examiner understand the etiology of the reading problem and assist with prescriptive interventions that are evidence based in this area of skill deficit (Naglieri, 2001; Teeter, 1997). The exact procedure for examining the Sequential/*Gsm* scale along with the KTEA-II is described later in this chapter in the section, "Integration of the KABC-II and KTEA-II."

In summary, the KABC-II and KTEA-II study comparing the reading disability group with a nonclinical reference group found that there were significant differences between the two groups on all of the scales and composites of both tests. The reading disability group indicated overall low-average information processing abilities that were evidenced by significant deficits on academic tests measuring reading decoding, fluency, and comprehension skills and low-average functioning in oral language skills.

KABC-II Math Disability Study

The KABC-II was administered to 96 students with learning disabilities in mathematics. The sample consisted of 59 males and 37 females from varied SES and ethnic backgrounds (details can be found in the KABC-II manual).

Overall, the study found larger-difference scores between the mathematics disability group and the nonclinical reference group than for the reading and written expression disability groups (Kaufman & Kaufman, 2004a, pp. 126–128). Although the range of mean scores on the indexes was not large for the children with math disabilities (82.0 to 84.6; see Rapid Reference 6.8), the greatest standard score difference between the mathematics disability group and the nonclinical reference group (about 16 points) was on the Planning/*Gf* scale. This depression is not an uncommon observation and has been addressed with interventions in many studies (Montague & Bos, 1986; Rourke, 1989; Strang & Rourke, 1985; Teeter & Semrud-Clikeman, 1998). These studies found that remediation strategies involving cognitive and metacognitive approaches, rules for problem solving, and step-by-step problem solving with feedback helped children with mathematics difficulties plan solutions to mathematical problems.

How do scores on the KABC-II of children with math disabilities evidence on measures of academic achievement? As a point of comparison, the scores for this group on the KTEA-II are illustrated in Rapid Reference 6.9. As would be expected, the group performed poorly on the Mathematics composite (mean standard score = 77.2), although the group also averaged about 77 on the Reading and Written Language composites as well. The group's Below Average mean scores in virtually all areas of achievement on the KTEA-II undoubtedly reflect the fact that 81% of the sample had reading disabilities as well as math disabilities. The math disability group's weakness in written language is also probably related to the fact that both academic subjects rely on the planning and organizing of information—hence the relatively low Planning/*Gf* index on the KABC-II.

In summary, the KABC-II and KTEA-II study comparing the math disability group with a nonclinical reference group found that there were significant differences between the two groups on all of the scales and composites of both tests. The math disability group evidenced overall Low Average information processing abilities that resulted in significant deficits on academic tests measuring mathematics, reading decoding, and written language skills.

KABC-II Written Expression Disability Study

The study conducted with children with learning disabilities in the area of written expression had 122 subjects. There were 76 males and 46 females with a variety of SES and ethnic backgrounds (details can be found in the KABC-II manual). Rapid Reference 6.8 shows their KABC-II index profile.

In view of the fact that about one-third of the students with written expression disabilities also had reading disabilities, it is not surprising that the pattern of performance for the written expression group was similar to the pattern for the reading group; their highest index was on the Simultaneous/*Gv* scale, followed by the Planning/*Gf* index. However, again, the range of mean indexes is less than 4 points.

The group's lowest index was on the Learning/*Glr* scale. Written expression does place a large demand on examinees, not only in terms of integrating all levels of information, but also in terms of rapidly changing thoughts and ideas as the material develops. This type of activity stretches every cognitive functional system, and perhaps the Learning/*Glr* scale suffers the most when a child has problems with overall sequential, simultaneous, and planning activities. Indeed, it follows that the evidence-based intervention techniques that work best for children with written expression deficits are those that are based on cognitive and metacognitive strategies (Teeter, 1997).

How are written expression deficits evidenced on achievement tests? Rapid Reference 6.9 shows the results of the same group of children's performance on the KTEA-II. The writing disability group had the lowest scores on the Reading Decoding composite (77.3), followed closely by the Reading composite (77.4), Reading Fluency composite (77.5), and Written Language composites (77.5). It appears that for this group reading and writing activities are equally difficult. Again, this finding is consistent with the fact that 34% of the children in the written expression sample also had notable difficulties in reading. Similarly, the strongest achievement area for both the reading disability and writing disability groups was on the Oral Fluency composite.

The overall problems with sequential processing, planning, and learning in the writing process would definitely require intervention strategies that support remediation in these areas. Evidence-based interventions for written expression disabilities have been suggested by Bos and Van Reusen (1991), Englert (1990), and Graham and Harris (1987). The interventions focus mainly on cognitive and metacognitive strategies to help organize, plan, edit, and revise writing samples.

In summary, the KABC-II and KTEA-II study comparing the writing disability group with a nonclinical reference group found that there were significant differences between the two groups on all of the scales and composites of both tests. The writing disability group indicated overall Low Average information processing abilities that evidenced in significant deficits on academic tests measuring reading decoding, written language, and reading fluency.

Conclusion

All in all, the advantages of having direct comparisons of ability and achievement with the KABC-II and the KTEA-II should prove to be very useful in the years to come. The emphasis in learning disability diagnosis has, thankfully, shifted away from the discrepancy analysis and gone back to where it really always should have been: the comprehensive assessment. The definition of learning disabilities is not slated to change any time in the near or distant future, and therefore it will still remain, for the most part, a diagnosis by exclusion. Given that in order to obtain a diagnosis of SLD, the learning difficulties cannot be primarily due to emotional, social, physical, or cultural causes, we must make sure that the comprehensive assessment ensures that all of these areas are investigated and excluded from the primary diagnosis. Just as important, the second phase of the comprehensive assessment must identify in detail the cognitive and processing strengths and weaknesses of the child. This must be done with the best tools available, and we are lucky to be living in a time when all of the major ability batteries have been revised and are at their psychometric best.

The third phase of the comprehensive assessment is just as important as the first two phases and consists of evidence-based prescriptions for interventions that are directly related to the child's strengths or weaknesses. The latter is now being informed by neuropsychological research that is beginning to determine critical periods of brain development that respond to either strength or weakness remediation strategies, and sometimes both at the same time (Teeter, 1997).

There is a link between the brain and behavior, and it is important that brain-behavior research informs the assessment process. Both the KABC-II and the KTEA-II were founded on brain-behavior theory and research, and hopefully they will continue to support the comprehensive assessment process and research for evidence-based intervention.

ASSESSMENT OF ETHNIC GROUPS

The problem of potential cultural bias in ability tests has long been a subject of fierce debate and has been a theme of controversy throughout the history of mental measurement (Jensen, 1980; Lichtenberger & Kaufman, 1998; Reynolds, 2000).

There has been a great deal of evidence indicating that Whites outperform other ethnic groups on tests of ability. The reasons for this disparity may be due to genetic influences, child rearing practices, language differences, transactional and reciprocal models of child development, educational variables, or cultural bias in the tests that are used to measure ability (Lichtenberger et al., 2000; Reynolds, 1997). Evaluating and understanding these reasons is very important when it comes to interpreting scores for some ethnic groups.

Much of the controversy about cultural bias in the tests has hovered around the interpretation of differences in mean global scores between groups. However, much more goes into the design and development of limiting ethnic bias in tests than the examination of mean score index differences. The latter is one way of examining bias in ability assessment, but there are many more. Test developers have the burden of designing and evaluating their tests by many means, including design parameters that support different cultural sensitivity, item bias analyses, reliability and validity data, factor analyses, and validity studies to name just a few.

KABC-II (and K-ABC) Test Development and Ethnic Assessment

The authors of the KABC-II and the test publisher, American Guidance Service (AGS), revised the K-ABC with the intent to produce a battery that continued to minimize global score differences between ethnic children and White children. All of the clinical data from studies and reviews of the K-ABC over the previous 20-year period were examined. The overall analysis pointed to several variables in the development of the original K-ABC that successfully resulted in substantially smaller discrepancies between children from varied ethnic backgrounds and children from the mainstream:

- The elimination of knowledge-based subtests from the global score indexes and the reduced emphasis on language and crystallized abilities for measuring overall cognitive ability
- Design of subtests that were based on research that indicated fewer cultural differences (e.g., Face Recognition and Gestalt Closure)
- The reduced verbal load for the examiner and the examinee on each subtest that is a part of a global scale

- The development of novel subtests that were designed to be intrinsically interesting to children of all ages
- The simplification of administration and scoring thereby freeing the examiner to observe *how* the child took the test as much as the correctness of content
- The inclusion of teaching items where examiners were encouraged to modify wording, use gestures, and explain introductory items
- The inclusion of subtest designs based on a theoretical model of brain function for assessing cognitive processes, as opposed to the assessment of acquired knowledge

This historical analysis also included how the original K-ABC was used with different cultural groups not only in North America but also in Europe, Africa, and Asia. There was a great deal of information from many countries relating to the translated and adapted versions of the K-ABC (e.g., Conant et al., 1999; Kim, Goak, Jang, & Han, 1995; Mardell-Czudnowski, 1995; Melchers & Preuss, 1991, 2003; Voyazopolous, 1994; Wolke & Meyer, 1999). In addition, edited books, studies, and other publications clearly marked the strengths and weaknesses of the K-ABC in a cross-cultural context (e.g., Kamphaus & Reynolds, 1987; Lichtenberger et al., 2000; Reynolds et al., 1997; Samuda, Feuerstein, Kaufman, Lewis, & Sternberg, 1998).

After studying the history of the original K-ABC, the authors developed broad objectives for the revision and pilot tested new items and subtests on small and then larger groups of children. The Kaufmans specifically included a few tasks in the original K-ABC, such as Face Recognition, which were known to produce small differences across cultures. However, they did not develop any new subtests for the KABC-II based on this consideration. Instead, all new tasks had to meet two main criteria: (1) They had to measure one of the basic theoretical constructs measured by the KABC-II, and (2) they had to capture the interest of children and adolescents across a broad age range.

The latter criterion stemmed from an unexpected research finding with the original K-ABC—one of the subtests that produced among the *smallest* differences between White children and African American children was Faces and Places (Kaufman & Kaufman, 1983b, Table 4.35), an Achievement subtest that was arguably the most culture-loaded task on the entire battery. This finding of reduced ethnic differences was found as well with the similar Famous Faces subtest on the Kaufman Adolescent and Adult Intelligence Test (KAIT; Kaufman & Kaufman, 1993) for African American and Hispanic individuals ages 11 to 24 (Kaufman, McLean, & Kaufman, 1995).

Reduced differences on a subtest that measures range of general knowledge was unexpected because the similar Information subtest has consistently produced among the *largest* race differences on Wechsler's scales (Kaufman, 1994a; Kaufman & Lichtenberger, 2002). The K-ABC Faces and Places subtest (and KAIT Famous Faces) changed the format by using the identification of visual stimuli instead of the schoollike oral questions but did not change the ability that was measured. The mere change in format, coupled with a more interesting, less schoollike approach to the assessment of range of general knowledge was apparently sufficient to reduce ethnic differences substantially.

Therefore, when developing new tasks for the KABC-II, interest value to children was regarded as the key to maintaining the original K-ABC's legacy of reduced ethnic differences. Hence, subtests like Atlantis, Rover, Story Completion, and the easy set of items on Triangles, Conceptual Thinking, and Verbal Knowledge (which replaced Faces and Places, a task that was correctly criticized for getting out of date too quickly) were developed.

Based on these test development guidelines and with the energetic, insightful help of a team of graduate students (Kaufman & Kaufman, 2004a, pp. x–xi), the tryout version of the KABC-II was developed; it was administered to 696 children ages 3 to 18 around the country. The tryout group primarily consisted of children from varied ethnic backgrounds. Two-thirds of the tryout sample was either African American or Hispanic American children. The only reason for this disproportionate number of children from ethnic backgrounds was to support item bias analyses as early in the process of test development as possible. The percentage of children from ethnic minorities in the tryout sample was much higher than in the tryout samples for other tests that were being developed at the same time (Reynolds & Kamphaus, 2003; Roid, 2003; Wechsler, 2003).

Possible sex or ethnic item bias on the tryout results was evaluated using the Rasch method in which each subtest is calibrated independently for each subgroup of interest, and the difference in an item's difficulty values between groups is tested for statistical significance. Items that showed differential item functioning were carefully reviewed in an effort to understand the cause of the difference, and most of the identified items were eliminated or modified. During the tryout phase, a group of 16 experts also reviewed the items, evaluating fairness to population subgroups such as ethnic group, sex, SES, education, and physical disabilities.

Ethnic Differences on the KABC-II

The next step in evaluating cultural fairness took place with the standardization sample. The primary purpose of test standardization is to gather data on a large sample of individuals that is representative of the population. The standardization data are used for final statistical evaluation of the difficulty, reliability, validity, and fairness of the items.

Tables 6.1 and 6.2 present mean KABC-II standard scores alongside comparable K-ABC standard scores for African American children, unadjusted for SES.

Table 6.1 Mean Global Indexes on the K-ABC and KABC-II for African American Children (*not adjusted* for SES)

Scale	K-ABC	KABC-II
MPI (MPC)	95.0	95.5
FCI	—	94.7
NVI	93.2	96.0
Age range	2½–12½	3–18
Sample size	805	465

Source. Means were computed from data presented in the K-ABC and KABC-II manuals (Kaufman & Kaufman, 1983b, Table 4.35; Kaufman & Kaufman, 2004a, Tables 8.7 & 8.8).

Note. Dash indicates that the K-ABC did not yield a FCI.

Table 6.2 Mean Scale Indexes on the K-ABC and KABC-II for African American Children (*not adjusted* for SES)

Scale	K-ABC	KABC-II
Learning/*Glr*	—	98.0
Sequential/*Gsm*	98.2	99.8
Simultaneous/*Gv*	93.8	93.5
Planning/*Gf*	—	94.3
Knowledge/*Gc* (Achievement)	93.7	93.9
Age range	2½–12½	3–18
Sample size	805	465

Source. Means were computed from data presented in the K-ABC and KABC-II manuals (Kaufman & Kaufman, 1983b, Table 4.35; Kaufman & Kaufman, 2004a, Tables 8.7 & 8.8).

Note. Dash indicates that the K-ABC only yielded sequential and simultaneous scores, not *Glr* or *Gf*.

The data are presented for the entire age range for each test (2.5 to 12.5 on the K-ABC and 3 to 18 on the KABC-II). As shown in Table 6.1, the mean KABC-II MPI and FCI are both virtually identical to the mean K-ABC Mental Processing Composite of 95; the mean NVI is higher by 3 points on the KABC-II than on the K-ABC. When comparing analogous scales on the old and new batteries (Table 6.2), the KABC-II yields a slightly higher Sequential score (99.8 versus 98.2). Means for the Simultaneous and Knowledge (Achievement) scales are virtually identical. These important results indicate that the KABC-II continues the tradition of the original K-ABC and provides indirect support for the Kaufmans' approach to test development that stressed both the theoretical relevance and child interest of new and modified subtests.

Mean KABC-II global scores (MPI, FCI, and NVI) for the normative sample by ethnicity, adjusted for sex and SES (mother's education), are presented separately for ages 3 to 6 (Table 6.3) and 7 to 18 (Table 6.4). For ages 3 to 6, these adjusted values are close to the normative mean of 100 for African American and Hispanic children (means of about 97 to 100); white children ages 3 to 6 averaged about 101. For ages 7 to 18, means are about 95 ± 5 for African American, His-

Table 6.3 Mean KABC-II Global Scores for Children Ages 3–6, by Ethnic Group (*adjusted* for gender and SES)

Scale	African American	Hispanic	White
MPI	98.7	98.2	100.9
FCI	98.0	96.6	101.6
NVI	96.7	99.7	100.8
Sample size	150	162	505

Source. Data are from the *KABC-II manual* (Kaufman & Kaufman, 2004a, Table 8.7).

Table 6.4 Mean KABC-II Global Scores for Children Ages 7–18, by Ethnic Group (*adjusted* for gender and SES)

Scale	African American	Hispanic	American Indian	Asian	White
MPI	95.2	96.5	96.5	104.6	101.9
FCI	94.5	95.8	95.6	103.9	102.4
NVI	93.1	98.3	97.0	103.4	102.0
Sample size	315	383	51	62	1,356

Source. Data are from the *KABC-II manual* (Kaufman & Kaufman, 2004a, Table 8.8).

panic, American Indian, Asian, and White children. (Means are not provided at ages 3 to 6 for American Indians and Asians because of small sample sizes.)

For children ages 7 to 18, African American children earned their highest mean index (adjusted for sex and SES) on the Sequential/*Gsm* scale (100) followed closely by the Learning/*Glr* scale (98). In contrast, for that same age range, Hispanic children scored highest on the Simultaneous/*Gv* and Planning/*Gf* indexes (99); the Simultaneous/*Gv* index was highest for American Indian children (101) and Asian children (105; Kaufman & Kaufman, 2004a, Table 8.8). Figures 6.6 and 6.7 show the mean score differences between Whites and other ethnic groups on the KABC-II indexes (data are graphed separately for children ages 3 to 6 and 7 to 18).

Most of the adjusted indexes for Hispanic children were close to 100 except for the Sequential/*Gsm* scale (95), where the language load on Word Order and Number Recall may have interfered with performance. This observation is consistent with K-ABC data and other tests that have verbal-nonverbal distinctions (Kaufman, 1994a; Kaufman & Lichtenberger, 2002).

Difference between Whites and African Americans are smaller on the KABC-

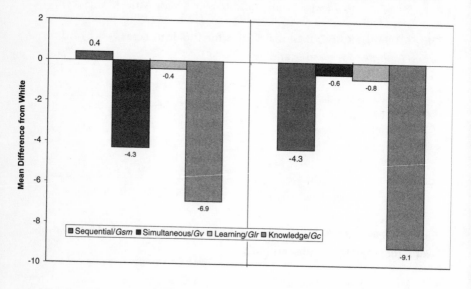

Figure 6.6 Mean score differences between Whites and two other ethnic groups on the four KABC-II indexes for children ages 3–6.

Source. Data are from the *KABC-II manual* (Table 8.7).

Notes. Data are adjusted for gender and mother's education. N = 114 for African American group and N = 124 for Hispanic group.

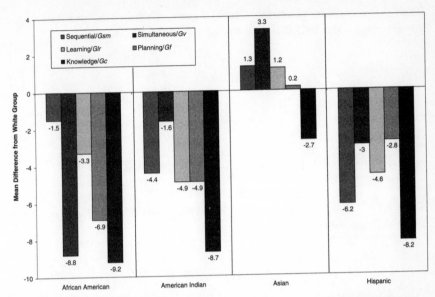

Figure 6.7 Mean score differences between Whites and other ethnic groups on the five KABC-II indexes for children ages 7–18.

Source. Data are from the *KABC-II manual* (Table 8.8).

Notes. Data are adjusted for gender and mother's education. N = 315 for African American group, N = 51 for American Indian group, N = 62 for Asian American group, and N = 124 for Hispanic group.

Table 6.5 Mean Global Scores on the WISC-III and KABC-II for African American Children (*not adjusted* for SES)

Scale	WISC-III Mean (ages 6–16, $N = 338$)	KABC-II Mean (ages 7–18, $N = 315$)
WISC-III FSIQ	88.6	—
KABC-II MPI	—	94.8
KABC-II FCI	—	94.0

Source. WISC-III data are from Prifitera and Saklofske (1998). KABC-II data are from Kaufman and Kaufman (2004a, Table 8.8).

II than for the Wechsler scales (Kaufman & Lichtenberger, 2002). African American children and adolescents scored about .5 SD higher on the KABC-II FCI and MPI than on the WISC-III Full Scale IQ (see Table 6.5). In addition, standard score differences between Whites and African Americans (adjusted for SES and other background variables) are smaller on the KABC-II than the WISC-III (see

Table 6.6 Differences between Global Scores of Whites and African Americans on the WISC-III and KABC-II (*adjusted* for SES)

Scale	WISC-III Mean (ages 6–16, $N = 338$)	KABC-II Mean (ages 7–18, $N = 315$)
WISC-III FS-IQ	+11.0	—
KABC-II MPI	—	+6.7
KABC-II FCI	—	+7.9

Source. WISC-III data are from Prifitera, Weiss, and Saklofske (1998). KABC-II data are from Kaufman and Kaufman (2004a, Table 8.8).

Table 6.7 Global Score Differences for Whites and African Americans on Several Tests (*adjusted* for SES)

Test	Mean Difference
Woodcock-Johnson—Revised (WJ-R)	12
WISC-III	11
Stanford Binet—Fourth Edition (Binet-4)	8
Cognitive Assessment System (CAS)	5
KABC-II MPI (without *Gc*)	5
KABC-II FCI (with *Gc*)	6.5

Source. WISC-III data are from Prifitera, Weiss, and Saklofske (1998). WJ-R and Binet-4 data are from Wasserman and Becker (2000). CAS data are from Naglieri, Rojahn, Aquilino, and Matto (2004).

Note. Mean differences are adjusted for SES and other variables, depending on the study. KABC-II data are for ages 3–18.

Table 6.6) and are generally smaller than the differences reported for other tests as well. Table 6.7 summarizes the results for several individually administered cognitive batteries. Only the CAS (Naglieri & Das, 1997) produced differences between Whites and African Americans as small as the 5-point difference on the MPI.

Results of these analyses of ethnic differences, both with and without adjustment for background variables, indicate that the KABC-II continues to have small differences between White children and children from ethnic backgrounds.

Fletcher-Janzen's Study of American Indian Children from Taos

To further understand the American Indian perspective on the KABC-II Fletcher-Janzen (2003) conducted a study with the Taos Pueblo tribe of New

Mexico. She initially tested 46 Taos Pueblo children and adolescents on the KABC-II during the standardization phase of development and then tested a random sample of the same subjects (*N* = 30) on the WISC-IV an average of 18 months later (Fletcher-Janzen, 2003). The coefficients of correlation between the global scores on the two instruments were strong, with the WISC-IV Full Scale IQ correlated with the FCI at .84 and with the MPI at .86. These coefficients indicate that the two tests are in strong agreement about what is being measured. However, the global scale differed by about half a standard deviation, with the FCI averaging 7.4 points higher than the WISC-IV Full Scale IQ and the MPI about 8.4 points higher. Table 6.8 shows the subtest, scale, and index correlation coefficients for this Taos study.

For those readers who are interested in examining the actual scores for this study, Table 6.9 shows the means and standard deviations on comparable KABC-II and WISC-IV scales for the Taos study. The smallest differences between the test scores were noted on the Fluid-Nonverbal scales (1 to 4) points and the largest differences were predictably on the measures of Crystallized-Verbal and Memory scales (7 points).

The Taos study brought forth some interesting results that also need to be investigated with other populations (AGS has several similar studies in progress). The numerical results essentially indicate that the KABC-II and the WISC-IV measure the same constructs, but members of the Taos Pueblo community earn higher overall scores on the KABC-II. Additional research is needed to under-

Table 6.8 Correlation Coefficients for the KABC-II and WISC-IV Comparative Study with Taos Pueblo Indian Children

	KABC-II							
WISC-IV	Sim/ *Gv*	Plan/ *Gf*	Se/ *Gsm*	Lrn/ *Glr*	Knowl/ *Gc*	MPI	FCI	NVI
PCI	.65	.75	.50	.52	.54	.78	.76	.78
WMI	.51	.55	.53	.58	.38	.70	.66	.57
PSI	.38	.36	.22	.20	.09	.39	.34	.34
VCI	.41	.57	.49	.45	.71	.59	.65	.58
FSIQ	.73	.78	.58	.59	.58	.86	.84	.80

Source. Data are adapted from Fletcher-Janzen (2003).

Note. *N* = 30 except for Planning/*Gf* where *N* = 21. Sim/*Gv* = Simultaneous/*Gv*; Plan/*Gf* = Planning/*Gf*; Se/*Gsm* = Sequential/*Gsm*; Lrn/*Glr* = Learning/*Glr*; Knowl/*Gc* = Knowledge/*Gc*.

Table 6.9 Means and Standard Deviations of KABC-II and WISC-IV Scales for Taos Pueblo Indian Children

Scale	N	Mean	SD
KABC-II			
Simultaneous/Gv	30	99.0	14.4
Planning/Gf	21	99.1	13.5
Sequential/Gsm	30	94.6	14.0
Learning/Glr	30	94.9	11.6
Knowledge/Gc	30	92.9	9.7
WISC-IV			
PCI	30	95.1	14.1
WMI	30	87.6	13.2
PSI	30	88.8	14.1
VCI	30	85.4	9.7

Source. Data are adapted from Fletcher-Janzen (2003).

Note. Mean global scores are as follows: FS-IQ = 86.7; KABC-II MPI = 95.1; KABC-II FCI = 94.1.

stand the reasons for the discrepancy (including studies that test children on both tests at the same point in time, in counterbalanced order).

The Taos Pueblo study results are also interesting because this particular tribe of American Indians has a culture that has been essentially cloistered for the past 1,000 years. From a very early age, the children are exposed to three languages: English, Spanish, and their own oral language, Tiwa. The Taos Pueblo culture has a dramatically different worldview from the mainstream in terms of concepts of time, community, language, communication style, nonverbal communication, spirituality, and economics. Yet on KABC-II subtests that measure novel and fluid cognitive processes, these children perform as well as any in the mainstream of American life. This fact merges the necessity of evaluating cognitive ability tests with the understanding that qualitative information instructs the cultural bias evaluation of tests just as much as quantitative information. For these children, scoring to the best of their ability and scoring well on the KABC-II determines placement decisions that affect quality of life.

Ethnic Versus Socioeconomic Differences on the KABC-II

Overall, as demonstrated, the ethnic group differences are modest on the KABC-II. Indeed, compared to the amount of variance accounted for by SES (mother's

Table 6.10 Percent of Variance in KABC-II Scales Accounted for by Ethnicity and Mother's Education Level

Scale/Index	By Ethnicity[a]		By Mother's Education Level[b]	
	Ages 3–6	Ages 7–18	Ages 3–6	Ages 7–18
Sequential/Gsm	1.3	2.3	10.3	6.2
Simultaneous/Gv	1.4	4.4	17.6	5.1
Learning/Glr	0.2	1.6	12.1	6.4
Planning/Gf	—	2.7	—	7.6
Knowledge/Gc	6.0	6.9	22.2	17.6
MPI	0.5	3.7	18.0	10.8
FCI	1.7	5.0	22.5	14.2
NVI	1.2	4.5	13.9	9.4

[a]Percentage of variance accounted for by ethnicity, controlling for sex and mother's education. From the *KABC-II manual* (Kaufman & Kaufman, 2004a, Tables 8.7 and 8.8).

[b]Percentage of variance accounted for by the linear relationship between test scores and mother's education level. From the *KABC-II manual* (Kaufman & Kaufman, 2004a, Table 8.6).

education level; see Table 6.10), the amount of variance accounted for by ethnicity is much smaller.

At ages 3 to 6, ethnic differences account for less than 1 to 2% of the variance in both the MPI and FCI, in contrast to a huge 18 to 22% of the variance accounted for by SES (mother's education). At ages 7 to 18, the percents are 4 to 5% (ethnic differences) versus 11 to 14% (SES). The profile of KABC-II Scale Indexes reflect the same general weighting for SES over ethnic differences in determining children's scores. Notably, and consistent with the Kaufmans' recommendation that the Luria model is the model of choice for children from bilingual and nonmainstream backgrounds, the Knowledge/Gc index produced the highest percents of variance at ages 3 to 18 for both ethnicity (6 to 7%) and SES (18 to 22%; see Table 6.10).

This finding is not inconsistent with other research in the area of ability testing. Socioeconomic status, in this case measured by parental education level, accounts for much more variance in scores (on any tests) than other cultural variables (Centers for Disease Control and Prevention, 1993; McKenzie & Crowcroft, 1994; Wong, Strickland, Fletcher-Janzen, Ardila, & Reynolds, 2000). However, consistently controlling for parental education level does not necessarily directly or accurately control for SES differences because income information

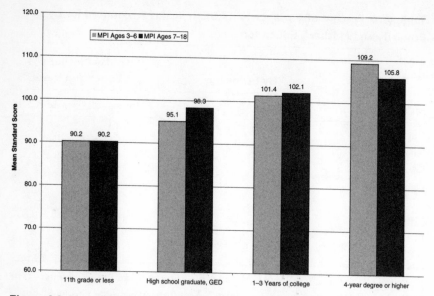

Figure 6.8 Mean MPI for the KABC-II norm sample by age and mother's education.

Source. From Table 8.6 of the *KABC-II manual* (Kaufman & Kaufman, 2004).

Note. Groups score progressively higher as maternal education increases.

(which is much more precise) is not gathered. Test publishers generally find that parental education level is information that parents are much more willing to reveal than dollar amounts about income. Therefore, while the scores for different ethnic groups are adjusted for parental education level, this might not present all relevant information about SES influence on test scores.

One clear trend noted in Figure 6.8 is that both the 3 to 6 and 7 to 18 age groups scored progressively higher as mother's education increased. These data are consistent with a wide array of data on other instruments (Kaufman & Lichtenberger, 2002, Chapter 4), including the original K-ABC (Kaufman & Kaufman, 2004a, Tables 4.34 and 4.35), and suggest an overall pattern that is understandable in light of the major role that the home environment and parental modeling have in the cognitive development and knowledge acquisition of children.

Conclusions about Ethnic Assessment

Overall, the KABC-II appears to be continuing the tradition set by the K-ABC for smaller global score differences between White and other ethnic groups.

While the KABC-II seems to be highly correlated with other tests of ability, the global scores that clinicians seek to obtain on a daily basis will be higher for ethnic students on the KABC-II than nearly all other ability batteries. This result was by design.

One other factor that might assist the cultural validity of the KABC-II is that sample items, instructions, and teaching can be done in the child's native language. In addition, examiners can accept verbal responses that are said in the child's native language as long as they are correct. (The details of administration and procedures for bilingual children are explained in more detail in the section on bilingual assessment in this chapter.) Not only will this process allow for ease of administration, but it also demonstrates that the KABC-II is adept at obtaining information about the child's cognitive processes, not cognitions confounded by problems with language interpretation.

The lowest index for *all* of the ethnic groups was on the Knowledge/*Gc* scale and was most likely related to language and educational variables. As might be expected, the Knowledge/*Gc* scale accounted for quite a bit of the SES variance for ages 3 to 6 (22.2%) and 7 to 18 (17.6%). In addition, the FCI was slightly lower for all ethnic groups than the MPI, again reflecting the influence of the Knowledge/*Gc* scale and supporting the use of the MPI rather than the FCI for some populations.

SOCIOECONOMIC (SES) NORMS

The original K-ABC offered special sociocultural norms as a supplement to the conventional age-based standard scores yielded by the test. These supplementary norms were provided separately for African American children and White children, with each ethnic group further classified by SES (parents' education). These sociocultural norms made it possible for examiners to compare children's cognitive abilities directly to other children from similar ethnic and sociocultural backgrounds, providing adjunct information to supplement the profile of standard scores derived from representative, age-based norms.

The inspiration for the sociocultural norms came from Jane Mercer's (1979) concept of the Estimated Learning Potential (ELP), which was a standard score derived from an administration of the WISC-R that takes into account a child's sociocultural background by use of multiple regression techniques. The ELP "enables one to make inferences concerning the child's probable potential for future learning" (Mercer, 1979, p. 143). That notion was seen as the principal advantage of the K-ABC sociocultural norms, especially since many of the children identified as having "probable potential" would go otherwise undetected.

The intended use of the sociocultural norms was described as follows in the original *K-ABC Interpretive Manual* (Kaufman & Kaufman, 1983b):

> The sociocultural norms should be used in much the same way that one uses local norms. Since test scores are known to be a function of an individual's subcultural and socioeconomic environments, these supplementary norms allow comparison of a child's K-ABC performance with the performance of other children from backgrounds that have certain commonalities. It is not possible truly to equate environments, or to identify reference groups that had precisely the same opportunities for learning as the specific child being evaluated. Racial background and parental education are only two of many variables that affect the type of learning opportunities available to children, and there are many individual variations in the quantity and quality of learning experiences *within* each sociocultural reference group. Nevertheless, subcultural and socioeconomic variables do exert a reasonably potent force on the child's learning environment, and reference groups that "control" for these factors represent valid yardsticks for gauging a child's test performance. However, the interpretive value of these supplementary comparisons will be enhanced by keeping in mind the inherent limitations in *any* attempt to equate children's backgrounds.
>
> It is generally true that opportunities for learning are greater in higher, rather than lower, socioeconomic homes. In that sense, the sociocultural percentile ranks are indexes of how well children have learned in view of their opportunities; they also may reflect the emphasis placed on acculturation to the dominant culture. (p. 166)

The Kaufmans and AGS decided not to offer sociocultural norms for the KABC-II, largely because there is question about the advisability of offering separate norms by racial background; informal feedback from K-ABC examiners suggested that sometimes these separate norms were misused in clinical practice, despite the careful guidelines presented by the test authors. In addition, limiting the sociocultural norms to African Americans and Whites raised questions about separate sociocultural norms for other ethnic groups such as Hispanic, American Indian, and Asian groups.

Nonetheless, the KABC-II authors believe in principle in the potential value of the sociocultural norm concept. In fact, the goals of providing sociocultural percentiles, when they are used in the ways indicated in the preceding quote from the K-ABC manual, are valuable and of great potential benefit to clinicians. And race or ethnicity really has a small role in the usefulness of the supplementary norms. As shown previously, the KABC-II yields small ethnic differences, and these differences are extremely small when contrasted with the role of SES (see Table 6.10, Figure 6.8).

Consequently, we have opted to provide an analog to the K-ABC's sociocultural norms, based solely on SES (mother's education)—*SES norms.* As was done for the original K-ABC, these norms are presented with percentile ranks, not standard scores, to underscore their roles as supplements. Yet as supplements, these percentile ranks will provide examiners with useful adjunct information regarding how well the child has managed to develop his or her cognitive abilities in light of opportunities available within the home environment.

Two SES tables are presented at the end of this book, one for ages 3 to 6 (Appendix E) and one for ages 7 to 18 (Appendix F). Separate norms are presented for four SES categories, based on mother's education: (1) 11 years of schooling or less, (2) high school graduate or GED, (3) 1 to 3 years of college, and (4) 4-year degree or higher. Because mean global KABC-II scores (and standard deviations) were remarkably similar *within* each of the four categories, only two SES norms tables had to be developed. For example, consider the 3- to 6-year-old children of mothers with 1 to 3 years of college: Their mean FCI, MPI, and NVI spanned the narrow range from 94.5 to 95.3, with similar SDs (13.4 to 14.4). Therefore, Appendix E permits examiners to enter the same column with a 3- to 6-year-old's FCI, MPI or NVI to determine its SES percentile rank. That same rule applies to Appendix F for ages 7 to 18.

The tables include children from a variety of ethnic backgrounds and are applicable to all children evaluated with the KABC-II, regardless of ethnic background. Norms for the four SES categories in Appendix E are based on sample sizes ranging from 101 to 269; for Appendix F the range is 328 to 695.

To illustrate the use of the SES norms tables, consider Javier, a Hispanic boy 9 years of age who earned an MPI of 93. He was diagnosed as having a reading disability and has just begun an intervention program. His mother dropped out of school after grade 8. Enter Appendix F (for ages 7 to 18) with the MPI of 93 in the section for children whose mothers completed 11 or less years of schooling. His MPI of 93 corresponds to the 60th percentile rank. Whereas the MPI of 93 corresponds to the 32nd percentile relative to conventional norms, the SES norms tell the examiner that relative to other children who were exposed to a similar range of educational and cultural opportunities, he performed better than 60% of his SES peers.

In contrast, Ken, a 10-year-old Japanese boy with written expression problems, also earned an MPI of 93. Ken's mother graduated college, so enter Appendix F in the section labeled "4-Year Degree or Higher." This time, the MPI of 93 corresponds to the 18th percentile. That range from 60th to 18th percentile is huge and reinforces just how powerful a force can be exerted by one's background. (Note that in Appendix F the precise value of 93 did not appear in the norms for "4-Year Degree or Higher," so the 18th percentile was interpolated based on the values for the 15th and 20th percentiles.)

In view of the SES percentile rank of 60 that corresponds to Javier's MPI of 93, one has to feel optimistic about his success in the intervention program that was recommended to improve his reading ability. In contrast, one has less reason for optimism for Ken, whose identical MPI ranked him at only the 18th percentile relative to children from comparable SES backgrounds.

Whether children with high SES percentile ranks and relatively low national percentile ranks really do have an untapped potential for future learning remains a research question that demands attention. Nevertheless, Kaufman and Kaufman (1983b) stated: [W]e feel intuitively that children who have apparently made the most of their opportunities, and have succeeded where others with similar backgrounds have failed, possess some special qualities that should be harnessed and exploited for their own benefit (p. 167).

Appendixes E and F were derived from data on mother's education. However, if information about mother's education is unavailable or believed to be unreliable, then use other more reliable data to enter Appendix E or F. Perhaps the father's education is known. If not, try to find out specific occupational information about the mother or father to select the appropriate reference group for the child. Consider the amount of formal schooling that is generally associated with an occupation, and then select the most appropriate SES group. As a general rule of thumb: (1) professional, technical, and managerial positions = 4-year degree or higher; (2) clerical or sales positions = 1 to 3 years of college; (3) skilled workers = high school graduate or GED; and (4) semiskilled or unskilled workers = eleventh grade or less. If specific educational and occupational data are unavailable, then it is best not to use the SES norms.

Ultimately, the child's socioeconomic background is far more influential than his or her ethnic background concerning its impact on the KABC-II profile. We encourage examiners to use the SES percentile ranks provided in Appendixes E and F as adjuncts to the global indexes whenever there is reason to believe that this adjunct interpretation will facilitate greater insight into the child's current level of functioning and, possibly, response to intervention.

INTEGRATION OF THE KABC-II AND THE KTEA-II

The KABC-II and the KTEA-II are designed to fit hand in glove. The advantages of conorming the two batteries are numerous: The theoretical basis for the ability test and the achievement tests are similar and cohesive; administration and interpretive systems are similar in design; more accurate comparisons can be made between achievement and ability; each test can enhance the diagnostic reach of the other; and the combination of tests conveniently provides a cohesive and large portion of a comprehensive assessment.

This section introduces the reader to the design and make up of the KTEA-II and the Cattell-Horn-Carroll (CHC) broad and narrow abilities that both the KABC-II and KTEA-II were designed to assess. Different aspects of the integration of the KABC-II and the KTEA-II are explored by examining theoretical, quantitative, clinical, qualitative, and procedural points of view. It should be noted that the formal integration of the KABC-II and the KTEA-II is in its infancy because the batteries have just been published. There are limits to the amount of prepublication research that can be performed. We look forward to the future field research that will explore and define the boundaries of KABC-II-KTEA-II integration.

Description of the KTEA-II

The *Kaufman Test of Educational Achievement, Second Edition* (KTEA-II; Kaufman & Kaufman, 2004b) is an individually administered measure of academic achievement. The test is available in two versions: the Brief Form, which assesses the achievement domains of reading, math, and written expression for ages 4.5 to old age (Kaufman & Kaufman, in press); and the Comprehensive Form, for ages 4.5 to 25 years, which covers a wider range of achievement domains and, in addition, provides an analysis of students' errors. The description of the KTEA-II in this section is taken directly from the KTEA-II Comprehensive Form manual (Kaufman & Kaufman, 2004b).

The KTEA-II Comprehensive Form represents a substantial revision of the earlier editions (Kaufman & Kaufman, 1985, 1998). Due to the expanded age range of the KTEA-II Comprehensive Form, the five retained subtests from the original K-TEA have been modified to allow for the testing of children and young adults from preschool age through college age. In addition, nine new subtests have been added to allow for assessment of a broad range of achievement domains and related skills.

The KTEA-II Comprehensive age norms are provided for 4 through 25 years, and grade norms are provided for kindergarten through grade 12. Like the original, the KTEA-II Comprehensive Form is a curriculum-based diagnostic instrument that is attractive and engaging. It provides norm-referenced and, through its error analysis systems, criterion-referenced assessment in the domains of reading, mathematics, written language, and oral language.

The KTEA-II Comprehensive Form has a number of special features that make it particularly useful as a tool for assessing academic achievement. It measures achievement in reading, mathematics, written language, and oral language and allows the examiner to administer a single subtest or any combination of subtests to assess achievement in one or more domains. All seven specific learning disability areas identified in IDEA are measured: basic reading skills, reading comprehension, mathematics calculation, mathematics reasoning, oral expression, listening comprehension, and written expression.

The KTEA-II Comprehensive Form, like that of the K-TEA, was developed from a clinical model of assessment in order to provide more than a profile of norm-referenced scores. Curriculum experts helped define the specific subskills measured by each subtest and the different types of errors students are likely to make on each subtest, and standardization data guided the construction of the final error analysis system. This system offers clear direction for instructional interventions in all content areas by allowing the examiner to compare a student's pattern of errors to that of the standardization sample.

Pairs of KTEA-II Comprehensive Form subtests—Reading Comprehension and Listening Comprehension, and Written Expression and Oral Expression—were developed to have similar formats to enable useful comparisons to be made between each pair of subtests. These comparisons help the examiner distinguish specific problems in reading or writing from more general language problems.

Composites

Eight of the fourteen KTEA-II Comprehensive Form subtests are grouped into four domain composites: Reading, Mathematics, Written Language, and Oral Language. As shown in Figure 6.9, the Comprehensive Achievement composite comprises six of the subtests that contribute to the domain composites from grade 1 through age 25, and four subtests from age 4.5 through kindergarten. At all grades and ages, each of the four domains is represented in the Comprehensive Achievement composite. The other six Comprehensive Form subtests measure skills related to reading, and these subtests contribute to four additional composites, as shown in Figure 6.10.

Subtests

Examiners may choose to administer a single subtest or any combination of subtests in order to assess a student's academic achievement in one or more domains or to obtain the desired composite score(s). The subtests are described briefly in Table 6.11, organized by content area. The table indicates the age and grade range at which each subtest may be administered. Regardless of whether grade or age norms are being used, selection of subtests is guided by the student's grade level.

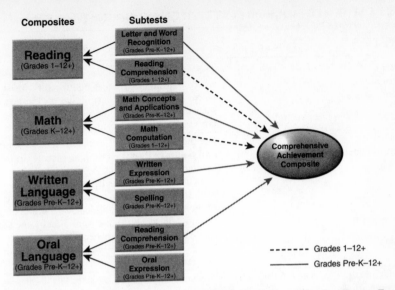

Figure 6.9 Composite structure of the KTEA-II Comprehensive Form: Four domain composites and the Comprehensive Achievement Composite.

Source. From the *KTEA-II manual.*

Notes. "Pre-K" means the subtest or composite starts at age 4-6. "12+" means the subtest or composite goes up to age 25-11.

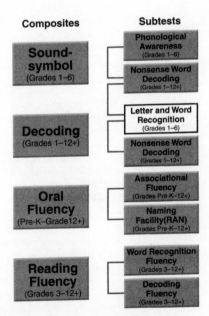

Figure 6.10 Composite structure of the KTEA-II Comprehensive Form: Composites formed by the reading-related subtests.

Source. From the *KTEA-II manual.*

Table 6.11 Brief Description of KTEA-II Comprehensive Form Subtests

Subtest	Range	Description
Letter & Word Recognition	ages 4-6 through 25-11	The student identifies letters and pronounces words of gradually increasing difficulty. Most words are irregular to ensure that the subtest measures word recognition (reading vocabulary) rather than decoding ability.
Reading Comprehension	grade 1 through age 25-11	For the easiest items, the student reads a word and points to its corresponding picture. In following items, the student reads a simple instruction and responds by performing the action. In later items, the student reads passages of increasing difficulty and answers literal or inferential questions about them. Finally, the student rearranges five sentences into a coherent paragraph, and then answers questions about the paragraph.
Math Concepts & Applications	ages 4-6 through 25-11	The student responds orally to test items that focus on the application of mathematical principles to real-life situations. Skill categories include number concepts, operation concepts, rational numbers, measurement, shape and space, data investigations, and higher math concepts.
Math Computation	grade K through age 25-11	The student computes solutions to math problems printed in a student response booklet. Skills assessed include addition, subtraction, multiplication, and division operations; fractions and decimals; square roots, exponents, signed numbers, and algebra.
Written Expression	ages 4-6 through 25-11	Kindergarten and pre-kindergarten children trace and copy letters and write letters from dictation. At grades 1 and higher, the student completes writing tasks in the context of an age-appropriate storybook format. Tasks at those levels include writing sentences from dictation, adding punctuation and capitalization, filling in missing words, completing sentences, combining sentences, writing compound and complex sentences, and, starting at Spring of Grade 1, writing an essay based on the story the student helped complete.
Spelling	grade 1 through age 25-11	The student writes words dictated by the examiner from a steeply graded word list. Words were selected to match acquired spelling skills at each grade level, and for their potential for error analysis. Early items require students to write single letters that represent sounds. The remaining items require students to spell orthographically regular and irregular words of increasing complexity.

Table 6.11 Continued

Subtest	Range	Description
Listening Comprehension	ages 4-6 through 25-11	The student listens to passages played on a CD and then responds orally to questions asked by the examiner. Questions measure literal and inferential comprehension.
Oral Expression	ages 4-6 through 25-11	The student performs specific speaking tasks in the context of a real-life scenario. Tasks assess pragmatics, syntax, semantics, and grammar.
Phonological Awareness	grades 1 through 6	The student responds orally to items that require manipulation of sounds. Tasks include rhyming, matching sounds, blending sounds, segmenting sounds, and deleting sounds.
Nonsense Word Decoding	grade 1 through age 25-11	The student applies phonics and structural analysis skills to decode invented words of increasing difficulty.
Word Reading Fluency	grade 3 through age 25-11	The student reads isolated words as quickly as possible for one minute.
Decoding Fluency	grade 3 through age 25-11	The student applies decoding skills to pronounce as many nonsense words as possible in one minute.
Associational Fluency	ages 4-6 through 25-11	The student says as many words as possible in thirty seconds that belong to a semantic category or have a specified beginning sound.
Naming Facility (RAN)	ages 4-6 through 25-11	The student names objects, colors, and letters as quickly as possible.

Integrating the KABC-II and KTEA-II—Quantitative Analyses

Relationships between the KABC-II and the KTEA-II

Coefficients of correlation between KABC-II global scores and scores on achievement tests were presented and discussed in Chapter 1. Overall, the FCI and MPI correlated substantially (mean r = .71 to .79) with the KTEA-II, WJ III, WIAT-II, and PIAT-R total achievement composites (Rapid Reference 1.17). They also demonstrated good correlations with specific composites measured by the KTEA-II, most notably with Reading, Math, and Written Language (r s in the mid-.60s to mid-.70s); coefficients with Oral Language were a little lower (mid-.50s to mid-.60s; see Rapid Reference 1.8). Correlations between KABC-II global scores and specific academic areas such as Reading and Math (as measured by the WJ III, WIAT-II, and PIAT-R) were comparable in magnitude to the values presented in

Rapid Reference 1.8 for the KTEA-II (see Kaufman & Kaufman, 2004a, pp. 118–126).

In general, achievement correlations with FCI were higher than with MPI, although the differences were typically small. This relationship is to be expected because the FCI includes the Knowledge/*Gc* scale that comprises subtests that are related to acquired knowledge and achievement. Relative to correlations involving the FCI and MPI, relationships between NVI and specific academic areas tended to be substantially lower (except for correlations with math achievement).

Rapid References 6.10 and 6.11 extend the focus of cognitive-achievement relationships by showing how each KABC-II scale index correlates with major KTEA-II composites. In each Rapid Reference, asterisks are used to indicate the KABC-II index that correlates highest (**) and second-highest (*) with each KTEA-II composite.

As shown, the Knowledge/*Gc* scale was the strongest correlate of all areas of achievement for ages 7 to 18 (Rapid Reference 6.10). For this age group, the Knowledge/*Gc* index correlated .75 with KTEA-II Comprehensive Achievement, about .70 with Reading and Oral Language, and about .60 with Math and Written Language. The second-best correlate for ages 7 to 18 was typically Planning/*Gf* (*r*s of .51 to .63), although Learning/*Glr* was the second-best correlate of Written Language (.53). The poorest relationships with all areas of academic achievement for ages 7 to 18 tended to be analogs of the original KABC-II processing scales—Sequential/*Gsm* and Simultaneous/*Gv* (*r*s of .40 to .54).

The strong relationship between the Knowledge/*Gc* index and all areas of achievement for school-age children and adolescents was anticipated, given that the scale is designed to measure the depth and breadth of knowledge acquired from one's culture (including schooling). The good correlations with achievement for the new KABC-II scales—Planning/*Gf* and Learning/*Glr*—attest to the importance in the classroom of the ability to solve problems and learn new material during a clinical evaluation of general cognitive ability. The fact that the original KABC-II processes had the lowest correlations with KTEA-II achievement for ages 7 to 18 suggests that the revisions to the K-ABC during the development of the second edition, most notably by expanding the processes and abilities that the overall battery measures, improved its relationship with academic achievement. Notably, though, the MPC yielded by the original K-ABC compared quite favorably to global scores yielded by other tests in its ability to predict school achievement (Naglieri & Bornstein, 2003).

Intriguingly, the patterns of relationship between ability and achievement ob-

KABC-II Scale Index Correlations with KTEA-II Composites (ages 7–18 years)

KTEA-II Composite

KABC-II Scale	Total	Reading	Math	Written Language	Oral Language
Learning/*Glr*	.58	.55	.49	.53*	.48
Sequential/*Gsm*	.50	.48	.44	.44	.44
Simultaneous/*Gv*	.54	.47	.53	.40	.43
Planning/*Gf*	.63*	.56*	.59*	.51	.51*
Knowledge/*Gc*	.75**	.71**	.62**	.59**	.68**

Source. Data are adapted from Kaufman and Kaufman (2004b).

Note. Total = Comprehensive Achievement Composite; N = 2,025. All correlations were corrected for the variability of the norm group, based on the standard deviation obtained on the KTEA-II, using the variability correction of Cohen, Cohen, West, and Aiken (2003, p. 58).

**Highest correlate of each KTEA-II Achievement Composite.

*Second-highest correlate of each KTEA-II Achievement Composite.

KABC-II Scale Index Correlations with KTEA-II Composites (ages 4.5–6 years)

KTEA-II Composite

KABC-II Scale	Total	Reading	Math	Written Language	Oral Language
Learning/*Glr*	.54	.58**	.52	.62**	.42
Sequential/*Gsm*	.59	.57*	.57*	.58	.49
Simultaneous/*Gv*	.65**	.57*	.65**	.59*	.50*
Knowledge/*Gc*	.60*	.49	.49	.47	.62**

Source. Data are adapted from Kaufman and Kaufman (2004b).

Note. Total = Comprehensive Achievement Composite; N = 491 for Total and Oral Language; N = 301 for Math; N = 122–124 for Written Language. All correlations were corrected for the variability of the norm group, based on the standard deviation obtained on the KTEA-II, using the variability correction of Cohen et al. (2003, p. 58).

**Highest correlate of each KTEA-II Achievement Composite.

*Second-highest correlate of each KTEA-II Achievement Composite.

served for school-age children and adolescents differed quite a bit from the patterns seen at ages 4.5 to 6 years (Rapid Reference 6.11), when academic abilities are first emerging. Despite its obvious link to vocabulary and acquisition of facts, the Knowledge/*Gc* index was *not* the highest correlate of achievement for young children. That distinction went to the Simultaneous/*Gv* index ($r = .65$ with KTEA-II Comprehensive Achievement), with Knowledge/*Gc* (.60) and Sequential/*Gsm* (.59) in a virtual deadlock for second best. So contrary to ages 7 to 18, the KABC-II descendants of the original K-ABC processing scales were among the best correlates of achievement for ages 4.5 to 6 years. In addition, rather than the Knowledge/*Gc* scale emerging as the automatic best predictor of each area of achievement, the highest correlates for young children varied by area. Simultaneous/*Gv* was the highest correlate of Math (.65), Learning/*Glr* was best for Written Language (.62), and Knowledge/*Gc* was best for Oral Language (.62). Three of the four indexes (all *except* Knowledge/*Gc*) were about equal as predictors of Reading (.57 to .58).

Thus, for ages 7 to 18, mental processes such as reasoning and planning were important for academic achievement but not as important as a child's previously acquired knowledge. For ages 4.5 to 6, the roles were reversed. During the stage when school skills are emerging, the amount of knowledge a child has already acquired is secondary to the cognitive processes that are needed to learn to read, write, compute, and speak. Indeed, the one aspect of achievement for which Knowledge/*Gc* was easily the best predictor was Oral Language—undoubtedly relating to the fact that both subtests for this age group (Riddles and Expressive Vocabulary) emphasize children's oral language skills.

The increase in the Knowledge/*Gc* scale's importance from ages 4.5 to 6 to 7 to 18 probably reflects the increased experience with language and academic information as age increases. Also, the strong correlations at ages 4.5 to 6 between Simultaneous/*Gv* and Achievement most likely relates to the fact that this scale measures *both* Visual Processing (*Gv*) and Fluid Reasoning (*Gf*) for young children because a separate Planning/*Gf* scale does not emerge until age 7.

The change in the role that the Knowledge/*Gc* scale plays in the prediction of achievement scores for 4.5 to 6 versus 7 to 18-year-old children is evident from data on global KABC-II and the achievement standard scores summarized in Chapter 1 (Rapid Reference 1.17: (1) FCI correlated .74 with overall KTEA-II Achievement for grades prekindergarten and kindergarten as opposed to about .80 for grades 1 to 12; (2) FCI and MPI were about equal as predictors of overall KTEA achievement from prekindergarten through grade 2, but FCI was decidedly better at grades 3 to 12. The younger children, ages 4.5 through grade 2, have simply not had as much academic experience; therefore, cognitive processing and academic knowledge are still, oftentimes, not as easily distinguished.

Another interesting and related finding from Rapid Reference 1.17 is that *both* FCI and MPI correlated substantially higher with total achievement on the WJ III and WIAT-II at the older grade levels than at the earlier grade levels (mean *r* for FCI = .83 for grades 6 to 10 versus .71 for grades 2 to 5; for MPI, the difference was .80 versus .64).

Further examination of Rapid References 6.10 and 6.11 indicates that coefficients between KABC-II scale indexes and the five major KTEA-II composites ranged from .40 to .75 with median values of .53 (ages 7 to 18) and .57 (4.5 to 6). Most values (about 70%) were in the .50 to .75 range, indicating an acceptable level of relationship between the individual scales of the KABC-II and major KTEA-II composites. If the majority of values were below this moderate range, then there would be a concern that there would not be a reasonable level of association between the two tests. On the other hand, individual scales indicating much higher levels would raise the issue of redundancy and the possibility that the tests measure the same constructs. Even the highest correlation of .75 between Knowledge/*Gc* and total KTEA-II achievement for ages 7 to 18 denotes an overlap of 56%, indicating that each test has its own uniqueness. Therefore, the fact that the majority of coefficients fall in this moderate to strong area indicates an acceptable level of relationship between the two tests.

The KABC-II scales that correlate most highly with the Comprehensive Achievement scale of the KTEA-II differ, again, by age level. The Knowledge scale, as expected, has the highest correlation coefficients with the Comprehensive Achievement scale across all age levels except ages 4.6 and grade 1. The latter groups have highest coefficients on the Simultaneous and Sequential scales, respectively, rather than the Knowledge scale. This is another way of reflecting the make up of the FCI, MCI, and Comprehensive Achievement relationship. The increase in Knowledge scale importance probably reflects the increased experience with language and academic information as age increases.

The KTEA-II offers a number of supplementary composites in addition to the five major academic areas focused on in this chapter and in Chapter 1 (e.g., Sound-Symbol). Though the data are not presented here, one composite yielded relatively low correlation coefficients with the MPI, FCI, and the NVI—Oral Fluency (composed of the Associational Fluency and Number Facility-Rapid Automatized Naming [RAN] subtests) with most values in the .20s and .30s. This finding is not surprising because the Oral Fluency subtests focus on speed and retrieval, which is more a speech task than a processing or achievement task. This composite is designed to be a screening measure for expressive language, so its distant relationship to the KABC-II processing scales is appropriate, but still helpful to have in a comprehensive assessment.

What do these correlation coefficients mean? In practical terms, they mean that you can interpret the two test batteries together and be confident that they relate to each other very well. The scores you obtain on one test with an individual child will be appropriately related to the scores on the other tests.

Calculating Significant Differences between KABC-II and KTEA-II Scores

Another quantitative method of understanding the relationship between the KABC-II and the KTEA-II can be gained by examining significant differences between standard scores on both batteries. One of the benefits of conorming an achievement battery with a measure of cognitive abilities is that it provides a basis for more accurate comparisons between achievement and ability.

The two primary methods of comparing ability with achievement are the simple-difference method and the regression (or predicted-score) method. In the former, a standard score from an ability test is compared with achievement standard scores, and the differences may be evaluated for statistical significance or unusualness. In the regression method, the correlation in the population between the ability and achievement scores is used to calculate the expected (average) achievement standard score for students having a given ability score, and the individual student's actual achievement score is compared with this predicted value. Both the simple-difference method and the regression method require that the achievement test be scored using age norms because ability tests typically do not provide grade norms. Interpretive tables for both methods are provided in the KTEA-II manual (Kaufman & Kaufman, 2004b) although we prefer the regression approach to the simple-difference method because it has a stronger psychometric rationale.

Integrating the KABC-II and KTEA-II—Theory

The integration of the KABC-II and KTEA-II was designed to sample the spectrum of broad and narrow abilities defined by the CHC model. The CHC model includes 10 broad abilities and about 70 narrow abilities (Flanagan & Ortiz, 2001). The KABC-II addresses five of the CHC broad abilities: Short-Term Memory (*Gsm*); Visual Processing (*Gv*); Long-Term Storage and Retrieval (*Glr*); Fluid Reasoning (*Gf*); and Crystallized Ability (*Gc*). The KTEA-II Comprehensive Form measures three additional broad abilities: Auditory Processing (*Ga*), Reading and Writing (*Grw*), and Quantitative Knowledge/*Gq* ability. It also measures *Glr* narrow abilities that increase the breadth of the *Glr* narrow abilities measured by the KABC-II when the two batteries are administered together. The KABC-II also indirectly measures one of the *Gq* narrow abilities (i.e., Mathematics Achievement, by virtue of the fact that Rover and Block Counting each require the child to count).

There are two broad abilities of the CHC model that are not measured by either the KABC-II or the KTEA-II: Processing Speed (*Gs*), and Decision Speed/Reaction Time (*Gt*; see the Don't Forget box). These two broad abilities are not measured by either battery because they are only concerned with speed, not quality, of processing; they lack the requisite complexity for inclusion; and they are weak measures of *g* in Carroll's (1993) factor analytic survey (Kaufman & Kaufman, 2004a). Measures of *Gs* are readily available in other tests, most notably the WJ III and WISC-IV (see case report of Vanessa in Chapter 7), but *Gt* is not measured by any major test battery.

Figure 6.11 displays the alignment of narrow abilities measured by the KABC-II and KTEA-II, grouped by the pertinent broad ability. Alone, the KABC-II measures 14 narrow abilities, including 2 or more associated with each of 5 broad abilities. For the KTEA-II, the corresponding values are 19 narrow abilities and 6 broad abilities. The 2 batteries together measure 8 broad abilities and 33 narrow abilities. The total of 33 is just under half of the 70 or so narrow abilities hypothesized, and often documented empirically, by Carroll (1993).

Rapid References 6.12 through 6.19 provide specific information regarding the precise KABC-II and KTEA-II subtests that are believed to measure each of the 34 narrow abilities. The Rapid References are organized by broad ability (e.g., Rapid Reference 6.12 covers the subtests that measure *Glr* narrow abilities, Rapid Reference 6.13 is confined to *Gsm* narrow abilities, and so forth). For definitions of the five broad abilities measured by the KABC-II, see Chapter 3 (Rapid References 3.1 to 3.5).

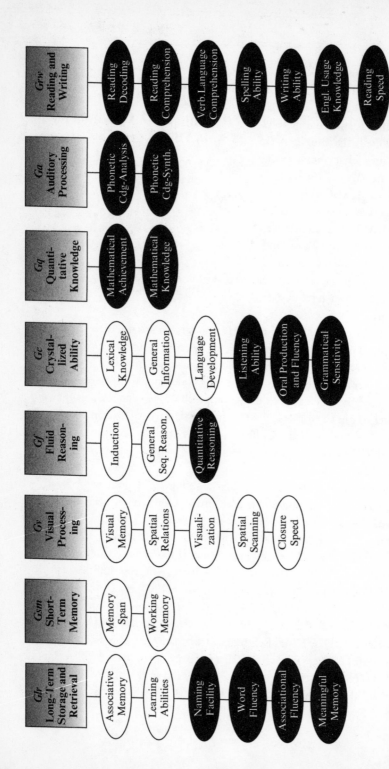

Figure 6.11 CHC Broad and Narrow Abilities measured by the KABC-II and the KTEA-II.

Notes. The CHC Broad Abilities are shown in gray squares. CHC Narrow Abilities that are measured by only KABC-II subtests are represented by white ovals; Narrow Abilities that are measured only by KTEA-II subtests are represented by black ovals. Two KABC-II subtests also measure math achievement but are primarily measures of other narrow abilities.

≡ *Rapid Reference 6.12*

CHC Analysis: Long-Term Storage & Retrieval *(Glr)* Narrow CHC Abilities Measured by KABC-II and KTEA-II Subtests

Glr **Narrow Ability**

Associative Memory
   KABC-II Atlantis
   KABC-II Rebus
   KABC-II Atlantis Delayed
   KABC-II Rebus Delayed

Learning Abilities
   KABC-II Atlantis Delayed
   KABC-II Rebus Delayed

Naming Facility
   KTEA-II Naming Facility/RAN

Associational Fluency
   KTEA-II Associational Fluency (category items, e.g., foods, animals)

Word Fluency
   KTEA-II Associational Fluency (category items, e.g., words that start with the /d/ sound)

Meaningful Memory
   KTEA-II Listening Comprehension

One of the most important expectations that you may have about using the KABC-II and the KTEA-II together is that there is a cohesive theoretical design that acts like an umbrella over the two tests. This expectation is met in that there are no redundancies between the tests that result in a waste of time. (No examiner has time to waste duplicating subtests!) The explanation for what is cognitive processing and what is achievement on the KABC-II and KTEA-II is theoretically based and evidence based, and the results of combining the two tests will give the examiner a comprehensive and fruitful examination of the child's cognitive abilities and how they translate into academic skills.

That is not to say that the two batteries do not overlap in broad or narrow abilities; as is evident from Figure 6.11 and Rapid References 6.12 to 6.19, there is some overlap. However, there is no redundancy. For example, both batteries mea-

≡Rapid Reference 6.13

CHC Analysis Short-Term Memory *(Gsm)* Narrow CHC Abilities Measured by KABC-II (KTEA-II subtests do not measure any *Gsm* Narrow Abilities)

Gsm Narrow Ability

Memory Span
  KABC-II Word Order (without color interference)
  KABC-II Number Recall
  KABC-II Hand Movements

Working Memory
  KABC-II Word Order (with color interference)

Note. Success on KTEA-II Phonological Awareness and Listening Comprehension is also dependent, to some extent, on *Gsm*.

---

sure *Glr* and *Gc* narrow abilities, but each measures a separate set. When they do measure the same narrow ability, they do it in quite different ways: Mathematical Achievement is a minor aspect of two KABC-II subtests, but this *Gq* ability is the major thrust of Mathematics Computation; in contrast, the *Gf* narrow ability of Induction is a key component of the KABC-II Planning/*Gf* subtests.

Flanagan and Ortiz (2001) suggest that you need at least two different primary narrow ability measures to adequately measure a broad ability from a cross-battery perspective. Examiners who integrate the KABC-II with the KTEA-II should easily be able to achieve adequate measurement of seven broad abilities: *Gv, Gf, Gc, Glr, Gsm, Grw,* and *Gq*. However, assessment of *Ga* depends on a single KTEA-II subtest (Phonological Awareness) that is only normed from age 4.5 to grade 6.

Of course, no one battery can cover the CHC model in its entirety, but the KABC-II and the KTEA-II—like the WJ III Cognitive and Achievement Batteries—provide a substantially positive start for the clinician to examine a child's performance from a CHC perspective. To supplement the KABC-II via Cross Battery Assessment, using CHC theory as a foundation, see Dawn Flanagan's section later in this chapter. For more in-depth study of the theory and assessment approach, as it pertains to other instruments such as the original K-ABC and Wechsler's scales, consult publications by Flanagan and her colleagues (Flanagan & Kaufman, 2004; Flanagan, McGrew, & Ortiz, 2000; Flanagan & Ortiz, 2001; Flanagan, Ortiz, Alfonso, & Mascolo, 2002; McGrew & Flanagan, 1998).

Long-Term Storage & Retrieval (Glr)

The KABC-II Core battery measures a single *Glr* narrow ability (Associative Memory); an additional narrow ability is assessed when examiners administer the supplementary Delayed Recall scale (Atlantis Delayed and Rebus Delayed each measure *both* Associative Memory and Learning Abilities). But to obtain rich measurement of *Glr* examiners need to administer a variety of KTEA-II subtests. Listening Comprehension, Associational Fluency, and Naming Facility/RAN all relate to the CHC requirement of the child engaging in activities that measure efficiency of how well information is stored and retrieved.

Listening Comprehension demands that the child listens and encodes a story and then manipulate the information to answer questions about the story. Although, "long-term storage and retrieval" implies that there is a long time between encoding and retrieval, this is not necessarily the case because the information has to be retrieved by association for whatever time interval has lapsed. The CHC model calls the narrow ability measured by Listening Comprehension *Meaningful Memory*.

The Naming Facility/RAN subtest was given its label based both on the CHC narrow ability that it measures (Naming Facility) and on the popular neuropsychological subtest that inspired it (Rapid Automatized Naming, or RAN). The Associational Fluency subtest is also named after a CHC narrow ability, but, in actuality, this subtest measures two different narrow abilities. The category items (e.g., name as many kinds of toys as you can) measure Associational Fluency, whereas the items that focus on naming as many words as possible that start with a specific sound (such as /k/) measure Word Fluency. For purposes of reliability, these two narrow abilities are subsumed by a single standard score. Inferences about the separate narrow abilities are only possible if the child performs at notably different levels on the two kinds of items (e.g., a child who can reel off a string of words that begin with particular sounds but is stymied and hesitant when retrieving categorical words). See Rapid Reference 6.12 for an outline of the Long-Term Storage & Retrieval (*Glr*) narrow abilities.

Short-Term Memory (Gsm)

The primary subtest that measures auditory short-term memory on the KABC-II is Number Recall. The CHC model mostly mentions auditory short-term memory tests for *Gsm* but visual and haptic activities such as Hand Movements also measure *Gsm*. The three subtests together measure different modalities of short-term memory and also how short-term memory can evolve into working memory.

All three KABC-II *Gsm* subtests (Number Recall, Word Order, and Hand

Movements) measure Memory Span. In addition, Word Order has a color interference task that definitely requires the narrow ability of Working Memory. Consequently, for young children (ages 3 to 5 or 6), who are not likely to reach the color interference items in Word Order, the KABC-II measures only a single CHC narrow ability—Memory Span. However, for children 6 to 7 or older, the KABC-II measures both Memory Span and Working Memory. See Rapid Reference 6.13 for an outline of the Short-Term Memory (*Gsm*) narrow abilities.

Visual Processing (Gv)

The KABC-II provides rich measurement of five *Gv* narrow abilities although examiners need to administer supplementary subtests such as Gestalt Closure (Closure Speed) and Hand Movements (Visual Memory) to measure all five. See Rapid Reference 6.14 for an outline of the Visual Processing (*Gv*) narrow abilities.

≡Rapid Reference 6.14

CHC Analysis: Visual Processing *(Gv)* Narrow CHC Abilities Measured by KABC-II (KTEA-II subtests do not measure any *Gv* Narrow Abilities)

Gv Narrow Ability

Visual Memory
   KABC-II Face Recognition
   KABC-II Hand Movements

Spatial Relations
   KABC-II Triangles

Visualization
   KABC-II Triangles
   KABC-II Conceptual Thinking
   KABC-II Block Counting
   KABC-II Pattern Reasoning
   KABC-II Story Completion

Spatial Scanning
   KABC-II Rover

Closure Speed
   KABC-II Gestalt Closure

Note. Success on KTEA-II Written Expression is also dependent, to some extent, on Visual Processing.

Fluid Reasoning (Gf)

Fluid reasoning is specifically measured by the subtests that constitute the Planning/*Gf* scale (Pattern Reasoning, Story Completion), and also by subtests on the Simultaneous/*Gv* scale (Rover, Conceptual Thinking) and the Knowledge/*Gc* scale (Riddles). KTEA-II Mathematics Concepts and Applications is primarily a *Gq* task, but it also requires considerable *Gf* for success, specifically the narrow ability Quantitative Reasoning. On the Planning/*Gf* scale, Pattern Reasoning primarily measures the narrow ability of Induction whereas Story Completion measures *both* Induction (figuring out what the story is about) and General Sequential Reasoning, or deduction (selecting and sequencing the correct pictures). See Rapid Reference 6.15 for an outline of the Fluid Reasoning (*Gf*) narrow abilities.

Crystallized Ability (Gc)

The narrow ability of Lexical Knowledge is measured by all three Knowledge/*Gc* subtests, with Riddles (Language Development) and Verbal Knowledge (General Information) each measuring an additional *Gc* narrow ability as well. When the KABC-II and KTEA-II are administered together, the measurement of *Gc* narrow abilities expands to six, indicating breadth of coverage of this broad ability. See Rapid Reference 6.16 for an outline of Crystallized Ability (*Gc*) narrow abilities.

≡ *Rapid Reference 6.15*

CHC Analysis: Fluid Reasoning (*Gf*) Narrow CHC Abilities Measured by KABC-II and KTEA-II Subtests

Gf Narrow Ability

Induction
    KABC-II Conceptual Thinking
    KABC-II Pattern Reasoning
    KABC-II Story Completion

General Sequential Reasoning
    KABC-II Story Completion
    KABC-II Rover
    KABC-II Riddles

Quantitative Reasoning
    KTEA-II Mathematics Concepts & Applications

Note. Success on KABC-II Rebus and four KTEA-II subtests (Reading Comprehension, Listening Comprehension, Oral Expression, and Written Expression) is also dependent, to some extent, on Fluid Reasoning.

≡ *Rapid Reference 6.16*

CHC Analysis: Crystallized Ability *(Gc)* Narrow CHC Abilities Measured by KABC-II and KTEA-II Subtests

Gc Narrow Ability

General Information

    KABC-II Verbal Knowledge (items that measure general information)

    KABC-II Story Completion

Language Development

    KABC-II Riddles

Lexical Knowledge

    KABC-II Riddles

    KABC-II Verbal Knowledge (items that measure vocabulary)

    KABC-II Expressive Vocabulary

Listening Ability

    KTEA-II Listening Comprehension

Oral Production and Fluency

    KTEA-II Oral Expression

Grammatical Sensitivity

    KTEA-II Oral Expression

    KTEA-II Written Expression

Note. Success on KABC-II Rebus is also dependent, to some extent, on Grammatical Sensitivity.

Auditory Processing (Ga)

Ga "requires the perception, analysis, and synthesis of patterns among auditory stimuli as well as the discrimination of subtle differences in patterns of sound" (Flanagan & Ortiz, 2001, p. 18). It is assessed on the KTEA-II by the supplementary Phonological Awareness and measures both the analytic and synthetic narrow abilities associated with the *Ga* broad ability. However, the KTEA-II subtest is of appropriate difficulty primarily for young children (prekindergarten to grade 2) and is only standardized through grade 6. In addition, it yields an overall score rather than separate scores for its two narrow abilities. Nonetheless, the KTEA-II Error Analysis procedure for Phonological Awareness permits examiners to determine whether the child performed at a Strong, Average, or Weak level on the separate sections of the subtest (Kaufman & Kaufman, 2004b). Hence, the error analysis allows examiners to compare the child's ability on the two *Ga* narrow abilities that it measures. See Rapid Reference 6.17 for an outline of Auditory Processing (*Ga*) narrow abilities.

≡Rapid Reference 6.17

CHC Analysis: Auditory Processing *(Ga)* Narrow CHC Abilities Measured by KTEA-II (KABC-II subtests do not measure any *Ga* Narrow Abilities)

Ga Narrow Ability

Phonetic Coding—Analysis

   KTEA-II Phonological Awareness (Section 1—Rhyming; Section 2—Sound Matching; Section 4—Segmenting; Section 5—Deleting Sounds)

Phonetic Coding—Synthesis

   KTEA-II Phonological Awareness (Section 3—Blending)

Note. Deficits in certain *Ga* narrow abilities, like Speech Sound Discrimination, may impact performance negatively on such tests as KABC-II Riddles, Word Order, and Number Recall, and KTEA-II Listening Comprehension.

≡Rapid Reference 6.18

CHC Analysis: Quantitative Knowledge *(Gq)* Narrow CHC Abilities Measured by KTEA-II and KABC-II Subtests

Gq Narrow Ability

Mathematical Knowledge

   KTEA-II Mathematics Concepts & Applications

Mathematical Achievement

   KTEA-II Mathematics Computation

   KABC-II Rover

   KABC-II Block Counting

Quantitative Knowledge (Gq)

Gq measures the individual's store of accumulated mathematical knowledge (Flanagan & Ortiz, 2001). It is different from the *Gf* narrow ability of Quantitative Reasoning because *Gq* is more about what the child knows than how the child reasons with quantitative information. Math Concepts and Applications measures quantitative Reasoning to some extent, but that subtest is primarily a measure of *Gq,* as is Mathematics Computation. Taken together, both KTEA-II subtests that make up the Math Composite measure the two *Gq* narrow abilities, providing thorough measurement of the *Gq* broad ability. See Rapid Reference 6.18 for an outline of Quantitative Knowledge (*Gq*) narrow abilities.

≡ Rapid Reference 6.19

CHC Analysis: Reading & Writing *(Grw)* Narrow CHC Abilities Measured by KTEA-II (KABC-II subtests do not measure any *Grw* Narrow Abilities)

Grw Narrow Ability

Reading Decoding
   KTEA-II Letter & Word Reading
   KTEA-II Nonsense Word Decoding

Reading Comprehension
   KTEA-II Reading Comprehension (paragraph items)

Verbal (Printed) Language Comprehension
   KTEA-II Reading Comprehension (items requiring student to do what a sentence tells them to do)

Spelling Ability
   KTEA-II Spelling

Writing Ability
   KTEA-II Written Expression

English Usage Knowledge
   KTEA-II Written Expression

Reading Speed
   KTEA-II Word Recognition Fluency
   KTEA-II Decoding Fluency

Reading & Writing *(Grw)*

Grw is measured by achievement tests (Flanagan & Ortiz, 2001). The KTEA-II provides thorough measurement of five key *Grw* narrow abilities: Reading Decoding, Reading Comprehension, Spelling Ability, Writing Ability, and Reading Speed. It also measures two additional *Gc* abilities to some extent—Verbal (Printed) Language Comprehension and English Usage Knowledge. Several of the new subtests added to the KTEA-II Comprehensive Form (Nonsense Word Decoding, Written Expression, Word Recognition Fluency, and Decoding Fluency) greatly enriched the measurement of *Grw* narrow abilities relative to the original K-TEA. See Rapid Reference 6.19 for an outline of Reading and Writing *(Grw)* narrow abilities.

Clinical Analysis of the Integration of the KABC-II and KTEA-II

CHC theory and quantitative analyses (especially correlational) provide valuable ways of integrating the KABC-II and KTEA-II, but it is important to remember that (1) the KABC-II is built on a dual theoretical foundation (Luria's neuro-psychological approach as well as CHC psychometric theory), and (2) both the KABC-II and KTEA-II are individually administered clinical instruments that afford examiners rich opportunities for qualitative observations. We cannot en-vision the examiner obtaining the full benefit of an analysis of the KABC-II and KTEA-II without including the important *process and qualitative* information. This information comes from observing a child in a standardized setting that mini-mizes unnecessary interactions (e.g., wording in instructions) *and* maximizes op-portunities to actively engage learning processes (e.g., dynamic subtests like At-lantis and Rebus) with the child.

This section on clinical analysis fully takes into account the neuropsychologi-cal processing model developed by Luria and addresses brain functions and pro-cesses involved in cognitive *and* achievement tests. For example, the Phonologi-cal Awareness test on the KTEA-II is a subtest that requires the child to remember and manipulate sounds and words. This subtest is a wonderful mea-sure of auditory skills (*Ga*) but also working memory and cognitive sequencing. These latter skills are specifically measured by the Sequential/*Gsm* scale, indicat-ing that a complete understanding of the young child's performance on KTEA-II Phonological Awareness requires examiners to compare that performance to the child's success (or lack of it) on KABC-II Sequential/*Gsm* subtests.

It is not a coincidence that these kinds of tasks reflect years of research based on auditory-sequential skills and the phonemic awareness skills needed for read-ing (e.g., Hooper & Hynd, 1985; Kamphaus & Reynolds, 1987; Lichtenberger et al., 2000; Lichtenberger, 2001) and associated with left-hemispheric processing (James & Selz, 1997; Lyon et al., 2003; Reynolds et al., 1997).

For each section that follows, discussion emphasizes functional processing abilities that will hopefully help examiners with construct and skill analyses. Both the CHC and Luria theoretical approaches reflect an aspect of comprehensive as-sessment that needs to be buttressed by qualitative or process information. Fur-thermore, all cognitive and achievement test data must be interpreted in the con-text of other important information such as history, medical status, medications, family involvement, quality of teaching, developmental stage, social and emotional functioning, visual-motor functioning, and responses to prior interventions.

Sequential Processing, Short-Term Memory, Phonological Awareness, and Listening Comprehension

As indicated in the note to Rapid Reference 6.13, we believe that KTEA-II Phonological Awareness and Listening Comprehension are each dependent, to some extent, on the CHC *Gsm* broad ability. The process rationale for each sub-test follows.

Process rationale for Phonological Awareness   It is important to understand both the Lurian and CHC ways of interpreting the Sequential/*Gsm* scale because there is a great deal of research literature that combines sequential processing and auditory short-term memory with the type of phonological processing skills that are measured by the KTEA-II Phonological Awareness subtest (Siegal, 1997; Teeter, 1997). The combination of this KTEA-II subtest and the KABC-II Sequential/*Gsm* subtests provides a large window of opportunity for evaluating reading problems and the more phonologically based subtypes of learning disabilities (see the section of this chapter on identifying learning disabilities)

As a primary measure of auditory short-term memory, the Sequential/*Gsm* Core subtests help the examiner evaluate the critical listening skills that children need in the classroom. The Phonological Awareness subtest measures sound-symbol connections but because of the way it is set up, it also measures auditory short-term memory and sequencing skills. This is an interactive subtest where the child has to listen very closely to the examiner and then reproduce sounds and manipulate word syllables and sounds. In the last part of Phonemic Awareness, the child also has to hold a multisyllable word in working memory and then remove a syllable to form a new word.

A skilled examiner can retrieve a lot of information by assessing behavioral clues about how well the child can remember sounds and use working memory. Does the child attempt to reproduce the sound? Does the child miss the examiner's cues and ask for repetitions? Is the child shy and too embarrassed to verbalize? Does the child get the sounds right but in the wrong order? When you move to the part of Phonological Awareness that needs working memory does the child's behavior shift dramatically? Does the child pay attention, or do you have to cue each item?

The reading research literature indicates that many early reading problems stem from a learning disability subtype called "auditory-linguistic or phonological form of dyslexia" (Spreen, 2001; Teeter, 1997). This is not to say that visual and other processing deficits are not important subtypes of reading problems, but for the moment, let us explore the relationship between the processing and production of phonology in young readers.

Phonological processing is basically the ability to understand and use the sound components of language. The KABC-II Phonological Awareness subtest comprises five different activities that correspond to Adams's (1990) five levels of phonemic awareness tasks in ascending order of difficulty: rhyming, sound matching, blending, segmenting, and manipulating phonemes.

Phonological processing is closely related to problems in speech perception, naming and vocabulary ability, and auditory short-term memory with sounds.

When phonological awareness deficits are present, reading comprehension suffers because the cognitive processes that are required for comprehension are tied up in decoding and word recognition (Stanovich, 1992). This leaves the child with a myopic focus on the elements of the text and little resources for fluid reading and comprehension.

Young children who have reading problems can be helped by evaluating their ability to understand the phonetic/linguistic parts of reading. If we know which parts are problematic, then we will be able to better describe interventions that are targeted to the child's specific deficit. There is evidence to support interventions in phonemic awareness with young elementary-aged children not only from an academic outcome perspective but also from neuropsychological growth perspective in that neural networks that support reading can be enhanced with the appropriate instruction (Lyon et al., 2003).

As indicated, the KABC-II scale that has an important part in the assessment of phonological awareness skills, especially in younger readers, is the Sequential/*Gsm* scale. The primary task of the Sequential/*Gsm* scale is to measure how the child processes information in a linear, step-by-step fashion. How a child performs on the Sequential/*Gsm* scale can illuminate whether the child has the prerequisite auditory sequencing and short-term memory skills to be able to put sounds together with symbols while he or she is decoding a word (Das, Naglieri, & Kirby, 1994; Kirby & Williams, 1991; Naglieri, 2001).

Process Rationale for Listening Comprehension   The Listening Comprehension subtest on the KTEA-II also supports the Sequential/*Gsm* scale because it straddles auditory short-term memory, auditory working memory, and auditory long-term encoding. The tasks are presented in a pure auditory form and therefore should be compared with Phonological Awareness and the Sequential/*Gsm* Core subtests. Does the child remember well on Phonological Awareness with small, short-term auditory segments and then do very poorly on Listening Comprehension that requires a much higher auditory memory load? Or—the opposite—does the child not do well with small pure auditory segments but when the task is put in story form on Listening Comprehension the child performs quite well? Answers to these types of processing questions will help with differential diagnosis later on.

The Simultaneous/Gv Scale and Written Expression

You may wish to supplement the Simultaneous/*Gv* scale with Written Expression, even if you do not administer any other KTEA-II subtest, just to check out the visual motor aspects of written expression activities and how they relate to some of the visual motor activities on the KABC-II subtests like Rover or Triangles. These comparisons may help you figure out why a child has poor handwriting or poor visual organization on writing tasks. Remember when you were administering the Written Expression test to the child. Did you observe the child having trouble holding the pencil? Did the child lose his or her place a lot? Did the child write a lot of words or letters in a reversed way? Were there multiple erasures? Did the child have trouble figuring out where he or she should write the responses even though you were pointing to the correct starting point?

If you do suspect that achievement in writing is partly due to visual-motor issues, then it would be appropriate to pursue this hypothesis further by administering tests designed specifically for assessing visual-motor problems. As shown in the note to Rapid Reference 6.14, we believe that KTEA-II Written Expression is dependent, to some extent, on the CHC *Gv* broad ability.

Planning, Reasoning, and Executive Functions: How They Apply to Rover and Rebus and to Several KTEA-II Subtests

Rapid Reference 6.14 indicates that Rover measures the *Gf* narrow ability of General Sequential Reasoning (deduction). Other subtests (Rebus and four KTEA-II tasks) are mentioned in the note to that Rapid Reference as being dependent, to some extent, on the *Gf* broad ability. The process rationale for each of these subtests follows.

Process Rationale for Rover Rover was designed to explore the child's ability to create numerous ways to solve a problem and then choose the best plan. Like the game of chess, however, Rover also has a visual-spatial component that is just as essential as planning ability in order to efficiently navigate the game board. When Rover was initially developed, it was intended as a measure of Planning/*Gf*. However, confirmatory factor analyses of the National Tryout sample clearly pinpointed Rover as a measure of simultaneous and visual processing. Because the child has to look for different ways a dog can get to a bone on a maplike game board containing rocks, weeds, and grass, it is ultimately the child's visual mapping ability that plays the most important part in solving the problems.

Nonetheless, Rover was included in the KABC-II because regardless of its scale membership, the task presented an interesting challenge to children and adolescents, measures *both Gf* and *Gv* narrow abilities and demands intact executive functions for success. If a child has poor planning or executive functions, performance on this subtest is severely impacted. Even though the child's visual-spatial mapping abilities lead the way, the child still has to figure out several plans, hold them in working memory, and then determine the value of the best plan. The latter is, most definitely, an executive functioning task.

Indeed, in a KABC-II study of 56 children with ADHD, a group that is notorious for having deficits in executive functions (Barkley, 2003), the ADHD children had significantly lower scores ($p < .001$) on Rover than their nonclinical peers (Kaufman & Kaufman, 2004a). They also had significantly lower scores on more pure measures of executive functions such as the Planning/*Gf* Pattern Reasoning and Story Completion subtests ($p < .01$).

When you are evaluating the Planning/*Gf* scale, therefore, consider the child's performance on Rover. Was the child organized? Did the child take the time to look for all of the possible ways, or did the child just blurt out the first answer? Also look at the style of processing. Did the child take time and think about the routes and then count out the final plan (reflective style), or did the child charge right in and then have to self-correct (impulsive style)? Rover can supplement the Planning/*Gf* scale by helping you look at the differences in subtest scores and including the processing and qualitative aspects of how the child obtained the scores. If you note executive function-type deficits during Rover, also see if these deficits were evident on Pattern Reasoning and Story Completion. Also, examine your qualitative observations of the child's strategy generation and then administer other tests of executive functions to test your hypotheses.

Process Rationale for Rebus   The CHC model places Rebus safely in the narrow ability category of Associative Memory (MA), where the examinee is required to learn the word associated with a particular rebus drawing and then read phrases and sentences composed of these drawings. Although Rebus primarily measures a *Glr* narrow ability, it still requires a great deal of organization, not just retrieval.

Rebus also measures the process of how a child responds to the teaching-learning situation. Unlike other subtests (except Atlantis), the child has to learn more and more information and then apply the information. It is similar to a classroom situation only it is strictly controlled and measurable because the examiner gives standardized teaching prompts. This is a subtest where the examiner feeds information and rehearsal to the child step-by-step. The examiner is constrained by only being able to teach in a standardized fashion; however, this constraint also frees the examiner to look at how the child responds to teaching. This is a *dynamic and controlled process* and provides key qualitative data to the KABC-II examiner.

The reason why Rebus is considered to depend on *Gf* to some extent is because during administration the test demands executive functions to be at maximum alert. Many researchers (e.g., Goldberg & Bougakov, 2000) liken the executive functions to an orchestra conductor. The first and second functional areas of the brain, if you will, are the actual musicians in the orchestra all designed to play certain instruments at certain times. The orchestra conductor is the third functional area of the brain (frontal lobe area) that has to direct complex cognitive functions that require input, processing, prioritizing, organizing, planning, and output.

Rebus taxes the orchestra conductor because there are many first and second functional unit tasks like paying attention to each tiny word or picture, processing the visual information, processing the auditory information, melding the symbol and sound, only learning exactly what the examiner is teaching at paced intervals, organizing the reading of symbols and their sounds into coherent and meaningful sentences, and checking for mistakes and comprehension. It takes quite a conductor to direct the Rebus symphony!

There are many qualitative or behavioral indicators during Rebus that can give the examiner clues as to problems with attention or executive functions. Many young children on Rebus will try very hard to learn the words and their matching symbols and then be completely oblivious to the fact that they are reading meaningful sentences. Therefore, if they make a mistake on a word and the meaning of the sentence disappears, they do not mentally register the lack of meaning, they simply just continue to read isolated symbols. On the other hand, children who do have developing executive or metacognitive functions will notice the break in comprehension and skip back to where they think they went wrong and try to figure out the mistaken symbol. This behavior is indicative of the orchestra conductor checking where lower functions went wrong, and it also makes for a difference in scores because the child self-corrects.

An alert examiner will know by the presence or absence of self-corrective behaviors if the child has problems with organization. A low score on Rebus could mean that there is a problem with transferring information from short or recent memory to long-term memory (as the *Glr* classification implies, but a low score could also mean that there is trouble with planning or executive functions. Hence, a comparison with the strong planning subtests like Pattern Reasoning and Story Completion is appropriate. Therefore, while Rebus factorially belongs on the Learning/*Glr* scale of the KABC-II, it can also assist in the exploration of the child's fluid reasoning ability measured on the Planning/*Gf* scale.

Process Rationale for KTEA-II Written Expression, Reading Comprehension, Math Applications, Oral Expression, and Listening Comprehension   There are four subtests on the KTEA-II that require not only academic knowledge but also organizational, deductive, inductive, and planning skills. Written Expression, Reading Comprehension, Oral Expression, and Listening Comprehension all require "higher levels of cognition" (Sattler, 2001), "cognitive load" (Raney, 1993), or "higher-complex abilities" (Mather, Wendling, & Woodcock, 2001). Sattler and Mather and colleagues describe primary academic tasks in a hierarchy ranging from ones requiring low levels of cognition, such as letter identification, to those that require higher levels, such as reading comprehension and the construction of written text. Figure 6.12 illustrates the hierarchical relationship among achievement areas and subtests on the KTEA-II Comprehensive Form with respect to their level of cognitive processing.

Informally interpreting these subtest scores alongside the subtests that truly measure *Gf* narrow abilities acknowledges that the more sophisticated skills needed for these upper-level academic tasks should be assessed in a cognitive processing way. Again, the skilled and observant examiner watches how the child takes these achievement tests and looks for behavioral clues to see if the child has the organization and planning skills to do a good job.

For example, during Reading Comprehension, the child has to pick the best of several responses to answer the question about comprehension correctly. Watch for processing style here. Does the child read the passage quickly and impulsively pick an answer (impulsive, inattentive style), or does the child read the passage and then spend quite a bit of time reading the possible answers and deliberating on the correctness of a response (reflective style)? Does the child have so many problems decoding the reading passage that they miss the overall story? Observe the child's

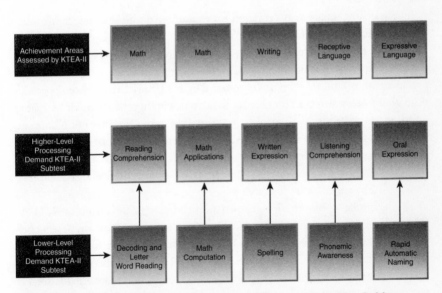

Figure 6.12 KTEA-II Hierarchy of Cognitive Processing Load by Achievement Area, Higher-Level Processing Subtests, and Lower-Level Processing Subtests.

eye movements. Does the child read from left to write with occasional loops back to check for comprehension (fluid movements), or do the child's eyes flicker back and forth, lose place, skip lines, or other nonfluid movements (poor eye tracking/ nonfluid movements)? These types of observations can give valuable clues as to what factors bring about a low score on reading comprehension.

Comparing these kinds of observations with other subtests that require organization, executive functions, and fluid reasoning may give the examiner some keys as to why reading comprehension performance is problematic for a child. Perhaps the problem is not that that the child does not know math facts, perhaps it is because the child cannot *organize* the math facts to be able to apply them to a problem. If the child does have problems with organization and other *Gf* subtests, then the remediation plan calls for including prescriptions about organization (not necessarily the drilling of math facts).

Similar observations about Written Expression, Oral Expression, and Listening Comprehension need to be made by the examiner because all of these subtests need the child to have good *Gf* skills. The beauty of comparing these scores with subtests on the Planning/*Gf* scale is that the process of how a child utilizes upper level cognitive skills to perform academic tasks is being compared, not just the concrete details that the teacher probably already knows about (e.g., reading and math levels).

There is also a quantitative method for examining the child's reasoning ability on the KTEA-II via its Error Analysis procedure. Reading Comprehension and Listening Comprehension deliberately include items that measure inferential thinking (*Gf*) as well as literal recall of facts. The items on each subtest have been preclassified as either *Literal* or *Inferential*. The KTEA-II Error Analysis procedure, therefore, permits examiners to determine whether the child performed at a Strong, Average, or Weak level on each type of item (Kaufman & Kaufman, 2004b). Hence, if the child's category on the Inferential items of Reading Comprehension, Listening Comprehension, or both is classified as Weak or Strong, that classification can be used to corroborate other quantitative and qualitative data about the child's reasoning ability.

From a process point of view, information and data gleaned from the KTEA-II high-level subtests can help the examiner look at how well the orchestra conductor organizes complex tasks and large bodies of information. If you do suspect that the child might have executive function deficits, then it is appropriate to test further with tests that are specifically designed to measure this area. If you do not feel comfortable incorporating measures of executive functions into the comprehensive assessment, then a referral to a colleague who is familiar with these measures is an appropriate course of action.

Auditory Processing (Ga) and Several Auditory Tasks on the KABC-II and KTEA-II

As indicated in the note to Rapid Reference 6.17, we believe that KTEA-II Listening Comprehension and three KABC-II subtests (Riddles, Number Recall, Word Order) are dependent, to some extent, on the CHC *Ga* broad ability. The process rationale for these subtests follows.

Process Rationale for Listening Comprehension, Riddles, Number Recall, and Word Order
These subtests do not measure the CHC-defined Auditory Processing/*Ga* because they are more to do with auditory memory and the keeping of auditory input long enough to come up with an answer. The primary subtests that measure *Ga*—like KTEA-II Phonological Awareness—are more concerned with the discrimination of sounds and with phonemic analysis and synthesis. Nonetheless, Listening Comprehension and the three KABC-II subtests still all use auditory input as the main processing vehicle and that, by nature, is serial and sequential. Because most of these auditory processes take place in similar places in the brain and have resultant brain-behavior similarities (e.g., language problems, reading problems), the examiner should make an effort to distinguish auditory memory from auditory discrimination. Both processes require different intervention strategies and have different influences on academic performance.

Listening Comprehension, in particular, is a supportive subtest for *Ga* because it measures the kind of listening comprehension that students must do in school—that is, comprehension of relatively formal speech rather than casual or naturalistic speech. This would serve the purpose of enhancing the relevance of the test score to a school-based evaluation. The Listening Comprehension subtest also has a second important design objective: to parallel the passage items of the Reading Comprehension subtest. The primary difference between the two subtests is that Listening Comprehension requires the students to listen to the passages on a CD and then answer questions spoken by the examiner. Because students perform similar tasks in Listening Comprehension and Reading Comprehension, a significantly lower score on the latter subtest may suggest the presence of a reading problem rather than a more general deficit in language development (Stanovich, 1992).

Integrating the KABC-II and KTEA-II—Qualitative/Behavioral Analyses

By comparing QIs on the KABC-II and the KTEA-II, you can see how a child behaviorally responds to different types of tests. (For more detailed information about QIs, the reader is directed to the KABC-II and the KTEA-II manuals and the QIs section elsewhere in this book.) Examine the following scenarios to determine if there are any differences on performance for each battery (see the Don't Forget box for a summary).

DON'T FORGET

Compare QIs on KABC-II and KTEA-II

Look for differences in performance...
with affect and motivation
with self-confidence
between modalities
with cognitive load

Look for Differences with Affect and Motivation

Does the child enjoy the novel game-like activities on the KABC-II but then become quiet, sullen, or bored on the KTEA-II, or vice versa? Does the child act nervous and unsure on the KABC-II but cheer up with familiar tasks on the KTEA-II? Look for changes in behavior going from novel process tasks to familiar academic tasks.

Look for Differences with Self-Confidence

Does the child try hard on the KABC-II subtests and know when he or she performed well? Does the child verbalize self-confidence with statements like: "I'm good at this!" or "This is easy!" Do these self-confident statements reach over into the KTEA-II test performance? Or does the child falter, say self-depreciating statements, or act unsure? Look for changes in behavior (verbalization about the self) when tasks change from process oriented to academic.

Look for Differences between Modalities

Some children have specific and significant processing styles. Many times their behavior will reflect these visual, auditory, haptic, and verbal strengths and weaknesses. Look for changes in behavior when the modality of the task changes. Does the child pay attention better when he or she has tasks that are visual and get fidgety when the tasks are auditory with no visual stimulus? Does the child chatter on verbal subtests and act unsure on visual-spatial tasks?

Look for Differences in Behavior with Cognitive Load

The KABC-II changes cognitive load from subtest to subtest and especially from basal to ceiling items on each subtest. The KTEA-II has four specific subtests that have a higher cognitive load because they require complex skills (see Figure 6.12 on page 263). Look for changes in behavior when the load level changes or items go from easy to difficult. Does the child do well on simple tasks and then get confused on ones where he or she has to organize? What strategies does the child employ on both batteries when the child starts to approach ceiling items: gives up, gets impulsive, acts like it is an enjoyable challenge, or gets frustrated, angry, or oppositional?

Look for How the Child Responds When You Teach on the Learning Scale of the KABC-II and Interactive Subtests on the KTEA-II

Note any changes in behavior when you administer the Atlantis and Rebus subtests on the KABC-II. These subtests are different from the other subtests because they are interactive, and the examiner basically teaches the child each item and then requests retrieval of the information. It is important to note how a child responds to the interactive and regimented pace. Atlantis and Rebus are dynamic subtests where there is a more intense social dependency between the examiner and the examinee, and the behaviors and social strategies that the child uses in this type of teaching-learning arrangement are valuable information.

You may also want to compare the QIs from Atlantis and Rebus with Written Expression, Phonological Awareness, Listening Comprehension, and Oral Expression subtests from the KTEA-II. They also are interactive subtests where the examiner engages the child throughout the test. Does the child enjoy engaging with you? Is the child nervous about being so interactive with you? Does the child act dependent and need you to lead him or her, or is the child defiant, impatient, or oppositional? It would be interesting to mention these types of behaviors to the child's teacher and see if the child's responses are similar in the classroom.

Qualitative observations need to be supported by other data. If you observe behaviors that you believe are disruptive and that hurt the child's performance on the KABC-II or the KTEA-II, check your observations out with staff and teachers to see if these QIs are present in other settings and not just the testing situation. Also, look at the scores for these subtests. If you believe that the QIs lowered the child's scores, then interventions for those behaviors may just well help the child perform better in the classroom. Remember, QIs are not just about negative behaviors. QIs can provide us with valuable information about how a child gets around a disability or weakness. Watching how a child naturally compensates for learning or behavioral deficits is very valuable information, and it should be included in any prescriptive recommendations.

Integrating the KABC-II and KTEA-II—Procedural Options

There are many ways to integrate the results of the KABC-II and the KTEA-II. At this point in time, there is no definitive method of integrating the results of the two batteries because it may take years of research to define the best approach. Even then, no single approach will match the needs of all examiners. Each examiner brings a wealth of experience, internal norms, and beliefs to the use of these tests. Additionally, every examiner has areas of diagnostic specialties and special populations with whom he or she works and different needs and wants.

The approaches described for integrating the results of the KABC-II and the KTEA-II in this chapter have been varied in theoretical foundations, procedural complexity, and utility. It is a good idea for you to look over the different methods that have been offered and decide which work best for you. It is important and best practice to incorporate different interpretative systems for different circumstances.

Summary and Conclusions

Clinicians and researchers in the field will be integrating the wealth of information gained from combining the KABC-II and the KTEA-II in the years to come. Fortunately, both test batteries are old familiar faces to many examiners and they have been integrating the ability and achievement data from these batteries for some time already. However, it is exciting to have the KABC-II and the KTEA-II conormed for the current revisions. The advantages of having ability and achievement information from theory to intervention should facilitate the difficult processes of determining the strengths and weaknesses of a child and providing prescriptive advice for those who work with the children on a daily basis.

SUPPLEMENTING THE KABC-II USING CROSS-BATTERY METHODS, BY DAWN P. FLANAGAN

The purpose of this section of the chapter is to provide brief guidelines for supplementing the KABC-II using cross-battery methods to gain additional information about a child's cognitive capabilities when deemed necessary. This section provides a brief description of the cross-battery approach. In addition, a step-by-step approach to supplementing the KABC-II is presented.

The Cross-Battery Approach

The CHC cross-battery approach was designed to spell out how practitioners can conduct assessments that approximate the total range of broad cognitive abilities more adequately than any single intelligence battery (Carroll, 1997, p. 129). According to Carroll (1998), this approach "can be used to develop the most appropriate information about an individual in a given testing situation" (p. xi). Likewise, Kaufman (2000) stated that the approach can serve to "elevate [test] interpretation to a higher level, to add theory to psychometrics and thereby to improve the quality of the psychometric assessment of intelligence" (p. xv).

Flanagan and colleagues define the CHC cross-battery approach as a time-efficient method of cognitive assessment that is grounded in contemporary psychometric theory and research on the structure of intelligence. It allows practitioners to measure a wider range (or a more in-depth but selective range) of abilities than that represented by a single intelligence battery (Flanagan & Ortiz, 2001; McGrew & Flanagan, 1998). The cross-battery approach is based on three foundational sources or pillars of information.

Contemporary Theory

The first pillar of the cross-battery approach is CHC theory. This theory was selected as the foundation for the approach because it is the most well-validated theory of the structure of cognitive abilities within the psychometric tradition (Daniel, 1997; Horn & Blankson, in press; McGrew, in press). The CHC theory was described in detail in Chapter 1.

Broad CHC Ability Classifications of Tests

The second pillar of the approach is defined by all existing *broad* cognitive and academic ability classifications of individual tests and subtests. Many of these classifications are based on theory-driven factor analyses of cognitive ability tests, such as those presented in the KABC-II Manual (Kaufman & Kaufman, 2004a; see also Flanagan & McGrew, 1998; Keith, Fine, Taub, Reynolds, & Kranzler, 2004; Keith, Kranzler, & Flanagan, 2001; Woodcock, 1990). Classification of tests at the broad ability level is necessary to improve upon the validity of cognitive assessment and interpretation. Specifically, broad ability classifications ensure that the CHC constructs that underlie assessments are minimally affected by *construct irrelevant variance* (Messick, 1989, 1995). In other words, knowing which tests measure what abilities enables clinicians to organize tests into *construct relevant* clusters—clusters that contain only measures that are *relevant to* the construct or ability of interest. (See Flanagan and Ortiz [2001] for an in-depth discussion.) The broad ability classifications of the KABC-II subtests were based primarily on the results of the factor analyses presented in the manual. These classifications were supported by an independent expert consensus study (Caltabiano & Flanagan, 2004).

Narrow CHC Ability Classifications of Tests

The third pillar of the approach is defined by all existing *narrow* cognitive and academic ability classifications of individual tests and subtests. These classifications were generated from expert consensus studies (e.g., Caltabiano & Flanagan, 2004; Flanagan et al., 2002; McGrew, 1997). To date, over 70 experts have been included in such consensus studies, resulting in over 10,000 individual ratings. The CHC narrow ability classifications are necessary to improve further upon the validity of intellectual assessment and interpretation. Specifically, narrow ability classifications were necessary to ensure that the CHC broad ability constructs that underlie assessments are well represented. According to Messick (1995), *construct underrepresentation* is present when an "assessment is too narrow and fails to include important dimensions or facets of the construct" (p. 742).

Interpreting the KABC-II Number Recall subtest as a measure of the broad Short-term Memory (*Gsm*) ability is an example of construct underrepresentation. This is because Number Recall measures only *one* narrow aspect of *Gsm* (i.e., Memory Span). At least one additional *Gsm* subtest that measures a narrow ability that is *qualitatively different* from Memory Span (i.e., Working Memory) is necessary to include in an assessment to ensure adequate representation of the broad *Gsm* construct. In other words, *two or more qualitatively different (narrow ability) measures of a broad ability* are needed for adequate (broad ability) construct representation (see Comrey, 1988; Messick, 1989, 1995). The aggregate of Number Recall (a measure of *Gsm*-Memory Span) and Word Order (a measure of *Gsm*-Memory Span and Working Memory[1]), for example, would provide a good estimate of the broad *Gsm* ability because these subtests are strong measures of *Gsm* (Kaufman & Kaufman, 2004a) and represent qualitatively different aspects of this broad ability. As mentioned earlier, all broad abilities on the KABC-II may be assessed by two or more subtests (core or supplementary) that measure qualitatively different narrow ability aspects of the broad ability.

In addition to interpreting a single subtest as a measure of a broad CHC ability, construct underrepresentation occurs when the aggregate of two or more measures of the *same* narrow ability is interpreted as measuring a broad ability. For example, the KABC-II Learning/*Glr* scale is primarily a measure of Associative Memory, a narrow *Glr* ability. As such, the Learning/*Glr* scale of the KABC-II would need to be supplemented with one or more tests that measure aspects of *Glr other than Associative Memory* before inferences about a child's broad *Glr* ability could be drawn. Kaufman and Kaufman (2004a) provide information beyond the Core Learning/*Glr* scale in their optional interpretive step (see Chapter 3). In short, a broad CHC ability cluster will yield far more information—and, hence,

---

[1] Word Order assesses Working Memory when the interference task is introduced.

be a more valid measure of a construct—if it contains more differentiated subtests (Clark & Watson, 1995).

It is important to understand that Kaufman and Kaufman (2004a) designed the KABC-II subtests to be complex. Therefore, the CHC narrow ability descriptions of their subtests often cut across broad ability domains. For example, Rover is primarily a measure of *Gv*-Spatial Scanning but, at a secondary level, it involves the ability to reason deductively (i.e., *Gf*-General Sequential Resoning, or *Gf*-RG). Whereas most test authors highlight the primary narrow ability measured by their subtests, placing less emphasis on secondary narrow ability classifications (e.g., Woodcock, McGrew, & Mather, 2001), Kaufman and Kaufman include secondary narrow ability classifications. These secondary ability classifications are meant to reflect the complexity of the KABC-II subtests. Indeed, most test authors would agree that it is not uncommon for a test's secondary narrow ability classifications to be associated with a broad ability domain that is different from that which is represented by its primary narrow ability classification. Therefore, when only primary narrow ability classifications are considered, it is clear that the KABC-II scales include subtests that are relevant to the construct intended to be measured by the scale.

The CHC broad and narrow ability classifications of cognitive and academic tests have been organized into CHC cross-battery worksheets that may be used to guide test organization and interpretation. The most current cross-battery worksheets are found in Flanagan and colleagues (2002) and at the following URLs—http://www.cross-battery.com or http://alpha.fdu.edu/psychology/. Rapid References 6.12 through 6.17 listed the narrow abilities measured by each KABC-II and KTEA-II subtest. Flanagan and colleagues provide detailed instructions on how to use these worksheets in practice.

In summary, the latter two pillars of the cross-battery approach assist in circumventing two ubiquitous sources of invalidity in assessment—construct irrelevant variance and construct underrepresentation. Taken together, the three pillars underlying the cross-battery approach provide the necessary foundation from which to organize assessments of cognitive abilities that are theory driven, comprehensive, and valid. The paragraphs that follow describe how to organize and interpret KABC-II-based CHC cross-battery assessments.

Application of the CHC Cross-Battery Approach

To ensure that CHC cross-battery assessment procedures are psychometrically and theoretically defensible, it is recommended that practitioners adhere to several guiding principles. These principles are described briefly in the following paragraphs.

Guiding Principle 1

When constructing CHC broad ability clusters, select tests that have been classified through an acceptable method, such as through theory driven factor analyses or expert consensus content validity studies. All subtests included on existing cross-battery worksheets (e.g., Flanagan et al., 2002), as well as the KABC-II and KTEA-II subtests, were classified through these methods.

Guiding Principle 2

When constructing CHC broad ability clusters, include two or more qualitatively different narrow ability indicators for each CHC domain to ensure appropriate construct representation. For example, when supplementing the KABC-II Core battery to include measurement of *Ga,* choosing the *Ga* cluster from the WJ III would allow you to draw inferences about the broad *Ga* ability because each subtest comprising this cluster measures a different narrow *Ga* ability (i.e., Sound Blending measures Phonetic Coding: Synthesis and Incomplete Words measures Phonetic Coding: Analysis). However, because recent research seems to support a single Phonetic Coding ability, rather than a dichotomous (Analysis-Synthesis) one (see McGrew, in press, for a summary), the administration of the WJ III Auditory Attention subtest would broaden *Ga* assessment further, as it measures the narrow *Ga* abilities of Speech-Sound Discrimination and Resistance to Auditory Stimulus Distortion.

Guiding Principle 3

When conducting CHC cross-battery assessments, select tests that were developed and normed within a few years of one another to minimize the effect of spurious differences between test scores that may be attributable to the Flynn effect (Flynn, 1984). Flanagan and colleagues (2002) most recent cross-battery worksheets include only those tests that were normed within a 10-year timeframe.

Guiding Principle 4

Select tests from the smallest number of batteries to minimize the effect of spurious differences between test scores that may be attributable to differences in the characteristics of independent norm samples (McGrew, 1994). In most cases, using select tests from a single battery to augment the constructs measured by any other major intelligence battery is sufficient to represent the breadth of broad cognitive abilities adequately as well as to allow for at least three qualitatively different narrow ability indicators of most broad abilities. An examination of the conormed WJ III COG and ACH batteries and the conormed KABC-II and

KTEA-II batteries shows that a total of nine broad cognitive abilities may be measured through approximately three to five qualitatively different indicators for each broad ability. Furthermore, nearly 40 narrow abilities are represented across these batteries, and close to half of them can be assessed adequately through the use of two or more subtests. In short, the careful selection of tests from the Woodcock and Kaufman batteries, following cross-battery principles and procedures, should provide sufficient information about a child's cognitive and academic capabilities for most purposes.

Guiding Principle 5

Use *clusters* from a single battery whenever possible. For example, if an intelligence battery contains only one measure of *Gs,* then select a *Gs cluster* from another battery and administer the *Gs* tests comprising that cluster. You may or may not wish to administer the single measure of *Gs* from your Core battery. By obtaining the *Gs* cluster from another battery, you ensure that the estimate of this construct is based on actual norms rather than an arithmetic average of subtest scores from different batteries. With regard to the Kaufman batteries, the KTEA-II contains only one measure of *Ga* (i.e., Phonological Awareness), the WJ III COG contains three (i.e., Sound Blending, Incomplete Words, and Auditory Attention). Therefore, the latter battery provides a more comprehensive assessment of *Ga* that can be interpreted alone or in combination with the KTEA-II *Ga* subtest.

In summary, the pillars and guiding principles underlying the CHC cross-battery approach provide the necessary foundation from which to conduct comprehensive assessments of the broad and narrow CHC abilities that define the structure of intelligence in the current psychometric theory and research literature. The paragraphs that follow demonstrate how to supplement the KABC-II using the cross-battery approach.

KABC-II Step-By-Step Cross-Battery Assessment

Interpretation of the KABC-II was discussed in Chapter 3 of this book. The CHC cross-battery approach is used here to demonstrate organization of KABC-II–based assessments and to expand upon KABC-II interpretation guidelines. Specifically, the cross-battery approach is used to augment KABC-II assessments by allowing for (1) greater *breadth* in the measurement of broad abilities (e.g., adding *Ga* and *Gs* to KABC-II assessments) and (2) greater *depth* in the measurement of broad abilities (e.g., adding qualitatively different measures of narrow abilities within broad ability domains). Additionally, the cross-battery approach is

≡Rapid Reference 6.20

The Steps of KABC-II Cross-Battery Assessment

Step 1. Determine whether assessment of *Ga* and *Gs* is necessary or desired.

Step 2. Determine whether there is a need to administer supplementary KABC-II subtests.

Step 3. Determine whether it is necessary or desirable to achieve more in-depth measurement of broad cognitive abilities assessed by the KABC-II.

Step 4. Determine whether the measurement of a specific or narrow ability is necessary or desirable.

used to aid in hypothesis testing based on the results of an initial KABC-II or KTEA-II assessment (Rapid Reference 6.20 summarizes the steps of this approach).

Cross-Battery Step 1: Determine Whether Assessment of Ga and Gs Is Necessary or Desired

If Ga is necessary to assess, such as in a referral for reading difficulties in a young child, then the KTEA-II phonological processing test may be administered. In addition, you may choose to assess *Ga* more broadly through the administration of the subtests that comprise the WJ III *Ga* or Phonemic Awareness Cluster (see Guiding Principle 5). Perhaps the broadest measurement of *Ga* abilities, particularly as they apply to phonological processing, may be obtained through special-purpose tests. For example, the Comprehensive Test of Phonological Processing (CTOPP; Wagner, Torgesen, & Rashotte, 1999) includes seven *Ga* subtests (Flanagan et al., 2002).

If Gs is necessary to assess, then you may administer the *Gs* subtests from the WJ III, which is recommended when you use the WJ III to assess *Ga* (see Guiding Principle 4). When *Ga* is either not considered necessary to assess or is assessed by an instrument other than the WJ III, then you may use either the WJ III *Gs* Cluster or the Wechsler Intelligence Scale for Children—Fourth Edition (WISC-IV; Wechsler, 2003) Processing Speed Index (PSI) to augment the KABC-II.

Use the following guidelines for deriving and interpreting CHC (broad and narrow) ability clusters:

I. *Interpret a cluster only when the child's performance on the subtests comprising the cluster is consistent (or common), indicating a unitary ability or construct.*

    A. For clusters derived from *actual norms,* use existing guidelines for determining consistency within broad ability domains. For KABC-II clusters (i.e., Learning/*Glr*, Simultaneous/*Gv*, Sequential/*Gsm*, Planning/*Gf*, and Knowledge/*Gc*), use the critical values on pages 3 and 23 of the Record Form; for WISC-IV Indexes, use the criteria specified in Flanagan and

Kaufman (2004)—for example, the construct underlying the PSI—*Gs*—should only be interpreted when the difference between the subtest scaled scores comprising this index is not unusual (i.e., ≤ 4 points).

B. For clusters that are derived from *averaging* test scores from either the same or different batteries, use the following guidelines recommended by McGrew and Flanagan (1998) and Flanagan and Ortiz (2001)[2]

1. Convert subtest scores to a scale having a mean of 100 and a standard deviation of 15.

2. Report subtest scores with a confidence interval corresponding to ± 1 SEM (68%), which is ± 7 (McGrew & Flanagan, 1998).

3. If the confidence bands corresponding to the two subtest scores that comprise an ability cluster touch or overlap, then the ability presumed to underlie the cluster is considered unitary and, therefore, a cluster may be obtained by averaging the two converted scores. If the bands do not touch or overlap, then the ability presumed to underlie the cluster is nonunitary and, therefore, cannot be interpreted.

4. Report clusters (both broad and narrow) with a confidence interval corresponding to ± 1 SEM (68%), which is ± 5 (McGrew & Flanagan, 1998).

Although an index is considered uninterpretable when the variability among the subtests that comprise it is uncommon, it makes sense to look at the normative classifications of the scaled scores to determine whether a general conclusion may be made about a child's range of observed functioning in the ability presumed to underlie the index (Flanagan & Kaufman, 2004). Specifically, when all subtest scaled scores within an index are either ≤ 8 or ≥ 12, a statement may be made about performance as in the following examples:

- If the variability among subtest scaled scores comprising an index is uncommon and all scaled scores are ≥ 12, then describe the child's range of observed functioning in the ability presumed to underlie the index as a notable integrity as follows: *The Simultaneous/Gv index, a measure of visual processing, represents Andrea's ability to analyze and synthesize visual stimuli as well as reason with visual information. The variability among Andrea's performances on the tasks that comprise the Simultaneous/Gv index (Rover = 12; Triangles = 18) was un-*

---

[2] This averaging technique is used mainly at the *narrow* ability level (i.e., to generate narrow ability clusters). Because the newest intelligence tests provide at least adequate representation of the broad abilities they measure, actual norms for broad ability clusters are available and, therefore, the averaging technique is not necessary.

common in the normative population, indicating that her overall Gv *ability cannot be summarized in a single score. However, it is clear that Andrea's* Gv *ability is a notable integrity for her because her performance on the tasks that comprise the Simultaneous/* Gv *index ranged from Average/Normal Limits to Upper Extreme/Normative Strength.*

- If the variability among subtest scaled scores comprising an index is uncommon and all scaled scores are ≤ 8, then describe the child's range of observed functioning in the ability presumed to underlie the index as a notable limitation as follows: *The Sequential/*Gsm *index, a measure of short-term memory, particularly Memory Span, represents Andrea's ability to apprehend and hold information in immediate awareness and use it again within a few seconds. The variability among Andrea's performances on the tasks that comprise the Sequential/*Gsm *index (Number Recall = 7; Word Order = 2) was uncommon in the normative population, indicating that her overall* Gsm *ability cannot be summarized in a single score. However, Andrea's* Gsm *ability is a notable limitation for her because her performance on the tasks that comprise the Sequential/*Gsm *index fell at or below the 16th percentile, indicating a Normative Weakness compared to her same-age peers.*

II. *Use norm-based clusters whenever they are available.* For example, when supplementing the KABC-II with measures of *Ga*, the WJ III *Ga* Cluster or Phonemic Awareness Cluster is preferable to an arithmetic average of one subtest from the KTEA-II (i.e., Phonological Awareness) and one subtest from the WJ III ACH (e.g., Sound Awareness).

Cross-Battery Step 2: Determine Whether There Is a Need to Administer Supplementary KABC-II Subtests

Administration of supplementary tests is considered necessary whenever the lower of the two subtest scaled scores comprising an index is a Normative Weakness (i.e., a scaled score < 7) and the higher of the two subtest scores is *well* within the average range of ability or higher (i.e., a scaled score ≥ 10), *regardless of whether the index represents a unitary ability.* In other words, when the difference between the subtest scaled scores within an index *exceeds* one standard deviation (i.e., ≥ 4 points) and the lower of the two scores suggests a deficiency, *it is worthwhile to conduct follow up assessment,* particularly in the narrow ability (or abilities) presumed to underlie the lower of the two subtest scaled scores. The following example illustrates a situation in which the administration of supplementary KABC-II subtests is necessary.

John (age 8) received a Riddles scaled score of 5 (Normative Weakness) and a Verbal Knowledge scaled score of 13 (Average range of ability). The 8-point difference between these two Knowledge/*Gc* scaled scores occurred in less than

10% of the KABC-II standardization sample (i.e., it exceeded the critical value of 5 points; see page 3 of the KABC-II Record Form), which rendered the Knowledge/*Gc* index uninterpretable. Riddles, the lower of the two scores, is < 7 and Verbal Knowledge, the higher of the two scores, is ≥ 10. Therefore, you should administer the supplementary *Gc* subtest appropriate for John's chronological age—i.e., Expressive Vocabulary. After administering and scoring this subtest, use the following guidelines:

Step 2a: Determine whether Expressive Vocabulary and Riddles represent a unitary construct using the same critical value that was used to determine whether Verbal Knowledge and Riddles represented a unitary construct (i.e., 5 points). If Expressive Vocabulary and Riddles represent a unitary construct, then calculate the Knowledge/*Gc* index based on these two subtests (using Table D.2).[3] Interpret the broad *Gc* ability and describe Verbal Knowledge as a Personal Strength within the area of *Gc*. Then, go to Step 3. If Expressive Vocabulary and Riddles do not represent a unitary construct, do not calculate and interpret the Knowledge/*Gc* index and go to Step 2b.

Step 2b: Determine whether Expressive Vocabulary and Verbal Knowledge represent a unitary construct using the same critical value that was used to determine whether Verbal Knowledge and Riddles represented a unitary construct (i.e., 5 points). If Expressive Vocabulary and Verbal Knowledge represent a unitary construct, then calculate the Knowledge/*Gc* index based on these two subtests (using Table D.2). Interpret the broad *Gc* ability and describe Riddles as a Normative Weakness within the area of *Gc*. Then, go to Step 3. If Expressive Vocabulary and Verbal Knowledge do not represent a unitary construct, do not calculate the Knowledge/*Gc* index.

Note that there may be times when the supplementary subtest scaled score falls somewhere between the two Core subtest scaled scores. For example, a child may receive a scaled score of 6 on Riddles and a scaled score of 12 on Verbal Knowledge, suggesting the need to administer a supplementary subtest (i.e., Expressive Vocabulary). If, for example, the child obtains an Expressive Vocabulary scaled score of 9, then you will find that this scaled score is not unusually different from either the Riddles *or* the Verbal Knowledge scaled scores (i.e., the mag-

---

[3] It is important to note that Table D.2 provides norms based only on the combination of Core battery subtests (Riddles and Verbal Knowledge at age 8). Although the test authors allow these norms to be used when a supplementary test is used in place of a core battery test (Riddles and Expressive Vocabulary age 8), these norms were not based on the latter alternative combination of tests (Kaufman & Kaufman, 2004a).

nitude of the difference between the Expressive Vocabulary scaled score of 9 and the other two scaled scores of 6 and 12, respectively, is not ≥ 5). When this occurs, you should examine the narrow abilities that underlie each subtest (see Rapid Reference 6.16 for a list of these narrow *Gc* abilities).

Expressive Vocabulary and Verbal Knowledge both *primarily* measure the narrow CHC ability of Lexical Knowledge (VL). Additionally, Verbal Knowledge measures General Information (KO). Although success on the Riddles subtest also depends on VL, this test, unlike Expressive Vocabulary and Verbal Knowledge, requires that the child *reason* with verbal information. In other words, the Riddles subtest measures *Gf* as well as *Gc*. Therefore, it makes sense to calculate a Knowledge/*Gc* cluster based on Expressive Vocabulary (scaled score = 9) and Verbal Knowledge (scaled score = 12) using Table D.2, excluding the subtest (Riddles) that measures a construct other than *Gc* (i.e., *Gf*). In this scenario, you may conclude that the child's fund of general information and acquired vocabulary knowledge is within the Average range of ability compared to same age peers, but when he or she is required to reason with this information, performance declines. This interpretation should be supported by other data sources (e.g., information from the Planning/*Gf* scale).

It is beyond the scope of this chapter to provide a detailed set of guidelines for interpreting all possible performance outcomes when KABC-II Supplementary subtests are administered in addition to Core battery subtests. Therefore, the reader is referred to Flanagan and colleagues (2002) for a set of detailed general interpretation guidelines that may be applied to KABC-II subtest performance.

Cross-Battery Step 3: Determine Whether It Is Necessary or Desirable to Achieve More In-Depth Measurement of Broad Cognitive Abilities Assessed by the KABC-II

For example, the *Glr* cluster on the KABC-II is mainly a measure of Associative Memory (see Rapid Reference 6.12); therefore, *Glr* is underrepresented on the *Core* battery. If a more detailed assessment of *Glr* is considered necessary, then you may administer the KABC-II delayed recall subtests (see interpretive Step 3A in Chapter 3) or the KTEA-II *Glr* subtests (e.g., Listening Comprehension, Naming Facility/RAN, and Associational Fluency). Alternatively (or in addition to, depending on the depth of measurement desired), you may administer *Glr* tests from the WJ III or from other more specialized batteries, such as the Children's Memory Scale (Cohen, 1997) or the CTOPP (which provides three measures of Naming Facility; Flanagan et al., 2002). The CHC cross-battery worksheets may be particularly useful in identifying the most appropriate tests for evaluating any broad ability in more depth (Flanagan & Ortiz, 2001; Flanagan et al., 2002).

Cross-Battery Step 4: Determine Whether the Measurement of a Specific or Narrow Ability Is Necessary or Desirable

Much of the research on the relations between cognitive abilities and academic achievement highlights narrow CHC abilities. For example, Naming Facility, a narrow *Glr* ability, and Phonetic Coding, a narrow *Ga* ability, show substantial and consistent positive correlations with basic reading skills (e.g., Morris et al., 1998; see Flanagan et al., 2002 for a summary of this research). Only a few narrow abilities are represented adequately on most intelligence batteries.

The KABC-II represents adequately the narrow abilities of Memory Span (i.e., Number Recall and Word Order [without interference task] or the Sequential/*Gsm* index), Associative Memory (i.e., the Learning/*Glr* Index) and Visual Memory (i.e., Face Recognition and Hand Movements[4]). Although the KABC-II Learning/*Glr* Index provides an estimate of the narrow Associative Memory ability and the Sequential/*Gsm* index provides an estimate of the narrow Memory Span ability (for children who do not receive the interference component of the Word Order subtest), a Visual Memory narrow ability cluster will need to be derived following the information in Step 1 (section B).

Measurement of narrow CHC abilities may be useful in hypothesis testing (see Step 6 of KABC-II interpretation described in Chapter 3). For example, the Visual Memory cluster may be particularly informative when there is an observed reading difficulty that is not explained by difficulties in phonemic awareness or rapid automatized naming. Although research has not consistently demonstrated a relationship between the broad *Gv* ability and reading achievement, the narrow *Gv* ability of Visual Memory is related to reading. Specifically, orthographic processing, which involves visual memory and visual shape constancy, is important to the development of a sight word vocabulary (Mather, 2002).

With regard to reading, the KTEA-II provides good measurement of *Glr* fluency abilities (e.g., Naming Facility/RAN, Associational Fluency, Word Recognition Fluency and Decoding Fluency)—some of which may be even more important than phonemic awareness (e.g., Naming Facility/RAN) in predicting basic reading skills. Using the subtests from the KTEA-II (Rapid Reference 6.12), you can examine specific aspects of fluency as well as the global construct of fluency.

For example, Word Recognition Fluency and Decoding Fluency together provide a specific *reading fluency* estimate. Calculation of a Reading Fluency cluster may provide an indication of the degree to which an individual has automatized basic reading skills (e.g., decoding). Average or better performance in this area

---

[4] Hand Movements also involves Memory Span.

would suggest that the child has not only acquired basic skills necessary for reading but also has achieved automaticity in these skills. Deficient performance in the area of reading fluency may suggest that the child has a fundamental decoding deficit, has not learned an appropriate strategy for decoding words, or that decoding skills have not yet been automatized.

Reading Fluency can be compared to other fluency abilities, such as Naming Facility and Associational Fluency to determine whether, for example, fluency is impaired more globally or only as it relates to reading decoding. Moreover, when all fluency subtests are Below Average, this may suggest a deficit in a basic psychological process—that is, Processing Speed or *Gs*. Because *Glr*-Naming Facility tests correlate at least moderately with *Gs* tests (Woodcock et al., 2001), *Gs* should be assessed directly when KTEA-II Naming Facility and Fluency test performance is Below Average.

SUMMARY

This section provided a brief description of the CHC cross-battery approach. Steps for supplementing the Core KABC-II subtests with additional (sub)tests were offered as a means to improve upon the breadth and depth of measurement of cognitive abilities when deemed necessary vis-à-vis a review of initial KABC-II data. Although space does not allow for a more detailed description of the application and utility of cross-battery procedures, the steps outlined here provide the information needed to further test hypotheses about variation in a child's KABC-II score profile.

 TEST YOURSELF

1. **In the KABC-II clinical sample of children who are deaf or hearing impaired, the lowest scores were noted on**
   (a) Sequential/*Gsm*.
   (b) Simultaneous/*Gv*.
   (c) Learning/*Glr*.
   (d) Planning/*Gf*.
   (e) Knowledge/*Gc*.

2. **A definitive diagnosis of Autism can be made simply on the basis of a Simultaneous/*Gv* > Sequential/*Gsm* pattern on the KABC-II.** True or False?

3. The extended floor on many KABC-II subtests and the out-of-level testing procedures have improved the KABC-II's usefulness in assessing children with more extreme levels of mental retardation. True or False?

4. The diagnosis of ADHD is primarily made on the basis of the results of tests of cognitive ability like the KABC-II. True or False?

5. As a group, children with Reading Disabilities earned mean scores on the KABC-II Knowledge/*Gc* scale that were similar to their mean scores on the other KABC-II scales. This pattern is likely due to the fact that the Knowledge/*Gc* subtests do not require complex verbal responses and measure verbal concepts that are accessible within the everyday environment, as opposed to being specifically taught in school. True or False?

6. Differences between global scores of Whites and African Americans on the WISC-III are typically about 11 points when parents' education is controlled. In contrast, the differences between these groups on the MPI and FCI of the KABC-II are

   (a) slightly higher—about 14–15 points.

   (b) about the same—about 10–11 points.

   (c) lower—about 6–8 points.

   (d) 0 points.

7. Which ethnic group, on average, scores higher than Whites on the KABC-II global scales?

   (a) African American

   (b) Hispanic

   (c) American Indian

   (d) Asian

8. When the KTEA-II is administered alongside the KABC-II, which additional three broad CHC abilities are measured?

9. The percentile ranks offered in the KABC-II's socioeconomic (SES) norms provide examiners with useful adjunct information regarding how well the child has managed to develop his or her cognitive abilities in light of opportunities available within the home environment. True or False?

10. There are two broad abilities of the CHC model that are not measured by either the KABC-II or the KTEA-II: Processing Speed *(Gs)*, and Decision Speed/Reaction Time *(Gt)*. These two broad abilities are not measured by either battery because

   (a) they are only concerned with speed, not quality, of processing.

   (b) they lack the requisite complexity for inclusion.

   (c) they are weak measures of g in Carroll's (1993) factor-analytic survey.

   (d) all of the above

Answers: 1. e; 2. False; 3. True; 4. False; 5. True; 6. c; 7. d; 8. Quantitative Ability *(Gq)*, Auditory Processing *(Ga)*, Reading and Writing *(Grw)*; 9. True; 10. d.

Seven

ILLUSTRATIVE CASE REPORTS

This chapter includes the case studies of four children who were referred for psychoeducational evaluations. The KABC-II profile of Vanessa J. was presented in Chapter 3 to illustrate the interpretive steps. The culmination of that interpretive process is presented here in Vanessa's case report. The second case report describes the case of Allisonbeth, a 3-year-old girl who was referred for an assessment to determine whether her cognitive abilities were in the gifted range. The third case report describes the case of Pedro, a 10-year-old bilingual boy with ADHD and a potential learning disability. The fourth case report describes the case of Alex, a 5-year-old boy referred to assess his readiness for kindergarten.

The goals of this chapter are to bring all other facets of this book together to demonstrate how the KABC-II may be used as part of a comprehensive battery and to demonstrate the cross-validation of hypotheses with behavioral observations, background information, and supplementary test scores. The basic outline for each report includes the following: reason for referral, background information, appearance of client and behavioral observations, tests administered, test results and interpretation, summary diagnostic impression, and recommendations. All of the test data are presented in a psychometric summary at the end of each report.

As in all illustrative cases presented throughout this book, the identifying data of the clients have been changed to protect their confidentiality.

CASE REPORT I

Name: Vanessa J.
Age: 11 years, 2 months
Grade: Fourth
Examiner: Dr. Nadeen L. Kaufman

Referral and Background Information

Vanessa J., an 11-year-old fourth grader, was referred for psychoeducational evaluation by her father, Walter J. Mr. and Mrs. J. brought Vanessa in for an evaluation because of their concern and feelings of helplessness about their daughter's academic difficulties. Vanessa has had problems with reading and related academic skills such as phonics and spelling since kindergarten. Vanessa's parents hope to learn what is causing her difficulties and to find a way to help her.

Vanessa lives with her parents and older sister, Natalia (age 14). Vanessa's mother, Mrs. J., was born in the Dominican Republic and came to live in America about 25 years ago at the age of 16. Mrs. J. speaks English adequately and has continued to take adult education classes such as English as a Second Language. She dropped out of school after grade 10, but expects to take the exam for a GED soon. She currently is a semiskilled worker at a local dry cleaner. Mr. J., an African American man in his early 40s, is a high school graduate and has taken a few adult education courses on history and literature at a nearby high school. He works as a uniformed doorman in a residential apartment building in Brooklyn, New York.

Vanessa's family's academic history revealed that Mr. J. had trouble reading in the early grades; his mother forced him to read an hour a day, and he hated it. His brother has a master's degree and works in a bank. His sister quit high school the first chance possible, and he is worried that Vanessa will ultimately do the same thing.

Information about Vanessa was obtained from the parent interview and from a form, filled out by both parents, concerning Vanessa's developmental, medical, and educational history. Her parents said that Vanessa has experienced reading-related difficulties throughout her entire school career, which began with attendance at Head Start as a 4-year-old. She entered kindergarten at the same Catholic elementary school that her older sister Natalia attended. Problems appeared with early reading skills almost immediately, and she was required to repeat second grade "because she couldn't keep up with reading," according to her father. Examination of Vanessa's kindergarten school records indicated that she had difficulty with all writing activities and saying numbers and the alphabet. In contrast, her behavior and work habits have been areas in which she has excelled. By second grade she was failing phonics, spelling, and vocabulary, with slightly better performance in reading and grammar. She received good grades in mathematics and had no behavioral problems, but her teachers repeatedly asked her to "practice phonics worksheets every day." When she repeated second grade, she continued to have the same academic problems and math began to fall as well. Both her teacher and principal sent home notes stating, "It is absolutely essential that she *read* every day," but also said that "she tries very hard."

When the examiner asked Vanessa how she felt about having to repeat second grade, she answered, "It was OK, because I still had some friends," emphasizing that social things are more important than academics. She added, "In first grade I liked the Priest; he called me Miss J.—like he treated you with respect." She also felt accepting about attending summer school for math following third grade: "I'm not a good reader so it messed up my math."

On the Iowa Tests of Basic Skills that were administered to Vanessa at the end of second grade, she earned the following National Percentile Ranks:

Iowa Tests of Basic Skills Area	Percentile Rank
Reading—vocabulary	15
Reading comprehension	8
Word analysis	8
Reading total	**10**
Language—listening	13
Oral language	42
Language total	**22**
Math—concepts	15
Problems	16
Computation	63
Math total	**21**

These are the only standardized test scores on record, and there was no remedial or extra help given while Vanessa attended this Catholic school. At the end of third grade, her parents were told that she could not continue there. Vanessa now attends fourth grade at the local public school in the predominantly African American section of Brooklyn where the family lives. English is the primary language spoken in the home, although both daughters speak Spanish reasonably well, an advantage when talking on the phone and occasionally visiting their mother's side of the family in the Dominican Republic. Mr. J. is of African American descent and stated that he only speaks English.

Mrs. J.'s pregnancy with Vanessa was uneventful, and early developmental milestones were all reached within normal limits. Other than her academic problems and a bout of chicken pox, Vanessa has experienced few problems. About a year ago, a doctor recommended that Vanessa wear eyeglasses to correct her vision, but she refused, calling glasses "ugly." She recently agreed to comply and has begun to wear them.

Vanessa's older sister, Natalia, is an A student who has been accepted with a scholarship at an excellent private high school in downtown Manhattan starting in the fall. Natalia frequently helps Vanessa with her homework, and Vanessa is worried about losing her sister's help in the fall. Mr. J. also reported that he and his wife are concerned that Vanessa will suffer when her "good-natured and patient" older sister is not available to help Vanessa with her homework. Natalia's school success is much valued by the family, and they are aware that the demands of the private high school will not leave time for Natalia to help Vanessa. According to Mr. and Mrs. J., Natalia is the academic one in the family and is also sociable and attractive. Mr. J. referred to Vanessa as "the adventurous one—fearless and clever."

Vanessa also provided the examiner with background information, all of which was confirmed by Mr. J. There was no library in the parochial school she attended; books were available only in a mobile library bus that came to the school once a week for the whole school. She was aware that her second grade teacher (the first year she was in grade 2) did not have a degree to teach. After school, Vanessa goes to an apartment in the building she lives in. She stays in this apartment with many other children, where there is little or no one-on-one supervision, until her parents get home. Both Vanessa and her sister are allowed to travel by New York City subways, although this is the first year Vanessa is allowed to go without Natalia accompanying her. Vanessa is alert to her environment and has street smarts and good adaptive skills.

Both parents describe Vanessa as mature and responsible. They feel that Vanessa has a fine sense of humor and a warm, sociable personality, but they need help to understand what can be done to aid their daughter become an adequate reader and a better student.

Behavioral Observations

Vanessa, a pretty, tan-skinned 11-year-old girl, was accompanied to the evaluation by her father and older sister. She remained quiet but involved as the two of them helped make her comfortable with the testing environment by their easy conversation with the examiner. After they left together, Vanessa maintained a shy smile and compliant nature but did not offer spontaneous conversation until well into the first session. For the second session, she was obviously more relaxed, smiled more, and asked some questions. Throughout both sessions, Vanessa responded well to encouragement and incorporated feedback quickly and effectively. Her test performance was characterized by patience, perseverance, frustration tolerance, and motivation to succeed. She seemed to love the one-on-one attention.

It was evident that physical appearance is very important to Vanessa; she was well groomed with nails polished and long brown hair neatly pulled back in a ponytail. At the first testing session, she wore gold earrings, a gold charm bracelet, a red T-shirt, and Capri-length pants.

When the examiner commented on Vanessa's stylish eyeglasses, her face conveyed her disagreement and embarrassment with a wrinkle of her nose and twist of her mouth. These nonverbal gestures enhanced Vanessa's ability to communicate, as her verbal language was sparse. Shrugs of a shoulder, excellent eye contact, and an aura of personal warmth characterized the two testing sessions, with most of her oral language either single words and phrases, or runs of several phrases together, spoken with surprisingly appropriate intonation and voice inflection.

Another significant feature of Vanessa's language production was frequent dysnomia and more general dysphasia. During a KABC-II subtest requiring Vanessa to name a pictured object, she knew the correct ideas or concepts but had trouble with labels. When shown a picture of a mailbox, for example, she said "where you put letters, or cards, like if you send a birthday card to a friend." On a subtest, which presents an incomplete inkblot drawing and required Vanessa to name it, she could not think of the word *eagle* for the sample item, but replied, "a bird, the one that stands for the U.S." This type of response occurred many times during the evaluation. Often she said, "I'm close to getting it," trying so hard to concentrate and retrieve a label or a word that she was able to talk about but not simply saying its name. Vanessa felt comfortable skipping over items she did not know on some tasks (e.g., tests of paired-associate learning), but she experienced obvious discomfort when she was unable to retrieve a label when she really knew its meaning. Despite her frustration, Vanessa displayed remarkable perseverance and poise while trying to remember vocabulary words. When she would finally realize that her effort was fruitless, she would calmly say, "I can't think of the name [word]," and automatically start telling as much as she possibly could about the object or concept.

When responding to verbal questions, she asked for repetition frequently and was very slow to answer; she typically remained silent until the answer came to her or else she gave a shy smile and a shrug. On a verbal task that does not use any visual stimuli for school-age children, Vanessa would first attempt to show the answer rather than speak it (e.g., she pointed to buttons on her shirt top instead of saying the word *button*). She generally used a lot of manual expression, such as making believe she was hitting a nail with a hammer instead of saying the word *hammer.*

She didn't know the meaning of many words used in verbal questions on both the KABC-II and KTEA-II and often asked what specific words meant (e.g., *spear, bill*). When the examiner explained that Vanessa needed to give her best answer, she was adept at guessing the meaning from context. She used context clues effectively when trying to read, an area of great difficulty for her. For example, she didn't know the word *drink* but correctly responded to the command, *Pretend to drink a glass of milk.* On a subtest that required her to learn symbols that represented words, when she did not remember the word that went with a particular symbol, she also relied on context clues (e.g., she said *game* instead of *playing*). She had difficulties with grammatical tenses, a problem that was notable on the symbol-word subtest, when she interchanged past and future tenses and on the KTEA-II Oral Expression subtest. On the latter task, she made obvious grammatical errors ("dry theirselves") and spoke in fragments and run-on sentences.

Despite the grammatical and structural errors on the KTEA-II, Vanessa was much more competent at oral communication when saying something spontaneously as opposed to being required to retrieve a specific word or answer a question that imposes linguistic constraints on her verbal product. However, she did have some notable speech problems. Her articulation was poor—many of her words were unclear, with one sound blending into another. For example, she pronounced *refrigerator* as "fidjator." She said *beard* as "beer" and left off the last consonant on many other words as well. She had trouble saying *crown*. Articulation errors were noted throughout both cognitive and achievement testing. She said "lello" for "yellow" on a math subtest. On Phonological Awareness, she said *birdhouse* as "burr-house" and *rain* as "ray." When reading out loud, she tended to ignore the last letters of a word, much like she does in speaking out loud; she read *heard* as "hear" and *several* as "severe."

Vanessa had auditory discrimination problems as well as articulation difficulties. During a measure of receptive vocabulary and general information, she had trouble hearing the sound differences in words spoken by the examiner: For example, when asked to "Point to pile," she heard "tile" at first and questioned the examiner. She had extreme difficulty understanding the passages presented by audiocassette for the KTEA-II Listening Comprehension subtest, saying things like, "What was that?" or "I missed some words," or "This is *hard*." When items were spoken out loud by the examiner to determine whether her difficulties were due to the audiotape presentation, Vanessa showed no improvement in her performance. On a task requiring her to repeat a random sequence of letters and numbers, her errors frequently included a letter given in the response that rhymed with the actual letter spoken by the examiner (e.g., D for B, A for J).

Vanessa displayed visual-perceptual difficulties. When asked to draw a picture of her family doing something together, she erased a lot, counted the people a few times, and drew (right-handed) in a slow, careful, nondistractible style. She broke the pencil point three times. She made many erasures on all written work. She worked unusually slowly during a psychomotor paper-and-pencil task. She realized several errors after she made them (groaning to let the examiner know) but knew she had no time to erase and change the errors. She had difficulty visualizing stimuli and holding them in working memory even briefly. On visual-motor tasks that can benefit from visual memory, she frequently looked back and forth from code to box before responding.

To help her visualize, she sometimes turned her whole head upside down to better picture the stimulus. When solving items on a design-copying task (using foam shapes), she demonstrated a preference for solving problems sequentially, working systematically, usually from the top down. Here she used both color and lines as cues but got confused when the lines were removed and ultimately lost the gestalt of designs.

On tasks that were challenging for Vanessa, she used a variety of compensatory strategies to help her. For example, during a task that required her to plan the best path on a grid, she blocked out alternate paths with her other hand while thinking about a particular move. On a counting task, she blocked out one-half of the stimuli to count the correct number and then used her hand again to cover up the ones already counted. Similar strategies were employed when reading words; she used her hand to hide part of words to help her "read" better (e.g., *fist* was separated into *fi* and *st*) but she still couldn't figure the word out. In general, throughout the evaluation, she had effective means of self-compensation. When solving verbal math problems on the KTEA-II, she used paper and pencil to rewrite facts for several items that she could not solve immediately. When computing math items, Vanessa compensated for not knowing the multiplication tables by adding (e.g., 39×9 was written with series of 9s, the 18s, all added together laboriously; even 9×7 was done this way).

Assessment Procedures

- Clinical Interview with Mr. and Mrs. J.
- Clinical Interview with Vanessa J.
- Kaufman Assessment Battery for Children—Second Edition (KABC-II)
- Wechsler Intelligence Scale for Children—Fourth Edition (WISC-IV; selected scales and subtests)
- Kaufman Test of Academic Achievement Second Edition (KTEA-II)—Comprehensive Form (Form A)
- Kinetic Family Drawing (KFD)

Test Results and Interpretation

Assessment of Cognitive Abilities

Vanessa was administered the KABC-II to obtain a comprehensive picture of her mental processing and cognitive abilities. The KABC-II is based on a double theoretical foundation, Luria's neuropsychological model and the CHC psychometric theory. It offers five scales, each given a label that reflects both theoretical models: Sequential/*Gsm*, Simultaneous/*Gv*, Learning/*Glr*, Planning/*Gf*, and Knowledge/*Gc*. (From the perspective of CHC theory, *Gsm* = short-term memory; *Gv* = visual processing; *Glr* = long-term storage and retrieval; *Gf* = fluid reasoning; and *Gc* = crystallized ability.)

Examiners are given the option of selecting either the Luria model or the CHC model of the KABC-II, based on the child's background and the reason for referral. (Knowledge/*Gc* is excluded from the Luria model because measures of language ability and acquired knowledge may not provide fair assessment of some children's cognitive abilities—e.g., those from bilingual or nonmainstream backgrounds). Although some Spanish is spoken in the J's household, English is Vanessa's primary language. This fact, coupled with the referral reason (possible reading disability) led the examiner to administer the CHC model of the KABC-II, which yields the FCI as the global measure of general cognitive ability (see the Don't Forget box).

Vanessa earned a KABC-II Fluid Crystallized Index (FCI) of 93, ranking her at the 32nd percentile and classifying her overall mental processing ability as falling within the Average range. The chances are 90% that her true FCI is between 88 and 96. However, she displayed considerable variability in her standard scores on the five theory-based scales that compose the FCI with indexes ranging from 127 on Sequential/*Gsm* to 80 on Simultaneous/*Gv*. This wide variation in indexes (47 points, which equals more than 3 SDs), renders her FCI meaningless as an estimate of global ability; it is merely the midpoint of greatly varying abilities. Unlike the FCI, all five of Vanessa's scale indexes were interpretable, as she performed consistently on the tasks that compose each separate scale (see the Don't Forget box).

Vanessa's Sequential/*Gsm* index

> ### DON'T FORGET
> Remember to explain the following in your KABC-II reports:
> 1. The fact that examiners choose either the Luria or CHC model
> 2. The difference between the Luria and CHC model
> 3. Why you chose the Luria or CHC model

> ### DON'T FORGET
> Clearly state when either the FCI or the MPI is not meaningful due to variability within the KABC-II's indexes.

of 127 (96th percentile) is in the Above Average range and is a Normative Strength for her (relative to other 11-year-olds). In contrast, her Simultaneous/ *Gv* Index of 80 (9th percentile) is in the Below Average range and is a Normative Weakness. Her other three indexes, which range from 87 to 94, are all within the Average Range.

Vanessa's short-term memory is an important strength for her, a key asset. This strong ability was evident from Vanessa's Above Average index on the Sequential/*Gsm* scale. Her score was significantly higher than her own Average level of cognitive ability. In addition, her standard score of 127 was so much higher than her Average overall ability that differences that large occurred less than 10% of the time in the standardization sample. Vanessa's relative strength in this domain was corroborated by an additional measure of short-term memory and working memory—the Working Memory index (WMI) of the WISC-IV. Although her WMI of 107 (68th percentile) is probably a spuriously low estimate of her short-term memory because several of her errors on the Letter-Number Sequencing subtest seemed due to her auditory discrimination problem (she misheard some letters), Vanessa's Average WMI, even if it is an underestimate of her ability, supports her good short-term and working memory. Vanessa's level of skill in this area provides valuable information for any possible diagnosis of a reading disability and for formulating scientifically based interventions.

In contrast to her strength in short-term memory, her problems with visual processing represent a high-priority concern for Vanessa. Her visual processing difficulties were apparent from her Below Average performance on the Simultaneous/*Gv* scale. She performed significantly below what is typical for children her age as well as compared to her own overall ability. Furthermore, visual perceptual difficulties were observed clinically throughout the evaluation (e.g., turning her head upside down to better visualize stimuli, losing the gestalt of the designs when constructing designs). Additional support for her visual processing problems was found in her Below Average PSI of 80 (9th percentile) on the WISC-IV. She had great difficulty retaining the simple visual stimuli, even briefly, during the two PSI subtests, which greatly slowed down her performance and resulted in drawing several incorrect symbols on one of these subtests. Her quick performance on the Planning/*Gf* subtests attests to her adequate processing speed when visualization is not required for successful performance. Another support for Vanessa's visual processing problems is her performance on a task requiring her to copy a sequence of hand movements (50th percentile). Although she performed at an Average level on this Supplementary KABC-II task, her score is significantly lower than her scores on the Core Sequential/*Gsm* subtests. This subtest is also the only Sequential/*Gsm* task that measures *visual* memory.

Vanessa performed about equally well when applying her visual perception to meaningful stimuli such as pictures of people and things (16th percentile) or to abstract designs and symbols (27th percentile), suggesting that her problems with visual perception and visual processing pertain to a variety of visual stimuli (see the Don't Forget box). She also performed much higher on visual tasks that can be responded to with little or no motor coordination (50th percentile) versus those that require gross motor coordination for success (7th percentile). Indeed, she performed relatively well (50th percentile) on a visualization subtest requiring her to count blocks, including those that are

> # DON'T FORGET
>
> Although you calculate new standard scores for the clusters in the planned clinical comparisons of step 5, we recommend that you don't report these additional standard scores. Remember, you can talk about what the results from step 5 mean using percentile ranks or just by describing which ability is better or worse.

> # DON'T FORGET
>
> Remember to insert example QIs where relevant to support hypotheses. For example, Vanessa's unusual perseverance and unusual level of focus were noted here.

partially or completely hidden from view. That score was significantly higher than her scores on the Core Simultaneous/*Gv* subtests. Vanessa persevered with nondistractible concentration on the Block Counting items, which aided her performance (see the Don't Forget box). However, it is possible that the fact that she did need to rely on gross motor coordination to respond was likely an aid. In fact, poor motor coordination conceivably played a role in her relatively low PSI on the WISC-IV, along with the visual perceptual problems she displayed by continually looking back at the stimulus symbols before responding. And Vanessa broke several pencil points during the evaluation. Vanessa's visual processing and visual perceptual difficulties are primary and her visual-motor coordination is secondary regarding the school learning problems she is experiencing.

To obtain yet further information about visual processing, as well as to build rapport, Vanessa was administered an informal drawing test, the Kinetic Family Drawing (KFD). During this task (in which she was asked simply to draw a picture of her family doing something together), she erased a lot, counted the people a few times, broke the pencil point, and was slow, careful, and nondistractible. Vanessa drew her family members with care, thinking about each one in turn, deciding what activity most characterized them. She drew her sister, Natalia, first and put a book in her hands to show her reading. Of notable interest was that even though each figure had a prop to indicate the action, the figures themselves were merely sticks attached to heads, with little arm and leg branches. Vanessa had a wealth of ideas (many expressed in words), but her communication of these ideas with paper and pencil was sparse and incomplete. Her difficulties in expressing her many ideas in her drawings are a reflection of her visual processing and motor coordination problems.

Like her weakness in visual processing, Vanessa's acquired knowledge of words and facts (crystallized ability) is also a relative weakness. This weakness is consistent with the learning problems she has displayed in school since she was a 4-year-old in Head Start. Her difficulty in this area was highlighted in her Knowledge/*Gc* Index of 87 (19th percentile), which is a significant Personal Weakness for her. Although this score is in the Average range compared to children her age, she performed significantly lower on this index than her overall level of cognitive performance. During the administration of the Core Knowledge/*Gc* subtests, Vanessa's serious word retrieval difficulties and auditory discrimination problems negatively affected her scores. Her word retrieval problems especially impacted her performance on the Supplementary Expressive Vocabulary subtest (2nd percentile), which was significantly and substantially lower than her scores on the two Core Crystallized/*Gc* subtests. In addition, Vanessa's Below Average performance (5th percentile) on a Supplementary Simultaneous/*Gv* subtest that requires verbal responses reflects her difficulties with both visual processing and word retrieval.

To broaden the assessment of Vanessa's crystallized ability, two WISC-IV Verbal Comprehension subtests were administered. Her performance on a verbal test of general factual knowledge (25th percentile) is consistent with her performance on KABC-II measures of acquired knowledge, but her High Average ability on a task tapping common sense and social judgment (95th percentile) is well above her scores on all other measures of crystallized ability. This high score reflects a surprising strength for Vanessa in view of her learning and language problems. While answering many of the socially relevant questions on this subtest, she demonstrated her street smarts and social awareness, and she also made use of her excellent short-term memory. For example, she repeated the entire long stimulus sentence verbatim, sometimes two or three times out loud, before pausing to consider its meaning. Her use of verbal memory seemed to provide delay time to allow her to compensate for slow verbal processing. Vanessa is alert to her environment, especially in an incidental, self-directed way as opposed to didactic school lessons. In addition, her ability to verbalize her ideas in spontaneous speech, when she did not have to worry about retrieving a particular word, was efficient, as noted earlier.

In contrast to her widely ranging abilities in the domains of visual processing and short-term memory, Vanessa functions consistently within the Average range in her ability to learn new material and to solve novel problems using fluid reasoning. These abilities were noted in her scores on the Learning/*Glr* scale (standard score = 94; 34th percentile) and the Planning/*Gf* scale (standard score = 90; 25th percentile). All subtests on these two scales require visual perception of stimuli, both abstract and meaningful. It is, therefore, conceivable that Vanessa's visual processing and visual perceptual difficulties may have attenuated her indexes on these scales to some extent. In addition, her language problems may have also impacted her score on the Symbol-Word Learning subtest (Learning/*Glr* scale) because of the need to learn verbal labels for abstract symbols. It is noteworthy that Vanessa scored within the Average range on the Supplementary Delayed Recall scale (27th percentile), indicating that she was able to retain the newly learned paired associates (taught by the examiner during the administration of the Learning/*Glr* subtests) after an interval of about 20 minutes—despite participating in other cognitive tasks and without advance warning that she would be retested. The fact that Vanessa did score within the Average range on the scales that measure learning, delayed recall, and reasoning (coupled with the 95th percentile that she scored on the reasoning-oriented WISC-IV Comprehension subtest) suggests that she has some intact abilities that should be capitalized on when planning her educational interventions.

Assessment of Academic Achievement

Vanessa was administered the KTEA-II Comprehensive Form, which is an individually administered test of academic achievement, to measure her skills in reading, math, written language, and oral language. Her standard scores on the KTEA-II Comprehensive Form composites (based on grade norms) varied widely, rendering her Comprehensive Achievement composite of 76 ± 4 (5th percentile) meaningless. She scored within the Average range on Written Language (97 ± 6; 42nd percentile) and Mathematics (91 ± 6; 27th percentile) but scored at the juncture of the Below Average and Lower Extreme levels on Reading (70 ± 4; 2nd percentile) and Oral Language (70 ± 8; 2nd percentile). Both Reading and Oral Language represent Normative Weaknesses for Vanessa and are areas of great concern for both diagnostic purposes and as academic skills that require educational intervention.

Vanessa's reading skills were consistently Below Average, whether she was reading words (3rd percentile on Letter and Word Recognition), sounding out nonsense words using phonics skills (6th percentile on Nonsense Word Reading Decoding), demonstrating understanding of what she reads (5th percentile on Reading Comprehension), or rapidly decoding real words and nonsense words

(5th percentile on Reading Fluency Composite). She also scored in the Below Average range on the prereading skill of phonological processing (13th percentile on Phonological Awareness). Consequently, Vanessa's reading problems are pervasive, extending to all aspects of the reading process.

When reading real words, she was generally hesitant; she did not know many words by sight and has to sound them out, stopping for long pauses. Her typical style was to start sounding out the word until she thought of a word that it *may* be; then she guessed; for example, *understood* was misread as "undoorable"; *truth* was misread as "turtle." As mentioned earlier, she tended to ignore the last letters of a word, much like she did when speaking out loud, and she attempted to compensate for her visual perceptual problems by using her hand to cover up parts of words she was trying to sound out (just as she used her hand to block out interfering visual stimuli during cognitive tasks). She read very slowly during Reading Comprehension and was able to make use of context when she could not read some of the words in a sentence. During Nonsense Word Decoding she made many reversals (e.g., she saw Ds as Bs) and tried to make nonsense words into real words (e.g., she said "soap" instead of *snope* and "ring" instead of *rell*). Vanessa also demonstrated Below Average ability on two Supplementary KTEA-II subtests that measure cognitive processes that have been shown by research to be especially difficult for children with reading problems: Phonological Awareness (13th percentile), a measure of phonological processing, and Naming Facility/RAN (10th percentile), a measure of rapid automatized naming (RAN). During the administration of Phonological Awareness, Vanessa displayed poor auditory discrimination and articulation.

Vanessa's responses on several KTEA-II subtests were further examined by error analysis to identify specific areas of academic skill strengths and weaknesses. On Phonological Awareness, Vanessa was identified as being weak in the subskill of word segmentation. When asked to divide words that are presented aloud into their constituent sounds, Vanessa had difficulty dividing the word into the appropriate parts. For example, for the word *blackboard,* Vanessa segmented it into three sounds—*black-ack-board.* For the word *cat,* Vanessa segmented it into the following sounds: *ca-at.* Vanessa's difficulty with being able to identify and segment sounds she hears may play a role in her difficulties with reading and spelling. She found blending sounds together easier than segmenting them. Perhaps the more difficult task for her required more simultaneous thinking, whereas the blending of sounds allowed her to process with her better sequential skills.

Within the area of Written Language, Vanessa scored in the Average range both on Written Expression (70th percentile) and Spelling (19th percentile). Nonetheless, her ability to express her ideas in writing (70th percentile) was markedly higher than her ability to spell (19th percentile). During Written Expression, Vanessa erased a great deal and reversed letters ("List go" for *Let's go*); she demonstrated knowledge of few rules of spelling on both Written Language subtests (e.g., "makeing" for *making*). However, the Written Expression subtest does not penalize for incorrect spelling and rewards students for their ability to express their ideas in writing. This aspect of school achievement is clearly an area of relative integrity for Vanessa.

Vanessa showed a significant number of specific skill weaknesses across academic areas related to reading. Vanessa had great difficulty pronouncing and spelling the correct vowel sounds in words. For example, for the nonsense word *trame,* Vanessa pronounced the word *trem* with a short /e/ sound. Similarly, for the word *high,* she pronounced the word *hand,* indicating a difficulty with long vowel sounds (as well as the silent letters *gh*). Vanessa also displayed considerable difficulties spelling or reading consonant digraphs within words. She spelled *bath* as *baf.* Other skill deficits included pronouncing silent letters in words (e.g., pronouncing the silent *k* in *kneel*); incorrectly writing suffixes/inflections when spelling words (e.g., writing *spoking* for the word *spoken;* and incorrectly pronouncing consonant blends (e.g., pronouncing *brother* as *bother*).

Vanessa's Low Average Oral Language Composite represented a combination of Low Average performance on Oral Expression (10th percentile) and Lower Extreme performance on Listening Comprehension (< 1st percentile). Though both scores are Normative Weaknesses for Vanessa, her ability to express her ideas in words (standard score = 81) was substantially higher than her ability to understand passages that she listened to on an audiocassette (standard score = 60). In addition, Vanessa scored in the Average Range on the Associational Fluency subtest (standard score = 98; 45th percentile), a task requiring her to rapidly name as many things as possible within a brief time span. She was notably better when naming things in categories (e.g., animals) than naming words that start with a particular sound (e.g., the sound that *D* makes), but her overall Average score on this KTEA-II subtest, along with the 95th percentile she earned on WISC-IV Comprehension, indicate that it is her oral *comprehension* rather than her oral *expression* that reflects Vanessa's most serious oral language concern in the classroom. Vanessa complained about having considerable difficulty understanding the audiocassette. To determine the effect of the taped presentation, the examiner read several of the Listening Comprehension passages to Vanessa (from Form B of the KTEA-II), but that modification did not appear to improve her ability to understand the content of the passages.

Vanessa's ability to understand information via reading versus listening was also assessed. Vanessa's standard score of 76 (5th percentile) on Reading Comprehension is significantly higher than her standard score of 60 (< 1st percentile) on Listening Comprehension, but both types of comprehension are of concern because she performed well below other children in fourth grade in these areas. She understands relatively little of what she reads and what she hears, greatly limiting her ability to learn within the classroom or from books. She had a weak ability to comprehend both literal and inferential items. The literal comprehension weakness suggests that Vanessa has difficulty recalling information that is explicitly stated in a text or dialogue. Weaknesses for answering the inferential items suggest that she has difficulty combining information across several clauses or has difficulty understanding the main idea of a passage.

In addition to comparing Vanessa's understanding of printed and spoken language, Vanessa's ability to express ideas in writing versus speaking was assessed. Her Average Written Expression standard score of 108 (70th percentile) is significantly and substantially higher than her Below Average standard score of 81 (10th percentile) on Oral Expression. This difference is notable because her ability to express her ideas in writing reflects a considerable academic strength that is important to consider when planning educational interventions for her. In fact, her standard score on Written Expression might be a slight underestimate of her writing ability because her auditory discrimination problem led to some errors. For example, she heard *fan* as "fin" and then wrote the wrong answer according to how it sounded to her. On both the Oral and Written Expression subtests, Vanessa displayed weak skills in the category of word form errors. This means that she had difficulty with subject-verb agreement, plurals, and tense shifts in her responses. For example, in one response she stated, "After she got the popcorn, she **asking** the boy if he could fill up the cup with soda."

Vanessa's performance in mathematics reveals Average functioning in the basic skills of computation (23rd percentile) and the application of mathematical principles to solve word problems (34th percentile). Vanessa's consistency on the two subtests indicates that her Math Composite of 91 provides a good overview of her skills in mathematics. She used her fingers for counting everything, even small addition items, like 8 + 4. She did not know the multiplication tables and other number facts that (as a fourth grader) she should know, especially given her exceptional short-term memory. As indicated previously, Vanessa spontaneously tried to compensate for her deficits. She persevered on math problems that required multiplication by performing repeated additions (e.g., she wrote down 7 + 7 = 14; 14 + 7 = 21; and so forth, to try to solve 7×9).

Vanessa displayed several weak areas in Math Concepts and Applications. She had difficulty with concepts related to time and money, number concepts, and problems involving subtraction. She showed weaknesses in computing subtraction, multiplication, and division problems. She also displayed little mastery of basic multiplication facts and had a difficult time when regrouping was required to correctly solve two-digit subtraction problems. For example, when given the problem 58 – 39, Vanessa computed the difference as 39. Although she correctly borrowed from the tens place (the 5 in the number 58), she crossed out the entire number when the borrowing occurred. Thus, when solving the problem, she brought the 3 (from the tens place in the number 39) directly down into the difference. Along with subtraction with regrouping, Vanessa displayed considerable difficulties with multiplication and division problems. Although Vanessa answered several early multiplication items correctly, any multiplication items that required regrouping were answered incorrectly. It is not surprising, given Vanessa's difficulty with multiplication, that she also showed a weakness in computing division problems; conceptually, these two skills are related, and a weakness in multiplication often leads to difficulties with division.

Comparison of Ability and Achievement

Vanessa's KABC-II Indexes ranged from 80 to 127 (from the 9th to the 96th percentile). Similarly, her scaled scores on the six selected WISC-IV subtests administered to her ranged from the 9th to the 95th percentile. No overall standard score can be used to meaningfully reflect Vanessa's diverse array of abilities. However, she performed at an Above Average level on the KABC-II Sequential/*Gsm* scale and the WISC-IV Comprehension subtest. She scored within the Average range on the KABC-II Planning/*Gf*, Learning/*Glr*, and Knowledge/*Gc* scales, and on the WISC-IV Working Memory scale and Information subtest. Her only Below Average cognitive scores were on the KABC-II Simultaneous/*Gv* scale, the WISC-IV Processing Speed scale, and the Supplementary KABC-II Expressive Vocabulary and Gestalt Closure subtests. Based on clinical observations, these Below Average scores are clearly the result of her visual perceptual and language problems. Vanessa's cognitive ability is Average to Above Average. As such, her abilities are commensurate with her achievement, as measured by the KTEA-II, in the areas of mathematics and written language. However, her abilities are substantially better than her achievement in reading and oral language, especially listening comprehension.

The KABC-II provides reliable measures of five of the 10 broad abilities that make up the CHC theory of intelligence. When the KTEA-II and the selected WISC-IV subtests administered to Vanessa are added to the mix, it is possible to provide reliable estimates of Vanessa's standard scores on 9 of the 10 CHC broad abilities (note that some of these abilities are, in actuality, academic achievement). These scores for Vanessa are presented in a table at the end of this report. Because the KABC-II and WISC-IV yield *age-based* scores, the KTEA-II standard scores shown in the table are derived from *age* norms such that all of Vanessa's scores are on a common yardstick (hence her KTEA-II standard scores in this table are slightly different from her *grade-based* scores discussed earlier and shown in her KTEA-II test profile. An examination of the CHC summary reveals the striking contrast between Vanessa's Average to Above Average abilities in short-term memory, associative memory, fluid reasoning, quantitative knowledge, and written language (19th to 96th percentile) as compared to (1) her Below Average processing abilities in auditory (phonological) processing, naming facility/RAN, visual processing, and processing speed (7th to 12th percentile); and (2) her Below Average to Lower Extreme achievement in reading, listening ability, and oral production (1st to 10th percentile). From a CHC perspective, Vanessa's intact abilities tend to be in Short-Term Memory (*Gsm*), Fluid Reasoning (*Gf*), and Quantitative Knowledge (*Gq*), and her weaknesses tend to be in Visual Processing (*Gv*), Processing Speed (*Gs*), Crystallized Ability (*Gc*), and Reading (*Grw*).

Diagnostic Impression

Vanessa's difficulties are complex, and, although the problems were recognized early in her education, they received little formal intervention in academic settings. Vanessa displays significant deficits in the area of visual processing. Her deficit in this basic psychological process, coupled with her phonological difficulties and general expressive language deficits, has led to the development of a Reading Disorder (DSM-IV-TR). Throughout the testing, Vanessa's verbal expression was sparse, she had word finding difficulties, and made vocabulary and grammatical errors. Thus, she likely also has an Expressive Language Disorder (DSM-IV-TR). Finally, her persistent omissions of sounds (e.g., final consonants) and substitutions of sounds, which interfere with her functioning in social and academic settings, require a diagnosis of Phonological Disorder (DSM-IV-TR). The combined areas of learning disability require intense and immediate intervention, both to keep her from falling further behind her peers, and to limit the damaging effects of low self-esteem and poor self-concept. Luckily, Vanessa has a supportive, intact family and personality strengths that will facilitate her progress.

Recommendations

1. Vanessa needs thorough evaluation of speech and hearing, performed by a speech pathologist with experience in language disorders. An

audiologist should evaluate her hearing as she might have a slight hearing deficit (especially at certain speech frequencies, where it might exist subtly).

2. Because she did not wear eyeglasses for a long time after they were prescribed, she should have a visual acuity test. The optometrists should also assess Vanessa's visual depth perception and eye muscle coordination as it relates to reading.

3. To ensure that Vanessa learns rules or new facts, turn learning new bits of information into a game like *Concentration* or quizlike paired associate learning with multiple sets to ensure appropriate application.

4. Because of listening comprehension difficulty and poor vocabulary, Vanessa needs one-to-one instruction to learn most important new information. Find a tutor who can develop a consistent, supportive, therapeutic relationship with her to facilitate learning.

5. When teaching Vanessa new information, provide facts in small increments so that she doesn't get lost. Repetitive exercises are not necessary to teach new information because Vanessa has a good working memory (in fact, she will be bored or lose motivation with them). Instead, help her fully understand new information by incorporating it in a variety of applications. For example, apply math concepts such as multiplication to cooking, buying groceries, or building things.

6. Vanessa has great frustration tolerance, perseverance, motivation to succeed, and desire to please. However, because of her persistent academic failure, she has learned that she is not the academic one in the family. To ensure that she continues to have motivation on academic tasks, help her develop appropriate academic goals so that she will believe the tasks are within her capability.

7. She has acquired many phonics skills, but because of her auditory discrimination problems, she hears many vowels differently. Speech intervention and reading intervention need to be conducted side by side.

8. Vanessa's vocabulary problem is more a difficulty in retrieving specific labels than in missing the concepts—when one word is specifically required to be recalled, she has trouble finding it, even though she can express enough information to demonstrate knowledge. Nonetheless, the range and breadth of her vocabulary has necessarily been limited by her problems in understanding what she reads and hears. She would benefit from regularly scheduled language therapy sessions to expand her expressive abilities.

9. Use a programmed instruction style to develop her vocabulary—computerized and sequential approaches to help improve her reading, vocabulary, and spelling. Games with animated praise and small steps should

be effective. Her ability to learn multiplication tables and other number facts will be enhanced by self-competition and instant feedback—and by her good short-term and working memory—even though rote learning is inherently boring.

10. Vanessa's visual perceptual-motor difficulties are accentuated by her slow processing style. She desires to be correct and to succeed, but sometimes her perfectionistic, reflective approach hurts her. To remove some of these obstacles, create an atmosphere for intervention in which mistakes are okay and judgments about performance are withheld.

11. Vanessa learns extremely well in incidental learning environments (field trips in school, going shopping with her older sister). She would benefit from a Big Sister mentor relationship, which could foster such learning experiences outside of school.

12. When planning educational interventions, consider her age and gender. Although she is reading at the second grade level, her interests are not the same as 8-year-olds'. To keep her from being so bored with second grade reading level content, select reading materials such as cosmetic brochures, instructions on nail polish, maps about the New York City subway system, and so forth. Emphasize hands-on learning in all content areas.

13. The following books will provide useful suggestions for educational interventions that will take into account Vanessa's strength in short-term memory (sequential processing) and her weakness in visual (simultaneous) processing: (1) From a Luria theoretical perspective—J. A. Naglieri and E. B. Pickering, 2003, *Helping Children Learn: Intervention Handouts for Use in School and at Home,* Baltimore: Paul H. Brookes, and (2) From a CHC theoretical perspective—N. Mather and L. Jaffe, 2002, *Woodcock-Johnson III: Recommendations, Reports, and Strategies,* New York: Wiley.

14. Teach Vanessa how to use spell checker programs and provide her with a variety of software so she can understand how to begin to write something comprehensible to others—like in E-mail messages to friends. Currently, she needs much help from her sister to read E-mails and compose her own. Vanessa expresses her ideas well in writing but needs to improve her spelling and basic writing skills, such as grammar, so she will not be self-conscious and ask family members for help. She is social and will enjoy the pleasure of communicating independently with friends in written language.

15. Vanessa would benefit from participating in a school-based program to enhance her self-efficacy and increase academic self-regulation. An

example of such a program, called "Self-Regulation Problem-Solving Process," appeared in T. J. Cleary and B. J. Zimmerman, 2004, "Self-Regulation Empowerment Program: A School-Based Program to Enhance Self-Regulated and Self-Motivated Cycles of Student Learning," *Psychology in the Schools 41*(5), 537–550.

16. Find additional ways of measuring Vanessa's learning. Alternate forms of assessing gains can include drawing, acting out, or preparing a lesson for her to give to others. These new approaches could break old patterns of failure as well as provide her with better means of communicating what she really can do. Vanessa needs to incorporate her excellent adaptive skills into the arena of school learning and increase her self-confidence.

17. Make sure Vanessa has a library card for the closest public library and have a weekly time that a parent can accompany her to the library, even if only to browse at magazines while there.

18. Help Vanessa practice her functional skills in age-appropriate activities. For example, Vanessa can be in charge of some of the family's grocery shopping: She might write out a short list, prepared with a parent, then be the one in charge to pick the items out, pay for them, and take them home. Such an activity will be appreciated by people she cares about and will help her develop the feeling of success and independence based on her skills.

19. A better method of communication between the school and Vanessa's parents should be developed. For example, designate one teacher or school counselor to convey Vanessa's academic needs to her parents and communicate back to them ways that they can stay involved and be in more control of Vanessa's learning. Such a system of communication will be a valuable source of help and support.

Psychometric Summary for Vanessa J.: KABC-II, CHC Model

Scale	Standard Score (mean = 100; SD = 15)	90% Confidence Interval	Percentile Rank
Sequential/*Gsm*	127	[117–133]	96
Number Recall	15		95
Word Order	14		91
Hand Movements	10		50
Simultaneous/*Gv*	80	[73–89]	9
Rover	7		16
Triangles	6		9
Block Counting	10		50
Gestalt Closure	5		5
Learning/*Glr*	94	[87–101]	34
Atlantis	8		25
Rebus	10		50
Planning/*Gf*	90	[92–100]	25
Story Completion	7		16
Pattern Reasoning	10		50
Knowledge/*Gc*	87	[81–93]	19
Verbal Knowledge	8		25
Riddles	7		16
Expressive Vocabulary	4		2
Fluid-Crystallized Index (FCI)	93	[88–98]	32
Supplementary Scale			
Delayed Recall	92	[86–98]	30
Atlantis Delayed	8		25
Rebus Delayed	9		37

Note. Italicized subtests are Supplementary and not included in the calculation of the indexes.

WISC-IV, Selected Subtests

Scale	Standard Score (mean = 100; SD = 15)	90% Confidence Interval	Percentile Rank
Verbal Comprehension			
Comprehension	15		95
Information	8		25
Working Memory	**107**	**[100–113]**	**68**
Digit Span	11		63
Letter-Number Seq.	12		75
Processing Speed	**80**	**[75–90]**	**9**
Coding	7		16
Symbol Search	6		9

Note: A Verbal Comprehension Index could not be computed because only one of the three subtests that compose this scale was administered to Vanessa. The Information subtest is italicized because it is a Supplementary WISC-IV subtest.

KTEA-II Comprehensive Form (form A)

Composites and Subtests	Standard Score (+90% Confidence Interval) Grade Norms	Percentile Rank
Reading Composite (LWR + RC)	**70 ± 4**	**2**
Letter & Word Recognition (LWR)[a]	71 ± 5	3
Reading Comprehension (RC)[a]	76 ± 6	5
Reading-Related Composites		
Decoding Composite (LWR + NWD)	**74 ± 5**	**4**
Nonsense Word Decoding (NWD)	77 ± 7	6
Sound-Symbol Composite (NWD + PA)	**76 ± 7**	**5**
Phonological Awareness (PA)	83 ± 9	13
Reading Fluency Composite (WRF + DF)	**76 ± 7**	**5**
Word Recognition Fluency (WRF)	75 ± 4	5
Decoding Fluency (DF)	76 ± 6	5
Mathematics Composite	**91 ± 6**	**27**
Mathematics Concepts & Applications (MCA)[a]	94 ± 7	34
Mathematics Computation[a]	89 ± 9	23
Oral Language Composite	**70 ± 8**	**2**
Listening Comprehension[a]	60 ± 10	< 1
Oral Expression	81 ± 10	10
Oral Fluency Composite (AF + NF)	**84 ± 7**	**14**
Associational Fluency (AF)	98 ± 14	45
Naming Facility/RAN (NF)	81 ± 9	10
Written Language Composite	**97 ± 6**	**42**
Written Expression[a]	108 ± 10	70
Spelling	87 ± 6	19
Comprehensive Achievement Composite	**76 ± 4**	**5**

[a]Included in the Comprehensive Achievement Composite.

CHC Broad Ability	Standard Score	Percentile Rank	Source
Gf Fluid Reasoning	90	25	KABC-II
Gc Crystallized Ability			
Lexical Knowledge	87	19	KABC-II
Listening Ability	65	1	KTEA-II
Oral Production	81	10	KTEA-II
Gv Visual Processing	80	9	KABC-II
Gsm Short-Term Memory	127	96	KABC-II
	107	68	WISC-IV
Glr Long-Term Retrieval			
Associative Memory	94	34	KABC-II
Associational Fluency	97	42	
Naming Facility (RAN)	78	7	KTEA-II
Ga Auditory Processing	82	12	KTEA-II
Gq Quantitative Knowledge	87	19	KTEA-II
Grw Reading and Writing			
Reading	69	2	KTEA-II
Written Language	89	23	KTEA-II
Gs Processing Speed	80	9	WISC-IV

CASE REPORT 2

Name: Allisonbeth C.
Age: 3 years, 10 months
Examiner: Dr. Nadeen L. Kaufman

Background and Referral Information

Mr. and Mrs. C. contacted the examiner when the application for their daughter's admittance to a prestigious Manhattan preschool was rejected. As part of the application procedure, young Allisonbeth had been administered the Stanford-Binet-4th Edition, as an entrance exam screener for determining the requisite gifted status necessary for admission. The results of this assessment consisted of one overall number, 108, typed into a form with no further elaboration other than the rejection. Mr. and Mrs. C. requested this evaluation to learn the specifics of how they might facilitate their daughter's growth and development and to clarify if their daughter was or was not gifted.

Allisonbeth is the only child of a 49-year-old mother and 75-year-old father who are each presidents of different financial investment firms. Married nearly 25 years, they pursued their careers and originally did not plan to have children. They live in a penthouse condominium apartment with a governess employed to care for Allisonbeth while her parents work. Mrs. C.'s older sister is a classroom elementary school teacher and has told the family that she has been "monitoring Allisonbeth's academic achievement," and reassures them that "Allisonbeth is indeed gifted."

To facilitate the possibility of becoming pregnant, Mr. and Mrs. C. conceived Allisonbeth through in vitro fertilization. The pregnancy itself was uncomplicated, and Allisonbeth's early developmental milestones progressed normally. She has maintained excellent health, and started attending nursery school two mornings a week once she was toilet trained, at about age 20 months. There are no siblings. The family's live-in governess is a certified preschool teacher who has taught Allisonbeth to use a computer and spends time each day on prereading activities through a wide variety of software. Every evening before sleep, the family ritual includes the governess presenting Mr. and Mrs. C. with a report card for Allisonbeth's learning, and they reward her accordingly, starting with "Level One," sitting in front of the monitor. In this manner, Mr. and Mrs. C. feel assured of Allisonbeth's future academic success.

Appearance and Behavioral Characteristics

Allisonbeth arrived accompanied by both her parents. All three were dressed up, which, as Mr. C. pointed out, was the family's usual style for any outing. Allisonbeth, who was playfully referred to by her parents as "Alpha-Bet," is a beautiful little girl, of age-appropriate height and weight, with long blond hair curled in rows like Shirley Temple. A cute pink bow held a lock of hair up from her forehead, cascading it down to frame the front of her face. Allisonbeth was well dressed in a matching pink and brown long-sleeved cotton knit shirt and pants outfit. Even though she was willing to approach the examiner with a shy smile, she remained a bit clingy to her two parents. Mr. and Mrs. C. pointed things out in the office in attempts to facilitate the requisite separation, but her response was to become *less* secure. She interacted with the examiner giving only partial attention, always keeping the location of her parents in sight. When they attempted to leave, telling her they'd be back soon, she ran back to them, saying she was hungry. In this manner, she cleverly switched requests in unsuccessful attempts to manipulate her parents. Finally, Mr. C. left, promising to bring her back a muffin, while Mrs. C. went into an adjoining vacant office, showing Allisonbeth where she'd be staying while Allisonbeth had a play date with the examiner.

Allisonbeth's manipulation characterized the early part of the evaluation; it soon developed into a more confident, assertive tone that bordered on oppositional behavior. It is clear that Allisonbeth has a definite need to be in charge, to set her own goals, and to determine what the rules will be for interactions between herself and others. When the examiner enabled this tendency to be allowed within the confines of a broader set of rules (e.g., "we have to take turns—now it's your turn to answer . . ."), Allisonbeth was redirectable. When a fair agreement was negotiated (e.g., "you can have a taste of this after this game is finished"), Allisonbeth participated agreeably. Without these conciliations, however, it was difficult to engage Allisonbeth's complete attention and cooperation, even for a short time. Indeed, once the actual testing began, it became apparent that keeping Allisonbeth's attention focused long enough for her to participate at optimum performance required continual effort. The examiner was able to make this effort in her interaction with Allisonbeth, typically with compromises and conciliations, and, thus, the results of the present evaluation are deemed accurate and valid.

This task of engaging Allisonbeth was considerably easier if the activity at hand contained pictures or manipulatable materials to engage her interest; she had more difficulty sustaining attention when only words and no visual or physical stimuli were available. One exception to this behavior occurred during the administration of a subtest that required her to copy the examiner's hand movements, where she had both a visual and a three-dimensional stimulus to observe (i.e., the examiner's hand), yet she had a hard time sustaining attention long enough for the initial items to be validly administered. Whenever Allisonbeth's attention waned, the examiner redirected her face and attention carefully before the start of each new item in the subtest.

Allisonbeth was a slow worker when coordination or higher-level cognitive reasoning was required. These observations applied to the standardized tests administered to her and to informal drawing and writing tasks as well. One informal task also revealed Allisonbeth's oppositional tendencies. When asked to draw a girl, she refused, saying she would draw a dog. She used her right hand to draw and write and held the pencil correctly. However, on a standardized test of putting colored blocks together to match a design (WPPSI-III Block Design), she did not code the order of red to white in forming her responses and couldn't determine how to use a half-red, half-white block in creating the block designs. She also rotated and reversed her designs and left broad gaps between the blocks (however, these errors are not penalized on this task). On the paper-and-pencil task for which Allisonbeth decided to draw a dog, the resulting squiggle had no recognizable parts, nor did she verbalize while drawing. Yet, when asked, "How many legs does a dog have?" she answered "Four," then proceeded to put four vertical strokes of the pencil in a row next to the squiggle she called a dog. These strokes were not placed to resemble legs under an animal's body, which might have been positioned to hold weight. Her pencil point eventually ripped the paper, and she continued making hundreds of little vertical lines across many new pages, evidence of perseveration.

Verbal tasks elicited quick, frequently impulsive responses, and Allisonbeth rarely elaborated when questioned further. When prodded, she tended to perseverate on the response already given. Perseveration also occurred when she did not know a specific answer and happily shouted out answers to previous items. In this way she did not display awareness of failure or hesitate on questions to indicate indecisiveness.

Allisonbeth's language ability was well developed. She articulated clearly, and her sentences were age appropriate in length and grammatical structure. For example, when the examiner asked her a question in casual conversation, she said coyly, "I'm not telling you!" When responding to specific verbal question in standardized tasks, her verbal knowledge was sporadic; some items she knew correctly, others not at all, with great inconsistency. If a response didn't pop into her mind immediately, she attempted to manipulate the task requirement into one she was more skilled at, namely reciting letters of the alphabet. The alphabet, perhaps reflecting her parents' reinforcing nickname, became the topic of Allisonbeth's only spontaneous commentary during the evaluation: After putting blocks together to match abstract designs, she started putting the blocks together to make a giant C. She indicated that she feels competent in her letter knowledge and that she has received many compliments for her letter-naming skills.

Allisonbeth was able to take care of body needs appropriately; she asked to go to the bathroom by herself with no difficulty. She also fed herself little spoonfuls of chocolate ice cream when allowed to after completed subtests according to preagreement rules. When the evaluation was over, she didn't want to leave and was eventually coaxed to leave the assessment room by a reminder about Daddy coming with a muffin.

Assessment Procedures

- Kaufman Assessment Battery for Children—Second Edition (KABC-II)
- Wechsler Preschool and Primary Scale of Intelligence—Third Edition (WPPSI-III)
- Informal measures of drawing, writing, and arithmetic ability
- Clinical Interview with Mr. and Mrs. C.

Test Results and Interpretation

Allisonbeth was administered the KABC-II and the WPPSI-III. The WISC-IV and KABC-II and WPPSI-III are each individually administered tests of a child's intellectual and processing ability, and each provides scales to identify the child's cognitive strengths and weaknesses.

The KABC-II is based on a double theoretical foundation, Luria's neuropsychological model and the CHC psychometric theory. For 3-year-olds, in general, the KABC-II yields only a global score; however, the test has a built-in special procedure for obtaining a complete profile of scores for 3-year-old children believed to be Above Average. Because Allisonbeth was referred for possible giftedness and was nearly 4 years old when tested, this special procedure was applied. It involves administering the 4-year level of the KABC-II to a 3-year-old and then using out-of-level norms to obtain the profile of scores. Though the 4-year level of the KABC-II is administered in this out-of-level procedure, the standard scores are, nonetheless, based on the performance of children Allisonbeth's same age (3 years, 10 months).

In addition to a global score, the 4-year level of the KABC-II offers four scales, each given a label that reflects both theoretical models: Sequential/*Gsm,* Simultaneous/Gv, Learning/Glr, and Knowledge/Gc. (From the perspective of CHC theory, Gsm = short-term memory; Gv = visual processing; Glr = long-term storage and retrieval; and Gc = crystallized ability.)

Examiners are given the option of selecting either the Luria model or the CHC model of the KABC-II, based on the child's background and the reason for referral. (Knowledge/Gc is excluded from the Luria model because measures of language ability and acquired knowledge may not provide fair assessment of some children's cognitive abilities—e.g., those from bilingual or nonmainstream backgrounds). Based on Allisonbeth's enriched background and her referral for possible giftedness, the CHC KABC-II model was chosen. This model yields the FCI as the global measure of general cognitive ability. To administer the 4-year level of the KABC-II to Allisonbeth, it was necessary to administer the Core 3-year battery (seven subtests) plus an additional two subtests (Rebus and Number Recall) that ordinarily are not administered until age 4.

Allisonbeth earned a KABC-II FCI of 111, ranking her at the 77th percentile and classifying her overall cognitive ability as falling within the Average range. The chances are 90% that her true FCI is between 106 and 116. Her indexes (standard scores) on the four theory-based scales that compose the FCI ranged from 99 on the Simultaneous/Gv scale (47th percentile) to 118 on the Knowledge/Gc scale (88th percentile).

Allisonbeth demonstrated well-developed language and vocabulary skills in addition to a strong base of knowledge. These strengths were evident from her performance on the Knowledge/Gc index of 118. She performed better than 88 of 100 of children her age, and her performance was significantly higher than her own level of Average cognitive ability (a Personal Strength). Her Knowledge/Gc index is significantly higher than her Learning/Glr index of 103 (Average range, 58th percentile), indicating that her acquired knowledge is better developed than her ability to learn new information taught by the examiner (e.g., the nonsense names assigned to pictures of fish, plants, and shells). Allisonbeth's strong performance on measures of acquired knowledge was exemplified by tasks that measure receptive language (pointing to the correct picture of a word or fact spoken by the examiner), expressive language (giving the name of pictured concrete object), and both types of language (solving a verbal riddle).

In contrast to her strong performances on tests of acquired knowledge, Allisonbeth performed less well on tests of visual processing and nonverbal reasoning. Although her performance on the Simultaneous/Gv scale (standard score = 99; 47th percentile) was not as strong as her performance on the other indexes, her score was in the Average range relative to other children almost 4 years of age and is no cause for concern.

Additional information about Allisonbeth's cognitive abilities was obtained from the WPPSI-III. The WPPSI-III comprises four subtests in the Core battery for 3-year-olds, two that yield a Verbal IQ and two that yield a Performance IQ. Overall, on the four WPPSI-III subtests, Allisonbeth earned a Full Scale IQ of 112, ranking her general intelligence at the 79th percentile and classifying her ability level as High Average when using the WPPSI-III classification system (her ability level would be considered Average range using the KABC-II definition, i.e., 85 to 115). With 90% confidence, her true WPPSI-III Full Scale IQ is within the range from 106 to 117. Regardless of the descriptive classification system that is used, Allisonbeth's Full Scale IQ of 112 is virtually identical to her FCI of 111, and both global scores are entirely consistent with the Stanford-Binet-IV global composite of 109 that she earned when tested for entrance to preschool. Allisonbeth does not meet the intellectual criteria for giftedness. Her overall ability level is Average to High Average. She is a bright child who has benefited from much enrichment but does not qualify as gifted.

Allisonbeth's pattern of scores on the WPPSI-III were also consistent with those on the KABC-II, indicating that her language abilities are better developed than her visual processing and nonverbal reasoning abilities. Evidence for this finding was the fact that her WPPSI-III Verbal IQ of 116 (86th percentile) is significantly higher than her Performance IQ of 105 (63rd percentile), indicating that she was able to express her intelligence better when responding verbally than when manipulating concrete materials. Taken together, the results of both tests paint the picture of a young girl whose Above Average acquisition of words and facts significantly exceeds her Average level of problem-solving ability, spatial visualization, and skill at learning new information. Her areas of strength (often referred to as *crystallized* ability) have undoubtedly been enhanced by her enriched environment and by her caring parents and governess. The other abilities measured by the KABC-II and WPPSI-III are less influenced by an enriched environment. Her Average level on the other cognitive scales probably reflects her fluid abilities, which are associated with skill at solving novel problems. However, it is important to note that the best predictor of school achievement is crystallized ability, suggesting that her future academic success is likely to be Above Average rather than Average.

The findings from nonstandardized assessment procedures further supported the results from the KABC-II and WPPSI-III. Informal assessment revealed that whereas she can count, she does not possess one-to-one correspondence. Other informal tasks demonstrated Allisonbeth's success in writing recognizable letters from her name: A, L, I, N, E, T, and H, but letters possessing curves were very poor efforts, consistent with the earlier mentioned fine-motor-skill level and with her drawings of circles and straight lines. Alternatively, she could dictate her full name loudly and clearly. Despite her good language skills, Allisonbeth did not catch on to problem-solving types of task demands when presented with the standard set of instructions (e.g., KABC-II Conceptual Thinking) and needed much teaching on those items where teaching was allowed.

Because Allisonbeth was distractible and had a limited attention span, one must rule out the possibility that her relatively weaker areas of functioning were primarily due to an attentional problem. In the examiner's judgment, that was not the case. The KABC-II Sequential/*Gsm* scale, which measures short-term memory, is quite susceptible to distractibility. Allisonbeth earned an index of 112 on that scale (79th percentile), and also scored at the 84th percentile on the Supplementary Hand Movements subtest—a test of visual memory that required much effort by the examiner to sustain Allisonbeth's attention. In addition, Allisonbeth performed almost identically on the WPPSI-III and KABC-II, even though the subtests that comprise the WPPSI-III are *not* particularly susceptible to distractibility—in contrast to the KABC-II Learning/*Glr* and Sequential/*Gsm* subtests, which are among the tasks that are *most* impacted by attentional problems.

Recommendations and Suggestions for Enrichment

1. The results of this evaluation helped to clarify that Allisonbeth has Average to Above Average abilities but does not score in the Gifted range of ability. As Allisonbeth's parents clearly have high expectations for their daughter based on their prior belief that she may be gifted, they could benefit from sessions with a counselor to help them develop a more realistic understanding of Allisonbeth's cognitive strengths and weaknesses. Having realistic expectations for Allisonbeth's future school performance should help Allisonbeth to not feel undue pressure to succeed. A recommendation for a good counselor in close proximity is Dr. Angela R.

2. Mr. and Mrs. C. should consider enrolling Allisonbeth in a small group activity oriented program that requires child-to-child interaction— this will reduce the one-to-one adult attention she receives, even in her current nursery school, and help her acquire better peer-oriented social skills. Examples are a Dalcroze music and dance/rhythm group or an age-appropriate group sport that does not stress competition (like soccer)— this will improve her coordination and motor skills at the same time as facilitating peer-group skills she needs to reduce the ability to be in a group of age mates and only focus on the adult, whom she can likely manipulate.

3. The emphasis in parental time spent alone with Allisonbeth should broaden the goals to focus on the we and less on the struggle for power. If the power struggle continues, she will become more challenging to get to comply as she gains more reasoning ability. Also, it will help Allisonbeth's cognitive growth to supplement concern with the traditional reading emphasis of academic preschool content with added emphasis on discovery, spontaneous learning, and interest development. This type of enrichment can be enhanced by frequent and short visits to children's hands-on museums. A Montessori experience might be good to focus her attention on sensory development and independence.

4. Since Allisonbeth already has mastered some computer skills and enjoys playing on the computer, Mr. and Mrs. C. should consider purchasing software that uses attractive visual materials, is interactive, and fosters the growth of reasoning and problem-solving skills. The software she currently uses emphasizes reading-oriented games. New software should also include reading-related activities and should include a voice that instructs or talks, to take advantage of her strong language skills while enhancing her reasoning skills.

5. Allisonbeth will also benefit from noncomputer visual-motor activities, such as manipulating puzzles or blocks, using paper and pencil, and counting and sorting form boxes.

6. Mr. and Mrs. C. might want to evaluate the behavior/conduct/discipline style of the governess to see if she is subtly reinforcing the struggle for control issues. A stress on cooperation rather than competition needs to be maintained by all adults who interact with her to the degree this is possible. Observing her in nursery school might provide additional information on this topic.

7. Allisonbeth should be encouraged to complete tasks that stretch her attention span gradually by increasing expectations and providing reinforcement for successful behavior, regardless of correctness or goodness of performance.

8. An easy-to-care-for plant or goldfish might encourage the development of responsibility to other living things and increased awareness of others' needs; this activity may improve Allisonbeth's compliance as a learning experience that is oriented to the rights of others. Along the same goal lines, acting out skits where she must identify with someone else's different life circumstances may help her develop more emotional empathy for others.

Psychometric Summary for Allisonbeth C.: KABC-II, CHC Model, Out-of-Level Norms (4-Year Level)

Scale	Standard Score (mean = 100; SD = 15)	90% Confidence Interval	Percentile Rank
Sequential/*Gsm*	112	[104–118]	79
Number Recall	11		63
Word Order	13		84
Hand Movements	*13*		84
Simultaneous/*Gv*	99	[90–108]	47
Conceptual Thinking	11		63
Face Recognition	7		16
Triangles	11		63
Learning/*Glr*	103	[95–111]	58
Atlantis	10		50
Rebus	11		63
Knowledge/*Gc*	118	[110–124]	88
Riddles	12		75
Expressive Vocabulary	14		91
Verbal Knowledge	*12*		75
Fluid-Crystallized Index (FCI)	111	[106–116]	77

Note. Italicized subtests are Supplementary and do not contribute to the global score indexes.

WPPSI-III

Scale	Standard Score (mean = 100; SD = 15)	90% Confidence Interval	Percentile Rank
Verbal IQ	116	[110–120]	86
Receptive Vocabulary	14		91
Information	12		75
Performance IQ	105	[97–112]	63
Block Design	11		63
Object Assembly	10		50
Full Scale IQ	112	[106–117]	79

CASE REPORT 3

Name: Pedro G.
Age: 10 Years, 10 Months
Grade: Fourth
Examiner: Michelle Lurie, Psy.D.

Referral and Background Information

Pedro G., age 10 years, 10 months, was referred for an evaluation by his pediatrician, Dr. O. Dr. O. is currently completing a comprehensive evaluation of Pedro for ADHD and requested a psychoeducational testing to rule out any potential learning disability. In addition, Mr. and Mrs. G. hope to obtain information regarding how best to meet Pedro's needs once they return to Mexico. Pedro lives with his biological parents, 9-year-old brother, and 4-year-old sister in Plano, Texas. The family is originally from Mexico City, Mexico. They moved to Texas a year ago when Mr. G.'s company transferred his position to Plano. However, the family plans to return to Mexico within the next 6 months. The primary language spoken in his home is Spanish, although all the family members are bilingual.

According to Mrs. G., she had a normal pregnancy, and Pedro was born weighing 3.5 kg. Childhood developmental milestones were within normal limits. At age 3, Pedro was hospitalized for Salmonellas, and he had his tonsils removed at the age of 7. Pedro has sleep difficulties, taking a long time to fall asleep and waking up during the night and very early in the morning. Pedro was diagnosed with ADHD in Mexico at the age of 9. He was treated with Ritalin; however, Pedro complained of dizziness and depression, and his parents stopped his medication after 9 months. Mr. and Mrs. G. noted that Pedro complains of insomnia and that he is often tired. He frequently complains of dizziness, particularly after exercise or when in mass. Before moving to the United States, Pedro had received various treatments for his ADHD, such as multisensory teaching and computerized treatments. His parents indicated that they questioned the effectiveness of these treatments.

In an interview with Dr. O. regarding Pedro's current medical condition, he noted that his overall diagnostic impression of Pedro is "ADHD primarily inattentive type." He stated that the side effects Pedro reportedly experienced when on Ritalin could be a wear-off effect, which can occur when the doses are too far apart. The doctor commented that Ritalin or another stimulant medication could be tried again. Dr. O. also indicated that Pedro is being treated for multiple allergies. According to Dr. O., Pedro may have a tic disorder, possibly a variant of

Tourette's Syndrome. The symptoms which Mr. and Mrs. G. reported to Dr. O. include both vocal tics, such as animal noises, as well as motor tics, such as eye blinking and grimacing. Pedro has never received treatment for his mild tic disorder.

Mr. and Mrs. G. indicated that Pedro is having a great deal of difficulty in school, both academically and socially. He is in fourth grade in public school in the Plano Independent School District, and he has been at this school since moving to Texas. His primary difficulties are in classes that are verbally demanding. He has difficulty keeping up with the changing requirements in the classroom and struggles with reading and problem solving in mathematics. Further difficulties were reported with Pedro's writing and spelling skills. He tends to spell phonetically, confusing rules he has learned in Spanish with those applicable to English. According to his parents, Pedro struggles to attend to details. For example, when focusing on his spelling, he will neglect his punctuation and capitalization. Mr. and Mrs. G. noted that Pedro's current teacher, Mrs. S., emphasizes the importance of details, and Pedro is often graded down in this area. Many of these difficulties appear to result from the discrepancy between Pedro's education in Mexico and that in the United States. In Mexico, Pedro attended a bilingual private school in which he was performing at an Average level. In this school, Pedro was consistently given the same assignments and tests every week, which created a predictable environment for him. The emphasis in Mexico was placed on grammar and vocabulary, and very little reading was done in either Spanish or English. In contrast, his education in public school in the United States has demanded more reading and has a much less consistent pattern of assignments each week.

In an interview with Mrs. S., she indicated that although Pedro had made progress over the past few months, he would not have done so without the individualized assistance she is providing. Mrs. S. noted that she needs to call on Pedro "at least a hundred times a day" in order to get his attention. She commented that he is easily distracted, particularly in class discussions, during which he loses concentration as soon as the other children begin talking. Mrs. S. further indicated that Pedro prefers working on worksheets than participating in class discussions but that he does not finish the words and sentences or even the math problems he is working on and tends to hand in incomplete work. According to Mrs. S., in a discussion with Pedro he indicated that he does not always understand her vocabulary. Since this discussion, Pedro appears to be more comfortable asking Mrs. S. to clarify instructions when necessary. Mrs. S.'s primary concerns are that Pedro has poor study skills and is unable to work independently.

According to Mr. and Mrs. G., homework is another area of difficulty for Pedro. They report that without supervision, Pedro tends to become stuck on a section of the homework and is unable to move on. Consequently, his homework takes him a substantial amount of time and is very frustrating. His parents describe Pedro as "unmotivated." They are concerned that should he fail fourth grade, he will be in the same grade as his younger brother, who they describe as a high achiever in all areas. One of the primary concerns of Mr. and Mrs. G. is that Pedro may require special accommodations in school, which are unavailable in Mexico.

Pedro has struggled to make friends since his move to the United States. His parents indicated that Pedro is very sensitive to the teasing that goes on in the classroom and that he acts in an immature manner around his peers. Similar problems were noted in Mexico. Mr. and Mrs. G. commented that Pedro had low self-esteem before but that it has become worse since the move. They noted that Pedro cries easily, that he often "acts silly" and behaves "like a ninny." His parents described Pedro as very fidgety and nervous, and they commented that he is very badly affected by failure. They indicated that Pedro "gives up easily" and becomes frustrated and irritable.

Appearance and Behavioral Characteristics

Pedro is a slightly built, attractive boy with sandy-blond hair and freckles on his nose. At both testing sessions, he was casually dressed in a school uniform of blue sweatpants, shirt, and sneakers. Pedro arrived at the first testing with a bag of licorice in his hand, and he brought along a bottle of Gatorade to the second session. Pedro was friendly and responsive to the examiner, and rapport was easily established. He described his difficulty adjusting to his new school, commenting that "the beginning of the year was hard," and he shared several jokes with the examiner at various times during the testing. Pedro spoke with a slight accent, and at times his language appeared stilted. He made some errors, such as confusing "mother" and "father" and "brother" and "sister." Pedro was unable to tell the examiner his exact address and indicated that his phone number had "some 5s and 8s but I don't remember the order." Despite these difficulties, Pedro appeared to clearly understand the examiner's instructions.

Throughout the testing, Pedro tended to verbally mediate as he worked. When drawing pictures, he spontaneously narrated the scene for the examiner to hear, and when presented with passages to read, he chose to read out loud. Pedro's ability to pay attention to the task presented was inconsistent. He had to be encouraged to refocus his attention on several occasions, and he tended to fidget constantly and swing in his chair, particularly when faced with higher-level items. At those times, Pedro would stare at the clock or at a picture on the wall and had to be prompted to attend to the task. However, it was often difficult to determine whether Pedro was distracted or whether he was focusing on the task. At various times throughout the testing, although Pedro did not appear to be paying attention, he was able to answer the question or complete the task he was working on accurately. At other times, Pedro became completely focused and engrossed in a task and was able to attend throughout the presentation of a subtest, even as the items became challenging.

On several occasions, especially during one test of immediate sequential memory (pointing to pictures of words said by the examiner, sometimes after an interference task), Pedro fidgeted and displayed excessive motor activity. During a receptive language subtest, Pedro began biting on a paper cup, gradually tearing and sucking on the cup until it was torn into pieces. During a visualization task (counting sets of blocks where some blocks are hidden from view), he began pulling on the label of the Gatorade bottle until it came loose, and then fidgeted with it on the table top. Mild facial tics, such as a stretching of his mouth and a widening of his eyes, were apparent during the first session, but they were not noted at the second testing. After concentrating intently during a subtest that measured Pedro's ability to learn new information (i.e., the nonsense names of pictures), he complained of feeling dizzy; however, no other somatic complaints were noted.

Pedro appeared to be confident about what he did and did not know. He persevered throughout the testing; however, when he was unable to answer a question, he stated calmly "this is too hard for me, I won't do this one." On the Mathematics Computation subtest, when faced with long division problems and two-digit multiplication problems, Pedro commented "I certainly won't do those," and "those will take me too long." This behavior was also evident on the Reading Comprehension subtest. Pedro did not appear to be uncomfortable stating that he did not know an answer. Given Pedro's level of motivation and his ability to complete all tasks presented to him, this assessment is a valid measure of Pedro's cognitive, language, and academic abilities.

Assessment Procedures

- Clinical Interview with Mr. and Mrs. G.
- Clinical Interview with Pedro G.
- Kaufman Assessment Battery for Children—Second Edition (KABC-II)
- Kaufman Test of Academic Achievement Second Edition (KTEA-II)—Comprehensive Form (Form A)

- Developmental Test of Visual Motor Integration (4th ed.; VMI-4)
- Intermediate Visual and Auditory Continuous Performance Test (IVA)
- Behavior Assessment System for Children (BASC): Parent Rating Scale (Spanish Version)
- Behavior Assessment System for Children (BASC): Teacher Rating Scale
- Kinetic Family Drawing (KFD)
- Draw-a-Person test
- Peabody Picture Vocabulary Test—Third Edition (PPVT-III)

Test Results and Interpretation

Assessment of Cognitive, Visual-Motor, and Language Abilities

To obtain a comprehensive picture of Pedro's mental processing and cognitive abilities, Pedro was administered the KABC-II. The KABC-II is based on a double theoretical foundation, Luria's neuropsychological model, and the CHC psychometric theory. It offers five scales, each given a label that reflects both theoretical models: Sequential/*Gsm,* Simultaneous/*Gv,* Learning/*Glr,* Planning/*Gf,* and Knowledge/*Gc.* (From the perspective of CHC theory, *Gsm* = short-term memory; *Gv* = visual processing; *Glr* = long-term storage and retrieval; *Gf* = fluid reasoning; and *Gc* = crystallized ability.)

Examiners are given the option of selecting either the Luria model or the CHC model of the KABC-II, based on the child's background and the reason for referral. (Knowledge/*Gc* is excluded from the Luria model because measures of language ability and acquired knowledge may not provide fair assessment of some children's cognitive abilities—e.g., those from bilingual or nonmainstream backgrounds.) Pedro was administered the Luria model of the KABC-II because he is bilingual, and Spanish is the primary language spoken in the home. However, to obtain additional information about Pedro's ability, he was additionally administered the Knowledge/*Gc* scale as a supplement that did not factor into his overall global score. The Luria model yields a global score called the Mental Processing Index (MPI).

The KABC-II also offers a third global score option, the Nonverbal scale, which comprises subtests that can be administered gesturally and responded to nonverbally. Because Pedro speaks and understands English well, the examiner felt that the MPI was likely to provide a good estimate of Pedro's overall cognitive functioning. However, the Nonverbal scale was administered as well to provide an estimate of his global ability without the influence of any oral English language. (The Nonverbal scale, which yields the Nonverbal index or NVI, includes some subtests that contribute to the MPI plus a few Supplementary subtests.)

Pedro earned a KABC-II MPI of 116, ranking him at the 86th percentile and classifying his overall mental processing ability as Above Average. The chances are 90% that his true MPI is within the 111 to 121 range. He displayed considerable variability in his standard scores on the four theory-based scales that compose the MPI with indexes ranging from 130 on Simultaneous/*Gv* to 97 on Sequential/*Gsm*. This wide variation in indexes renders his MPI meaningless as an estimate of global ability and is nothing more than the midpoint of diverse abilities. In addition, as discussed in the following, his lowest indexes may have been affected by his ability to speak and understand English (his second language). Consequently, the Nonverbal scale probably reflects the best estimate of Pedro's cognitive ability. He earned a Nonverbal index (NVI) of 135, which ranks him at the 99th percentile and classifies his global nonverbal ability in the Upper Extreme category (90% confidence interval = 127 to 139).

Unlike the MPI, all four of Pedro's scale indexes were found to be interpretable, as he performed consistently on the tasks that compose each separate scale. Pedro was administered the Knowledge/*Gc* scale as a supplement to the MPI, but that index was found *not* to be interpretable because he displayed considerable variability on the two Core Knowledge/*Gc* subtests (scoring at the 84th percentile on a task requiring him to solve riddles and at the 9th percentile on a receptive language subtest requiring him to point to the picture that represented a particular word or fact). Therefore, Pedro's Knowledge/*Gc* index of 90 could not be meaningfully interpreted.

Pedro demonstrated well-developed reasoning and problem-solving ability when solving problems that depend either on spatial visualization and simultaneous processing of information or on verbal mediation. These skills were evident in Pedro's performance on the Simultaneous/*Gv* scale (index = 130, percentile rank = 98) and on the Planning/*Gf* scale (index = 121, percentile rank = 92). Relative to his own Above Average level of ability, these scores were Personal Strengths. In addition, his scores on both of these scales were significantly higher than typical 10-year-olds' (Normative Strengths). Furthermore, his standard score of 130 on Simultaneous/*Gv* was *substantially* higher than his Above Average overall ability (a difference that large occurred less than 10% of the time in the standardization sample).

His strong ability to apply his reasoning skill in verbal and visual tasks is exemplified by his performance on specific Simultaneous/*Gv* and Planning/*Gf* subtests. For example, Pedro performed exceptionally well (98th percentile) on the Triangles subtest, which required him to assemble several identical two-colored triangles to match a picture of an abstract design, and on Story Completion (91st percentile), which required him to fill in the missing pictures in an incomplete story. Respectively, these two problem-solving tasks depend primarily on visualization and verbal mediation requiring him to assemble several identical two-colored triangles to match a picture of an abstract design (98th percentile).

Pedro's ability to solve problems that depend on simultaneous processing of information (integrating many stimuli at once) and visualization is a key asset for him (noted on the Simultaneous/*Gv* index). Pedro was able to apply excellent reasoning and simultaneous processing strength to a language task as well, as evidenced by his good performance (84th percentile) on a subtest requiring him to integrate clues to identify a concrete or abstract verbal concept. His strong skills on a variety of problem-solving tasks provide strong support that this well-developed ability will provide valuable information for diagnostic purposes and for planning any educational interventions that might be necessary.

In contrast to these areas of integrity for Pedro, he displayed difficulties—relative to his Above Average ability level—in his sequential processing of information (solving problems one step at a time) and in his ability to learn new information. These areas of relative deficit were noted in his Sequential/*Gsm* scale (index = 97, percentile rank = 42) and Learning/*Glr* scale (index = 100, percentile rank = 50). His performance on both of these scales was significantly lower than his overall Above Average level of cognitive ability. However, both indexes are in the Average range compared to other 10-year-olds. In addition, both the Sequential/*Gsm* and Learning/*Glr* scales require verbal abilities, suggesting that his Personal Weaknesses may relate to the fact that English is Pedro's second language. Furthermore, he was fidgety and seemed to have limited attention span during some of the tasks on the Sequential/*Gsm* and Learning/*Glr* scales.

The effect of Pedro's English skills was noted on the Sequential/*Gsm* scale. For example, Pedro scored at the 37th percentile on a subtest measuring his ability to point to silhouettes of common objects in the same order as these objects were named by the examiner. This subtest (Word Order) includes a 5-second interference task that requires the child to name a series of colors before pointing to the silhouettes. This color naming was very disruptive for Pedro. He had difficulty retrieving the names of several of the colors, such as "gray." It is also likely that the verbal comprehension required on this subtest created a problem for Pedro. When originally presented with the silhouettes, he called the "cup" a "teapot." Clearly, Pedro's language background may have impacted his performance on this subtest.

Nonetheless, even if his scores were attenuated to some extent on the Core Sequential/*Gsm* subtests, both of which involve language, it is important to note that Pedro's performance on the Supplementary Sequential/*Gsm* subtest (Hand Movements, which is included on the Nonverbal scale) was almost identical to his scores on the two Core subtests (he earned scaled scores of 9, 10, and 11 on the three Sequential/*Gsm* subtests, all in the Average range). Therefore, Pedro conceivably does have a relative weakness in his sequential processing of information and short-term memory, especially in contrast to his strong skills in simultaneous processing and reasoning abilities. That discrepancy is further illustrated by one of the planned clinical comparisons that is included in the KABC-II interpretive system: Problem Solving Ability versus Memory and Learning. Pedro's performance on the Problem Solving grouping of subtests (98th percentile) is significantly higher than on the Memory and Learning grouping (45th percentile), and this discrepancy is uncommonly large in magnitude. However, it is feasible that the unusually large magnitude of the difference is due, in part, to the role that language ability plays on the Memory and Learning subtests and also to the attentional problems that were displayed during some subtests.

On the Learning/*Glr* scale, Pedro scored at the 75th percentile on a subtest (Atlantis) that required him to learn the nonsense names assigned to pictures of fish, plants, and shells. In contrast, he scored at the 25th percentile on a subtest requiring him to learn a new language (Rebus), namely to associate new visual symbols with familiar words and to read sentences composed of these symbols. Although his variability on these two subtest scores was not unusually large (i.e., his Learning/*Glr* index was interpretable), his test behaviors on the two tasks were notable. On Atlantis, Pedro's strong visual processing, together with the fact that he was recalling meaningless names (which are not related to any culture or language), seemed to facilitate both his confidence and his test performance. By contrast, he struggled with the English words he had to memorize and attach to abstract symbols as he tried to read sentences in this new language. Pedro made use of the context of the symbols within each sentence to help recall their meaning, but he did not approach this task with confidence. The KABC-II provides a Supplementary Delayed Recall scale, which was administered to see how well Pedro was able to remember the nonsense names of pictures and the new symbolic language about 20 minutes later in the test session (after other subtests were administered). He earned a standard score of 97 (42nd percentile) on the Delayed Recall scale, indicating that his retention of the newly learned associations was consistent with his initial learning of the material (Learning/*Glr* index of 100). Again, he performed a bit better in his retention of the nonsense word associations (63rd percentile) than in how well he remembered the new Rebus language (25th percentile).

Clearly, Pedro's indexes on two of the four scales that compose the MPI were likely depressed to some extent because of his language abilities. The unusually high NVI of 135 that Pedro obtained is a better estimate of his overall cognitive functioning than his MPI of 116, although it is notable that both of these global scores are above the Average range and categorize his overall ability as a Normative Strength relative to other 10-year-old children.

To further assess Pedro's visual-motor and nonverbal abilities, he was administered Developmental Test of Visual Motor Integration (VMI-4); his paper-and-pencil coordination and drawings were also evaluated with the Kinetic Family Drawing (KFD) and Draw-a-Person tests. On the VMI-4, Pedro was asked to copy various geometric forms. He scored Above Average (94th percentile) on this test, consistent with his NVI on the KABC-II. On the unstructured drawing tasks, Pedro appeared to grip the pencil appropriately and drew people that were age-appropriate and of good quality. In fact, Pedro performed better on the KABC-II visual-perceptual tasks that require gross motor coordination (99th percentile) than on those—such as counting blocks when some blocks are hidden from view—that demand little or no motor coordination (66th percentile). Pedro is especially able to demonstrate his outstanding reasoning ability when expressing himself via motor coordination.

The variability Pedro displayed on the Supplementary KABC-II Knowledge/*Gc* scale was noteworthy. As indicated, he performed at the 84th percentile on the Riddles subtest (receptive and expressive language) compared to the 9th percentile on the Verbal Knowledge subtest (receptive language). He was also administered the Supplementary Expressive Vocabulary subtest (expressive language), on which he performed at an average level (63rd percentile). Whereas his performance on Riddles was partly a reflection of Pedro's exceptional reasoning ability, he was also aided by the fact that the KABC-II accepts correct responses given in Spanish. On eight items, Pedro answered Riddles correctly in Spanish (e.g., *paraguas* for "umbrella" and *tinta* for "ink"), and he likewise was given credit for his Spanish responses to six Expressive Vocabulary items (e.g., *flecha* for "arrow" and *lengua* for the "tongue" of a shoe). However, on Verbal Knowledge, where he had to *point* to pictures that corresponded to a word (such as "agile") or a fact (such as "where the gold rush of 1849 began"), he was not able to compensate by relying on Spanish, and he was also not exposed to a number of the facts because he was raised primarily in Mexico, not the United States.

To further examine Pedro's receptive language in English, he was administered the Peabody Picture Vocabulary Test (PPVT-III), which is limited to vocabulary and does not measure general factual information. Pedro struggled on the PPVT-III, in which he was required to identify the picture named by the examiner. He often asked for these words to be repeated, and his score (8th percentile, Below Average) was virtually identical to his score on KABC-II Verbal Knowledge. On the basis of these results, it is clear that Pedro may have some difficulty understanding English words used in his everyday environment. This problem is supported by the report of his teacher, Mrs. S., who said that Pedro indicated that he does not always understand the words she is using. Pedro's Verbal Knowledge and PPVT-III scores are a reflection of his bilingual and bicultural background and do not reflect a cognitive deficit of any kind. Although Pedro may have some difficulties with word retrieval (in English), his strong abstract reasoning and analytic abilities assist him in the formation of verbal concepts.

Assessment of Academic Achievement

To assess Pedro's academic achievement in reading, math, written language, and oral language, he was administered the KTEA-II Comprehensive Form, which is an individually administered test of academic achievement. Pedro's standard scores on the main KTEA-II Comprehensive Form Composites (based on grade norms) were all within the Average range: Reading (104 ± 4; 61st percentile), Mathematics (96 ± 6; 39th percentile), Oral Language (95 ± 8; 37th percentile), and Written Language (95 ± 6; 37th percentile), Comprehensive Achievement (95 ± 4; 37th percentile).

Pedro's standard scores on the separate KTEA-II subtests spanned the wide range from 85 on Listening Comprehension (16th percentile) to 127 on the Supplementary Nonsense Word Decoding subtest (96th percentile). Despite this extreme subtest variability, all of his subtest standard scores were within the Average Range (85 to 115), except for the aforementioned Nonsense Word Decoding subtest and the Letter and Word Recognition subtest (120, 91st percentile), on which he performed Above Average.

Pedro's standard score on Letter and Word Recognition was 33 points (greater than 2 SDs) higher than his standard score of 87 on Reading Comprehension, a discrepancy that is both statistically significant and substantial in magnitude. That finding indicates that Pedro is more proficient at recognizing and correctly pronouncing a list of words in isolation than understanding and correctly answering questions about passages. Pedro made excellent use of his phonetic skills to sound out the words presented on Letter and Word Recognition; however, his percentile rank of 19 on Reading Comprehension indicates that he was not always able to extract the meaning of the words.

Indeed, Pedro's standard score of 127 on Nonsense Word Decoding (sounding out nonsense words) attests to his excellent phonics ability, as does his standard score on the Supplementary Decoding Composite 126 ± 5; 96th percentile). Pedro's errors on the Spelling subtest provided further confirmation of his reliance on phonics; for example, he spelled *spoken* as *spokun* and *reached* as *reacht*. However, he was not nearly as successful in spelling words as in decoding words. His standard score of 94 on the Spelling subtest (34th percentile) was well below his Decoding Composite (96th percentile), although it was consistent with the standard score of 97 (42nd percentile) that he earned on the Written Expression subtest. Consequently, Pedro's Written Language Composite of 95 provides a good estimate of his ability to express his ideas in writing and to spell in English, but his Reading Composite of 104 is not meaningful in view of his wide disparity between decoding words and understanding their meaning.

A brief informal assessment was conducted in Spanish to compare Pedro's performance in his native language. When reading in Spanish, Pedro had very little difficulty decoding high-level words; however, his pace and tempo were slow, and this style was similar to how he read in English. On the informal spelling test administered in Spanish, Pedro missed 5 out of 15 words. An analysis of his errors indicated confusion between the representation of sounds in Spanish and English, such as when he wrote a "y" for "ll."

Pedro's performance on the KTEA-II Reading Comprehension subtest was inconsistent, and he was able to answer some difficult higher level questions and struggled on some easier ones. It is likely that his difficulty interpreting the question, as indicated by several statements such as "I don't understand," impacted his performance. It is important to recognize, as well, the impact that Pedro's academic background may have had over his performance. In Mexico, Pedro was taught English with very little emphasis on reading. It is only since he began attending school in the United States that he has had more exposure to reading comprehension, and this appears to be an area of difficulty for him.

Like Pedro's Reading Composite, his Oral Language Composite of 95 (37th percentile) represented the midpoint of his substantially better ability to express his ideas in English (108 on Oral Expression, 70th percentile) than to understand spoken English (85 on Listening Comprehension, 16th percentile). The Listening Comprehension subtest is presented on audiocassette. Pedro indicated his difficulty on this task, commenting that it was difficult to understand the audiotape. Findings on the oral language and written language tasks are consistent with each other, as Pedro performed strikingly better expressing his ideas in speaking and writing than in understanding the spoken or written word. These KTEA-II results are also consistent with the KABC-II findings. Pedro performed notably better on Knowledge/*Gc* subtests that emphasize expressive, rather than receptive, language. Pedro benefited on the KABC-II by being allowed to respond in Spanish or English—he was able to perform equally well on the KTEA-II expressive tasks—even though the KTEA-II relies does not give credit for correct Spanish responses.

Pedro's performance in mathematics reveals consistent functioning in the basic skills of computation and quantitative concepts (93) and also in the ability to apply mathematical principles to solve word problems (99), indicating that Pedro's Math Composite of 93 (Average range, 39th percentile) provides a good overview of his skills in mathematics.

Examination of the nature of Pedro's errors on reading and spelling subtests supported his phonics approach to spelling and to reading. In the error analysis for Letter and Word Recognition, Pedro was characterized as weak in unpredictable letter patterns. For instance, he pronounced *ocean* as *ok-ee-an, shoes* as *shows,* and *heard* as *heerd.* He also showed a weakness in the consonants/double consonant and hard/soft C, G, S categories—he consistently mispronounced the *g* sound in words like *guess* and *guarded.* In addition, Pedro was categorized as weak with respect to silent letters on Letter and Word Recognition (he pronounced the *k* in *kneel,* and the *gh* in *high*), on Nonsense Word Decoding (he pronounced the *k* in *knurtle* and the *n* in *sulfemn*), and on Spelling (he spelled *wrongly* as *rongly* and *knocked* as *nocked*). And, as on Letter and Word Recognition, Pedro was weak in unpredictable patterns on Spelling (he wrote *sed* instead of *said* and *peepul* instead of *people*). He also was weak in suffixes/inflections. He spelled *spoken* as *spokun* and *reached* as *reacht.*

Error analyses on Reading Comprehension and Listening Comprehension assess how well a student performs on literal versus inferential questions. On both of these subtests, Pedro was categorized as weak on literal comprehension questions and average on inferential comprehensions. These results are consistent with Pedro's well-developed reasoning abilities. He performed better when answering inferential questions, which require thinking skills, than when answering literal questions (i.e., recalling facts explicitly stated in the passages).

Error analysis for Oral Expression revealed a weakness in word meaning errors. Pedro confused pronouns such as using *he* when referring to a girl. Pedro also incorrectly used adjectives and verbs. For example, he said, "The small girl" when referring to a young girl and used the verb *grabbed* instead of *collected* when referring to a bus driver receiving bus fares. On Written Expression Pedro's weaknesses included sentence structure, capitalization, and punctuation. Examination of his incorrect responses revealed that he consistently wrote run-on sentences when trying to describe complex situations that occurred in the written expression booklet. Also, he consistently failed to capitalize proper nouns (people's names, places, etc.) and had great difficulty with the editing items that required him to place correct punctuation marks throughout a piece of text.

On math subtests, Pedro was found to be weak on concepts and applications problems that involved subtraction with regrouping, multiplication, and long division. For example, in the computation subtest, when presented with the problem "411 − 84," Pedro did not regroup, and simply subtracted the smaller number from the larger regardless of their position. Thus, his answer was 473. His errors in two-digit multiplication and long division reflected an inability to correctly finish the problems. Pedro would complete part of the problems correctly but fail to finish them.

Integration of Ability and Achievement

In evaluating the consistency of Pedro's cognitive and achievement scores, it is clear that overall he has functions in the Average range in most areas, coupled with exceptional reasoning ability and reading decoding ability. Some of his test results appeared to be negatively impacted by language and cultural factors (including teaching styles in Mexico)—notably his Average range of performance on the KABC-II Sequential/*Gsm* and Learning/*Glr* scales and on the KTEA-II Reading Comprehension and Listening Comprehension subtests and his Below Average scores on the PPVT-III and KABC-II Verbal Knowledge subtest. Whereas Pedro's Upper Extreme NVI of 135 may reflect the best estimate of his overall cognitive functioning, this index may be indicative primarily of his overall nonverbal ability, not general cognitive ability. That is to say, even though several of Pedro's KABC-II scores may have been depressed to some extent because English is his second language and because of attentional difficulties, it is, nonetheless, feasible that he does have relative weaknesses in sequential processing of information, learning ability, and memory.

If the NVI is used as the best estimate of his functioning, then he does demonstrate substantial discrepancies between ability and KTEA-II achievement in most areas. But because it is unclear the extent to which language factors, cultural factors, teaching styles in Mexican schools, and even attentional problems may have impacted Pedro's performance on the achievement subtests, a diagnosis of learning disability is not appropriate.

Assessment of Attention and Concentration Abilities

Pedro was administered the IVA, which is a test developed to help in the identification and diagnosis of ADHD. It involves a similar situation to that which children are exposed to in the classroom and requires sustained attention to a repetitive task. During the administration, Pedro attended and appeared motivated to perform to the best of his ability. The results indicate that the administration was valid and can be interpreted. Pedro's performance reflected a directed and steady focus of attention; however, his auditory reaction speed and mental processing speed were slow. This test supports Pedro's relative strength and greater ability for mental processing in the visual modality. It further indicates that Pedro's visual strength is at its peak when task demands are high, and he is stimulated by activity. He performs less well when test demands are low and his attention is free to wander. On the basis of these results it is evident that Pedro's attentional difficulties do not meet ADHD diagnostic criteria. However, it is important to note that while Continuous Performance Tests rarely identify a false positive, they are known to, at times, identify a false negative. In other words, this test alone cannot definitively rule out a diagnosis of ADHD. Multiple factors including reports of his behavior in multiple settings need to be considered. On the cognitive and achievement tests, many of Pedro's lowest scores were on the subtests that are sensitive to distractibility and attention difficulties (e.g., measures of sequential processing, immediate memory, learning ability, and listening comprehension). Pedro may use his strength on simultaneous holistic problem solving as a compensating mechanism when working on tasks requiring a high level of attention. On those tasks involving purely temporal linear problem-solving skills, Pedro's attention difficulties appeared most evident. Another compounding factor is that it is not always clear when Pedro is attending and when he is distracted by external stimuli. This ambiguity makes it more difficult to obtain a definitive conclusion regarding the influence of attentional difficulties on Pedro's profile.

Rating scales from the BASC were administered to Pedro's mother and father (who responded jointly to the Parent Rating Scale, Spanish version) and to Mrs. S., Pedro's teacher (who filled out the Teacher Rating Scale). In this way, further information was obtained on a wide array of potentially problematic behaviors. Pedro's parents had moderate concerns about his internalization of problems, withdrawal, atypical symptoms (like tics), social skills, and school problems (ratings on pertinent scales ranged from the 85th to 92nd percentile). On the Teacher Rating Scale, Mrs. S. expressed mild to moderate concerns about Pedro's attentional problems, adaptability, study skills, and social skills (76th to 90th percentile). These ratings corroborate and validate much of the other data collected that point to an ADHD diagnosis.

Summary and Diagnostic Impressions

Pedro G., aged 10 years, 10 months, and in the fourth grade, was born in Mexico and relocated to the United States a year ago. The G. family plan is to return to Mexico City within the next 6 months. Pedro was referred for an evaluation by his pediatrician, Dr. O., who is currently assessing Pedro for ADHD. The aim of this psychoeducational evaluation was to rule out a learning disability and to provide Mr. and Mrs. G. with recommendations to help their son. Pedro has had previous educational and medical treatments for ADHD in the past; however, none of these proved to be very successful. Mr. and Mrs. G.'s primary concern is that Pedro may require various accommodations in school, which are unavailable in Mexico. They hope that the outcome of this evaluation will provide them with information about how to best meet Pedro's needs.

Pedro was friendly and responsive to the examiners throughout the testing. His attention appeared to be inconsistent, and he frequently had to be encouraged to attend to the task. There was some evidence of fidgeting and excessive motor activity, such as when Pedro started chewing and tearing apart his paper cup and swinging on his chair.

Pedro's cognitive, visual-motor, and language abilities were examined with the KABC-II, VMI-4, PPVT-III, and drawing tests. Pedro's intellectual functioning in the nonverbal sphere is exceptional (in the Upper Extreme range), but his scores in some other areas (such as memory and learning) were in the Average range. Pedro has notable cognitive strengths in his reasoning and problem solving and can apply that ability when correct solutions depend mostly on visualization or verbal mediation. He demonstrated relative weaknesses in sequential processing of information, memory, and learning, but those relatively lower scores were within the Average range and might have been attenuated by language, cultural, and attentional factors. This testing provided evidence of some difficulty in word retrieval and receptive language processing in the English language.

Pedro's academic achievement, as evidenced on the KTEA-II, was mostly within the Average range, with the exception of his Above Average ability to decode words. He had relative difficulty with reading comprehension and understanding spoken language, although he was able to express himself in English (whether talking or writing) quite well. Pedro's relatively low scores on reading and listening comprehension were both undoubtedly related to linguistic factors and to different teaching styles in Mexican schools. However, his slow reading pace was noticed when reading both Spanish and English.

Pedro's performance on the IVA, a test requiring sustained attention to a repetitive task, indicates that he was able to maintain his focus of attention throughout the test. This test provides further support for Pedro's relative strength in visual processing and indicates some difficulty in auditory response speed. While this test does not support the diagnosis of ADHD, it should be noted that this test alone cannot definitively rule out a diagnosis of ADHD. Multiple factors, including reports of his behavior in multiple settings, need to be considered. Behavior rating scales filled out by his parents (Spanish version) and teacher supported a possible diagnosis of ADHD, emphasizing his difficulties with attention, social skills, and study skills.

Overall, it appears that Pedro's academic achievement is fairly consistent with his cognitive abilities. Although there are some notable discrepancies between his cognitive abilities and achievement in some areas, the possible role played by bilingualism, culture, and teaching styles (different in Mexico and the United States), within both the cognitive and achievement realms, precludes any diagnosis of a learning disability.

Recommendations

1. Pedro clearly benefits from individualized instruction. He should continue to sit toward the front of the class and would benefit from being placed in as small a class as possible, with few distractions and a highly structured, consistent routine.

2. Pedro will benefit from being encouraged to ask for help when he does not understand directions or has missed part of the instructions. It is essential to ensure that Pedro is paying attention before giving him oral instructions and to make oral instructions clear and concise.

3. Pedro will benefit from teaching methods which incorporate nonverbal input and visual reinforcement whenever possible, such as using gestures, drawing on the board, or modeling the steps of a process.

4. It is recommended that Pedro be taught strategies for monitoring his comprehension of text, such as paraphrasing the main idea of a paragraph after reading it. He could be taught to form a visual picture of the elements of the paragraph and could be encouraged to actually draw a semantic map of the material, using the main idea and supporting details to structure the map. It is recommended that Pedro be taught to relate new information to those ideas that he already understands by using analogies from his own experience. Before assigning independent reading, it would be useful to check that Pedro has the necessary vocabulary and background knowledge to understand the story. Pedro appears to make use of context clues when possible, and this should be further encouraged.

5. The following books also provide some useful suggestions for intervention that will take into account Pedro's strength in simultaneous (visual) processing and reasoning (planning) ability, as well as his possible weakness in short-term memory and sequential processing: J. A. Naglieri and E. B. Pickering, 2003, *Helping Children Learn: Intervention Handouts for Use in School and at Home,* Baltimore: Paul H. Brookes; N. Mather and L. Jaffe, 2002, *Woodcock-Johnson III: Recommendations, Reports, and Strategies,* New York: Wiley.

6. In order to increase Pedro's interest in reading, allow him to select materials that are high interest and low vocabulary. Establish a system of us-

ing reinforcers to increase the amount of time Pedro spends in daily reading, such as trading the number of pages he reads for points that may be exchanged for a specific reward at a later stage. In order for Pedro to see that reading can be fun, the family could play language games together, such as "Scrabble," "Up Words," or "Boggle." Pedro could also be encouraged to play computer games that require reading to get from one level to the next and to listen to taped books as he reads along. Pedro would benefit from hearing English being spoken at home. The family is encouraged to engage in discussions in English together at dinner time and to watch English TV programs.

7. Pedro's positive response to reinforcement could be used to sustain his attention by following a difficult assignment with an enjoyable activity. Pedro's frustration level could be monitored by understanding that sudden behavioral outbursts may be a signal that a task is too difficult or that a short break is needed. As indicated by Pedro's parents, Pedro has some difficulty accepting failure. When Pedro fails at a task, he would benefit from being provided with opportunities to succeed at another task. This will prevent him from developing a sense of helplessness and a lack of motivation toward learning.

8. Pedro's acting out behavior, as indicated by his parents, may be his attempt at copying in social situations that he finds confusing and difficult to understand. Pedro displayed a good sense of humor during the assessment, and he could be taught to use humor productively in social situations instead of acting "silly."

Psychometric Summary for Pedro G.: KABC-II, Luria Model

Scale	Standard Score (mean = 100; SD = 15)	90% Confidence Interval	Percentile Rank
Sequential/*Gsm*	97	[89–105]	42
Number Recall	10		50
Word Order	9		37
Hand Movements	11		63
Simultaneous/*Gv*	130	[120–136]	98
Rover	14		91
Triangles	16		98
Block Counting	9		37
Gestalt Closure	11		63
Learning/*Glr*	100	[93–107]	50
Atlantis	12		75
Rebus	8		25
Planning/*Gf*	121	[111–129]	92
Story Completion	14		91
Pattern Reasoning	13		84
Mental Processing Index (MPI)	116	[111–121]	86
Nonverbal Index (NVI)	135	[127–139]	99
Supplementary Scales			
Knowledge/*Gc*	90	[84–96]	25
Verbal Knowledge	10		50
Riddles	6		9
Expressive Vocabulary	11		63
Delayed Recall	97	[91–103]	42
Atlantis Delayed	1		0.1
Rebus Delayed	8		25

Note. Italicized indexes and subtests are Supplementary.

KTEA-II, Comprehensive Form (form A)

Scale	Standard Score (+ 90% Confidence Interval) Grade Norms	Percentile Rank
Reading Composite	**104 ± 4**	**61**
Letter and Word Recognition	120 ± 5	91
Reading Comprehension	87 ± 6	19
Nonsense Word Decoding	*127 ± 7*	*96*
Decoding Composite	**126 ± 5**	**96**
Mathematics Composite	**96 ± 6**	**39**
Mathematics Concepts and Applications	99 ± 7	47
Mathematics Computation	93 ± 9	32
Oral Language Composite	**95 ± 8**	**37**
Listening Comprehension	85 ± 10	16
Oral Expression	108 ± 10	70
Written Language Composite	**95 ± 6**	**37**
Written Expression	97 ± 10	42
Spelling	94 ± 6	34
Comprehensive Achievement Composite	**95 ± 4**	**37**

Note: The italicized subtest is Supplementary.

CASE REPORT 4

Name: Alex R.
Age: 5 years, 0 months
Grade: Prekindergarten
Examiner: Elizabeth Lichtenberger, Ph.D.

Reason for Referral

Alex R. is a 5-year-old attending a local preschool. He was referred to the clinic by his teacher for assessment of his readiness to begin kindergarten and to determine whether he may be showing early signs of a learning disability. Alex's teacher administered Early Screening Profiles (ESP) to him prior to this evaluation. From the results obtained on the ESP, questions were raised about Alex's visual processing ability and his overall level of maturity. The results of this evaluation will be used to determine if there are any difficulties that may be problematic for Alex when he begins kindergarten next fall.

Background Information

Alex lives at home with his parents, Mr. and Mrs. R., and his 8-year-old brother, Jake. Mr. R. is self-employed and Mrs. R. is a full-time homemaker. Mr. R. stated that Alex's brother currently receives a "low dose of Ritalin because he is mildly ADD." In Alex's prenatal history, Mrs. R. reported that she experienced premature dilation at 36 weeks, which required her to be on medication. She indicated that there were no other difficulties with his pregnancy, and Alex was born at 38 weeks after 12 hours of labor, weighing 7 pounds and 1 ounce. According to his parents, Alex has had no major illnesses or hospitalizations. About one year ago Alex was evaluated by a pediatric ophthalmologist. Mr. R. indicated that Alex was prescribed eyeglasses for "vision problems" and difficulty with a "stray eye." Alex wears his glasses daily.

According to his parents, Alex reached all of his developmental milestones within the normally expected time limits. He sat up at 6 months, said his first words at 9 months, walked at 14 months, and completed toilet training at 30 months. His parents noted that because of "nodules on his vocal cords," he had difficulty with his speech, and they accordingly took Alex to a speech therapist. Alex was in speech therapy for approximately one year. The speech therapist stated that through various exercises practiced at home and during speech therapy, the nodules on Alex's vocal cords were eliminated. According to the therapist, Alex had difficulty pronouncing several sounds, such as "L," "R," "Sh," "Ch," and "J." After approximately four months of speech therapy, Alex's difficulty pronouncing "Ls" was cleared up. The speech therapist reported that Alex still has difficulty pronouncing "R," "Sh," "Ch," and "J" sounds, which he felt "may lead to problems and frustration for Alex in learning phonics in school."

Alex has attended preschool since 18 months of age. His mother reported that during the first year of preschool he attended just one day a week, and since age two and a half, Alex has attended three days a week. Alex's current school includes approximately 30 preschoolers, with classroom size varying depending on the children's activity. Alex was observed during a typical day at preschool, with activities including music, story reading, art activities, free time, and show-and-tell. Alex was observed to interact well with his peers. He showed the ability to share and cooperate. He allowed other children to help him complete a puzzle he was working on and at another point allowed a student to play with blocks that he was already playing with. At times Alex demonstrated spurts of excessive energy. For example, he twirled around for a couple minutes at one time and inappropriately scattered puzzle pieces at another point. However, he was able to quiet himself down quickly and behaved overall very appropriately. Alex demonstrated the ability to work independently on a puzzle for a reasonable amount of time. He was quite persistent and patient in his work on solving the puzzle. He was quiet and attentive when his teacher read a story and was comfortable participating verbally when asked questions. Alex appeared self-confident as he presented four toys he had brought for show-and-tell.

According to his parents, Alex and his brother get along well, they "play together a lot, and are nice to each other." Alex's interests include playing with stuffed animals, cars, and his new puppy. His parents describe Alex as "active, petite, and a little immature." Alex reportedly follows his parents' directions at least 50% of the time, but they indicate that he can be "stubborn with certain issues." Overall, Mr. and Mrs. R. characterize Alex as an "easy child."

Appearance and Behavioral Characteristics

Alex is a 5-year-old boy, who is small for his age. He wears small wire-rim eyeglasses and seems comfortable with them. Alex speaks with slight speech articulation immaturities (difficulty especially articulating "R" and "Th"), which makes his sound slightly younger than he is. For example, he pronounced *World* as "Wald" and *Three* as "Free." His speech, along with his diminutive size, gave the impression that Alex is younger than his chronological age. Alex was tested on three separate occasions. Initially he was quite shy and requested that his mom join him in the testing room. During each of the sessions his mother escorted him to the room. Alex appeared more at ease once he was occupied by drawing with markers. He slowly warmed up to the examiner, first answering questions with nonverbal nods while still drawing and then progressed to short, quick verbal responses. Alex appeared to be more comfortable expressing himself through nonverbal rather than verbal communication. After a short period with his mother present in the room, Alex agreed that he was comfortable being left alone and seemed indifferent when his mom did leave the room. He demonstrated a good ability to use fantasy play while interacting with the examiner and also appeared to have a good sense of humor.

Alex tended to have a short attention span during many of the subtests. Tests that provided visual stimulation or manipulation of concrete objects held his attention much more than tests that were purely auditory in nature. Alex's inattention was accompanied by much fidgeting, resistance, and difficulty following directions. His fidgeting was evident when he kicked the table, played with pages of the easel, and picked his nose. Alex was resistant when he was tired of a task. This was exhibited in his attempts to close the pages of the examiner's easel, when he sank down in his chair until he was underneath the table, when he pulled his shirt over his face, and when he would make statements such as "this is the end" and "I wanna be done." Following directions was problematic for Alex during a task that required him to copy a design with triangular shaped blocks. Alex wanted to reconstruct the design his way, which was standing the triangles up on their side, instead of flat on the table as the examiner had instructed. After he was redirected multiple times, Alex still was able to follow directions only about 50% of the time.

Alex appears to enjoy tactile, visual, and kinesthetic stimuli but seems to find auditory stimulation less exciting. He repeatedly attempted to provide additional self-soothing stimulation for himself by sucking his thumb, putting the examiner's easel in his mouth, or by feeling the weight of the easel on his head. He enjoyed manipulating small rubber triangles with his hands and repeatedly asked to play with these items during other subtests. Alex was able to attend to auditory tasks better when he could occupy himself with concrete stimuli. For example, Alex was fidgeting and having difficulty attending to a task requiring him to listen to verbally presented questions. However, when Alex was allowed to hold onto and manipulate a stopwatch during the auditory task, he was able to calm down and focus his attention better. Similarly, Alex was allowed to play with small rubber triangles during an auditorily presented social comprehension task, and this seemed to allow him to redirect his attention so he was free to listen and respond appropriately.

Although Alex preferred visual stimuli, at times he became overwhelmed when the stimulus field was too crowded. This happened during two separate subtests. On one auditory-visual association task, Alex was shown a picture of a sea creature and told the sea creature's name. Then he was required to point out the sea creature from a group of others. When the number of creatures became too great for Alex, he could not remember any and just pointed to them all.

When faced with too much challenge, Alex responded with a decreased interest and effort and often responded in a silly manner. During a task that required him to repeat a series of hand gestures demonstrated by the examiner, Alex began to make up his own creative gestures when the items became difficult. Similarly, during more challenging items on a number recall task, he began to just say any random number that came to his mind. When encouraged by the examiner on other tasks to try a little harder to give a real instead of silly answer, he often came up with the correct answer. For example, on a task requiring Alex to identify a distorted picture, he identified one item as a "blood head," but after encouragement from the examiner, responded with the correct answer, "train." On challenging items Alex tends to give up easily. He responded to some items by saying they were "too hard" before even attempting to answer. Alex did not appear overly concerned or anxious about his performance and demonstrated low frustration tolerance. His random or silly responses were compensations that helped him deal with this frustration.

Alex tended to be quick to respond when he definitely knew the answer to a problem but was able to slow himself down to think about more difficult problems. During a design-copying task, Alex initially responded very rapidly, but as the designs became more difficult, he slowed down and took time to more carefully study the designs before copying them. He appeared to enjoy tasks that were administered quickly and responded to the problems likewise in a quick manner. Alex had difficulty with items that required a sequential problem-solving style. He had difficulty remembering a sequence of verbally presented numbers and a sequence of visually presented hand movements. Once each of the sequences got too long he lost all of the information presented to him. On one auditory-visual sequencing task, Alex was required to listen to a verbally presented list of objects and then point to the correct sequence of pictures on a page. Alex at times verbalized the correct order of items in the sequence but then would not be able to point them out correctly.

Tests Administered

- Kaufman Assessment Battery For Children—Second Edition (KABC-II)
- Developmental Test of Visual-Motor Integration—Fourth Edition (VMI)
- Wechsler Individual Achievement Test—Second Edition (WIAT-II)

- Wechsler Preschool and Primary Scale of Intelligence—Third Edition (WPPSI-III): selected subtest

Test Results and Interpretation

Alex was administered the KABC-II to obtain a comprehensive picture of his mental processing and cognitive abilities. The KABC-II is based on a double theoretical foundation, Luria's neuropsychological model, and the CHC psychometric theory. For 5-year-olds, it offers four scales, each given a label that reflects both theoretical models: Sequential/*Gsm,* Simultaneous/*Gv,* Learning/*Glr,* and Knowledge/*Gc.* (From the perspective of CHC theory, *Gsm* = short-term memory; *Gv* = visual processing; *Glr* = long-term storage and retrieval; and *Gc* = crystallized ability.)

Examiners are given the option of selecting either the Luria model or the CHC model of the KABC-II, based on the child's background and the reason for referral. (Knowledge/*Gc* is excluded from the Luria model because measures of language ability and acquired knowledge may not provide fair assessment of some children's cognitive abilities—e.g., those from bilingual or nonmainstream backgrounds). Taking into consideration that Alex is English speaking and that his referral reason involves evaluating a potential learning disability, the examiner decided to administer the CHC model of the KABC-II, which yields the FCI as the global measure of general cognitive ability.

Alex earned a KABC-II FCI of 103, ranking him at the 58th percentile and classifying his overall mental processing ability as falling within the Average range. The chances are 90% that his true FCI is between 98 and 108. However, he displayed considerable variability in his standard scores on the four theory-based scales that compose the FCI, with indexes ranging from 120 on Simultaneous/*Gv* to 86 on Learning/*Glr.* This wide variation in indexes (34 points, which equals more than 2 SDs) renders his FCI meaningless as an estimate of global ability; it is merely the midpoint of greatly varying abilities. Unlike the FCI, all four of Alex's scale indexes were interpretable, as he performed consistently on the tasks that compose each separate scale.

The low points of Alex's profile of cognitive abilities were affected by his distractibility during certain KABC-II tasks. Alex earned a Sequential/*Gsm* standard score of 88 (21st percentile) and a Learning/*Glr* standard score of 86 (18th percentile). Although both of these scores are within the Average range compared to other children his age, his performance on both of these scales was significantly below his average level of cognitive ability. The discrepancy between his average level of performance and his score on the Learning/*Glr* scale was also uncommonly large (i.e., it occurred in less than 10% of children his age), indicating that it was a weakness worth investigating further. The tasks on both the Sequential/*Gsm* and Learning/*Glr* scales are susceptible to the effects of distractibility—as noted in the behavioral observations, Alex did require much redirection to sustain an adequate level of attention during these tasks.

Alex's behavior during the Sequential/*Gsm* scale's three subtests (two Core and one Supplementary) exemplifies his difficulty attending. During a test requiring him to repeat with his hands a sequence of hand gestures, Alex had difficulty remembering a sequence of more than two gestures. On a test that requires recalling a sequence of verbally presented numbers, Alex had difficulty remembering a sequence of more than three numbers. On a task calling for integration of a verbally presented sequence of words and a response of pointing to the pictures of these objects, Alex could not remember a sequence of more than two items. Each of these subtests required a short period of sustained attention and the ability to recall the information presented. It appears the most critical factor affecting his relatively lower scores was his inability to remember due to his high distractibility when the stimuli were presented. Alex's performance on two subtests on the Learning/*Glr* scale also confirmed that his difficulty remembering may have been affected by his problem sustaining attention for an entire test. On both auditory-visual association tasks measuring long-term retrieval, Alex displayed signs of inattention (fidgeting, playing with the easel, looking away). He also appeared overwhelmed when the number of stimuli on these paired-association learning tasks became too great, and he became disinterested and wouldn't put forth his best effort. His performance on the Learning/*Glr* scale was at the 18th percentile.

Alex's performance on the Learning/*Glr* scale has important implications for learning at school. Compared to problem-solving abilities (91st percentile), Alex's memory and learning abilities were significantly weaker (16th percentile). This contrast in his abilities alerts us to the fact that he is capable of solving problems that are of interest to him and that are visually stimulating, but he has trouble learning and remembering information that is presented only in an auditory fashion or that he does not find interesting. Alex's tendency to easily lose focused attention will likely affect his ability to learn new information in school—especially if it is in an area that is not inherently interesting to him.

On tasks that are more resistant to the effects of distractibility, Alex performed much better. Many of Alex's stronger abilities were noted on tasks that required visual and holistic processing rather than step-by-step sequential processing or short-term memory. His strengths were evident in his Above Average performance on the Simultaneous/*Gv* scale (standard score = 120; 91st percentile). His visual processing abilities were stronger than most children his age and were greater than his overall level of cognitive ability. His strong visual organization and his alertness to his environment and visual detail aided him in completing tasks involving copying models with foam shapes, determining visual patterns, counting partially hidden blocks, and similar tasks. In addition to strong visual reasoning, his visual-motor skills were also well developed. For example, on the Developmental Test of Visual-Motor Integration (VMI-4), a design copying task, Alex scored at the 86th percentile, equivalent to a child a full year older than his own chronological age.

Alex's academic achievement, as measured by the WIAT-II, was in the Average range. In the area of mathematics, Alex scored at the 61st percentile (during math tasks he was required to identify numbers, count, compute, and demonstrate understanding of mathematical concepts). Although he spoke with some slight articulation difficulties, Alex's oral and written language abilities were commensurate with those of other children his age, as he scored at the 55th percentile on both of these tasks. Alex's lowest achievement score was in the area of Reading (though still in the Average range). He had difficulty identifying some letters and reading and pronouncing words (39th percentile). For example, Alex could only recognize an "A" and "E," but did know that they were letters in his name. An additional subtest measuring Alex's verbal comprehension, as well as common sense, social judgment, and social maturity, again showed his ability to achieve in the Average range (63rd percentile on WPPSI-III Comprehension subtest). His overall Average level of achievement was commensurate with his overall level of cognitive ability and was very similar to his performance on the KABC-II scale measuring acquired knowledge (Knowledge/Gc = 109; 73rd percentile). This level of similarity between his general cognitive ability and prekindergarten achievement indicates that, at this point, he is performing academically about where one would predict given his ability level.

Summary and Diagnostic Impressions

Alex R. is a 5-year-old boy who was referred for an evaluation to determine whether he may be exhibiting early signs of a learning disability and to determine his level of readiness for kindergarten. After being given a preliminary screening test by his teacher, questions were raised about his visual processing ability and level of maturity. During the evaluation, Alex was highly distractible, demonstrated low frustration tolerance, and had difficulty following directions. He was able to focus better on auditory tasks if he had something concrete to manipulate, which allowed him to redirect his attention.

The assessment shows Alex's abilities to encompass a wide range of intellectual functioning (Average to Above Average). Alex had strengths in visual processing, attention to visual detail, and holistic processing (Simultaneous/Gv standard score of 120). In contrast, his inattention and distractibility appeared to negatively affect his performance on tasks of short-term memory and of learning (Sequential/Gsm = 88 and Learning/Glr = 86). His performance on Achievement subtests showed Alex to have average acquisition of learned material in all areas.

Overall, Alex is a self-confident, strong-willed, petite young boy, who lacks strong concentration skills and motivation to keep on trying when a situation becomes challenging to him. He likes to take control of situations and can take several minutes to redirect if his behavior is problematic. Although he can be highly inattentive, he can become more focused if he is occupied with a concrete stimulus while following along with a more abstract auditory or visual task. From these test results Alex does not appear to have any visual processing difficulties, as earlier hypothesized from an initial screening. He is somewhat immature for his age, which is accentuated by his attentional problems, but does not possess any cognitive or academic deficits that would cause difficulty for him in a kindergarten setting. There is a possibility that Alex is demonstrating signs of a mild attention deficit, or he may merely be a bit younger developmentally in his self-control and impulse control.

Recommendations

1. Given Alex's attentional problems and level of maturity, it will be important to find an experienced kindergarten teacher for Alex who is willing to make some accommodations for him in the classroom. For example, when the class is expected to listen quietly to the teacher reading, Alex may need to also have his hands occupied with a small object or may need to doodle while listening.

2. Alex will benefit from being instructed through the use of hands-on activities. He enjoys feeling and manipulating objects and will likely stay focused longer with a task that allows him to do so.

3. Because of Alex's short attention span, lessons should be kept as brief as possible. Planned interruptions when longer lessons are given will be useful. For example, Alex may get up and get some more supplies after part of a lesson is complete. Incorporation of quiet activities and active ones within a lesson will also help to keep Alex's attention.

4. Alex's ability to better utilize a simultaneous or holistic processing style, rather than a sequential processing style, should be recognized in

teaching him. Knowledge of his good visual organization and attention to visual detail may also be useful in instructing Alex. The following books will provide useful suggestions for educational interventions that will take into account Alex's strong and weak abilities: (1) From a Luria theoretical perspective—J. A. Naglieri and E. B. Pickering, 2003, *Helping Children Learn: Intervention Handouts for Use in School and at Home,* Baltimore: Paul H. Brookes, and (2) From a CHC theoretical perspective—N. Mather and L. Jaffe, 2002, *Woodcock-Johnson III: Recommendations, Reports, and Strategies,* New York: Wiley.

5. Alex will benefit from practicing letters and numbers at home as much as possible. Such practice can be quite enjoyable through the use of various games or fun computer programs.

6. Given Alex's low tolerance for frustration and desire to do things his way, it will be useful for his teacher and his parents to set realistic behavioral goals for him and follow through with reinforcement when he does what is expected and with consequences when he does not follow these behavioral expectations. Reinforcement may be in the form of tangible or intangible rewards. For example, when appropriate behavior is demonstrated, classroom privileges, free time, and helping the teacher may be given as tangible rewards. Smiles, pats on the back, and praise may be given as intangible rewards.

7. It is recommended that if Alex's distractibility and attentional difficulties become unmanageable in the classroom and at home, a referral may be made to a pediatric psychiatrist for an evaluation to determine if he would benefit from pharmacological treatment along with a structured behavioral modification program.

Psychometric Summary for Alex R.:
Kaufman Assessment Battery for Children—Second Edition
(KABC-II) CHC Model

Subtest/Scale	Standard Score	90% Confidence Interval	Percentile Rank
Sequential/Gsm	88	[82–96]	21
Number Recall	9		37
Word Order	7		16
Hand Movements	8		25
Simultaneous/Gv	120	[112–126]	91
Triangles	12		75
Conceptual Thinking	14		91
Pattern Reasoning	13		84
Block Counting	10		50
Face Recognition	13		84
Gestalt Closure	15		95
Learning/Glr	86	[80–94]	18
Atlantis	8		25
Rebus	7		16
Delayed Recall	88		21
Atlantis Delayed	9		37
Rebus Delayed	7		16
Knowledge/Gc	109	[101–117]	73
Riddles	12		75
Expressive Vocabulary	11		63
Verbal Knowledge	13		84
Fluid Crystallized Index (FCI)	103	[98–108]	58

Note. Subtests shown in *italics* are Supplementary and are not used in the calculation of the indexes or global scales.

Wechsler Individual Achievement Test—Second Edition (WIAT-II)

Composite	Standard Score	90% Confidence Interval	Percentile Rank
Reading	96	[88–104]	39
Math	104	[96–112]	61
Written Language	102	[97–107]	55
Oral Language	102	[97–107]	55
Total Achievement	**101**	**[96–106]**	**53**

Developmental Test of Visual-Motor Integration (VMI-4)

Subtest	Standard Score	Percentile Rank	Age Equivalent
VMI	116	86	6.0

Wechsler Preschool and Primary Scale of Intelligence—Third Edition (WPPSI-III) Selected Subtest

Subtest	Scaled Score	Percentile Rank
Comprehension	11	63

Appendix A

KABC-II Interpretive Worksheet

STEP 1: INTERPRET THE GLOBAL SCALE INDEX

Scale Used (circle one)	Scale Index (Standard Score)	Confidence Interval (circle one) 90% or 95%	Is Global Scale Interpretable? (ages 4–18) Highest Index — Lowest Index = Range — Less than 23 points	Descriptive Category or Categories
FCI (CHC Model)	☐	(_ _ – _ _)	Y N	
MPI (Luria Model)			*If no, do not interpret*	
NVI				Percentile Rank ___

STEP 2: INTERPRET PROFILE OF SCALE INDEXES TO IDENTIFY STRENGTHS AND WEAKNESSES

Scale	Scale Index (Standard Score)	Subtest Scaled Scores High	Low	Range	Interpretable? *See critical values for Step 2A	Normative Weakness (NW) or Normative Strength (NS) <85	>115	Personal Weakness (PW) or Personal Strength (PS) Diff from Mean	PW or PS (p<.05)	Infrequent (<10%)
Sequential/*Gsm*	☐	—	—	—	Y N	NW	NS	—	PW PS	☐
Simultaneous/*Gv*	☐	—	—	—	Y N	NW	NS	—	PW PS	☐
Learning/*Glr*	☐	—	—	—	Y N	NW	NS	—	PW PS	☐
Planning/*Gf*	☐	—	—	—	Y N	NW	NS	—	PW PS	☐
Knowledge/*Gc*	☐	—	—	—	Y N	NW	NS	—	PW PS	☐
Index Mean (rounded)	☐ CHC model (include Knowledge/*Gc*) ☐ Luria model (omit Knowledge/*Gc*)									

Critical values for step 2A and steps 3A and 3B:
Minimum subtest scaled score range that occurs in <10% of the population

Scale	Age 4	Age 5	Age 6	Ages 7–9	Ages 10–12	Ages 13–18
Sequential/Gsm	6	5	5	5	5	5
Simultaneous/Gv	8	7	9	6	6	6
Learning/Glr	6	8	7	6	6	6
Planning/Gf	5	5	5	6	6	6
Knowledge/Gc	5	5	5	5	5	4
Delayed Recall		6	6	6	6	6

Critical values for determining Personal Strengths and Weaknesses in step 2C:
Statistically significant (<.05) or infrequent (<10%) differences from the mean of scale indexes

CHC Model

Scale	Age 4 Sig.	Age 4 10%	Age 5 Sig.	Age 5 10%	Age 6 Sig.	Age 6 10%	Ages 7–9 Sig.	Ages 7–9 10%	Ages 10–12 Sig.	Ages 10–12 10%	Ages 13–18 Sig.	Ages 13–18 10%
Sequential/Gsm	8	16	8	14	8	16	9	19	9	19	9	18
Simultaneous/Gv	9	15	7	14	7	13	9	16	9	16	9	17
Learning/Glr	8	15	7	14	7	15	8	17	7	17	7	16
Planning/Gf							9	15	9	14	9	15
Knowledge/Gc	8	13	8	14	8	14	8	14	7	14	8	14

Luria Model

Scale	Age 4 Sig.	Age 4 10%	Age 5 Sig.	Age 5 10%	Age 6 Sig.	Age 6 10%	Ages 7–9 Sig.	Ages 7–9 10%	Ages 10–12 Sig.	Ages 10–12 10%	Ages 13–18 Sig.	Ages 13–18 10%
Sequential/Gsm	7	14	7	13	7	15	8	19	8	18	8	17
Simultaneous/Gv	8	14	7	13	6	13	9	16	9	16	9	16
Learning/Glr	8	14	7	14	7	14	8	17	7	17	7	16
Planning/Gf							9	16	9	15	9	15
Knowledge/Gc	10	18	10	18	11	18	10	18	9	18	9	17

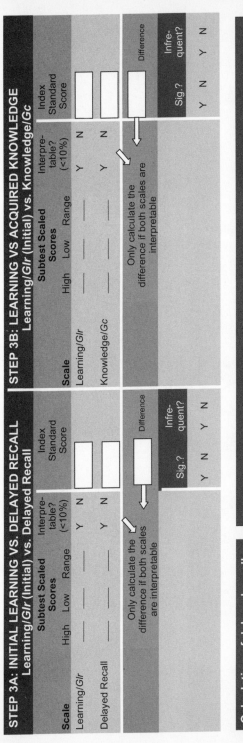

STEP 3A: INITIAL LEARNING VS. DELAYED RECALL
Learning/*Glr* (initial) vs. Delayed Recall

Scale	Subtest Scaled Scores High	Low	Range	Interpretable? (<10%)	Index Standard Score
Learning/*Glr*	—	—	—	Y N	☐
Delayed Recall	—	—	—	Y N	☐

Only calculate the difference if both scales are interpretable

Difference ☐

Sig.?	Infrequent?
Y N	Y N

STEP 3B: LEARNING VS ACQUIRED KNOWLEDGE
Learning/*Glr* (initial) vs. Knowledge/*Gc*

Scale	Subtest Scaled Scores High	Low	Range	Interpretable? (<10%)	Index Standard Score
Learning/*Glr*	—	—	—	Y N	☐
Knowledge/*Gc*	—	—	—	Y N	☐

Only calculate the difference if both scales are interpretable

Difference ☐

Sig.?	Infrequent?
Y N	Y N

Critical values for steps 3A and 3B: Differences between cluster scores that are statistically significant or infrequent

Clusters	Age 3 Sig.	10%	Age 4 Sig.	10%	Age 5 Sig.	10%	Age 6 Sig.	10%	Ages 7–9 Sig.	10%	Ages 10–12 Sig.	10%	Ages 13–18 .05	<10%
Learning/*Glr* (initial) vs. Delayed Recall	-	-	-	-	15	16	14	16	13	16	12	16	12	16
Learning/*Glr* (initial) vs. Knowledge/*Gc*	-	-	13	25	12	25	12	25	12	24	11	24	11	24

Calculation of delayed recall scale

Atlantis Delayed	—
Rebus Delayed	—
Sum	⬭
Standard Score	☐

STEP 4: SUPPLEMENTARY SUBTEST ANALYSIS FOR AGE 3

Scale	Global Scale Interpretable?	Sum of Scaled Scores	Mean Scaled Score	Supplementary Subtest	Scaled Score	Diff from Mean	Differences between supplementary subtest and mean scaled score that are significant or infrequent			
							Sig. (p<.05)	Sig.?	Infrequent (<10%)	Infrequent?
MPI	Y N	◯ / 5 =	▢	Number Recall	—	—	3.2	Y N	4.8	Y N
				Gestalt Closure	—	—	3.8	Y N	4.6	Y N
FCI	Y N	◯ / 7 =	▢	Number Recall	—	—	3.1	Y N	4.9	Y N
				Gestalt Closure	—	—	3.7	Y N	4.4	Y N

STEP 4: SUPPLEMENTARY SUBTEST ANALYSIS FOR AGE 4

Scale	Scale Interpretable in Step 2?	Sum of Scaled Scores	Mean Scaled Score	Supplementary Subtest	Scaled Score	Diff from Mean	Differences between supplementary subtest and mean scaled score that are significant or infrequent			
							Sig. (p<.05)	Sig.?	Infrequent (<10%)	Infrequent?
Sequential/Gsm	Y N	◯ / 2 =	▢	Hand Movements	—	—	3.5	Y N	5.0	Y N
Simultaneous/Gv	Y N	◯ / 3 =	▢	Gestalt Closure	—	—	3.8	Y N	5.0	Y N
Knowledge/Gc	Y N	◯ / 2 =		Verbal Knowledge	—	—	3.1	Y N	4.0	Y N

STEP 4: SUPPLEMENTARY SUBTEST ANALYSIS FOR AGE 5

Scale	Scale Interpretable in Step 2?	Sum of Scaled Scores	Mean Scaled Score	Supplementary Subtest	Scaled Score	Diff from Mean	Differences between Supplementary subtest and mean scaled score that are significant or infrequent			
							Sig. (p<.05)	Sig?	Infrequent (<10%)	Infrequent?
Sequential/*Gsm*	Y N	◯ / 2 =	☐	Hand Movements	—	—	3.5	Y N	5.0	Y N
Simultaneous/*Gv*	Y N	◯ / 3 =	☐	Gestalt Closure	—	—	3.6	Y N	5.0	Y N
				Face Recognition	—	—	4.0	Y N	6.0	Y N
				Block Counting	—	—	2.7	Y N	5.0	Y N
Knowledge/*Gc*	Y N	◯ / 2 =	☐	Verbal Knowledge	—	—	3.1	Y N	4.0	Y N

STEP 4: SUPPLEMENTARY SUBTEST ANALYSIS FOR AGE 6

Scale	Scale Interpretable in Step 2?	Sum of Scaled Scores	Mean Scaled Score	Supplementary Subtest	Scaled Score	Diff from Mean	Differences between Supplementary subtest and mean scaled score that are significant or infrequent			
							Sig. (p<.05)	Sig?	Infrequent (<10%)	Infrequent?
Sequential/*Gsm*	Y N	◯ / 2 =	☐	Hand Movements	—	—	3.5	Y N	5.0	Y N
Simultaneous/*Gv*	Y N	◯ / 4 =	☐	Gestalt Closure	—	—	3.9	Y N	5.3	Y N
				Block Counting	—	—	2.9	Y N	5.0	Y N
				Story Completion	—	—	3.1	Y N	7.0	Y N
Knowledge/*Gc*	Y N	◯ / 2 =	☐	Verbal Knowledge	—	—	3.1	Y N	4.0	Y N

STEP 4: SUPPLEMENTARY SUBTEST ANALYSIS FOR AGES 7–12

Scale	Scale Interpretable in Step 2?	Sum of Scaled Scores	Mean Scaled Score	Supplementary Subtest	Scaled Score	Diff from Mean	Differences between Supplementary subtest and mean scaled score that are significant or infrequent		
							Sig. (p<.05)	Sig?	Infrequent (<10%)	Infrequent?
Sequential/*Gsm*	Y N	◯ / 2 =	▢	Hand Movements	___	___	3.5	Y N	5.0	Y N
Simultaneous/*Gv*	Y N	◯ / 2 =	▢	Gestalt Closure	___	___	3.7	Y N	5.5	Y N
				Block Counting	___	___	3.2	Y N	5.5	Y N
Knowledge/*Gc*	Y N	◯ / 2 =	▢	Expressive Vocab.	___	___	3.1	Y N	3.5	Y N

STEP 4: SUPPLEMENTARY SUBTEST ANALYSIS FOR AGES 13–18

Scale	Scale Interpretable in Step 2?	Sum of Scaled Scores	Mean Scaled Score	Supplementary Subtest	Scaled Score	Diff from Mean	Differences between Supplementary subtest and mean scaled score that are significant or infrequent		
							Sig. (p<.05)	Sig?	Infrequent (<10%)	Infrequent?
Sequential/*Gsm*	Y N	◯ / 2 =	▢	Hand Movements	___	___	3.5	Y N	5.0	Y N
Simultaneous/*Gv*	Y N	◯ / 2 =	▢	Gestalt Closure	___	___	3.7	Y N	6.0	Y N
				Triangles	___	___	3.1	Y N	5.0	Y N
Knowledge/*Gc*	Y N	◯ / 2 =	▢	Expressive Vocab.	___	___	3.1	Y N	3.5	Y N

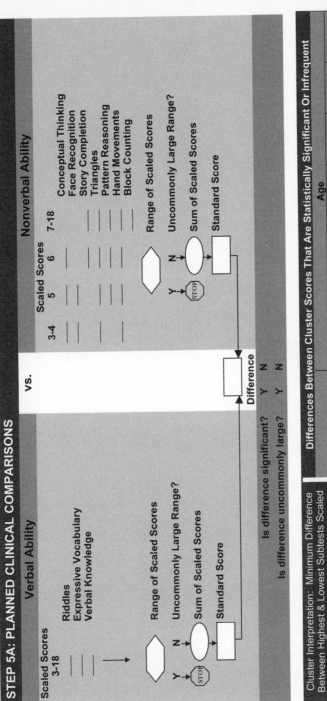

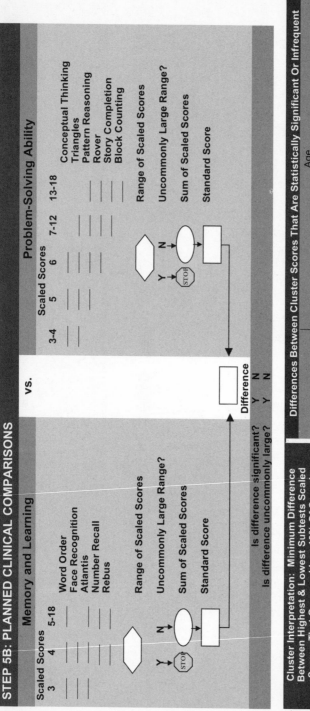

STEP 5B: PLANNED CLINICAL COMPARISONS

Memory and Learning vs. Problem-Solving Ability

Memory and Learning

Scaled Scores

| 3 | 4 | 5 | 6 | 7-12 | 13-18 |

- Word Order
- Face Recognition
- Atlantis
- Number Recall
- Rebus

Range of Scaled Scores

Uncommonly Large Range?

Sum of Scaled Scores

Standard Score

Is difference significant? Y N
Is difference uncommonly large? Y N

Difference Y N Y N

Problem-Solving Ability

Scaled Scores

| 3-4 | 5 | 6 | 7-12 | 13-18 |

- Conceptual Thinking
- Triangles
- Pattern Reasoning
- Rover
- Story Completion
- Block Counting

Range of Scaled Scores

Uncommonly Large Range?

Sum of Scaled Scores

Standard Score

Cluster Interpretation: Minimum Difference Between Highest & Lowest Subtests Scaled Scores That Occurred in < 10% Of Sample

Cluster	Age						
	3	4	5	6	7-12	13-18
Problem-Solving Ability	7	7	8	9	8	9
Memory and Learning	8	10	9	9	9	9

Differences Between Cluster Scores That Are Statistically Significant Or Infrequent

Cluster	Age													
	3		4		5		6		7-9		10-12		13-18	
	Sig. .05	Freq. <10%	Sig. .05	Freq. <10%	Sig. .05	Freq. <10%	Sig. .05	Freq. <10%	Sig. .05	Freq. <10%	Sig. .05	Freq. <10%	Sig. .05	Freq. <10%
Problem-Solving Ability vs. Memory and Learning	16	26	14	28	11	22	10	24	11	25	11	23	11	24

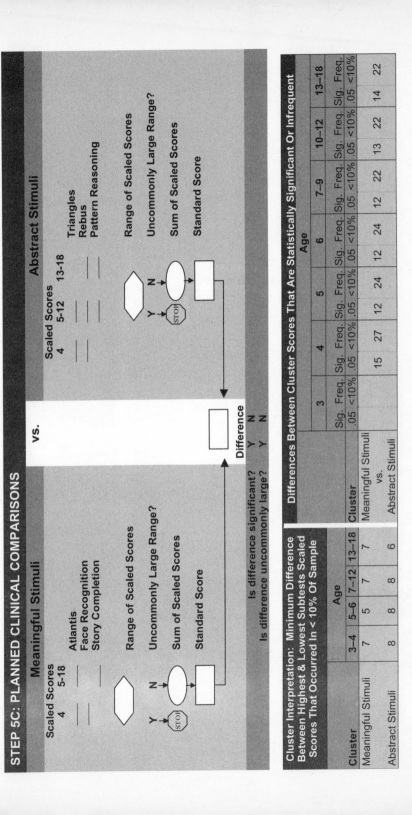

STEP 5C: PLANNED CLINICAL COMPARISONS

Meaningful Stimuli   vs.   Abstract Stimuli

Meaningful Stimuli

Scaled Scores
4   5-18

   Atlantis
   Face Recognition
   Story Completion

Range of Scaled Scores

Uncommonly Large Range?

Sum of Scaled Scores

Standard Score

Is difference significant? Y N
Is difference uncommonly large? Y N

Difference

Y N
Y N

Abstract Stimuli

Scaled Scores
4   5-12   13-18

   Triangles
   Rebus
   Pattern Reasoning

Range of Scaled Scores

Uncommonly Large Range?

Sum of Scaled Scores

Standard Score

Cluster Interpretation: Minimum Difference Between Highest & Lowest Subtests Scaled Scores That Occurred In < 10% Of Sample				
	Age			
Cluster	3-4	5-6	7-12	13-18
Meaningful Stimuli	7	5	7	7
Abstract Stimuli	8	8	8	6

Differences Between Cluster Scores That Are Statistically Significant Or Infrequent																
	Age															
	3		4		5		6		7-9		10-12		13-18			
Cluster	Sig. .05	Freq. <10%	Sig. .05	Freq. <10%	Sig. .05	Freq. <10%	Sig. .05	Freq. <10%	Sig. .05	Freq. <10%	Sig. .05	Freq. <10%	Sig. .05	Freq. <10%
Meaningful Stimuli vs. Abstract Stimuli			15	27	12	24	12	24	12	22	13	22	14	22

STEP 5D: PLANNED CLINICAL COMPARISONS

| Verbal Response | vs. | Pointing Response |

Verbal Response

Scaled Scores
4-6   7-18
___ ___ Number Recall
___ ___ Rebus
___ ___ Expressive Vocabulary
___ ___ Riddles

Range of Scaled Scores

Uncommonly Large Range?

Sum of Scaled Scores

Standard Score

Pointing Response

Scaled Scores
4   5-18
___ ___ Word Order
___ ___ Face Recognition
___ ___ Atlantis
___ ___ Verbal Knowledge

Range of Scaled Scores

Uncommonly Large Range?

Sum of Scaled Scores

Standard Score

Difference

Is difference significant?   Y N   Y N
Is difference uncommonly large?   Y N   Y N

Cluster Interpretation:: Minimum Difference Between Highest & Lowest Subtests Scaled Scores That Occurred In < 10% Of Sample

Clusters	Age	
	4	5–18
Verbal Response	8	8
Pointing Response	9	8

Differences Between Cluster Scores That Are Statistically Significant Or Infrequent

Cluster	Age													
	3		4		5		6		7–9		10–12		13–18	
	Sig. .05	Freq. <10%	Sig. .05	Freq. <10%	Sig. .05	Freq. <10%	Sig. .05	Freq. <10%	Sig. .05	Freq. <10%	Sig. .05	Freq. <10%	Sig. .05	Freq. <10%
Verbal Response vs. Pointing Response			12	20	12	20	12	20	12	18	12	18	11	18

STEP 5E: PLANNED CLINICAL COMPARISONS

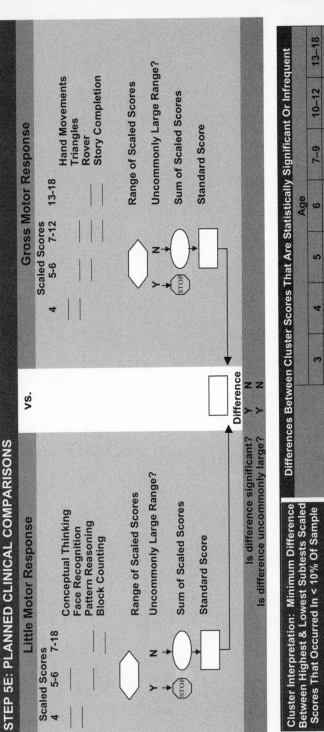

Little Motor Response

Scaled Scores
4	5-6	7-18	
			Conceptual Thinking
			Face Recognition
			Pattern Reasoning
			Block Counting

Range of Scaled Scores
Uncommonly Large Range?
Sum of Scaled Scores
Standard Score

vs.

Gross Motor Response

Scaled Scores
4	5-6	7-12	13-18	
				Hand Movements
				Triangles
				Rover
				Story Completion

Range of Scaled Scores
Uncommonly Large Range?
Sum of Scaled Scores
Standard Score

Difference
Is difference significant? Y N
Is difference uncommonly large? Y N

Cluster Interpretation: Minimum Difference Between Highest & Lowest Subtests Scaled Scores That Occurred In < 10% Of Sample

Cluster	Age 4	5-6	7-12	13-18
Little Motor Response	8	6	6	6
Gross Motor Response	7	5	8	7

Differences Between Cluster Scores That Are Statistically Significant Or Infrequent

	Age 3		4		5		6		7-9		10-12		13-18	
Cluster	Sig. .05	Freq. <10%	Sig. .05	Freq. <10%	Sig. .05	Freq. <10%	Sig. .05	Freq. <10%	Sig. .05	Freq. <10%	Sig. .05	Freq. <10%	Sig. .05	Freq. <10%
Little Motor Response vs. Gross Motor Response			17	29	13	25	13	25	12	22	13	22	15	25

STEP 6A: GENERATE HYPOTHESES TO EXPLAIN FLUCTUATIONS IN SCALES THAT ARE NOT INTERPRETABLE.

First Line of Attack: Examine planned clinical comparisons (from step 5) to identify possible hypotheses.

Was index found uninterpretable in step 2? (check box if yes)	Cluster that may provide hypotheses for the subtest variability in the index	Age	Core Subtests Relevant to the Clusters
Sequential/Gsm ☐	Verbal Response vs. Pointing Response	4–18	Number Recall (Verbal) vs. Word Order (Pointing)
	Abstract vs. Meaningful Stimuli	4	Face Recognition (Meaningful) vs. Triangles (Abstract)
	Memory & Learning vs. Problem Solving Ability	3–4	Face Rec. (Mem. & Learn.) vs. Triangles/Concep. Th. (Prob. Slv.)
Simultaneous/Gv ☐	Little Motor vs. Gross Motor Response	4	Face Recognition/Concept. Thinkg. (Little) vs. Triangles (Gross)
	Little Motor vs. Gross Motor Response	5	Concept Thinking/Pattern Reason. (Little) vs. Triangles (Gross)
	Little Motor vs. Gross Motor Response	6	Concept Th./Pattern Reason. (Little) vs. Triangles/Rover (Gross)
	Little Motor vs. Gross Motor Response	13–18	Block Counting (Little) vs. Rover (Gross)
Learning/Glr ☐	Verbal Response vs. Pointing Response	4–18	Rebus (Verbal) vs. Atlantis (Pointing)
	Abstract vs. Meaningful Stimuli	4–18	Rebus (Abstract) vs. Atlantis (Meaningful)
Planning/Gf ☐	Abstract vs. Meaningful Stimuli	7–18	Pattern Reasoning (Abstract) vs. Story Completion (Meaningful)
	Little Motor vs. Gross Motor Response	7–18	Pattern Reasoning (Little) vs. Story Completion (Gross)
Knowledge/Gc ☐	Verbal Response vs. Pointing Response	7–18	Riddles (Verbal) vs. Verbal Knowledge (Pointing)

Second Line of Attack: Examine how the Core subtests within each scale complement each other.

Consult Rapid References 3.3 through 3.7 to develop hypotheses.

Third Line of Attack: Examine Qualitative Indicators (QIs), behavioral observations, and background information.

Follow up hypotheses derived from QIs, behavioral observations, and background information by collecting supplemental data if necessary (e.g., administer additional subtests, contact further sources for collateral information).

Step 6B: GENERATE HYPOTHESES TO EXPLAIN SUPPLEMENTARY SUBTESTS THAT ARE INCONSISTENT WITH THE MEAN OF CORE SUBTESTS.

First Line of Attack: Determine which Supplementary subtests are significantly different from the Core Subtests.

a. Check box if Supplementary subtest is significantly different from mean of core subtests (see step 4 results).

b. Conduct only an informal examination of the planned Clinical comparisons, as most Supplementary subtests are excluded from the planned comparisons.

The following supplementary tests are included in step 5's clusters:

- Expressive Vocabulary (Gc subtest) is in the Verbal Ability cluster.
- Verbal Knowledge (Gc subtest) is in the Verbal Ability and Pointing Response clusters.
- Hand Movements (Gsm Subtest) is in the Gross-motor response and Nonverbal Ability clusters.
- Block Counting (Gv subtest) is in the Little Motor cluster.

Supplementary Subtest	Age 3	Age 4	Age 5	Age 6	Ages 7–12	Ages 13–18
Number Recall						
Gestalt Closure						
Hand Movements						
Verbal Knowledge						
Face Recognition						
Block Counting						
Story Completion						
Expressive Vocabulary						
Triangles						

Second Line of Attack: Examine how Supplementary and Core subtests within each scale complement each other.

Consult Rapid References: 3.4, 3.5, and 3.7 to develop hypotheses.

Third Line of Attack: Examine Qualitative Indicators (QIs), behavioral observations, & background information.

Follow up hypotheses derived from QIs, behavioral observations, and background information by collecting supplemental data if necessary (e.g., administer additional subtests, contact further sources for collateral information).

Appendix B

Table B.1 Standard Scores Corresponding to Sums of Subtest Scaled Scores for Planned Comparison Clusters: Delayed Recall, Verbal Ability, Meaningful Stimuli, and Abstract Stimuli

Sum of Scaled Scores	Delayed Recall Ages 5–18	Verbal Ability Ages 3–6	Verbal Ability Ages 7–9	Verbal Ability Ages 10–18	Meaningful Stimuli Ages 3–4	Meaningful Stimuli Ages 5–6	Meaningful Stimuli Ages 7–18	Abstract Stimuli Age 4	Abstract Stimuli Ages 5–12	Abstract Stimuli Ages 13–18	Sum of Scaled Scores
57		155	160	160					160		57
56		153	160	160					160		56
55		151	160	159					160		55
54		149	160	155					160		54
53		146	159	151					157		53
52		144	154	148					154		52
51		142	150	144					151		51
50		140	146	141					148		50
49		138	143	139					145		49
48		136	140	136					142		48
47		134	137	133					139		47
46		132	134	131					136		46
45		130	131	129					134		45
44		128	129	126					131		44
43		126	126	124					129		43
42		124	124	122					126		42
41		122	122	120		154			124		41
40		120	120	118		151		160	122		40
39		118	118	116		148		160	119		39
38	160	116	115	114	160		160	156	117	160	38
37	160	114	113	112	160		160		115	160	37
36	160	112	111	110	160		160		112	160	36

35	159	110	153	155	145	158	108	110	110	160	35
34	152	108	149	150	142	153	107	108	109	157	34
33	147	106	146	146	139	148	105	106	107	150	33
32	141	104	142	141	136	144	103	104	105	144	32
31	137	102	138	137	133	140	101	102	103	139	31
30	132	100	135	133	130	135	100	100	101	134	30
29	128	97	131	129	127	131	98	98	99	130	29
28	124	95	128	126	124	128	96	97	97	126	28
27	121	93	124	122	120	124	95	95	95	122	27
26	117	91	121	119	117	120	93	93	93	118	26
25	114	89	117	115	114	117	91	91	91	115	25
24	111	87	114	112	111	113	90	89	89	112	24
23	107	85	110	109	108	110	88	88	87	108	23
22	104	83	107	106	105	107	86	86	86	105	22
21	102	81	104	102	102	104	85	84	84	102	21
20	99	79	100	99	99	100	83	82	82	99	20
19	96	77	97	96	96	97	81	80	80	97	19
18	93	75	94	93	93	94	79	78	78	94	18
17	91	73	91	91	89	91	78	76	76	91	17
16	88	71	88	88	86	88	76	74	74	88	16
15	85	69	85	85	83	85	74	72	72	85	15
14	83	66	82	82	80	82	72	70	70	83	14
13	80	64	79	79	77	80	70	68	68	80	13
12	78	62	76	76	74	77	69	66	66	77	12
11	75	60	73	74	71	74	67	64	64	74	11
10	73	58	70	71	68	71	65	61	62	72	10
9	71	56	67	68	65	68	63	59	60	69	9
8	68	54	65	66	62	66	61	56	58	66	8
7	66	51	62	63	59	63	59	54	56	63	7
6	63	49	59	60	56	60	57	51	53	60	6
5	61	47	57	58	53	57	54	48	51	57	5
4	58	45	54	55	49	55	52	44	49	54	4
3	56	42	52	52	46	52	50	41	47	50	3
2	53		49	50	43	49				47	2

Appendix C

Table C.1 Standard Scores Corresponding to Sums of Subtest Scaled Scores for Planned Comparison Clusters: Problem-Solving and Memory & Learning

Sum of Scaled Scores	Problem-Solving						Memory and Learning			Sum of Scaled Scores
	Ages 3–4	Age 5	Age 6	Ages 7–9	Ages 10–12	Ages 13–18	Age 3	Age 4	Ages 5–18	
95								160		95
94								160		94
93								160		93
92								160		92
91								160		91
90								159		90
89								158		89
88								157		88
87								156		87
86								155		86
85								153		85
84								152		84
83								151		83
82								150		82
81								148		81
80								147		80
79								146		79
78								144		78
77								143		77
76			158	160	160	160		142	160	76

75	160	140			160	160	156	160	75
74	160	139			160	160	155	160	74
73	160	137			160	160	154	160	73
72	160	136			160	160	152	160	72
71	160	135			160	160	151	160	71
70	160	133			158	160	149	160	70
69	160	132			156	160	148	160	69
68	157	130			154	157	147	159	68
67	155	129			151	154	145	156	67
66	152	127			149	151	143	154	66
65	150	125			147	148	142	151	65
64	148	124			145	146	140	149	64
63	145	122			143	143	139	146	63
62	143	121			141	141	137	144	62
61	141	119			139	138	135	142	61
60	138	118		160	137	136	134	139	60
59	136	116		160	135	134	132	137	59
58	134	114		160	133	132	130	135	58
57	132	113		160	131	130	129	133	57
56	130	111		160	129	128	127	130	56
55	128	109	160	160	127	126	125	128	55
54	126	108	160	160	125	124	124	126	54
53	124	106	160	160	123	122	122	124	53
52	122	104	160	160	121	120	120	122	52
51	120	103	160	160	119	118	118	120	51
50	118	101	160	160	117	116	116	118	50
49	116	100	159	159	115	114	115	116	49
48	114	98	154	154	113	112	113	114	48
47	112	96	150	150	111	111	111	112	47
46	110	95	146	146	110	109	109	110	46

(continued)

Table C.I Continued

Sum of Scaled Scores	Problem-Solving						Memory and Learning			Sum of Scaled Scores
	Ages 3–4	Age 5	Age 6	Ages 7–9	Ages 10–12	Ages 13–18	Age 3	Age 4	Ages 5–18	
45		133	108	108	107	108	142	93	108	45
44		131	106	106	106	106	138	92	106	44
43		129	104	105	104	104	135	90	105	43
42		126	102	103	102	103	132	89	103	42
41		124	101	101	101	101	128	87	101	41
40		122	99	99	99	99	125	86	99	40
39		120	97	97	97	98	123	84	98	39
38	158	118	96	96	96	96	120	83	96	38
37	154	116	94	94	94	94	117	81	94	37
36	151	113	92	92	92	93	114	80	93	36
35	148	111	91	90	91	91	112	78	91	35
34	145	109	89	89	89	90	109	77	89	34
33	142	107	88	87	88	88	107	76	88	33
32	138	105	86	86	86	87	104	74	86	32
31	135	103	85	84	85	85	102	73	85	31
30	132	101	83	82	83	84	100	72	83	30
29	129	98	82	81	82	82	97	70	81	29
28	126	96	80	79	80	81	95	69	80	28
27	123	94	79	78	79	79	93	68	78	27
26	120	92	77	76	77	78	91	67	77	26

25	75	65	88	77	75	74	76	90	117	25
24	74	64	86	75	74	73	75	87	114	24
23	72	63	84	74	72	71	73	85	111	23
22	71	62	82	72	71	70	72	83	108	22
21	69	61	80	71	69	68	71	80	105	21
20	68	59	78	70	68	67	69	78	101	20
19	66	58	75	69	66	65	68	76	98	19
18	65	57	73	67	65	64	67	73	95	18
17	64	56	71	66	63	63	66	71	92	17
16	62	55	69	65	62	61	65	68	89	16
15	61	54	67	64	60	60	63	66	86	15
14	59	53	65	62	58	58	62	63	82	14
13	58	52	62	61	57	57	61	60	79	13
12	57	51	60	60	55	56	60	58	76	12
11	55	50	58	59	54	54	59	55	72	11
10	54	49	55	58	52	53	58	52	69	10
9	53	48	53	56	50	51	57	49	65	9
8	51	47	51	55	49	50	56	46	62	8
7	50	46	48	54	47	49	55	43	58	7
6	49	45	46	53	45	47	54	40	55	6
5	47	44	43	52	44	46	53	40	51	5
4	46		41	51	42	45	52	40	47	4
3			40					40	43	3
2									40	2

Appendix D

Table D.1 Standard Scores Corresponding to Sums of Subtest Scaled Scores for Planned Comparison Clusters: Verbal Response, Pointing Response, Little Motor, and Gross Motor

Sum of Scaled Scores	Verbal Response		Pointing Response		Little Motor		Gross-Motor				Sum of Scaled Scores
	Ages 4–6	Ages 7–18	Ages 3–4	Ages 5–18	Ages 3–4	Ages 5–18	Age 4	Ages 5–6	Ages 7–12	Ages 13–18	
76			160								76
75			160								75
74			160								74
73			160								73
72			160								72
71			160								71
70			160								70
69			160								69
68			158								68
67			155								67
66			153								66
65			151								65
64			149								64
63			147								63
62			145								62
61			143								61
60			140								60
59			138								59
58			136								58
57	160	160	134	160					160		57
56	160	160	132	160					160		56

55		160					160	130	160	160	55
54		160					160	128	160	159	54
53		160					160	126	160	156	53
52		158					157	124	160	154	52
51		154					154	122	160	151	51
50		151					151	120	156	149	50
49		148					148	118	152	146	49
48		145					145	116	148	143	48
47		142					142	114	144	141	47
46		139					139	112	140	138	46
45		136					136	110	137	136	45
44		133					134	108	134	133	44
43		131					131	106	131	131	43
42		128					128	105	128	128	42
41		125					126	103	125	126	41
40	160	123	149	160	160	160	123	101	122	124	40
39	157	120	147	160	156	160	121	99	120	121	39
38	154	118	144	159	153	160	118	97	117	119	38
37	150	115	142	153	149	155	116	95	115	116	37
36	147	113	139	149	145	151	113	94	112	114	36
35	144	111	137	144	142	146	111	92	110	112	35
34	140	108	134	140	138	142	109	90	108	109	34
33	137	106	131	136	135	138	107	88	105	107	33
32	133	104	129	132	131	134	104	87	103	105	32
31	130	101	126	129	128	131	102	85	101	103	31
30	126	99	123	126	125	127	100	83	99	100	30
29	123	97	120	122	122	124	98	82	97	98	29
28	119	95	117	119	118	120	95	80	94	96	28
27		93					93	78	92	94	27
26		91					91	77	90	91	26

Table D.I Continued

Sum of Scaled Scores	Verbal Response		Pointing Response		Little Motor		Gross-Motor				Sum of Scaled Scores
	Ages 4–6	Ages 7–18	Ages 3–4	Ages 5–18	Ages 3–4	Ages 5–18	Age 4	Ages 5–6	Ages 7–12	Ages 13–18	
25	89	88	75	89	117	115	116	114	88	116	25
24	87	86	74	87	114	112	113	111	86	112	24
23	85	84	72	85	110	109	110	108	84	109	23
22	83	82	70	83	107	106	107	105	82	106	22
21	80	80	69	81	104	103	104	102	80	102	21
20	78	78	67	79	101	100	101	99	78	99	20
19	76	76	66	77	98	97	98	96	76	96	19
18	74	75	64	75	94	94	95	93	74	93	18
17	72	73	63	73	91	91	92	90	72	90	17
16	70	71	61	71	88	89	89	87	70	87	16
15	67	69	60	70	85	86	86	84	68	85	15
14	65	67	58	68	81	83	82	81	66	82	14
13	63	65	57	66	78	80	79	78	64	79	13
12	61	63	56	64	75	77	76	75	62	77	12
11	59	61	54	62	71	75	72	72	60	74	11
10	57	59	53	60	67	72	68	69	58	72	10
9	55	57	51	59	63	69	65	66	56	70	9
8	53	55	50	57	59	66	60	63	54	67	8
7	50	53	49	55	55	64	56	60	52	65	7
6	48	51	47	53	51	61	51	57	50	63	6
5	46	49	46	51	46	58	46	54	48	61	5
4	44	47	45	50	41	55	40	51	46	59	4
3	42	45		48	40	53	40	48	44	57	3
2					40	50	40	45		55	2

Appendix E

Table E.1 Socioeconomic Status Norms: Converting the KABC-II Global Score (FCI, MPI, NVI) of Children Ages 3–6 Years to a Percentile Rank Based on Their Socioeconomic Status (Mother's Education)

	Mother's Educational Category: Global Index			
Percentile Rank	0–11 Years	High School Graduate or GED	1–3 Years of College	4-Year Degree or More
>99th	124–160	131–160	137–160	145–160
99th	119–123	126–130	131–136	140–144
95th	111–112	118	123–124	132
90th	107	112–113	118–119	126–127
85th	104	109–110	115–116	123–124
80th	101–102	106–107	113	120–121
75th	99	104–105	110–111	118–119
70th	97–98	102–103	108–109	116–117
65th	95–96	100–101	106–107	114–115
60th	93–94	98–99	105	112–113
55th	92	97	103–104	111
50th	90–91	95	101–102	109
45th	89	93	99–100	107
40th	87–88	91–92	98	105–106
35th	85–86	89–90	96–97	103–104
30th	83–84	87–88	94–95	101–102
25th	82	85–86	92–93	99–100
20th	79–80	83–84	90	97–98
15th	77	80–81	87–88	94–95
10th	74	77–78	84–85	91–92
5th	69–70	72	79–80	86
1st	57–62	60–64	67–72	73–78
<1st	40–56	40–59	40–66	40–72

Notes: Global Index = FCI, MPI, or NVI. Select the portion of the table that corresponds to Mother's Education. Enter the appropriate "Global Index" with the child's FCI, MPI, or NVI. Read across to determine the child's socioeconomic (SES) percentile rank. If a child's exact index does not appear in the table, interpolate. These SES percentile ranks were developed by applying a linear equating technique to data provided for ages 3–6 years by Kaufman and Kaufman (2004a, Table 8.6). Within each category of mother's education, the 50th percentile is based on the mean of the FCI, MPI, and NVI; the standard deviation used to obtain the remaining percentile ranks was pooled from the SDs of the three global scores.

Appendix F

Table F.1 Socioeconomic Status Norms: Converting the KABC-II Global Score (FCI, MPI, NVI) of Children Ages 7–18 Years to a Percentile Rank Based on Their Socioeconomic Status (Mother's Education)

	Mother's Educational Category: Global Index			
Percentile Rank	0–11 Years	High School Graduate or GED	1–3 Years of College	4-Year Degree or More
>99th	125–160	137–160	137–160	143–160
99th	119–124	131–136	131–136	137–142
95th	112	123	124	129
90th	107	117–118	119	123–124
85th	104	114	116	120–121
80th	101–102	111	113–114	117–118
75th	99	108–109	111	115–116
70th	97	106–107	109	113–114
65th	95	104	107	111–112
60th	93–94	102	105–106	109–110
55th	92	100–101	104	108
50th	90	98–99	102	106
45th	88	96–97	100	104
40th	86–87	95	98–99	102–103
35th	85	93	97	100–101
30th	83	90–91	95	98–99
25th	81	88–89	93	96–97
20th	78–79	86	90–91	94–95
15th	76	83	88	91–92
10th	73	79–80	85	88–89
5th	68	74	80	83
1st	56–61	60–66	67–72	70–75
<1st	40–55	40–59	40–66	40–69

Notes: Global Index = FCI, MPI, or NVI. Select the portion of the table that corresponds to Mother's Education. Enter the appropriate "Global Index" with the child's FCI, MPI, or NVI. Read across to determine the child's socioeconomic (SES) percentile rank. If a child's exact index does not appear in the table, interpolate. These SES percentile ranks were developed by applying a linear equating technique to data provided for ages 7–18 years by Kaufman and Kaufman (2004a, Table 8.6). Within each category of mother's education, the 50th percentile is based on the mean of the FCI, MPI, and NVI; the standard deviation used to obtain the remaining percentile ranks was pooled from the SDs of the three global scores.

References

Achenbach, T. M., & McConaughy, S. H. (2004). *School-based practitioners' guide for the Achenbach System of Empirically Based Assessment (ASEBA)* (4th ed.). Burlington, VT: University of Vermont, Research Center for Children, Youth, and Families.

Adams, M. J. (1990). *Beginning to read: Thinking and learning about print.* Cambridge, MA: MIT Press.

Allen, M. H., Lincoln, A. J., & Kaufman, A. S. (1991). Sequential and simultaneous processing abilities of high-functioning autistic and language-impaired children. *Journal of Autism and Developmental Disorders, 21,* 483–502.

American Psychiatric Association. (2000). *Diagnostic and statistical manual of mental disorders* (4th ed., text rev.). Washington, DC: American Psychiatric Association.

Anastasi, A., & Urbina, S. (1997). *Psychological testing* (7th ed.). Upper Saddle River, NJ: Prentice Hall.

Anastopoulos, A. D., Spisto, M. A., & Maher, M. C. (1994). The WISC-III Freedom from Distractibility factor: Its clinical utility in identifying children with Attention Deficit Hyperactivity Disorder. *Psychological Assessment, 6,* 368–371.

Anderson, R. J., & Sisco, F. H. (1977). *Standardization of the WISC-R Performance Scale for deaf children* (Series T, No. 1). Washington, DC: Gallaudet University, Office of Demographic Studies.

Aram, D. M., & Hall, N. E. (1989). Longitudinal follow-up of children with preschool communication disorders: Treatment implications. *School Psychology Review, 18,* 487–501.

Ardila, A. (1999). A neuropsychological approach to intelligence. *Neuropsychology Review, 9,* 117–136.

Ardila, A. (2002). Language representation and working memory with bilinguals. *Journal of Communication Disorders, 36*(3), 233–240.

Assesmany, A., McIntosh, D. E., Phelps, L., & Rizza, M. G. (2001). Discriminant validity of the WISC-III with children classified as ADHD. *Journal of Psychoeducational Assessment, 19,* 127–147.

Aylward, G. P., & MacGruder, R. W. (1986). *Test behavior checklist.* Brandon, VT: Clinical Psychology.

Barkley, R. A. (1990). *Attention-Deficit Hyperactivity Disorder: A handbook for diagnosis and treatment.* New York: Guilford Press.

Barkley, R. A. (1997). *ADHD and the nature of self-control.* New York: Guilford Press.

Barkley, R. A. (1998). *Attention-Deficit Hyperactivity Disorder: A handbook for diagnosis and treatment* (2nd ed.). New York: Guilford Press.

Barkley, R. A. (2003). Attention-Deficit/Hyperactivity Disorder. In E. J. Mash & R. A. Barkley (Eds.), *Child psychopathology* (2nd ed., pp. 75–143). New York: Guilford Press.

Barkley, R. A., DuPaul, G. J., & McMurray, M. B. (1990). A comprehensive evaluation of Attention Deficit Disorder with and without hyperactivity. *Journal of Consulting and Clinical Psychology, 58,* 775–789 .

Barnhill, G., Hagiwara, T., Myles, B. S., & Simpson, R. L. (2000). Asperger syndrome: A study of 37 children and adolescents. *Focus on Autism and Other Developmental Disabilities, 15*(3), 146–153.

Bellugi, U. B., Lichtenberger, L., Jones, W., Lai, Z., & St. George, M. (2000). The neurocognitive profile of Williams syndrome: A complex pattern of strengths and weaknesses. *Journal of Cognitive Neuroscience, 12*(3), 1–23.

Bigler, E. D., & Adams, W. V. (2001). Clinical neuropsychological assessment of child and adolescent memory with the WRAML, TOMAL, and the CVLT-C. In A. S. Kaufman & N. L. Kaufman (Eds.), *Specific learning disabilities and difficulties in children and adolescents* (pp. 387–429). New York: Cambridge University Press.

Bigler, E. D., Nussbaum, N. L., & Foley, H. A. (1997). Child neuropsychology in the private medical practice. In C. R. Reynolds & E. Fletcher-Janzen (Eds.), *The handbook of clinical child neuropsychology* (2nd ed., pp. 726–742). New York: Kluwer-Plenum.

Binet, A., & Simon, T. (1905). Methodes nouvelles pour le diagnostic du niveau intellectuel des anormaux [New methods for the diagnosis of the intellectual level of subnormals]. *L'Annee Psychologique, 11,* 191–244.

Bohline, D. S. (1985). Intellectual and effective characteristics of attention deficit disordered children. *Journal of Learning Disabilities, 18,* 604–608.

Bolen, L. M. (1998). WISC-III score changes for EMH students. *Psychology in the Schools, 35*(4), 327–332.

Boliek, C. A., & Obrzut, J. E. (1997). Neuropsychological aspects of Attention Deficit/Hyperactivity Disorder. In C. R. Reynolds & E. Fletcher-Janzen (Eds.), *The handbook of clinical child neuropsychology* (2nd ed., pp. 619–634). New York: Kluwer-Plenum.

Bornstein, H., Wollward, J. C., & Tully, N. (1976). Language and communication. In B. Bolton (Ed.), *Psychology of deafness for rehabilitation counselors* (pp. 19–42). Baltimore: University Park Press.

Bos, C. S., & Van Reusen, A. K. (1991). Academic interventions with learning-disabled students: A cognitive/metacognitive approach. In J. Obrzut & G. W. Hynd (Eds.), *Neuropsychological foundations of learning disabilities* (pp. 659–684). Orlando, FL: Academic Press.

Bower, A., & Hayes, A. (1995). Relations of scores on the Stanford-Binet Fourth Edition and Form L-M. Concurrent validation study with children who have Mental Retardation. *American Journal on Mental Retardation, 99*(5), 555–563.

Bracken, B. A., & McCallum, R. S. (1998). *Universal Nonverbal Intelligence Test (UNIT)*. Itasca, IL: Riverside Publishing.

Braden, J. P. (1984). The factorial similarity of the WISC-R Performance Scale in deaf and hearing samples. *Personal and Individual Differences, 5*(4), 403–409.

Braden, J. P. (1985). WISC-R deaf norms reconsidered. *Journal of School Psychology, 23,* 375–382.

Braden, J. P. (1994). *Deafness, deprivation, and IQ.* New York: Plenum Press.

Brady, K. D., & Denckla, M. B. (1994). *Performance of children with Attention Deficit Hyperactivity Disorder on the Tower of Hanoi task.* Unpublished manuscript, Johns Hopkins University School of Medicine.

Breen, M. J. (1988). ADHD girls and boys: An analysis of attentional, emotional, cognitive, and family variables. *Journal of Child Psychology and Psychiatry, 30,* 711–716.

Burgemeister, B. R., Blum, L. H., & Lorge, I. (1954). *Columbia Mental Maturity Scale.* New York: Harcourt Brace Jovanovich.

Burgemeister, B. R., Blum, L. H., & Lorge, I. (1972). *Columbia Mental Maturity Scale, 3rd ed.: Guide to administering and interpreting.* New York: Harcourt Brace Jovanovich.

Burgess, A. (1991). Profile analysis of the Wechsler intelligence scales: A new index of subtest scatter. *British Journal of Clinical Psychology, 30*(3), 257–263.

Caltabiano & Flanagan. (2004). *Content validity of new and recently revised intelligence tests: Implications for interpretation.* Unpublished manuscript.

Campbell, J. M., Bell, S. K., & Keith, L. K. (2001). Concurrent validity of the Peabody Picture Vocabulary Test—3rd Edition as an intelligence and achievement screener for low SES African American children. *Assessment, 8,* 85–94.

Canivez, G. L., & Watkins, M. W. (2001). Long-term stability of the Wechsler Intelligence Scale for Children—Third edition among students with disabilities. *School Psychology Review, 30*(2), 438–453.

Cantrill, J. L. (2003). Inhibition, working memory, and time sense in children with Attention Deficit Hyperactivity Disorder. *Dissertation Abstracts International, 63* (7-B). (UMI No. 95002-229)

Carroll, J. B. (1943). The factorial representation of mental ability and academic achievement. *Educational and Psychological Measurement, 3,* 307–332.

Carroll, J. B. (1993). *Human cognitive abilities: A survey of factor-analytic studies.* Cambridge, England: Cambridge University Press.

Carroll, J. B. (1997). The three-stratum theory of cognitive abilities. In D. P. Flanagan, J. L. Genshaft, & P. L. Harrison (Eds.), *Contemporary intellectual assessment: Theories, tests, and issues* (pp. 122–130). New York: Guilford Press.

Carroll, J. B. (1998). Foreword. In K. S. McGrew & D. P. Flanagan (Eds.), *The intelligence test desk reference (ITDR): Gf-Gc cross battery assessment* (pp. xi–xii). Boston: Allyn & Bacon.

Cattell, R. B. (1941). Some theoretical issues in adult intelligence testing. *Psychological Bulletin, 40,* 592.

Cattell, R. B. (1963). Theory of fluid and crystallized intelligence: A critical experiment. *Journal of Educational Psychology, 54,* 1–22.

Cattell, R. B., & Horn, J. L. (1978). A check on the theory of fluid and crystallized intelligence with description of new subtest designs. *Journal of Educational Measurement, 15,* 139–164.

Centers for Disease Control and Prevention. (1993). Use of race and ethnicity in public health surveillance summary of the CDC/ATSDR workshop. *MMWR Weekly* (No. RR-10). Washington, DC: Author.

Chow, D., & Skuy, M. (1999). Simultaneous and successive cognitive processing with nonverbal learning disabilities. *School Psychology International, 20,* 219–231.

Clark, L. A., & Watson, B. (1995). Constructing validity: Basic issues in objective scale development. *Psychological Assessment, 7,* 309–319.

Cohen, J., Cohen, P., West, S. G., & Aiken, L. S. (2003). *Applied multiple regression/correlation analysis for the behavioral sciences.* Mahwah, NJ: Erlbaum.

Cohen, M. (1997). *Children's Memory Scale.* San Antonio, TX: The Psychological Corporation.

Cohen, M. J., Hall, J., & Riccio, C. A. (1997). Neuropsychological profiles of children diagnosed as specific language impaired with and without hyperlexia. *Archives of Clinical Neuropsychology, 12*(3), 223–229.

Common Ground. (2002). *Specific learning disabilities: Finding common ground.* A report developed by the Learning Disabilities Roundtable Sponsored by the Division of Research to Practice, Office of Special Education Programs, U.S. Department of Education. Washington, DC: Author.

Comrey, A. L. (1988). Factor-analytic methods of scale development in personality and clinical psychology. *Journal of Consulting and Clinical Psychology, 56*(5), 754–761.

Conant, L. L., Fastenau, P. S., Giordani, B., Boivin, M. J., Opel, B., & Nseyila, D. D. (1999). Modality specificity of memory span tasks among Zairian children: A developmental perspective. *Journal of Clinical & Experimental Neuropsychology, 21,* 375–384.

Conners, C. K., & Jett, J. L., (2001). *Attention Deficit Hyperactivity Disorder in adults and children: The latest assessment and treatment strategies.* Kansas City, MO: Compact Clinicals.

Conners, C. K., Wells, K. C., Parker, J. D. A., Sitarenios, G., Diamond, J. M., & Powell, J. W. (1997). A new self-report scale for assessment of adolescent psychopathology: Factor structure, reliability, validity, and diagnostic sensitivity. *Journal of Abnormal Child Psychology, 25*(6), 487–497.

Conrad, R., & Weiskrantz, B. C. (1981). On the cognitive ability of deaf children with deaf parents. *American Annals of the Deaf, 126,* 995–1003.

Cook, T. W. (1937). Amount of material and difficulty of problem solving: The disk transfer problem. *Journal of Experimental Psychology, 20,* 288–296.

Cox, C. (1997). Neuropsychological abnormalities in Obsessive-Compulsive Disorder and their assessments. *International Review of Psychiatry, 9,* 45–60.

Crichfield, A. B. (1986). Psychometric assessment. In L. G. Steward (Ed.), *Clinical rehabilitation assessment and hearing impairment: A guide to quality assurance* (pp. 1–8). Silver Springs, MD: National Association of the Deaf.

Daleiden, E., Drabman, R. S., & Benton, J. (2002). The guide to the assessment of test session behavior: Validity in relation to cognitive testing and parent-reported behavior problems in a clinical sample. *Journal of Clinical Child Psychology, 31,* 263–271.

Daniel, M. H. (1997). Intelligence testing: Status and trends. *American Psychologist, 52*(10), 1038–1045.

Das, J. P., Kirby, J. R., & Jarman, R. F. (1979). *Simultaneous and successive cognitive processes.* New York: Academic Press.

Das, J. P., Naglieri, J. A., & Kirby, J. R. (1994). *Assessment of cognitive processes.* Needham Heights, MA: Allyn & Bacon.

Davidson, K. L. (1992). A comparison of Native American and White students cognitive strengths as measured by the Kaufman Assessment Battery for Children. *Roeper Review, 14,* 111–115.

DeCroly, I. (1914). Epreuve nouvelle pour l'examination mental [New approach for mental tests]. *L'Année Psychologique, 20,* 140–159.

Delis, D.C., Kaplan, E., & Kramer, J. H. (2003). *Manual for the Delis-Kaplan Executive Function System.* San Antonio, TX: The Psychological Corporation.

Denckla, M. B. (1994). Measurement of executive function. In G. R. Lyon (Ed.), *Frames of reference for the assessment of learning disabilities: New views on measurement issues* (pp. 117–142). Baltimore: Brooks Publishing.

Denny, G. R. (1997). Discriminating attention-deficit hyperactivity disordered, learning disabled, and typical school aged children: Evaluating an assessment battery for learning clinics and schools. *Dissertation Abstracts International, 58*(1-A). (UMI No. 95013-174)

Doyle, A. E., Biederman, J., Seidman, L. J., Weber, W., & Faraone, S. V. (2000). Diagnostic efficiency of neuropsychological test scores for discriminating boys with and without Attention Deficit Hyperactivity Disorder. *Journal of Counseling and Clinical Psychology, 68*(3), 477–488.

Durkin, M. S., & Stein, Z. A. (1996). Classification of Mental Retardation. In J. W. Jacobson & J. A. Mulick (Eds.), *Manual of diagnosis and professional practice in Mental Retardation* (pp. 67–73). Washington, DC: American Psychological Association.

Edwards, J., & Lahey, M. (1996). Auditory lexical decisions in children with specific language impairment. *Journal of Speech and Hearing Research, 39,* 1263–1273.

Ehlers, S., Nyden, A., & Gillberg, C. (1997). Asperger syndrome, autism and attention disorders: A comparative study of the cognitive profiles of 120 children. *Journal of Child Psychology and Psychiatry and Allied Disciplines, 38*(2), 207–217.

Eisenmajer, R., Prior, M., Leekam, S., Wing, L., Gould, J. Welham, M., & Ong, B. (1996). Comparison of clinical symptoms in autism and Asperger's Disorder. *Journal of the American Academy of Child and Adolescent Psychiatry, 35,* 1523–1531.

Englert, C. S. (1990). Unraveling the mysteries of writing through strategy instruction. In T. W. Scruggs & Y. L. Wong (Eds.), *Intervention research in learning disabilities* (pp. 186–223). Berlin: Springer-Verlag.

Faraone, S. V., Biederman, J., Lehman, B. K., & Spencer, T. (1993). Intellectual performance and school failure in children with Attention Deficit Hyperactivity Disorder and in their siblings. *Journal of Abnormal Psychology, 102*(4), 616–623.

Farrell, M. M., & Phelps, L. (2000). A comparison of the Leiter-R and the Universal Nonverbal Intelligence Test (UNIT) with children classified as language impaired. *Journal of Psychoeducational Assessment, 18*(3), 268–274.

Federal Register. 42:250 p. 65083. Washington, DC: U.S. Government Printing Office.

Field, M. (1987). Relation of language-delayed preschoolers' Leiter scores to later IQ. *Journal of Clinical Child Psychology, 16*(2), 111–115.

Fischer, M., Barkley, R., Fletcher, K., & Smallish, L. (1990). The adolescent outcome of hyperactive children diagnosed by research criteria, II: Academic, attentional, and neuropsychological status. *Journal of Consulting and Clinical Psychology, 58,* 580–588.

Flanagan, D. P., & Alfonso, V. C. (2000). Essentially, essential for WAIS-III users. *Contemporary Psychology: APA Review of Books, 45,* 528–533.

Flanagan, D. P., & Kaufman, A. S. (2004). *Essentials of WISC-IV assessment.* New York: Wiley.

Flanagan, D. P., & McGrew, K. S. (1998). Interpreting intelligence tests from contemporary *Gf-Gc* theory: Joint confirmatory factor analysis of the WJ-R and KAIT in a non-White sample. *Journal of School Psychology.*

Flanagan, D. P., McGrew, K. S., & Ortiz, S. O. (2000). *The Wechsler intelligence scales and* Gf-Gc *theory: A contemporary approach to interpretation.* Boston: Allyn & Bacon.

Flanagan, D. P., & Ortiz, S. O. (2001). *Essentials of cross-battery assessment.* New York: Wiley.

Flanagan, D. P., Ortiz, S. O., Alfonso, V. C., & Mascolo, J. (2002). *The achievement test desk reference (ATDR): Comprehensive assessment and learning disabilities.* Boston: Allyn & Bacon.

Fletcher-Janzen, E. (2003). *A validity study of the KABC-II and the Taos Pueblo Indian children of New Mexico.* Circle Pines, MN: American Guidance Service.

Flynn, J. R. (1984). The mean IQ of Americans: Massive gains 1932–1978. *Psychological Bulletin, 95,* 29–51.

Flynn, J. R. (1987). Massive IQ gains in 14 nations: What IQ tests really measure. *Psychological Bulletin, 101,* 171–191.

Fourqurean, J. M. (1987). A K-ABC and WISC-R comparison for Latino learning disabled children of limited English proficiency. *Journal of School Psychology, 25,* 15–21.

Frick, P. J., Kamphaus, R. W., Lahey, B. B., Loeber, R., Christ, M. A. G., Hart, E. L., & Tannenbaum, L. E. (1991). Academic underachievement and the Disruptive Behavior Disorders. *Journal of Consulting and Clinical Psychology, 59,* 289–294.

Gallaudet Research Institute. (2003). *Regional and national summary report of data from the 2001– 2002 Annual Survey of Deaf and Hard of Hearing Children & Youth.* Washington, DC: Author.

Gardner, H. (1993). *Multiple intelligences: Theory in practice.* New York: Basic Books.

Gilchrist, A., Green J., Cox, A., Burton, D., Rutter, M., & Le Couteur, A. (2001). Development and current functioning in adolescents with Asperger syndrome: A comparative study. *Journal of Child Psychology and Psychiatry, 42*(2), 227–240.

Glutting, J. J., & McDermott, P. A. (1988). Generality of test-session observations to kindergarteners' classroom behavior. *Journal of Abnormal Child Psychology, 16,* 527–537.

Glutting, J. J., & Oakland, T. (1993). *The guide to the assessment of test session behavior.* San Antonio, TX: The Psychological Corporation.

Glutting, J. J., Oakland, T., & McDermott, P.A. (1989). Observing child behavior during testing: Constructs, validity, and situational generality. *Journal of School Psychology, 27,* 155–164.

Glutting, J. J., Robins, P. M., & de Lancey, E. (1997). Discriminant validity of test observations for children with attention deficit/hyperactivity. *Journal of School Psychology, 35,* 391–401.

Glutting, J. J., Youngstrom, E. A., Oakland, T., & Watkins, M. W. (1996). Situational specificity and generality of test behaviors for samples of normal and referred children. *School Psychology Review, 25,* 94–107.

Goldberg, E., & Bougakov, D. (2000). Novel approaches to the diagnosis and treatment of frontal lobe dysfunction. In A. Christensen & B. P. Uzell (Eds.), *International handbook of neuropsychological rehabilitation* (pp. 93–112). New York: Kluwer-Plenum.

Golden, C. J. (1997). The Luria-Nebraska Children's Battery. In C. R. Reynolds & E. Fletcher-Janzen (Eds.), *The handbook of clinical child neuropsychology* (2nd ed., pp. 237–251). New York: Kluwer-Plenum.

Golden, J. (1996). Are tests of working memory and inattention diagnostically useful in children with ADHD? *ADHD Report, 4*(5), 6–8.

Goldstein, G., Beers, S. R., Siegel, D. J., & Minshew, N. J. (2001). A comparison of WAIS-R profiles in adults with high-functioning autism or differing subtypes of learning disability. *Applied Neuropsychology, 8*(3), 148–154.

Goldstein, G., Minshew, N. J., Allen, D. N., & Seaton, B. E. (2002). High-functioning autism and Schizophrenia. A comparison of an early and late onset neurodevelopmental disorder. *Archives of Clinical Neuropsychology, 17,* 461-475.

Golinkoff, M., & Sweeney, J. A. (1989). Cognitive impairments in depression. *Journal of Affective Disorders, 17*(2), 105–112.

Gordon, R. P., Stump, K., & Glaser, B. A. (1996). Assessment of individuals with hearing impairments: Equity in testing procedures and accommodations. *Measurement and Evaluation in Counseling and Development, 29*(2), 111–118.

Graham, S., & Harris, K. R. (1987). Improving composition skills of inefficient learners with self-instructional strategy training. *Topics in Language Disorders, 7,* 66–77.

Gregory, R. J. (1987). *Adult intellectual assessment.* Boston: Allyn & Bacon.

Grodzinsky, G. M., & Barkley, R. M. (1999). The predictive power of frontal lobe tests in the diagnosis of Attention Deficit Hyperactivity Disorder. *Clinical Neuropsychologist, 13,* 12–21.

Grodzinsky, G. M., & Diamond, R. (1992). Frontal lobe functioning in boys with Attentional-Deficit Hyperactivity Disorder. *Developmental Neuropsychology, 8,* 427–445.

Grossman, I., Kaufman, A. S., & Grossman, D. (1993). Correlations of scores on the Kaufman Short Neuropsychological Assessment Procedure and the Kaufman Adolescent and Adult Intelligence Test for a hospitalized depressed sample. *Perceptual and Motor Skills, 77,* 1055–1058.

Grossman, I., Kaufman, A. S., Mednitsky, S., Scharff, L., & Dennis, B. (1994). Neurocognitive abilities for a clinically depressed sample versus a matched control group of normal individuals. *Psychiatry Research, 51,* 231–244.

Groth-Marnat, G., Gallagher, R. E., Hale, J. B., & Kaplan, E. (2000). The Wechsler intelligence scales. In G. Groth-Marnat (Ed.), *Neuropsychological assessment in clinical practice: A guide to test interpretation and integration* (pp. 129–188). New York: Wiley.

Gruzelier, J., Seymour, K., Wilson, L., & Jolley, A. (1988). Impairments on neuropsychologic tests of temporohippocampal and frontohippocampal functions and word fluency in remitting Schizophrenia and affective disorders. *Archives of General Psychiatry, 45*(7), 623–629.

Ham, S. J. (1985). *A validity study of recent intelligence tests on a deaf population.* (Available from the Author, School Psychologist, North Dakota School for the Deaf, Devils Lake, ND 58301)

Hammen, C., & Rudolph, K. D. (2003). Childhood mood disorders. In E. J. Mash & R. A. Barkley (Eds.), *Child psychopathology* (2nd ed., pp. 233–278). New York: Guilford Press.

Hardy, S. T. (1993). *Proper and effective use of sign language interpreters by school psychologists.* Paper presented at the meeting of the National Association of School Psychologists, Washington, DC.

Hardy-Braz, S. T. (2003). *Enhancing school-based psychological services: Assessments and interventions with students who are deaf or hard of hearing.* Workshop presented at the meeting of the National Association of School Psychologists, Toronto, CN.

Harmony, T. (1997). Psychophysiological evaluation of neuropsychological disorders in children. In C. R. Reynolds & E. Fletcher-Janzen (Eds.), *The handbook of clinical child neuropsychology* (2nd ed., pp. 356–383). New York: Kluwer-Plenum.

Harrison, P. L. (1990). Mental Retardation: Adaptive behavior assessment, and giftedness. In A. S. Kaufman (Au.), *Assessing adolescent and adult intelligence* (pp. 533–585). Needham, MA: Allyn & Bacon.

Hebben, N., & Milberg, W. (2002). *Essentials of neuropsychological assessment.* New York: Wiley.

Henry, G. M., Weingartner, H., & Murphy, D. L. (1973). Influence of affective states and psychoactive drugs on verbal learning and memory. *American Journal of Psychiatry, 130*(9), 966–971.

Hinshaw, S. P., & Lee, S. L. (2003). Conduct and Oppositional Defiant Disorders. In E. J. Mash & R. A. Barkley (Eds.), *Child psychopathology* (2nd ed., pp. 144–198). New York: Guilford Press.

Hodapp, R. M., Leckman, J. F., Dykens, E. M., & Sparrow, S. S. (1992). K-ABC profiles in children with Fragile X syndrome, Down syndrome, and nonspecific Mental Retardation. *American Journal on Mental Retardation, 97*(1), pp. 39–46.

Hong, E. (1999). Test anxiety, perceived test difficulty, and test performance: Temporal patterns of their effects. *Learning and Individual Differences, 11,* 431–447.

Hooper, S. R., & Hynd, G. W. (1982, October). *The differential diagnosis of developmental dyslexia with the Kaufman Assessment Battery for children.* Paper presented at the meeting of the National Academy of Neuropsychologists, Atlanta, GA.

Hooper, S. R., & Hynd, G. W. (1985). Differential diagnosis of subtypes of developmental dyslexia with the Kaufman Assessment Battery for Children (K-ABC). *Journal of Clinical Child Psychology, 14,* 145–152.

Horn, J. L. (1965). *Fluid and crystallized intelligence: A factor analytic and developmental study of the structure among primary mental abilities.* Unpublished doctoral dissertation, University of Illinois, Urbana-Champaign.

Horn, J. L. (1968). Organization of abilities and the development of intelligence. *Psychological Review, 75,* 242–259.

Horn, J. L. (1989). Cognitive diversity: A framework of learning. In P. L. Ackerman, R. J. Sternberg, & R. Glaser (Eds.), *Learning and individual differences* (pp. 61–116). New York: Freeman.

Horn, J. L., & Blankson, N. (in press). Foundations for better understanding of cognitive abilities. In D. P. Flanagan & P. L. Harrison (Eds.), *Contemporary intellectual assessment: Theories, tests, and issues* (2nd ed.). New York: Guilford Press.

Horn, J. L., & Cattell, R. B. (1966). Refinement and test of theory of fluid and crystallized intelligence. *Journal of Educational Psychology, 57,* 253–270.

Horn, J. L., & Cattell, R. B. (1967). Age differences in fluid and crystallized intelligence. *Acta Psychologica, 26,* 107–129.

Horn, J. L., & Hofer, S. M. (1992). Major abilities and development in the adult period. In R. J. Sternberg & C. A. Berg (Eds.), *Intellectual development* (pp. 44–99). Boston: Cambridge University Press.

Horn, J. L., & Noll, J. (1997). Human cognitive capabilities: *Gf-Gc* theory. In D. P. Flanagan, J. L. Genshaft, & P. L. Harrison (Eds.), *Contemporary intellectual assessment: Theories, tests, and issues* (pp. 53–91). New York: Guilford Press.

Hu, L., & Bentler, P. M. (1999). Cutoff criteria for fit indexes in covariance structure analysis: Conventional criteria versus new alternatives. *Structural Equation Modeling, 6,* 1–55.

Ialongo, N., Edelsohn, G., Werthamer-Larsson, L., Crockett, L., & Kelhanm, S. (1996). Social and cognitive impairment in first-grade children with anxious and depressive symptoms. *Journal of Clinical Child Psychology, 25,* 15–24.

James, E. M., & Selz, M. (1997). Neuropsychological bases of common learning and behavior problems in children. In C. R. Reynolds & E. Fletcher-Janzen (Eds.), *The handbook of clinical child neuropsychology* (2nd ed., pp. 157–203). New York: Kluwer-Plenum.

Jensen, A. (1980). *Bias in mental testing.* New York: Free Press.

Jensen, A. (1984). The Black-White difference on the KABC: Implications for future tests. *The Journal of Special Education, 18*(3), 377–408.

Johnston, J., & Ellis Weismer, S. (1983). Mental rotation abilities in language disordered children. *Journal of Speech and Hearing Research, 26,* 397–403.

Kagan, J., & Klein, R. E. (1973). Cross-cultural perspectives on early development. *American Psychologist, 28,* 947–961.

Kamphaus, R. W. (1993). *Clinical assessment of children's intelligence: A handbook for professional practice.* Boston: Allyn & Bacon.

Kamphaus, R. W. (2003). Clinical assessment practice with the K-ABC. In C. R. Reynolds & R. W. Kamphaus (Eds.), *Handbook of psychological and educational assessment of children: Intelligence, aptitude, and achievement* (2nd ed., pp. 204–216). New York: Guilford Press.

Kamphaus, R. W., & Reynolds, C. R. (1987). *Clinical and research applications of the K-ABC.* Circle Pines, MN: American Guidance Service.

Kaplan, B. J., Crawford, S. G., Dewey, D. M., & Fisher, G. C. (2000). The IQs of children with ADHD are normally distributed. *Journal of Learning Disabilities, 33*(5), 425–432.

Kaufman, A. S. (1979). *Intelligent testing with the WISC-R.* New York: Wiley.

Kaufman, A. S. (1994a). *Intelligent testing with the WISC-III.* New York: Wiley.

Kaufman, A. S. (1994b). Practice effects. In R. J. Sternberg (Ed.), *Encyclopedia of intelligence* (Vol. II, pp. 828–833). New York: Macmillan.

Kaufman, A. S. (1994c). A reply to Macmann and Barnett: Lessons from the blind men and the elephant. *School Psychology Quarterly, 9,* 199–207.

Kaufman, A. S. (2000). Foreword. In D. P. Flanagan, K. S. McGrew, & S. O. Ortiz (Eds.), *The Wechsler intelligence scales and CHC theory: A contemporary approach to interpretation.* Boston: Allyn & Bacon.

Kaufman, A. S., Grossman, I., & Kaufman, N. L. (1994). Comparison of hospitalized depressed patients and matched normal controls on tests differing in their level of cognitive complexity. *Journal of Psychoeducational Assessment, 12,* 112–125.

Kaufman, A. S., & Kaufman, N. L. (1977). *Clinical evaluation of young children with the McCarthy Scales.* New York: Grune & Stratton.

Kaufman, A. S., & Kaufman, N. L. (1983a). *Kaufman Assessment Battery for Children (K-ABC) administration and scoring manual.* Circle Pines, MN: American Guidance Service.

Kaufman, A. S., & Kaufman, N. L. (1983b). *K-ABC interpretive manual.* Circle Pines, MN: American Guidance Service.

Kaufman, A. S., & Kaufman, N. L. (1985). *Kaufman Test of Educational Achievement* (K-TEA). Circle Pines, MN: American Guidance Service.

Kaufman, A. S., & Kaufman, N. L. (1990). *Administration and scoring manual for Kaufman Brief Intelligence Test* (K-BIT). Circle Pines, MN: American Guidance Service.

Kaufman, A. S., & Kaufman, N. L. (1993). *Manual for Kaufman Adolescent and Adult Intelligence Test (KAIT).* Circle Pines, MN: American Guidance Service.

Kaufman, A. S., & Kaufman, N. L. (1998). *Kaufman Test of Educational Achievement—Normative Update (KTEA-NU).* Circle Pines, MN: American Guidance Service.

Kaufman, A. S., & Kaufman, N. L. (Eds.). (2001). *Specific learning disabilities and difficulties in children and adolescents: Psychological assessment and evaluation.* New York: Cambridge University Press.

Kaufman, A. S., & Kaufman, N. L. (2004a). *Kaufman Assessment Battery for Children, second edition manual* (KABC-II). Circle Pines, MN: American Guidance Service.

Kaufman, A. S., & Kaufman, N. L. (2004b). *Kaufman Test of Educational Achievement, second edition manual* (KTEA-II). Circle Pines, MN: American Guidance Service.

Kaufman, A. S., & Kaufman, N. L. (in press). *Kaufman Test of Educational Achievement—Second Edition, Brief Form (KTEA-II Brief)*. Circle Pines, MN: American Guidance Service.

Kaufman, A. S., & Lichtenberger, E. O. (1999). *Essentials of WAIS-III assessment*. New York: Wiley.

Kaufman, A. S., & Lichtenberger, E. O. (2000). *Essentials of WISC-III and WPPSI-R assessment*. New York: Wiley.

Kaufman, A. S., & Lichtenberger, E. O. (2002). *Assessing adolescent and adult intelligence* (2nd ed.). Boston: Allyn & Bacon.

Kaufman, A. S., McLean, J. E., & Kaufman, J. C. (1995). The fluid and crystallized abilities of White, Black, and Hispanic adolescents and adults, both with and without an education covariate. *Journal of Clinical Psychology, 51,* 637–647.

Kaufman, N. L., & Kaufman, A. S. (1995). Review of the GATSB: Guide to the assessment of test session behavior for the WISC-III and the WIAT. *Journal of Psychoeducational Assessment, 13,* 318–325.

Keith, T. Z., & Dunbar, S. B. (1984). Hierarchical factor analysis of the K-ABC: Testing alternate models. *Journal of Special Education, 18,* 367–375.

Keith, T. Z., Fine, J. G., Taub, G. E., Reynolds, M. R., & Kranzler, J. H. (2004). Hierarchical, multi-sample, confirmatory factor analysis of the Wechsler Intelligence Scale for Children—fourth edition: What does it measure? (4th ed.). Manuscript submitted for publication.

Keith, T. Z., Kranzler, J., & Flanagan, D. P. (2001). Joint confirmatory factor analysis of the Cognitive Assessment System (CAS) and the Woodcock-Johnson tests of cognitive ability: What does the CAS measure? *School Psychology Review.*

Kellogg, J. S., Hopko, D. R., & Ashcraft, M. H. (1999). The effects of time pressure on arithmetic performance. *Journal of Anxiety Disorders, 13,* 591–600.

Kennedy, M. H., & Hiltonsmith, R. W. (1998). Relationship among the K-ABC Nonverbal Scale, the Pictorial Test of Intelligence, and the Hiskey-Nebraska Test of Learning Aptitude for speech- and language-disabled preschool children. *Journal of Psychoeducational Assessment, 6*(1), 49–54.

Kim, A. L., Goak, H. K., Jang, M. J., & Han, Y. M. (1995). A preliminary study on the validation of the K-ABC Mental Processing Test for Korean preschoolers. *Korean Journal of Child Studies, 16,* 81–95.

Kirby, J. R., & Williams, N. H. (1991). *Learning problems: A cognitive approach*. Toronto, Canada: Kagan and Woo.

Klin, A., Volkmar, F. R., Sparrow, S. S., Cicchetti, D. V., & Rourke, B. D. (1995). Validity and neuropsychological characterization of Asperger's syndrome: Convergence with nonverbal learning disabilities syndrome. *Journal of Child Psychology and Psychiatry, 36,* 1127–1140.

Kohs, S. C. (1923). *Intelligence measurement*. New York: Macmillan.

Konold, T. R., Maller, S. J., & Glutting, J. J. (1998). Measurement and non-measurement influences of session-session behavior on individually administered measures on intelligence. *Journal of School Psychology, 36,* 417–432.

Korkman, M., Kirk, U., & Kemp, S. (1998). *NEPSY: A developmental neuropsychological assessment*. San Antonio, TX: The Psychological Corporation.

Kovacs, M., & Goldston, D. (1991). Cognitive and social cognitive development of depressed children and adolescents. *Journal of the American Academy of Child and Adolescent Psychiatry, 30,* 388–392.

Krassowski, E., & Plante, E. (1997). IQ variability in children with SLI: Implications for use of cognitive referencing in determining SLI. *Journal of Communication Disorders, 30*(1), 1–9.

Kusche, C. A., Cook, E. T., & Greenberg, M. T. (1993). *Journal of Clinical Child Psychology, 22,* 172–195.

Lahey, M., Edwards, J., & Munson, B. (2001). Is processing speed related to severity of language impairment? *Journal of Speech, Language, and Hearing Research, 44*(6), 1354–1361.

Lane, H. S. (1976). Academic Achievement. In B. Bolton (Ed.), *Psychology of deafness for rehabilitation counselors* (pp. 19–42). Baltimore: University Park Press.

Lezak, M. D. (1995). *Neuropsychological assessment* (3rd ed.). New York: Oxford University Press.

Lichtenberger, E. O. (2001). The Kaufman tests—K-ABC and KAIT. In A. S. Kaufman & N. L. Kaufman (Eds.), *Specific learning disabilities and difficulties in children and adolescents* (pp. 97–140). New York: Cambridge University Press.

Lichtenberger, E. O., Broadbooks, D. Y., & Kaufman, A. S. (2000). *Essentials of cognitive assessment with KAIT and other Kaufman measures.* New York: Wiley.

Lichtenberger, E. O., & Kaufman, A. S. (1998). The K-ABC: Recent research. In R. J. Samuda (Ed.), *Advances in cross-cultural assessment* (pp. 56–99). Thousand Oaks, CA: Sage.

Lichtenberger, E. O., & Kaufman, A. S. (2004). *Essentials of WPPSI-III assessment.* New York: Wiley.

Lichtenberger, E. O., Kaufman, A. S., & Lai, Z. C. (2002). *Essentials of WMS-III assessment.* New York: Wiley.

Lichtenberger, E. O., Mather, N., Kaufman, N. L., & Kaufman, A. S. (2004). *Essentials of assessment report writing.* New York: Wiley.

Lincoln, A. J., Courchesne, E., Kilman, B. A., Elmasian, R., & Allen, M. (1988). A study of intellectual abilities in high-functioning people with autism. *Journal of Autism and Developmental Disorders, 18,* 505–524.

Loge, D. V., Staton, R. D., & Beatty, W. W. (1990). Performance of children with ADHD on tests sensitive to frontal lobe dysfunction. *Journal of the American Academy of Child and Adolescent Psychiatry, 29,* 540–545.

Lohman, D. F. (1994). Spatial ability. In R. J. Sternberg (Ed.), *Encyclopedia of human intelligence* (pp. 1000–1007). New York: Macmillan.

Lovejoy, D. W., Ball, J. D., Keats, M., Stutts, M. A., Spain, E. H., Janda, L., & Janusz, J. (1999). Neuropsychological assessment of adults with Attention Deficit Hyperactivity Disorder (ADHD): Diagnostic classification estimates for measures of frontal lobe/executive functioning. *Journal of the International Neuropsychological Society, 5,* 222–233.

Luckasson, R., Borthwick-Duffy, S., Coulter, D. L., Craig, E. M., Reeve, A., Schalock, R. L., Snell, M. E., Spitalnik, D. M., Spreat, S., & Tasse, M. J. (2002). *Mental Retardation: Definition, classification, and systems of supports* (10th ed.). Washington, DC: American Association on Mental Retardation.

Luria, A. R. (1966). *Human brain: An introduction to neuropsychology.* New York: Basic Books.

Luria, A. R. (1970). The functional organization of the brain. *Scientific American, 222,* 66–78.

Luria, A. R. (1973). *The working brain: An introduction to neuro-psychology.* London: Penguin Books.

Lyon, G., Fletcher, J., & Barnes, T. (2003). Learning Disabilities. In E. J. Mash & R. A. Barkley (Eds.), *Child psychopathology* (pp. 390–345). New York: Guilford Press.

Mahone, E. M., Hagelthron, K. M., Cutting, L. E., Schuerholz, L. J., Pelletier, S. F., Rawlins, C., Singer, H. S., & Denckla, M. B. (2002). Effects of IQ on executive function measures in children with ADHD. *Child Neuropsychology, 8*(1), 52–65.

Manjiviona, J., & Prior, M. (1995). Comparison of Asperger syndrome and high-functioning autistic children on a test of motor impairment. *Journal of Autism and Developmental Disorders, 25,* 23–39.

Mardell-Czudnowski, C. (1995). Performance of Asian and White children on the K-ABC: Understanding information processing differences. *Assessment, 2,* 19–29.

Mariani, M., & Barkley, R. A. (1997). Neuropsychological and academic functioning in preschool children with Attention-Deficit Hyperactivity Disorder. *Developmental Neuropsychology, 13,* 111–129.

Mather, N., & Jaffe, L. E. (2002). *Woodcock-Johnson III: Reports, recommendations, and strategies.* New York: Wiley.

Mather, N., Wendling, B. J., & Woodcock, R. W. (2001). *Essentials of WJ III tests of achievement and assessment.* New York: Wiley.

Matier-Sharma, K., Perachio, N., Newcorn, J. H., Sharma, V., & Halperin, J. M. (1995). Differential diagnosis of ADHD: Are objective measures of attention impulsivity, and activity level helpful? *Child Neuropsychology, 1,* 118–127.

Mayes, S. D., & Calhoun, S. L. (2003). Analysis of WISC-III, Stanford-Binet: IV, and Academic achievement test scores in children with autism. *Journal of Autism and Developmental Disorders, 33*(3), 329–341.

Mayes, S. D., Calhoun, S. L., & Crites, D. L. (2001). Does *DSM-IV* Asperger's Disorder exist? *Journal of Abnormal Child Psychology, 29*(3), 263–271.

Mayes, S. D., Calhoun, S. L., & Crowell, E. W. (1998). WISC-III Freedom from Distractibility as a measure of attention in children with and without Attention Deficit Hyperactivitiy Disorder. *2,* 217–227.

McCallum, R. S., Bracken, B. A., & Wasserman, J. D. (2001). *Essentials of nonverbal assessment.* New York: Wiley.

McCarthy, D. (1972). *Manual of the McCarthy scales of children's abilities.* New York: The Psychological Corporation.

McConaughy, S. H., & Achenbach, T. M. (2002). *Manual for the test observation form for ages 2–18.* Burlington, VT: University of Vermont, Research Center for Children, Youth, and Families.

McDermott, P. A., Fantuzzo, J. W., & Glutting, J. J. (1990). Just say no to subtest analysis: A critique on Wechsler theory and practice. *Journal of Psychoeducational Assessment, 8,* 290–302.

McGrew, K. S. (1994). *Clinical interpretation of the Woodcock-Johnson tests of Cognitive Ability—revised.* Boston: Allyn & Bacon.

McGrew, K. S. (1997). Analysis of the major intelligence batteries according to a proposed comprehensive *Gf-Gc* framework. In D. P. Flanagan, J. L. Glenshaft, & P. L. Harrison (Eds.), *Contemporary intellectual assessment: Theories, tests, and issues* (pp. 151–180). New York: Guilford Press.

McGrew, K. S. (in press). The Cattell-Horn-Carroll (CHC) theory of cognitive abilities: Past, present, and future. In D. P. Flanagan & P. L. Harrison (Eds.), *Contemporary intellectual assessment: Theories, tests, and issues* (2nd ed.). New York: Guilford Press.

McGrew, K. S., & Flanagan, D. P. (1998). *The intelligence test desk reference (ITDR):* Gf-Gc cross-battery assessment. Boston: Allyn & Bacon.

McGrew, K. S., Woodcock, R., & Ford, L. (2002). The Woodcock-Johnson Battery, third edition. In A. S. Kaufman & E. O. Lichtenberger (Aus.), *Assessing adolescent and adult intelligence* (2nd ed., pp. 561–628). Boston: Allyn & Bacon.

McKenzie, K. J., & Crowcroft, N. S. (1994). Race, ethnicity, culture, and science. *British Medical Journal, 39,* 286–287.

McLaughlin-Cheng, E. (1998). Asperger syndrome and autism: A literature review and meta-analysis. *Focus on Autism and Other Developmental Disabilities, 13*(4), 234–245.

Melchers, P., & Preuss, U. (2003). Kaufman-Assessment Battery for Children (K-ABC). *Deutschsprachige Fassung* (6. Auflage). Leiden: PITS.

Mercer, J. R. (1979). *System of Multicultural Pluralistic Assessment (SOMPA): Technical manual.* New York: The Psychological Corporation.

Messick, S. (1989). Validity. In R. Linn (Ed.), *Educational measurement* (3rd ed., pp. 104–131). Washington, DC: American Council on Education.

Messick, S. (1995). Validity of psychological assessment: Validation of inferences from persons' responses and performances as scientific inquiry into score meaning. *American Psychologist, 50,* 741–749.

Miller, J. N., & Ozonoff, S. (2000). The external validity of Asperger Disorder: Lack of evidence from the domain of neuropsychology. *Journal of Abnormal Psychology, 109*(2), 227–238.

Miller, L. S., Faustman, W. O., Moses, J. A., & Csernansky, J. G. (1991). Evaluating cognitive impairment in depression with the Luria-Nebraska Neuropsychological Battery: Severity correlates and comparisons with nonpsychiatric controls. *Psychiatry Research, 37*(3), 219–227.

Miller, T. L., & Reynolds, C. R. (Eds.). (1984). Special issue: The K-ABC. *Journal of Special Education, 18,* whole issue.

Minnick, N. (2000). The theory of activity. In C. R. Reynolds & E. Fletcher-Janzen (Eds.), *Encyclopedia of special education* (2nd ed.). New York: Wiley.

Montague, M., & Bos, C. (1986). The effect of cognitive strategy training on verbal math problem solving performance of learning disabled adolescents. *Journal of Learning Disabilities, 19,* 26–33.

Morris, R. D., Stuebing, K. K., Fletcher, J. M., Shaywitz, S. E., Lyon, G. R., Shankweiler, D. P., Katz, L., Francis, D. J., & Shaywitz, B. A. (1998). Subtypes of reading disability: Variability around a phonological core. *Journal of Educational Psychology, 90*(3), 347–373.

Murphy, K. R., Barkley, R. A., & Bush, T. (2001). Executive function and olfactory identification in young adults with Attention Deficit Hyperactivity Disorder. *Neuropsychology, 15*(2), 211–220.

Naglieri, J. A. (1985). Use of the WISC-R and K-ABC with learning disabled, borderline mentally retarded, and normal children. *Psychology in the Schools, 22*(2), 133–141.

Naglieri, J. A. (1999). *Essentials of CAS assessment.* New York: Wiley.

Naglieri, J. A. (2001). Using the Cognitive Assessment System (CAS) with learning disabled children. In A. S. Kaufman & N. L. Kaufman (Eds.), *Specific learning disabilities and difficulties in children and adolescents* (pp. 141–177). New York: Cambridge University Press.

Naglieri, J. A., & Bornstein, B. T. (2003). Intelligence and achievement: Just how correlated are they? *Journal of Psychoeducational Assessment, 21,* 244–260.

Naglieri, J. A., & Das, J. P. (1997). *Cognitive Assessment System interpretive manual.* Chicago: Riverside Publishing.

Naglieri, J. A., Goldstein, S., Iseman, J. S., & Schwebach, A. (2003). Performance of children with Attention Deficit Hyperactivity Disorder and anxiety/depression on the WISC-II and Cognitive Assessment Battery for Children. *Journal of Psychoeducational Assessment, 21,* 32–42.

Naglieri, J. A., Rojahn, J., Aquilino, S. A., & Matto, H. C. (2004). *Black White differences in intelligence: A study of the PASS Theory and Cognitive Assessment System.* Unpublished manuscript.

Nandakumar, R., Glutting, J. J., & Oakland, T. (1993). Mantel-Haenszel methodology for detecting item bias: An introduction and example using the guide to the assessment of test session behavior. *Journal of Psychoeducational Assessment, 11,* 108–119.

National Center for Health Statistics. (1994). Prevalence and characteristics of persons with hearing trouble: United States, 1990–1991. *Vital Health Statistics, 10*(188).

Neisser, U. (1967). *Cognitive psychology.* New York: Appleton-Century-Crofts.

NICHCY. (2004). National Dissemination Center for Children with Disabilities. Retrieved April 14, 2004 from http://www.nichcy.org/

Oakland, T., & Glutting, J. J. (1990). Examiner observations of children's WISC-R test related behaviors possible socioeconomic status, race, and gender effects. *Psychological Assessment: A Journal of Consulting and Clinical Psychology, 2,* 86–90.

Obrzut, A., Obrzut, J. E., & Shaw, D. (1984). Construct validity of the Kaufman Assessment

Battery for children with learning disabled and mentally retarded. *Psychology in the Schools, 21,* 417–424.

Office of Special Education Programs. (2004a). *NCLD update.* Retrieved April 14, 2004, from http://www.ed.gov/about/offices/list/osers/osep/newsarchive.html?exp=0

Office of Special Education Programs. (2004b). *Twenty-second annual report to Congress on the Implementation of the Individuals with Disabilities Education Act (IDEA).* Washington, DC: Author.

Ottem, E. (1999). Interpreting the WPPSI subtests scores of language impaired children— a structural approach. *Scandinavian Journal of Psychology, 40,* 319–329.

Ozonoff, S., Rogers, S. J., & Pennington, B. F. (1991). Asperger's syndrome: Evidence of an empirical distinction from high-functioning autism. *Journal of Child Psychology and Psychiatry, 32,* 1107–1122.

Pennington, B. F., Grossier, D., & Welsh, M. C. (1993). Contrasting cognitive deficits in attention deficit disorder versus reading disability. *Developmental Psychology, 29,* 511–523.

Pernicano, K. M. (1986). Score differences in WAIS-R scatter for schizophrenics, depressives, and personality disorders: A preliminary analysis. *Psychological Reports, 59,* 539–543.

Perugini, E. M. (1999). The predictive power of combined neuropsychological measures for Attention Deficit/Hyperactivity Disorder in children. *Dissertation Abstracts International, 60* (4-B). (UMI No. 95020-204)

Perugini, E. M., Harvey, E. A., & Lovejoy, D. W. (2000). The predictive power of combined neuropsychological measures for Attention-Deficit/Hyperactivity Disorder in children. *Child Neuropsychology, 6*(2), 101–114.

Perugini, E. M., Harvery, E. A., Lovejoy, D. W., Sandstrom, K., & Webb, A. H. (2000). The predictive power of combined neuropsychological measures for Attention Deficit Hyperactivity Disorder in children. *Child Neuropsychology, 6*(2), 101–114.

Phelps, L. (1998). Utility of the WISC-III for children with language impairments. In A. Prifitera & D. H. Saklofske (Eds.), *WISC-III clinical use and interpretation: Scientist-practitioner perspectives* (pp. 157–174). San Diego, CA: Academic Press.

Phelps, L., & Branyan, B. J. (1988). Correlations among the Hiskey, KABC Nonverbal Scale, Leiter, and WISC-R Performance Scale with public-school deaf children. *Journal of Psychoeducational Assessment, 6*(4), 354–358.

Phelps, L., Leguori, S., Nisewaner, J., & Parker, M. (1993). Practical interpretations of the WISC-III with language-disordered children. *Journal of Psychoeducational Assessment, 81,* 71–76.

Polkinghorne, D. E., & Gibbons, B. C. (1999). Applications of qualitative research strategies to school psychology research problems. In C. R. Reynolds & T. B. Gutkin (Eds.), *The handbook of school psychology* (3rd ed). New York: Wiley.

Porter, L. J., & Kirby, E. A. (1986). Effects of two instructional sets on the validity of the Kaufman Assessment Battery for Children—Nonverbal scale with a group of severely hearing impaired children. *Psychology in the Schools, 23,* 37–43.

Prifitera, A., Weiss, L. G., & Saklofske, D. H. (1998). The WISC-III in context. In A. Prifitera & D. H. Saklofske (Eds.), *WISC-III clinical use and interpretation: Scientist-practitioner perspective* (pp. 1–38). San Diego, CA: Academic Press.

Prins, P. J. M., Groot, M. J. M., & Hanewald, G. J. F. P. (1994). Cognition in test-anxious children the role of on-task and coping cognition reconsidered. *Journal of Consulting and Clinical Psychology, 62,* 404–409.

The Psychological Corporation. (2002). *WPPSI-III technical and interpretive manual.* San Antonio, TX: Author.

The Psychological Corporation. (2003). *WISC-IV technical and interpretive manual.* San Antonio, TX: Author.

Raney, G. E. (1993). Monitoring changes in cognitive load during reading: An event-related brain potential and reaction time analysis. *Journal of Experimental Psychology: Learning, Memory & Cognition, 19,* 51–69.

Rapport, M. D., DuPaul, G. J., Stoner, G., & Jones, J. T. (1986). Comparing classroom and clinic measure of Attention Deficit Disorder: Differential, idiosyncratic, and dose-response effects of methylphenidate. *Journal of Consulting and Clinical Psychology, 54,* 334–341.

Reitan, R. M. (1988). Integration of neuropsychological theory, assessment, and application. *The Clinical Neuropsychologist, 2,* 331–349.

Reynolds, C. R. (1997). Methods for detecting and evaluating cultural bias in neuropsychological tests. In E. Fletcher-Janzen, T. L. Strickland, & C. R. Reynolds (Eds.), *The handbook of cross-cultural neuropsychology* (pp. 180–203). New York: Wiley.

Reynolds, C. R., & Bigler, E. D. (1994). *Test of Memory and Learning.* Austin, TX: PRO-ED.

Reynolds, C. R., & Bigler, E. (1997). Clinical neuropsychological assessment of child and adolescent memory with the Test of Memory and Learning. In C. R. Reynolds & E. Fletcher-Janzen (Eds.), *The handbook of clinical child neuropsychology* (2nd ed., pp. 296–319). New York: Kluwer-Plenum.

Reynolds, C. R., & Kamphaus, R. W. (2004). *Behavior Assessment for Children, Second Edition* (BASC-2). Circle Pines, MN: American Guidance Service.

Reynolds, C. R., & Kamphaus, R. W. (2003). *Reynolds Intellectual Assessment Scales.* Lutz, FL: Psychological Assessment Resources.

Reynolds, C. R., Kamphaus, R. W., Rosenthal, B. L., & Hiemenz, J. R. (1997). Applications of the Kaufman Assessment Battery for Children (K-ABC) in neuropsychological assessment. In C. R. Reynolds & E. Fletcher-Janzen (Eds.), *The handbook of clinical child neuropsychology* (2nd ed., pp. 253–269). New York: Kluwer-Plenum.

Ricciardi, P. W., Voelker, S., Carter, R. A., & Shore, D. L. (1991). K-ABC sequential-simultaneous processing and language-impaired preschoolers. *Developmental Neuropsychology, 7,* 523–535.

Riccio, C. A., Ross, C. M., Boan, C., Jemison, S., & Houston, F. (1997). Use of the Differential Ability Scales (DAS) Special Nonverbal Composite among young children with linguistic differences. *Journal of Psychoeducational Assessment, 15*(3), 196–204.

Roid, G. H. (2003). *Stanford-Binet Intelligence Scales, fifth edition, technical manual.* Itasca, IL: Riverside Publishing.

Roid, G. H., & Miller, L. J. (1997). *Leiter International Performance Scale* (rev. ed.). Wood Dale, IL: C. H. Stoelting.

Rourke, B. (1989). Significance of Verbal-Performance discrepancies for subtypes of children with learning disabilities: Opportunities for the WISC-II. In A. Prifitera & D. Saklofske (Eds.), *WISC-II clinical use and interpretation* (pp. 139–156). San Diego, CA: Academic Press.

Rumsey, J. M. (1992). Neuropsychological studies of high-level autism. In E. Schopler & G. B. Mesibov (Eds.), *High-functioning individuals with autism* (pp. 41–64). New York: Plenum.

Samuda, R. J., Feuerstein, R., Kaufman, A. S., Lewis, J. E., & Sternberg, R. J. (1998). *Advances in cross-cultural assessment.* Thousand Oaks, CA: Sage.

Sattler, J. (1988). *Assessment of children* (3rd ed). San Diego, CA: Author.

Sattler, J. (2001). *Assessment of children: Cognitive applications* (4th ed.). San Diego, CA: Author.

Sattler, J. M., & Hardy-Braz, S. T. (2002). Hearing impairments. In J. M. Sattler (Ed.), *Assessment of children: Behavioral and clinical applications* (pp. 377–387). La Mesa, CA: Jerome M. Sattler, Publisher.

Schaefer, B. A. (2002). Review of Kaufman and Lichtenberger's (2000) *Essentials of WISC-III and WPPSI-R Assessment. Journal of Psychoeducational Assessment, 20,* 391–395.

Schaefer, B. A., & McDermott, P. A. (1999). Learning behavior and intelligence as explanations for children's scholastic achievement. *Journal of School Psychology, 37,* 299–313.

Schmelter-Davis, L. (1984). *Vocational evaluation of handicapped college students: Hearing, motor, and visually impaired* (Report No. ISBN-0-916855-01-5). Lincroft, NJ: Brookdale Community College. (Eric Document Reproduction Service No. ED264390)

Schrank, F. A., Flanagan, D. P., Woodcock, R. W., & Mascolo, J. T. (2002). *Essentials of WJ III Cognitive Assessment Battery*. New York: Wiley.

Schwean, V. L., & Saklofske, D. H. (1998). WISC-III assessment of children with Attention Deficit/Hyperactivity Disorder. In A. Prifitera & D. Saklofske (Eds.), *WISC-III clinical use and interpretation* (pp. 91–118). San Diego, CA: Academic Press.

Seidman, L. J., Biederman, J., Faraone, S. V., & Milberger, S. (1995). Effects of family history and comorbidity on the neuropsychological performance of children with ADHD: Preliminary findings. *Journal of the American Academy of Child and Adolescent Psychiatry, 34*(8), 1015–1024.

Seidman, L. J., Biederman, J., Faraone, S.V., Weber, W., & Ouellette, C. (1997). Toward defining a neuropsychology of Attention Deficit-Hyperactivity Disorder: Performance of children and adolescents from a large clinically referred sample. *Journal of Consulting and Clinical Psychology, 65,* 150–160.

Seidman, L. J., Biederman, J., Monuteaux, M. C., Doyle, A., & Faraone, S. V. (2001). Learning disabilities and executive function in boys with Attention Deficit Hyperactivity Disorder. *Neuropsychology, 15*(4), 544–556.

Semrud-Clikeman, M., Kamphaus, R., Teeter, P. A., & Vaughn, M. (1997). Assessment of behavior and personality in the neuropsychological diagnosis of children. In C. R. Reynolds & E. Fletcher-Janzen (Eds.), *The handbook of clinical child neuropsychology* (2nd ed., pp. 320–341). New York: Kluwer-Plenum.

Sherman, S. W., & Robinson, N. M. (1982). *Ability testing of handicapped people: Dilemma for government, science, and the public* (Report No. ISBN-0-309-03240-7). Washington, DC: National Academy of Sciences-National Research Council, Assembly of Behavioral and Social Sciences. (Eric Document Reproduction Service No. ED221560)

Siegal, L. S. (1999). Issues in the definition and diagnosis of learning disabilities: A perspective on Guckenberger v. Boston University. *Journal of Learning Disabilities, 32,* 304–319.

Siegal, M. (1997). *Knowing children: Experiments in conversation and cognition* (2nd ed.). Hove, England: Psychology Press.

Siegel, D. J., Minshew, N. J., & Goldstein, G. (1996). Wechsler IQ profiles in diagnosis of high-functioning autism. *Journal of Autism and Developmental Disabilities, 26,* 398–406.

Slate, J. R. (1995). Discrepancies between IQ and index scores for a clinical sample of students: Useful diagnostic indicators? *Psychology in the Schools, 32,* 103–108.

Slate, J. R., & Fawcett, J. (1995). Validity of the WISC-III for deaf and hard of hearing persons. *American Annals of the Deaf, 140*(4), 250–254.

Spearman, C. (1904). "General intelligence" objectively determined and measured. *American Journal of Psychology, 15,* 201–293.

Speltz, M. L, DeKlyen, M., Calderon, R., Greenberg, M. T., & Fisher, P. A. (1999). Neuropsychological characteristics and test behaviors of boys with early onset conduct problems. *Journal of Abnormal Psychology, 108,* 315–325.

Sperry, R. W. (1968). Hemisphere deconnection and unity in conscious awareness. *American Psychologist, 23,* 723–733.

Spragins, A. B. (1998). *Reviews of assessment instruments used with deaf and hard of hearing students, 1998 Update* [On-line]. Washington, DC: Gallaudet Research Institute. Retrieved April 21, 2004 from http://gri.gallaudet.edu/~catraxle/reviews.html

Spreen, O. (2001). Learning disabilities and their neurological foundations, theories, and subtypes. In A. S. Kaufman & N. L. Kaufman (Eds.), *Specific learning disabilities and difficulties in children and adolescents* (pp. 283–308). New York: Cambridge University Press.

Spruill, J. (1998). Assessment of Mental Retardation with the WISC-III. In A. Prifitera & D. Saklofske (Eds.), *WISC-III clinical use and interpretation* (pp. 73–90). San Diego, CA: Academic Press.

Stanovich, K. E. (1992). Developmental Reading Disorder. In S. R. Hooper, G. W. Hynd, & R. E. Mattison (Eds.), *Developmental Disorders: Diagnostic criteria and clinical assessment* (pp. 173–208). Hillsdale, NJ: Erlbaum.

Stanovich, K. E. (1999). The sociopsychometrics of learning disabilities. *Journal of Learning Disabilities, 32,* 350–361.

Staton, R. D., Wilson, H., & Brumback, R. A. (1981). Cognitive improvement associated with tricyclic antidepressant treatment of childhood major depressive illness. *Perceptual and Motor Skills, 53,* 2199–2234.

Stewart, L. G. (1986). Psychological assessment: One perspective. In L. G. Steward (Ed.), *Clinical rehabilitation assessment and hearing impairment: A guide to quality assurance* (pp. 9–25). Silver Springs, MD: National Association of the Deaf.

Strang, J. D., & Rourke, B. P. (1985). Adaptive behavior of children with specific arithmetic disabilities and associated neuropsychological abilities and deficits. In B. P. Rourke (Ed.), *Neuropsychology of learning disabilities: Essentials of subtype analysis* (pp. 302–328). New York: Guilford Press.

Street, R. F. (1931). The Gestalt Completion Test. *Contributions to Education* (No. 481). New York: Bureau of Publications, Teachers College, Columbia University.

Sullivan, P. M., & Montoya, L. M. (1997). Factor analysis of WISC-III with deaf and hard-of-hearing children. *Psychological Assessment, 9*(3), 317–321.

Sullivan, P. M., & Schulte, L. E. (1992). Factor analysis of WISC-R with deaf and hard-of-hearing children. *Psychological Assessment, 4,* 537–540.

Swisher, L., & Plante, E. (1993). Nonverbal IQ tests reflect different relations among skills for specifically language-impaired and normal children: Brief report. *Journal of Communication Disorders, 26*(1), 65–71.

Talland, G. A. (1965). *Deranged memory.* New York: Academic Press.

Teeter, P. A. (1997). Neurocognitive interventions for childhood and adolescent disorders: A transactional model. In C. R. Reynolds & E. Fletcher-Janzen (Eds.), *The handbook of clinical child neuropsychology* (2nd ed., pp. 387–417). New York: Kluwer-Plenum.

Teeter, P. A., & Semrud-Clikeman, M. (1997). *Child clinical neuropsychology: Assessment and interventions for neuropsychiatric and neurodevelopmental disorders of childhood.* Boston: Allyn & Bacon.

Terman, L. D. (1916). *The measurement of intelligence.* Boston: Houghton-Mifflin.

Tramontana, M. G., & Hooper, S. R. (1997). Neuropsychology of child psychopathology. In C. R. Reynolds & E. Fletcher-Janzen (Eds.), *The handbook of clinical child neuropsychology* (2nd ed., pp. 120–139). New York: Kluwer-Plenum.

Tsatsanis, K. D., Dartnall, N., Cicchetti, D., Sparrow, S. S., Klin, A., & Volkmar, F. R. (2003). Concurrent validity and classification accuracy of the Leiter and Leiter-R in low-functioning children with autism. *Journal of Autism & Developmental Disorders, 33*(1), 23–30.

Ulissi, S. M., Brice, P. J., & Gibbons, S. (1985, April). *The use of the KABC with the hearing impaired.* Paper presented at the meeting of the National Association of School Psychologists, Las Vegas, NV.

Ulissi, S. M., Brice, P. J., & Gibbins, S. (1989). Use of the Kaufman-Assessment Battery for Children with the hearing impaired. *American Annals of the Deaf, 134*(4), 283–287.

U.S. Department of Education. (2002). *Twenty-Fourth Annual Report to Congress on the Implementation of the Individuals with Disabilities Education Act.* Washington, DC: Author.

Valencia, R. R., Rankin, R. J., & Livingston, R. (1995). K-ABC content bias: Comparisons between Mexican American and White children. *Psychology in the Schools, 32,* 153–169.

Valli, C., & Lucas, C. (1995). *Linguistics of American sign language: An introduction* (2nd ed.). Washington, DC: Gallaudet University Press.

Velluntino, F. R., Scanlon, D. M., & Lyon, G. R. (2000). Differentiating between difficult-to-remediate and easily remediated poor readers: More evidence against the IQ-achievement discrepancy definition of reading disability. *Journal of Learning Disabilities, 33,* 223–38.

Vernon, M., & Andrews, J. F. (1990). *The psychology of deafness.* New York: Longman.

Vig, S., & Jedrysek, E. (1996). Stanford-Binet, fourth edition: Useful for young children with language impairment? *Psychology in the Schools, 33*(2), 124–131.

Vig, S., Kaminer, R. K., & Jedrysek, E. (1987). A later look at borderline and mentally retarded preschoolers. *Journal of Developmental and Behavioral Pediatrics, 8,* 12–17.

Vincent, K. R. (1991). Black/White IQ differences: Does age make the difference? *Journal of Clinical Psychology, 47,* 266–270.

Voyazopolous, R. (Ed.). (1994). *K-ABC-Pratique et fondements theoriques.* Paris: Las Pensee Sauvage.

Wagner, R. K., Torgesen, J. K., & Rashotte, C. A. (1999). *Comprehensive Test of Phonological Processing.* Austin, TX: Pro-Ed.

Warner, C., & Nelson, N. W. (2000). Assessment of communication, language, and speech. In B. Bracken (Ed.), *The psychoeducational assessment of preschool children* (3rd ed., pp. 145–185). Needham Heights, MA: Allyn & Bacon.

Wasserman, J. D., & Becker, K. A. (2000, August). Racial and ethnic group mean score differences on intelligence tests. In J. A. Naglieri (Chair), *Making assessment more fair—Taking verbal and achievement out of ability tests.* Symposium conducted at the annual meeting of the American Psychological Association, Washington, DC.

Watson, R. (1951). *Test behavior observation guide.* In R. Watson (Ed.), *The clinical method in psychology.* New York: Harper.

Wechsler, D. (1974). *Manual for the Wechsler Preschool and Primary Scale of Intelligence (WPPSI).* New York: The Psychological Corporation.

Wechsler, D. (1981). *Manual for the Wechsler Adult Intelligence Scale—Revised (WAIS-R).* San Antonio, TX: The Psychological Corporation.

Wechsler, D. (1991). *Wechsler Intelligence Scale for Children—Third edition* (WISC-III). San Antonio, TX: The Psychological Corporation.

Wechsler, D. (2002). *WPPSI-III administration and scoring manual.* San Antonio, TX: The Psychological Corporation.

Wechsler, D. (2003). *The Wechsler Intelligence Scale for Children—Fourth edition* (WISC-IV). San Antonio, TX: The Psychological Corporation.

Wecker, N. S., Kramer, J. H., Wisniewski, A., Delis, D. C., & Kaplan, E. (2000). Age effects on executive ability. *Neuropsychology, 14,* 409–414.

Weyandt, L. L., & Willis, W. G. (1994). Executive functions in school-aged children: Potential efficacy of tasks in discriminating clinical groups. *Developmental Neuropsychology, 19,* 27–38.

Whitworth, R. H., & Chrisman, S. M. (1987). Validation of the Kaufman Assessment Battery for Children comparing Anglo and Mexican-American preschoolers. *Educational and Psychological Measurement, 47,* 695–702.

Wolf, M. (1997). A provisional, integrative account of phonological and naming-speed deficits in dyslexia: Implications for diagnosis and intervention. In B. Blachman (Ed.), *Cognitive and linguistic foundations of reading acquisition: Implications for intervention research* (pp. 123–146). Hillsdale, NJ: Erlbaum.

Wolke, D., & Meyer, R. (1999). Cognitive status, language attainment, and prereading skills of 6-year-old very preterm children and their peers: The Bavarian Longitudinal Study. *Developmental Medicine and Child Neurology, 41,* 94–109.

Wong, T. M., Strickland, T. L., Fletcher-Janzen, E., Ardila, A., & Reynolds, C. R. (2000). Theoretical and practical issues in the neuropsychological assessment and treatment of culturally dissimilar patients. In E. Fletcher-Janzen, T. L. Strickland, & C. R. Reynolds (Eds.), *Handbook of cross-cultural neuropsychology.* New York: Kluwer-Plenum.

Woodcock, R. W. (1973). *Woodcock Reading Mastery Tests.* Circle Pines, MN: American Guidance Service.

Woodcock, R. W. (1990). Theoretical foundations of the WJ-R measures of cognitive ability. *Journal of Psychoeducational Assessment, 8,* 231–258.

Woodcock, R. W., & Johnson, M. B. (1977). *Woodcock-Johnson Psycho-Educational Battery.* Itasca, IL: Riverside Publishing.

Woodcock, R. W., & Johnson, M. B. (1989). *Woodcock-Johnson Tests of Cognitive Ability: Standard and supplemental batteries.* Chicago: Riverside Publishing.

Woodcock, R. W., McGrew, K. S., & Mather, N. (2001). *Woodcock-Johnson III: Tests of Cognitive Abilities.* Chicago: Riverside Publishing.

Yirmiya, N., & Sigman, M. (1991). High functioning individuals with autism: Diagnosis, empirical findings, and theoretical issues. *Clinical Psychology Review, 11,* 669–683.

Yoakum, C. S., & Yerkes, R. M. (Eds.). (1920). *Army mental tests.* New York: Henry Holt.

Zelazo, P. D., Carter, A., Reznick, J. S., & Frye, D. (1997). Early development of executive function: A problem-solving framework. *Review of General Psychology, 1*(2), 198–226.

Annotated Bibliography

Flanagan, D. P., & Ortiz, S. (2001). *Essentials of cross-battery assessment*. New York: Wiley.

This book describes the CHC (Cattell-Horn-Carroll)-based cross-battery assessment method, which systematically integrates tests from one of the major intelligence batteries with tests from other cognitive batteries or supplemental cognitive ability tests. The text covers key cognitive test batteries, assesses the relative strengths and weaknesses of the tests, gives valuable advice on clinical applications, and provides illustrative case reports. The book also includes practical interpretation worksheets and summary sheets for those who conduct cross-battery assessment.

Kaufman, A. S., & Kaufman, N. L. (Eds.). (2001). *Specific learning disabilities and difficulties in children and adolescents*. New York: Cambridge University Press.

This book contains 13 chapters written by experts in the field of learning disabilities. History and traditions are examined along with alternative cognitive approaches to learning disabilities assessment and remediation. In addition, several chapters focus on neuropsychological assessment and remediation and the assessment of memory. A summary chapter reviews current controversies and future issues.

Kaufman, A. S., & Kaufman, N. L. (2004a). *Manual for the Kaufman Assessment Battery for Children—Second edition (KABC-II)*. Circle Pines, MN: American Guidance Service.

This manual comes as part of the KABC-II kit. It provides a basic description of the KABC-II scales and subtests and the theories that were a driving force behind its development. Revisions from the previous version of the K-ABC are reviewed and correlations between the two editions are provided. The standardization procedures and process of norms development are detailed. Evidence of reliability and validity are provided in the text along with numerous related tables. A chapter is included on the basic guidelines for KABC-II interpretation, which is coupled with the necessary discrepancy and base-rate tables in the appendixes.

Kaufman, A. S., & Kaufman, N. L. (2004b). *Kaufman Test of Educational Achievement—Second edition (KTEA-II): Comprehensive Form*. Circle Pines, MN: American Guidance Service.

The manual of this test (included in the test kit) gives detailed information about KTEA-II test development, standardization, and the test's psychometric properties. It describes all of the subtests and scales and instructs examiners on how to score and analyze the KTEA-II data. Because the KTEA-II was conormed with the KABC-II, this manual provides a wealth of correlational data and information about how the tests are related.

Kaufman, J. C., Kaufman, A. S., Kaufman-Singer, J. L., & Kaufman, N. L. (in press). The Kaufman Assessment Battery for Children—Second edition (KABC-II) and the Kaufman Adolescent and Adult Intelligence Test (KAIT). In D. P. Flanagan & P. L. Harrison (Eds.), *Beyond traditional intellectual assessment: Contemporary and emerging theories, tests, and issues* (2nd ed.). New York: Guilford Press.

Provides a description and overview of the KABC-II that covers practical, psychometric, theoretical, and clinical topics. Includes the case report of 12-year-old Jessica, referred for school problems and possible depression, who was assessed with the KABC-II and KTEA-II. It also provides a description and overview of the KAIT.

Lichtenberger, E. O., Broadbooks, D. A., & Kaufman, A. S. (2000). *Essentials of cognitive assessment with the KAIT and other Kaufman measures.* New York: Wiley.

This book provides information on seven of the tests that the Kaufmans have developed: K-ABC, K-BIT, ESP, K-SEALS, K-FAST, K-SNAP, and KAIT. The content of the K-ABC chapter is research based and it presents a historical overview of empirical findings over nearly the past two decades. The K-ABC topics include learning disabilities, cross-cultural assessment, testing preschool-age children, and assessment of pediatric samples.

Lichtenberger, E. O., Mather, N., Kaufman, N. L., & Kaufman, A. S. (2004). *Essentials of assessment report writing.* New York: Wiley.

This book reviews the essential elements and structure of well-written psychological and psychoeducational reports. It covers all aspects of preparing a written report and provides numerous illustrative examples of clear, informative reports. It includes the case report of Brianna, an 18-year-old diagnosed with ADHD, who was assessed with the KABC-II and KTEA-II.

Samuda, R. J., Feuerstein, R., Kaufman, A. S., Lewis, J. E., & Sternberg, R. J. (1998). *Advances in cross-cultural assessment.* Thousand Oaks, CA: Sage.

This book addresses cross-cultural assessment from varied and broad perspectives. Cross-cultural assessment issues and alternatives are introduced from a theoretical point of view. Alternative approaches to assessing learning potential are offered in the book. Current concerns about linking assessment to intervention, nontraditional uses of aptitude tests, and a chapter reviewing the 1993 Buros-Nebraska symposium on multicultural assessment are also presented. Two chapters review the K-ABC with case studies and a detailed review of the cross-cultural assessment data conducted with the battery.

Teeter, P. A., & Semrud-Clikeman, M. (1997). *Child neuropsychology.* New York: Allyn & Bacon.

This book is a practical and comprehensive overview of child neuropsychology. It contains 12 chapters that cover topics ranging from anatomy and physiology to intervention paradigms. There is a section on clinical assessment that compares different assessment batteries and approaches to neuropsychological assessment. The section on child and adolescent disorders is comprehensive and includes learning disabilities and other educationally related problems. Case studies are presented for several different neuropsychological conditions.

Index

Acknowledgments

We are deeply grateful to a number of people who contributed to this book. Dr. Dawn Flanagan contributed a wonderful section on cross-battery assessment with the KABC-II, and also made significant contributions in helping us develop the expanded KABC-II interpretive system presented in this book. Dr. Michelle Lurie contributed a valuable case study that helped to highlight the benefits of the KABC-II with diverse ethnic populations. Steven Hardy-Braz helped develop the section on the use of the KABC-II for children who are deaf or hard of hearing by using his expertise in this domain. Dr. James C. Kaufman provided valuable research assistance on many topics for this book as well as the KABC-II itself. Dr. Darielle Greenberg created yet another useful index for this Essentials series. Finally, we would like to thank Tracey Belmont and the staff at Wiley for making the process of writing this book as smooth and enjoyable as possible.

About the Authors

Alan S. Kaufman, PhD and Nadeen L. Kaufman, EdD are at the Child Study Center at Yale University's School of Medicine. Alan is Clinical Professor of Psychology and Nadeen is Lecturer on the clinical faculty.

Elizabeth O. Lichtenberger, PhD is a licensed clinical psychologist in San Diego, California.

Elaine Fletcher-Janzen, EdD is a visiting Professor of Psychology at the University of Colorado, Colorado Springs.